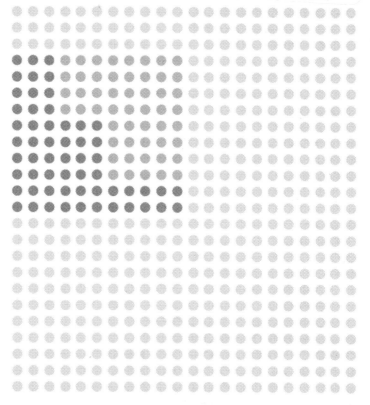

Contemporary Hollywood Stardom

Edited by
Thomas Austin
&
Martin Barker

A member of the Hodder Headline Group
LONDON
Distributed in the USA by Oxford University Press, Inc., New York

Acknowledgements

This book derives from the conference 'Film Stars in the '90s', held at the University of Sussex in 2001. Thanks to everybody who helped organise, and who participated in, this event. Apologies to those whose work we were unable to include in this collection. Thanks also to Charlotte Adcock and Martin Shingler, and to Lesley Riddle.

First published in Great Britain in 2003 by
Arnold, a member of the Hodder Headline Group,
338 Euston Road, London NW1 3BH

Distributed in the United States of America by
Oxford University Press Inc.
198 Madison Avenue, New York, NY10016

© 2003 Thomas Austin and Martin Barker

All rights reserved. No part of this publication may be reproduced or
transmitted in any form or by any means, electronically or mechanically,
including photocopying, recording or any information storage or retrieval
system, without either prior permission in writing from the publisher or a
licence permitting restricted copying. In the United Kingdom such licences
are issued by the Copyright Licensing Agency: 90 Tottenham Court Road,
London W1T 4LP.

The advice and information in this book are believed to be true and
accurate at the date of going to press, but neither the author[s] nor the publisher
can accept any legal responsibility or liability for any errors or omissions.

British Library Cataloguing in Publication Data
A catalogue record for this book is available from the British Library

Library of Congress Cataloging-in-Publication Data
A catalog record for this book is available from the Library of Congress

ISBN 0 340 809361 (hb)
ISBN 0 340 80937X (pb)

1 2 3 4 5 6 7 8 9 10

Typeset in 9.5 on 13pt Baskerville Book by Phoenix Photosetting, Chatham, Kent
Printed and bound in Great Britain by MPG Books Ltd.

Contents

Introduction – Martin Barker   1

Section 1 Star Systems

Introduction   25

1 Paul McDonald *Stars in the Online Universe: Promotion, Nudity, Reverence*   29

2 Barry King *Embodying an Elastic Self: The Parametrics of Contemporary Stardom*   45

3 Geoff King *Stardom in the Willennium*   62

4 Matt Hills *Putting Away Childish Things: Jar Jar Binks and the 'Virtual Star' as an Object
   of Fan Loathing*   74

5 Paul Wells *To Affinity and Beyond: Woody, Buzz and the New Authenticity*   90

Section 2 Star Performances

Introduction   103

6 Christine Geraghty *Performing as a Lady and a Dame: Reflections on Acting and Genre*   105

7 Sharon Marie Carnicke *From Acting Guru to Hollywood Star: Lee Strasberg as Actor*   118

8 Thomas Austin *Men in Suits: Costume, Performance and Masculinity in the Batman Films*   135

Section 3 Stars and their Audiences

Introduction   151

9 Ian Huffer *'What Interest does a Fat Stallone Have for an Action Fan?': Male Film
   Audiences and the Structuring of Stardom*   155

10 Máire Messenger Davies and Roberta Pearson *Stardom and Distinction:
   Patrick Stewart as an Agent of Cultural Mobility – A Study of Theatre and Film Audiences
   in New York City*   167

11 Joanne Lacey *'A Galaxy of Stars to Guarantee Ratings': Made-for-Television Movies and
   the Female Star System*   187

Section 4 Stars and Gender, Generation, Cultural Identity

Introduction   199

12 Peter Krämer *'A Woman in a Male-Dominated World': Jodie Foster, Stardom and 90s
   Hollywood*   201

13 Cynthia Baron *From Tormented Genius to Sexual Adventurer: Stars and Masculinity in the
   Jekyll and Hyde Films*   215

iii

14 Julian Stringer *Scrambling Hollywood: Asian Stars/Asian American Star Cultures*   229

15 Ewan Kirkland *'Peter Pan's my Dad?!?' The Man-Child Persona of Robin Williams*   243

Section 5 Star Controversies

Introduction   255

16 Alan Lovell *'I Went in Search of Deborah Kerr, Jodie Foster and Julianne Moore but got Waylaid ...'*   259

Contributors' details   271
Bibliography   273
Index   286

INTRODUCTION ☐

Martin Barker[1]

This book has two purposes. First, we want to contribute to the reawakening of star studies, after a period in which they have seemed to lose the energy that characterised their early 1980s life. We believe that the essays gathered here contribute much original thought to the field.[2] Second, we believe that stardom itself has changed significantly in the last decade, in ways that challenge a number of the ideas that became 'common sense' in star studies in that early, lively period.

Two events at the start of the 1990s symbolise the changes. In 1991 Michael Katzenberg, at the zenith of his career within the Disney Corporation, wrote a 28-page memo to Michael Eisner. He and Eisner had been hired in 1984 to turn around Disney's increasingly dismal fortunes – and they had succeeded, beyond anyone's expectations. The memo, leaked into legend, was a savage attack on the studios' addiction to stars, and their mega-salaries. At issue was the notion of 'bankability', the idea that the surest way to manage the risks associated with film productions was to have one, maybe several, 'names' which could help launch a film. This idea, which had particularly been promoted by the 1980s independent production companies (such as Miramax, Cinergi, CarolCo and New Line) had had its day, argued Eisner. Stars (and indeed their agents) were receiving inflated salaries. They were increasingly demanding 'points' (proportions of theatrical gross) in films, control over scripts, and in some cases, even effective say over direction. They were demanding – and sometimes receiving – rights over publicity regimes, merchandising and other intellectual property processes. Studios' dependence on a small crop of A-list stars was making them vulnerable to these demands.

And for what return? Eisner cited Warren Beatty's *Dick Tracy* (1990, USA) – a 'beautiful movie', he recently conceded (*Empire,* August 2001), but seen as a box-office failure.[3] Speaking from within Disney which, within four years, would become Hollywood's top studio, Katzenberg could say something more easily than other studios; Disney, under Eisner's and Katzenberg's leadership, was rediscovering – or reinventing – its animation roots.

The second event bears comparison. In 1993 Arnold Schwarzenegger released his (John McTierney-directed) *The Last Action Hero* (1993, USA). Arnie, perhaps more than anyone else, personified the heights to which stars had aspired during the 1980s. He was one of

1

the sure-fire guarantors of big movie money. Bidding for his presence was now a game in itself, and Columbia Pictures, recently acquired by Sony, had fought hard to win him. Acquiring the script idea from a couple of unknowns, they had spent $3 million just on developing it and wooing him. The film was important enough that Sony used it as the launch platform for its new sound system, Sony Dynamic Digital Sound (SDDS), hoping that cinemas would be willing to retool on the back of this guaranteed earner (Sergi, 1998: 165). It was very much Arnie's movie – his imprint can be found in everything, even down to the design of its poster. And he would use this movie to move forward his image to a new gentler phase, reducing the violence while keeping the muscular action and trademark catchphrases. The movie substantially overran its $60 million budget, but few worried – Arnie's name was sure to bring in the goods.

It was only when Columbia examined preliminary responses, and looked at the release-window competition, that nervous bells started clanging. Preview audiences were pretty bored. And Steven Spielberg's *Jurassic Park* (1993, USA) was scheduled for release one week earlier, with a potentially substantial audience overlap. On that film, the vibes were simply tremendous, the epicentre of which was the rumour of digital dinosaurs.

The Last Action Hero's death at the box office has echoed through Hollywood.[4] It was not that it lost money (in the end, after video, cable, television and the laid-off risks of licensed properties, few movies are absolute losers; *Last Action*'s eventual box office earnings amounted to $121 million on a budget of $60 million, with video adding at least $40 million worldwide), it was the way its 'failure' undercut a decade and a half's received wisdom. Columbia was deeply wounded by the experience, to the extent that some commentators wondered whether Sony would sell the company. The idea that certain star names gave such release security that they could be allowed to run the show was badly dented.

It is easy to exaggerate such changes. If in 1990 Katzenberg was attacking star power, in 1999 the *Guardian* in Britain was reporting that studio executives were 'grumbling' about hiked stars' fees, perks, etc., while alongside expensive star-driven flops like Harrison Ford in *Random Hearts* (1999, USA), Nic Cage in *Bringing Out The Dead* (1999, USA) and Kevin Costner in *For Love of the Game* (1999, USA) were such star-free hits as *American Pie* (1999, USA) and *The Blair Witch Project* (1999, USA); Tom Dewe Mathews commented, 'They're not just rich and famous. They're in charge' (*Guardian*, 19 November 1999). In 2000, Richard Corliss noted the same tendencies that Katzenberg was bemoaning a decade earlier:

> All right, Tom Cruise won, his *Mission Impossible* coasted to an easy
> victory in the summer box-office race, with $213 million in domestic
> grosses. Cruise did what movie stars are supposed to do: climb a rockface,
> save the girl and the world and, in the process, make a bundle for himself

and his backers. But take a look at the runners-up, and you will find a few surprises – unpleasant ones, for an industry that pays dearly for celebrity wattage to attract customers. The return on star investment is falling like a dotcom stock. Hollywood bosses have to wonder: Have we entered the poststar era?

('*So Much for Star Power*', Time, 4 September 2000: 75)

Still, the persistence of the complaints suggests new forces and new tensions in play. I am not attempting in this introduction to give some tidy summation. Rather, I want to point, perhaps provocatively, to some cases which raise difficult questions. These show the outlines of some changes. They may also query some primary emphases within film studies' approaches to stars and stardom to date. But before that, it may help to recapitulate the now broadly accepted understanding of stardom's historical development. I do this briefly, since this story has been well told by others.

STAGES IN THE HISTORY OF STARDOM

One of the most important outcomes of the 1980s tradition of work on stars was the construction of a history of relations between stars and their studio employers, as follows.

1. Stardom was not 'invented' in the mythological fashion that some early histories liked to tell it – although undoubtedly the showmanship of a figure like Carl Laemmle, 'stealing' Florence Lawrence and resurrecting her after planting the story of her death, played a role. But as Janet Staiger (1991) among others has shown, there is a prior history of popular theatrical touring companies promoting themselves via one famous figure, who embodied a style and a promise of performance. Far from being an invention of early showman film producers, star processes antedate cinema in theatre, sport and travelling shows – and of course these were among the formative influences on cinema itself.

2. Richard DeCordova (1990; 1991) has identified some distinct phases in the emergence of pre-stardom discourses, centred on discourses on acting, and the establishment of picture personalities. The first phase saw discussions (from around 1907) within trade magazines on the distinctiveness of screen acting, coupled with naming those who pre-eminently display the requisite skills. As this kind of talk permeated outwards, so public interest grew in the phenomenon of film acting *per se*. But because actors and actresses were hardly known off-screen, audience recognition of these traits encouraged predictable styles of performance, and the promotion of films as embodiments of these. It needed the conscious promotion of named actors on billboards, lobby cards and in press advertisements to establish the presence of individuals' distinctive aura and style across many films.

3. Overlaying this came an abiding fascination with personalities' off-screen lives. Fan magazines proliferated, gossip columns celebrated and damned with equal delight. This happened even as the growing companies were trying to secure respectability for their business, and therefore necessitated producing films whose themes and narratives marked them as serious, and opening cinemas in more middle-class districts. It also meant trying to control public discussions of cinema, as Paul McDonald captures: 'By representing the moral rectitude of performers' lives, star discourse promoted the image of the whole cinema business' (2000: 32). But the intensity and volume of fan interest continually undermined this effort. Gaylyn Studlar (1990; see also her larger 1996 study) captures this in her essay on women and the fan magazines of the 1920s, where she points up the fears about unbridled female sexuality which they both provoked and purveyed.

4. Generally, it is recognised that a distinct *system* of stardom, associated with the established oligarchy of Hollywood studios, was in place by the mid-1920s. Using the opportunity of the scandals around figures such as Fatty Arbuckle, and the rising demands for moral controls over films, the studios introduced vastly unequal contracts, tying stars for periods typically of seven years. With controls over the minutest aspects of stars' public and private lives, and with penalties for failure to perform, the studio system underpinned Hollywood's rise and survival even through the dark times of the Depression. Rent with arguments, challenged from time to time by organised labour (see Danae Clark, 1995) and by powerful, embittered individuals (perhaps most famously Bette Davies – see Spada, 1993), the system survived until the 1948 federal case against the studios – at which point, with varying rapidity, stars were shed. And of course some stars did 'escape', using their economic muscle and prestige to establish a 'stars' studio' in United Artists (Balio, 1976a).

5. Slowly, a new set of structural relations emerged across the 1950s, centred increasingly on the agents, and agencies. The big players (International Creative Management, Creative Artists Agency and William Morris) took on the job of packaging script, director, stars, financing together. But as Barry King (1986) has shown, whereas the studio system management of a star's image was essentially a studio operation, now stars had to look after their own careers. King examines stardom as a mode of labour, and distinguishes two predominant modes in which this was conducted: real versus formal subsumption. Within the former, stars were contractually bound to the studios, forbidden to use their labour and skills outside their owner's permissions. In return, paradoxically, the work of maintaining that which constituted their labour-power – their star persona – was largely performed by the studios. Following the Paramount decree, however, stars now had to labour, as 'sub-contractors', at maintaining and upgrading their personae. King illustrates this by comparing two parallel figures, one from each period: Clark Gable and Burt Lancaster. Among the differences he notes are differences in career continuities, and in the ways relations between image and character were managed. Where Gable follows a 'strategy of reducing all character to the star image personality' (1986: 176), Lancaster – by never committing himself to one studio alone, and by playing against his persona – developed a 'calculating use of star image that turns on discontinuities of character' (179).

Clearly, a crucial change, with long-term consequences, came with the 1948 Paramount decision. But what must also interest us are the ways in which that history has been understood within film studies.

DEVELOPMENTS IN STAR STUDIES

Although it might not seem so from some recent histories, critical studies of stars and stardom did not begin with Richard Dyer's 1979 publication, *Stars*. In fact, as Dyer himself makes clear, work had been under way for some time. American studies had developed from within the psychology of identity-formation (Klapp, 1962; Benson, 1974). Like much psychological work since, this approach suffers from a sense of timelessness – as though the 'human needs' stars were supposed to exist outside history, only entering the social process when they seek fulfilment (for a contemporary example, see Giles, 1999). Next, as film reviewing professionalised, a number of journalists had begun to write about the history of the phenomenon – notably Alexander Walker, whose *Stardom* (1970) remains a substantial contribution.

At the same time, historians of the film industry had already begun to publish on the political economy, and legal and contractual history, of the star system (see for instance Balio, 1976, and Kindem, 1982). Here, a quite different set of issues began to emerge, some of which have not been adequately addressed even now. Kindem, for instance, opens by emphasising the role of stars in achieving two simultaneous goals: 'to generate large audiences and differentiate entertainment programs and products' (1982: 79). This recognition of a need to differentiate has led to productive examination of differences within the studio oligopoly, their different preferences for kinds of stars. So, Gomery (1986) proposes a relationship between MGM's relative lack of cinema chains and its greater dependence on its star stable. Others have used this attention to business structures to tell the histories of particular studios – see for instance Ethan Mordden's (1988: especially 189–90) account of the rise of Columbia from minor to major.

There was also a strand of work deriving from the sociology of communications tradition, which was already seeking ways of studying stars' audiences (see Andrew Tudor (1974) for a summary of this work) – something that has only recently and with difficulty come to film studies' agendas. Finally, there are individual and sometimes idiosyncratic studies such as Hortense Powdermaker's (1950) anthropological examination of the Hollywood 'tribe', and stardom's place within it.

5

But although not the first, Dyer did provoke new questions. Famously, he invited examination of the role of stars within representation. What is the meaning of the 'character' that stars display? How does the endless talk surrounding stars relate to their on-screen personae? What kinds of pleasure, dream or compensation for life do stars offer their audiences? In short, what is their ideological function? Whether this was the best or only way to formulate these questions, the fact is that Dyer offered both an exciting new general approach, and a panoply of case studies including Bette Davies, Jane Fonda, Henry Fonda, John Wayne and Marlene Dietrich. He asked a whole series of detailed questions about the kinds and categories of stars, and their social and cultural functions.

Most influentially, drawing on the British cultural studies movement, Dyer developed his account of stardom as an ideological system in his second book *Heavenly Bodies* (1985), through case studies of Marilyn Monroe, Paul Robeson and Judy Garland. Dyer distinguishes two approaches: stardom as a phenomenon of production and as a phenomenon of consumption. Paul McDonald (1995 and 2000) is not alone in noting that emphasis fell almost entirely on the latter side – and construed in a distrusting way; to 'consume' stars was to ingest some distinctly unhealthy ideological E-numbers. But through this emphasis on images, the idea of an 'economic system' blurred and lost its specificity. (As Danae Clark (1995: 8) has commented, the 'aestheticisation' of star images has tended to elide the economy of work which defines the 'very structure of the acting profession'.) Hollywood seemed primarily a means for creating the image-systems necessary for ideological reproduction. Dyer gave a very definite role to stars in this:

> Capitalism justifies itself on the basis of the freedom (separateness) of anyone to make money, sell their labour how they will, to be able to express opinions and get them heard (regardless of wealth of social position). . . . [E]ven while the notion of the individual is being assailed on all sides, it is a necessary fiction for the reproduction of the kind society we live in. Stars articulate these ideas of personhood, in large measure shoring up the notion of the individual but also at times registering the doubts and anxieties attendant on it.
>
> *(Dyer, 1986: 11)*

This is big theory. There was of course acknowledgement of economic processes at work, but these seem quite gestural. Dyer wrote, 'Stars are made for profit. In terms of the market, stars are part of the way films are sold' (Dyer, 1986: 5). It wasn't easy to know how to do more, with this, than moralise about money-grubbing. It would take the examination of Hollywood as a historical system, within which stars labour, to make more of this. In the meantime Dyer's approach coalesced perhaps too comfortably with understandings of Hollywood as a 'patriarchal system'.

There is no doubting the bravura of Dyer's work, and the provocation it offered to many people. A rash of work emerged after Dyer's lead, much directly influenced by him. Christine Gledhill's book, for instance, gathered together a range of such work. Its confidence in the project is signalled in its opening sentence – the book 'offers a guide to studying stars and the phenomenon of stardom' (Gledhill, 1991: xiii) – at the same time as it notes that star studies were already having to take account of a wider set of knowledge than had previously been recognised.

Dyer's work became for a time the centre around which works revolved, illustrated by the way it appears in a recent academic dictionary:

> Whilst stardom itself is a kind of ideological construct, representative of a culture founded upon aspiration and material consumption, different types of stars can be seen as reflecting different, evolving societies. Dyer (1976: 6) quotes Raymond Durgnat's observation that 'The social history of a nation can be written in terms of its film stars' and Alexander Walker's that 'Stars are the direct and indirect reflection of the needs, drives and dreams of American society'. Despite the obvious dangers of reading the meaning of stars in such a direct way, there seem to be clear connections, at different historical moments, operating both ways between stardom and society.
>
> *(Blandford et al., 2001: 224)*

Unfortunately, Blandford *et al.* say nothing about what these dangers might be, or indeed if they might not undermine the grandeur of this project. One researcher who has gone further is Paul McDonald. In a first (1995) account, McDonald summarised four dominant approaches: textual, intertextual, psychoanalytic and audience-based. There, he says little about any conflicts among these. But in a supplementary chapter to the 1998 reprint of Dyer's *Stars*, McDonald summed up a number of the problems with Dyer's approach, citing a substantial body of work scattered across many sources, some far outside film studies' normal reach (journals of business and economics, for instance). And indeed it is the rising influence of studies of the 'New Hollywood', with which came an increasing attention to the political economy of film-making, that has most radically challenged star studies in recent years.

STARDOM IN THE NEW HOLLYWOOD

By the 1970s, many new factors were in play in Hollywood, such as changes in ownership of the major studios, rising negative costs on films, increased interdependence of film with television, the rise of the package system of film production, and the associated strengthening of the agencies who, among other roles, represent just about all the major stars. These were also new systems of marketing, and a messy set of changes lay ahead for the role and status of stars. With no attempt at completeness, I will now look at a few of these.

STARS AND INDEPENDENT PRODUCTION

During the 1970–80s, the film packaging process had allowed space for a number of independent production companies. Working, at least as much as the studios, with franchising properties (think *Teenage Mutant Ninja Turtles* (1990, USA), think *Robocop* (1987, USA), think *Nightmare on Elm Street* (1984, USA)), many of these film franchises were built around one star's embodiment of a *kind* of narrative: such as Sylvester Stallone and 'Rocky', Arnold Schwarzenegger and the 'Terminator' films (plus echoes of these in, for instance, *Total Recall*), Mike Myers and 'Austin Powers'.

In an important essay on these companies, Justin Wyatt (1998) has detailed their role in accelerating the salaries which stars can claim. Because of their more limited scope and clout, because of their greater dependence on finding and holding onto a franchise, the independent production companies of the 1970–80s had to emphasise the centrality of their stars – and in that process became very dependent upon them. The costs of hiring key stars could make but also break these smaller companies.

More than one of these 'dependent independents' failed to cope with the volatility of the film market in the mid-1990s. CarolCo failed due to cash-flow problems, along with poor returns on *Cutthroat Island* (1995, USA). In the same year Cinergi also failed, largely because of the box office deaths of *The Scarlet Letter* (1995, USA) and *Judge Dredd* (1995, USA). Other independents were snapped up by the studios, to become specialist branches. Most notably, Miramax was absorbed into the Disney Corporation, to become, along with Hollywood Pictures, an outlet for more adult fare. The mid-90s, then, saw a substantial change in the relations between the studios and the independent sector, to the extent that the Sundance Festival – until that point a focus for radical independent film-making – became effectively a talent show for the studios. With the decline in the independent sector, the conditions were now right for renewed studio controls. Yet in the same period new candidates for 'stardom' were making an appearance.

SPECIAL EFFECTS AS 'STARS'

For many years, Hollywood studio bosses have expressed fears about uncontrolled rising negative costs (up by more than 120 per cent between 1985–95, which far outstripped inflation). In 1996 after the launch of *Titanic* (1997, USA), long-time leader of the Motion Picture Association of America, Jack Valenti, spoke of the danger that these cost levels might become a precedent. And in 1998, *Red Herring*, the US venture capital magazine, discoursed upon Hollywood's dodgy economics. Noting also the worsening ratio between publicity costs and home box-office income, it turned to the one area which seemed to be sure-fire:

In the experience of one anonymous analyst from a major consulting firm, special effects action/adventure movies with budgets of at least $100 million are the only reliable moneymakers. The thinking is that startling special effects, highlighted in commercials and trailers, generate unstoppable momentum – even bad reviews fuel the fire. As the success of many such smartly marketed blockbusters shows, special effects can replace the traditional cornerstones of Hollywood films: *Star Wars* proved that a special effects film with no stars could still win big at the box office, and *Independence Day* proved that neither stars nor a story were essential. Special effects films are also extremely popular in foreign markets, where US films now derive half of their revenues.

(Jonathan Burke, 'Make Movies, Not War', Red Herring, January 1998:
80–1)

Although the article questions this view, it is clear that it is questioning a new received wisdom: special effects as the new 'stars'. There has been a commendable rise recently in interest in special effects as cinematic elements in their own right, and as indicators of wider cultural processes (see for instance LaValley, 1985; Bukatman, 1998; Landon, 1992; Prince, 1996; Pierson, 1999; Darley, 2000; King, 2001). But none of these addresses how star systems may be affected by the rising emphasis on special effects. Perhaps we need some new questions. For instance, how do the budgetary ratios between effects and stars affect on-set clout? How do the requirements of effects shape stars' performances, and the nature of their on-screen presence? *Lara Croft: Tomb Raider* (2000, USA) perhaps exemplifies such an encounter. Angelina Jolie playing Lara Croft brought to the part a sultry, muscular sexuality, posing and pouting frequently before launching into theatrical violence. Jolie is described in the book of the film as the 'embodiment' of Croft, Lara 'made flesh' – or in the most telling, highlighted summary, 'Angelina fills the screen with her personality. She is the film's best special effect' (Jones, 2001: 61). This may be a piece of rhetoric – but then is not stardom precisely built around such rhetorics?

DIRECTORS AS STARS

If special effects might be challenging the privileged position of stars, so might others. In his essay 'The New Hollywood' (one of the first, and still one of the best, to give an overview of the changes), Thomas Schatz (1993) names one shift particularly relevant to stardom: the rise of the director–superstar. In this period, marketers and publicists began to promote films on the name of their directors – as typified, of course, by Steven Spielberg.[5] Spielberg's abilities as a master of popular movie-making, rather than occasional serious film-maker, mark him as a superstar. In appearance something of a nerdy eccentric, this very quality makes Spielberg more cute and loveable, lifts him above all questions of wealth, politics, even of aesthetics (relatively failed and unpopular films, such as *1941* (1979, USA) or *A.I.* (2001, USA), are generously overlooked). When *Empire* magazine offered a Director's Special on Spielberg, its introductory panegyric spelled out the combination constituting his persona:

> [A]s his Stanley Kubrick collaboration *A.I.: Artificial Intelligence* hits
> British screens, *Empire* takes time to investigate, decipher and honour the
> life and works of the world's favourite helmer. Beards there have been,
> jumpers of extraordinary hue, but never a moment wasted: he has
> superseded stars, events and all the hype and hoopla of the Studio system to
> make 'A Film By Steven Spielberg' the most exciting words to ever appear
> on a screen . . .
>
> (Empire, *Director's Collection, 2001: 3*)

His very self-effacingness becomes the coinage, allowing commentators to overlook other contributors to his films even more than Spielberg himself does.

But it would be a mistake to limit the category to Spielberg alone, or to George Lucas (who might better be called a producer-superstar). Think how routinely studio advertising now incorporates expressions such as 'From the Director of . . .'. The names that readily play this part are James Cameron, Ridley Scott and, to a lesser extent, others such as Tim Burton. A much greater visibility of directors has been set in train. This has had several features: the director's cut (emerging particularly after the mid-1980s rise of domestic video), the director's commentary (associated with the rise of DVD, a phenomenon in itself – see Klinger, 2001) and 'specials' on directors from the new plethora of film magazines. Or as Alex Cox sardonically put it, 'Once treated as nuisances by studios, directors are back in demand for their DVD commentaries' (*Guardian*, 'Is DVD Worth It?', 23 February 2001: G2, 10). And once we pass beyond celebrating a new round of 'great names', we might see not only the economic benefits of repeated releases; as Brookey and Westerfelhaus (2002) argue, the Director's presence on a DVD may help to control errant readings.

STARS AS DIRECTORS

If directors could become stars, then stars would become directors – if allowed. For some time, studios wooed A-list stars into loyalty by offering finance deals enabling them to pursue their own projects, on condition that they appear in the studios' own next chosen vehicle. Such bankrolling deals led to the appearance – and almost immediate disappearance – of many a film; among others (Kim Basinger's) *I Dreamed of Africa* (2000, USA), (Kevin Costner's) *The Postman* (1997, USA) and (John Travolta's) *Battlefield Earth* (2000, USA). Such 'vanity deals', as they became contemptuously known, allowed various stars to create their own production companies. Some have been pretty successful – Clint

Eastwood is a good example. Many have been disastrous flops, and if the runes are right, their days are numbered. In 2000, John Patterson reported on the studios' effective withdrawal from these deals ('You're so Vain', *Guardian*, 22–8 July 2000: 9–10). A new austere financial climate at the millennium led to the cancellation of some projects – Michelle Pfeiffer's with Columbia, Melanie Griffith's and Antonio Banderas' with Warner Bros, among others. In the same article, Patterson quoted one Warners executive on the ending of their deal with Madonna: 'Hers may be the last of the old-fashioned vanity deals. I can't see our shareholders allowing us to sign such deals again.' The *Wall Street Journal* reiterated this, adding a studio complaint that 'some of these deals have been costing studios millions of dollars annually, but that many actors wind up making their movies elsewhere' (**us.imdb.com/StudioBrief**, 2 June 2000).

STAR STUDIES AFTER DYER

These are a few changes that have complicated our picture of stardom across the last three decades. Recent academic work on stardom has had plenty to say about these changing conditions. Among the recent developments has been greater attention to industrial contexts and questions of political economy. Paul McDonald's recent book (2000) provides more than an overview – it is a direct challenge to researchers to think more widely than matters of meaning and performance. He points to the importance of studying matters such as stars' contracts, and the complicated relations between stars' qualities as labour and as capital. He ends by posing an unanswered question about the relations between acting as labour, and actual performances by stars. Christine Geraghty (2000) opens her critical review by noting how profligate the term 'star' has become in light of, for instance, the new significance of sports stars and music stars. Geraghty suggests that it may help to distinguish several kinds of stardom: as celebrity (to which a sense of intimacy with people's private lives is central); as professional (for which the display of a particular specialist skill – be it football, kick-boxing or zany humour – is the core); and as performer (where the crafts of acting become pre-eminent). Her conclusions, that we may need to qualify just how far film stars are special, and examine the relations between them and other modes of stardom, are surely right. The much greater permeability between the worlds of film and for instance television and music undermines film stardom's exclusivity.

Another area of work to emerge has been the study of screen acting. An early major contribution was made by James Naremore (1988). Naremore offers a vocabulary and syntax for talking about acting, and about the ways in which the camera registers behaviour *as* acting. His argument becomes especially germane when he considers how attention to acting challenges current thinking about film stars. For instance, he queries Laura Mulvey's account of Marlene Dietrich by arguing, in effect, that Dietrich is never simply examined by the camera, but *plays* to it in ways that approach camp. Or in relation to James Cagney's death scene in *Angels With Dirty Faces* (1938, USA), he suggests that the compromising of Cagney's normal 'swagger-acting' prior to his execution *increases* the scene's ambiguity over whether he really has become a coward. Other important work since then has extended the interest in acting and performance (see for instance, Cardullo *et al.*, 1998, and Lovell and Krämer, 1999). Again, it is important that Lovell and Krämer have to position themselves to some extent *against* Dyer's work, because his account of stars, by separating them from actors, and making stardom primarily an ideological issue, renders irrelevant the examination of their acting (1999: 5).

A considerable range of other work could be added. Geoffrey Macnab (2000), for instance, has written about the relative failure of the British film industry to produce its own star system. Bruce Babington's (2001) edited collection on British stars also allows interesting comparisons, as its essays cover both stars who succeeded within the Hollywood system and those who did not. Ginette Vincendeau (2000) has performed the same essential function on French stardom.

There is a considerable volume of such work, and its effect seems to be to 'scatter' what seemed for a time a nicely self-contained and tidy story of Hollywood stardom. And if stars research within film studies has been opening out, we must remember the insights that may be gained by stepping over the portals into other domains. I will mention just a couple here.

1. In her acclaimed *No Logo*, Naomi Klein (2000) has touched interestingly on the contemporary meanings and functions of stars, albeit that her examples are primarily from rock and pop. Discussing the efforts by Canadian beer companies to use sponsored rock festivals as promotional vehicles, she tells of Molson's increasing discontent when (a) the names of stars bulked larger than those of the sponsors, and (b) the stars frequently insulted the product from the stage: 'Clearly fed up, in 1996 Molson held its first Blind Date concert' – a much more controlled publicity vehicle where, even if the stars misbehave, the winners are still the sponsors. Klein sums up the tendency:

> In *Advertising Age*'s annual 'Top Marketing 100' list of 1997's best brands, there was a new arrival: the Spice Girls (fittingly enough, since Posh Spice did once tell a reporter, 'We wanted to be a "household name". Like Ajax'). And the Spice Girls ranked number six in *Forbes* magazine's inaugural 'Celebrity Power 100', in May 1999, a new ranking based not on fame or fortune but on stars' brand 'franchise'. The list was a watershed moment in corporate history, marking the fact that, as Michael J Wolf says, 'Brands and stars have become the same thing.'
>
> *(Klein, 2000: 49)*

Of course there are important differences between the worlds of rock and film. 'Performance' in the popular music business is different from performance in a film, even if a steady number of pop stars attempt the transition. But Klein's point is still relevant to film stardom. Since the 1970s, films, and especially blockbuster film series, have existed as 'franchises'. In the form of merchandising, tie-ins and general intellectual property rights, this phenomenon has been extensively examined. Stars' relations to these franchises have been less studied: for instance, the issue of star-images on a range of products (from figurines to digitised versions in games, to images on clothing). Tom Hanks' contract with Disney for *Toy Story* (1995, USA) forbade the use of his image on Woody figurines. It has been suspected that Stallone withheld permission for his image to be used on Dredd merchandising – Stallone being among the very first to register a trademark in himself, in the 1970s. But these anecdotes relate only the stars' side of the story – we know even less about the studios' search for franchise control, except from the odd lawsuit. This aside, perhaps Klein's argument is also important, in as much as it is being made from outside the hermetic world of film studies. There is much to be learnt from wider developments in social, cultural and political theory, especially perhaps from work which positions Hollywood's production systems within the evolution of global capitalism (see for instance Miller, 1998).

2. Another area where work arising outside the film domain is relevant to film studies is the study of the phenomenon of celebrity. Dealing with a much broader array than just film stars, celebrity studies consider television, sport, fashion and modelling, the seeking or achieving of celebrity on bizarre grounds. These studies also frequently ask broader questions, and deploy a wider range of theoretical approaches. P. David Marshall, for instance, looks back to the work of Louis Althusser for his theoretical approach, arguing that 'the celebrity structures meaning, crystallizes ideological positions, and works to provide a sense and coherence to culture' (1997: ix–x). His examples range across Tom Cruise, Oprah Winfrey, New Kids On The Block and American presidents. Marshall's account hardly uses traditional filmic notions of a 'persona'. Instead he sees celebrities as commodities come to life – and functioning to warrant new styles of political authority.

Other work on celebrity has taken a rather different direction. Chris Rojek's broad-sweeping study of celebrity (2001) examines the ways in which notions of celebrity are connected with a broader redefinition of the public/private boundary. Rojek argues that as a whole society, we have moved from ascribed to achieved status, and that our ways of recognising celebrity have mirrored these changes. It is this very willingness to connect the study of fame and status with broader social theory of which we should perhaps take note, not simply that his examples run from film stars to mass murderers, and the Oklahoma City bomber. At the same time, others have begun to look at the new, apparently greater, permeability generated by new television show formats which make celebrities out of 'ordinary folks'. Jon Dovey (2000), for instance, explores the rise of the 'ordinary celebrity' in the context of the docusoap, and the people (for instance, the 'cheat' on the first British series of *Big Brother*; the woman who could not pass her driving test; the camp airline worker) who became famous for simply 'performing themselves'. Celebrity has become, in principle, accessible to anyone.

There is surely something important here. A swift examination of books in print with the word 'celebrity' in their title reveals more than 250 in the English language. Many are simply labelled 'Celebrity Bios', covering, indiscriminately, film, television, music, fashion and sports figures. Some have a distinct voyeuristic quality – take, for instance, *Celebrity Skins*, which lovingly details the tattoos of the famous (a forthcoming book on the same topic offers a set of transfers so that you can 'wear the same ones as them'). These speak of a diminished distance between the famous and the rest, which has critical implications for the classic picture of stardom as a 'world apart'.

UNFINISHED BUSINESS

There is a considerable body of work which addresses contemporary changes, much of it running counter to the 'big theories' from which star studies began. The main thrust of these came from two sources, as we have seen: from a will to see stars as representations, and as the solution to ideological crises. On both approaches, while there might be moments of tension and change, the norm was that stars were effective, coherent. Rather than start from this presumption, might we do better to try to learn from strange and awkward cases?

FAILURE

The first of these concerns *failure*. The obvious fact is that stars do fail, and even the most successful eventually fade – unless early death freezes and immortalises them. Given all the attention to the manipulation of star personae, to the management of public opinion, and so on, what can we learn from cases of failure? One film failure offers a case in point. *Judge Dredd* contributed greatly to the death of its parent company Cinergi, and did no favours to the star presence of its major star Sylvester Stallone. Yet the film may actually reveal much precisely *in and through* its failure, and might throw light on something which ought to concern us: the failure of star studies to replicate the promise of perhaps its most famous single case study. In his study of Marilyn Monroe, Richard Dyer claimed to reveal a really close 'fit' between her persona (Monroe as soft, almost amorphous sexuality, whose body promises infinite pleasures while her talk seems innocently unaware of what her body is doing) and the ideological tensions of a period (growing public recognition of female sexuality, tensions within the family increasingly orientated around consumption and leisure, and a will to remove women from the sphere of work). Was Dyer just a touch fortuitous in finding such a neat fit? Was this a special case? If stars *are* more than just filmic figures, why is it not easier to locate other cases where stars may resolve ideological tensions? Or perhaps we have looked for too tidy relations between stars and ideological processes? The most promising case since Dyer on Monroe has to be the many studies of 'musculinity' in 1980s action movies, which has been widely theorised as pointing to a crisis in masculinity 'contained' and perhaps magically resolved in the bodies of action heroes (see Tasker, 1993a; Kirkham and Thumim, 1993; Jeffords, 1994). The problem is that the 'crisis' is almost entirely an imputed one. Nothing like Dyer's careful research into wider discursive patterns of Monroe's period is to be found alongside the analyses of action movies; his study stands worryingly alone.

Judge Dredd posed problems. Born out of Thatcherite Britain, *Dredd* represented a totalitarian future – but in a way which turned its chief villain into its hero. Dredd is the law, but he is almost above the law. Its comic-book source managed this by walking a line between the character being humourless and the story overlaying a dark humour. IPC's Form Book, giving rules to merchandisers, captured this tension nicely:

> In character, Dredd is two-dimensional and machine-like. . . . Dredd never smiles. Though he is capable of a very black sense of humour, we can never be sure if he thinks his remarks are funny.

An additional problem was posed by the fact that *Dredd* was a British view of 'America', now being transformed by an American company.

This tested the producers. One of the film's scriptwriters, Steven de Souza, revealed their solution, a way to avoid the story 'warping into a moral vacuum':

> There's a temptation in the material that it's important not to give in to. I think anybody who reads the newspapers can see the frustration that people have with the court system. So it's important to show that Dredd is not a fascist, but that he's on the verge of becoming one and ultimately pulls back from it. . . . He helps the society to take a step towards real justice, as well, which is very much tied in with the idea of democracy.
>
> *(Killick, 1995: 48)*

'Fascism' as a concept has its own peculiar history within American political thinking. It has often been used by the Right as a ground for attacks on governmental, especially federal, acts. In the 1950s, partly through the work of Frankfurt School expatriates, it became one of the tools for critical tendencies within American society and culture: unless some controls were quickly imposed on, in particular, certain mass media, there was a danger of 'fascist personalities' being drawn to a Hitlerian leader. In short, fascism is not a descriptive concept, but one thoroughly imbricated into ideological struggles in the US.

It is therefore interesting to see that in the year following *Dredd*, another film emerged where again the issue was acknowledged – but this time the film-makers chose to ride the risks. *Starship Troopers* (1996, USA) took Robert Heinlein's highly controversial (1957) panegyric to authoritarian government (the novel was a treatise against 'peacemongers' who criticised America's acquisition of nuclear capabilities), and used it as a platform for discussing the dangers of an over-ordered, or fascist, society. Edward Neumeier, the main scriptwriter, discussed this in the book of the film:

> What I really liked about the idea of this movie was that it allowed me to write about fascism. That's amusing. It was also difficult to do – or do well. ... Because the message of the original book was pretty straightforward: Democracy is failing, and we need some strict controls on our culture. I retained this outlook in the *Starship Troopers* scripts. But I also wanted to play with it. To me, the whole spin of the movie was this: You want a world that works? Okay, we'll show you one. And it really *does* work. It happens to be a military dictatorship, but it works. That's the original rhythm I was trying to play with, just to sort of mess with the audience.
>
> *(Sammon, 1997: 12)*

The comparison is relevant, because with *Dredd* the producers clearly saw Stallone's star-persona as a means to defray these tensions. The script was fashioned around Stallone's star-image:

> Joel Silver told me that you can never forget who your star is, because the audience will never forget. ... The thing that Stallone does so well, is that he gets the shit kicked out of him, then he comes back. That's his myth, almost, ever since *Rocky*. So the presence of Stallone confirmed our sense that Dredd needed to get knocked down to his lowest point, because Sly is such a great fighter when he's coming back. It was a good plot device in the movie, but it was also very sympathetic to Stallone.
>
> *(Killick, 1995: 42)*

Late editing on *Judge Dredd* discloses the care which the producers took. An opening sequence in which the 'citizens' riot because the judges replace a promised park with another law enforcement barracks, was simply removed – which made the riot look like anarchistic violence that needed to be controlled.

But the star burst the bubble; in an 'outburst' widely reported at the point of the film's release, Stallone identified and praised a 'Dredd' political position:

Movie tough-guy Sylvester Stallone has stunned his Hollywood pals with an amazing right-wing outburst. The former *Rocky* and *Rambo* star wants a ruthless leader, like the fearless Judge Dredd in his new $50 million sci-fi movie, to clean up the world. Stallone believes society is in a sordid spiral of decline into a twilight zone of violence illustrated in his new fantasy epic. ... Now Stallone is calling for criminals who use guns to be hanged within 24 hours.

('*Judge Dredd to Rule the World*', Sunday Mirror, 2 July 1995)

In an important sense, then, Stallone's presence in *Dredd* could be seen as a conscious attempt to persuade him to function as Monroe's did in her films – to resolve away tensions, to marry the unmarriable. The key difference is that *Dredd* failed – the tensions burst through, the film died at the box office, and Stallone's own career nose-dived even further. This is not to suggest that the film failed because of the tensions over fascism – too many other factors were in play.[6] No, it was the attempt to use Stallone's persona to defray a perceived tension, reflected into the very form of the film which emerges. Dyer was only able to argue a parallelism; he did not attempt to demonstrate direct links between Monroe and 1950s sexual ideologies. Yet his writings presume that the parallelism was effective. The *Judge Dredd* case suggests where we might look for such links, but asks awkward questions about their effectiveness.

THE STAR VEHICLE

Might we raise another question from this: that perhaps the very concept of a 'star vehicle' is altering? In classical Hollywood, the notion of a star vehicle could be quite particular. Studios regularly researched combinations of titles, narrative outlines and (usually romantic) star combinations. Had they achieved the right formula so that the 'marquee value' of a star would add to the box office potential of a movie? (For the classic account of these practices, see Handel, 1950: Chapter 9.) Care has to be taken with this – a star often managed to make a part seem inevitably his/her own, even if s/he was fourth or fifth in line in original intent. Ron Base's *Starring Roles* gives many examples of how a part came late to a star, who then made it entirely their own. A good example is John Wayne acquiring the part of John Books in *The Shootist* (1976, USA), a part he badly wanted, but only acquired after Charles Bronson, Gene Hackman and Clint Eastwood had all turned it down (Shepherd and Slatzer, 1986: Chapter 21). Having gained the part, he proceeded to demand substantial script changes – including a change in the disease from which his character is dying, because he regarded bowel cancer as 'unmanly'. When he played the part, it unquestionably became 'his' vehicle. But Wayne was one of a passing breed of stars. What shall we say about the new breed?

There appears to be a greater tolerance of unevenness in stars' careers. Recently, a number of stars have managed to stay 'big', even in the face of contradictory evidence. Harrison Ford, for instance, after his high point in the 1980s, has been associated with some shaky box office staggerers (*Regarding Henry* (1991, USA) and *Sabrina* (1995, USA), for instance). Yet he has become widely known as the 'teflon star', to whose image no dirt sticks. Keanu Reeves is a good illustration of a star whose (in)ability to act has led to a wave-form career. He has had a series of big movies with (for instance) *Bill and Ted's Excellent Adventure* (1989, USA – US gross $40 million on a budget of under $10 million), *Bram Stoker's Dracula* (1992, USA – worldwide gross $192 million on a budget of $40 million), *Speed* (1994, USA – budget $30 million, worldwide gross over $280 million) and *The Matrix* (1999, USA – budget $63 million, worldwide gross in excess of $370 million). He has been part of cultish but relatively unsuccessful films such as *My Own Private Idaho* (1991, USA – budget $2.5 million, US gross $6 million), and played second fiddle while bringing a bit of popular appeal to otherwise art-house movies such as *Much Ado About Nothing* (1993, USA – grossed $22 million on a safe small budget of $8 million). He has also failed badly to bring appeal to other movies: *Even Cowgirls Get The Blues* (1993, USA – a US gross of $1.7 million to a budget of $8 million showed the limits of his sex appeal) and *Johnny Mnemonic* (1995, USA – budget $30 million, a worldwide gross of only $52 million). Perhaps his worst outing was as Shane Falco in *The Replacements* (2000, USA) which, perhaps on the back of his smash success in *The Matrix* began with a strong weekend, and then died irretrievably. On a $50 million budget (very high for a sports comedy), it managed a US gross of only $44 million, and very poor international earnings. Yet despite the fluctuations and the constant panning of his acting abilities, Reeves' career can hardly be said to have suffered.

The same seems true of Brad Pitt. Surprise winner to emerge from *Thelma and Louise* (1991, USA), his career has peaked and troughed regularly since – and this has been noticed. So commonplace is this that listings magazines will chart this uneven progress even as they publicise their offerings. Film Four, announcing its Brad Pitt season, ran a column entitled 'Box Office-O-Meter: how bankable is Brad Pitt?', listing the variations in his films' successes from 1991–2001 (*Film Four* magazine, October 2001). Yet it does not seem to have done great damage to his image. Indeed the clear box office weakness of *Fight Club* (1999, USA – on a budget of $63 million it earned only $37 million at the US box office) may even have redounded to his credit, as the film has become something of a specialist film with vociferous support from a young fan base.

That stars' careers contain both successes and failures is nothing new; it would be hard to find a star in any period who did not display this. But in the classical period, studios would have studied the form of their stars like racehorses; their stock and their bidding power would have risen or fallen fairly closely in line with their marquee value. Cathy Klaprat has studied Bette Davis's early career, arguing that 'stars were created, not discovered, counter to popular myths' (Klaprat, 1985: 351–2). According to Klaprat, Warner Bros took a number of years and experimented in various ways before hitting a winning formula – which then allowed the company to make one-off films which deliberately broke with that image. Failure therefore might not be directly ascribed to the star, because the studio had not yet found the right 'mix'. But after the dissolution of the system of studio ownership of stars, responsibility for success or failure transferred more directly to the stars – if their films performed badly, that was their fault. Now, but in a different mode, it seems the association is once again weaker. It is as if a number of stars are *less invested* in their individual films than they used to be.

Richard Corliss, quoted earlier, touches lightly on this:

> So why keep giving stars annuities? Because they are brand commodities who bring one more element – and, in the right mix, the crucial one – to the marketing of an expensive product. Because studio heads are nervous folks who want the insurance and the reassurance of a known name. And, not least, because the old guys know how to play the star game. They agree to keep appearing in movies that are recognizably big and bulky, with the special effects, the cartoon emotions, the apocalyptic ante all announcing that these movies have *size*.
>
> *(Corliss, 'So Much for Star Power', Time, 4 September 2000: 75)*

Corliss may have touched on something important – that one condition of recent stardom may be the willingness to play down to the requirements of high-energy, low-intellectual-demand blockbusters, where simple presence (the ability to *seem* deeply meaningful) is what makes these star vehicles. This might throw interesting light on the recent tendency for stars to take time out to return to the stage – as if to make sure that some meaning remains, after some of the particularly head-banging blockbusters have drained it out of them.

If there is truth in this, we should wonder if there is not an archetypal star for the turn of the millennium. It would have to be someone who, while commanding great attention for their movies, still seems to hold something in reserve; whose very presence and persona seem to withhold and almost comment ironically on the act of appearing in each movie. Such a star, surely, is Kevin Spacey. A meteoric rise to fame after his success in *The Usual Suspects* (1995, USA) led quickly to his acclaimed performance in the multi-Oscar-winning *American Beauty* (1996, USA). Since then, hardly a month goes by without him appearing somewhere – more than 50 major screen outings in 15 years, and a host of television appearances. Yet all the public presence leaves a puzzling gap: no authorised or unauthorised biography to date, and few details are known about Spacey's private life.

These gaps are, in some undefinable way, *incorporated into his star persona*. Spacey is an unknown, and loved as such.

If stardom depends on a dialogue between public persona and private person, it seems singularly lacking in his case. Spacey, of course, guards against invasions of his private life. He is notorious for declining to discuss anything more personal than his dog in interviews. Spacey functions as enigma. His on-screen presence is that of a mildly smiling, under-acting, gentle man. In a number of his early films, the narrative played on the possibility that *behind* this almost absence was something dangerous; *The Usual Suspects* is a clear case of this. However, while previewing *American Beauty*, the promotional magazine *Inside Film* used one of the taglines from *Suspects* ('And like that, he's gone ...') to dissolve the line between persona and simple acting skill:

> Kevin Spacey so submerges himself in his characters that he disappears before your very eyes. ... Kevin Spacey is not Kevin Spacey. That is, the Spacey seen on the screen over the past decade is not the real Spacey. ... Spacey knows the actor must constantly reinvent himself to stay ahead. And you can bet he's working 24:7 to make us believe in new lives, new stories. And like that, he's gone ...
>
> *(Jerry Glover,* Inside Film *18, 1999: 28–9)*

This suggests that Spacey is balanced between being actor and star, managing this by simultaneously denying us a private persona, and turning that denial into his persona.[7] Perhaps most revealing is the hint that this is a planned strategy. If Spacey might be an archetypal contemporary star, this public balancing act may be worth closer scrutiny.

ANIMATION AND VOICEOVERS

The fact that by the 1990s a number of processes were overlaid on each other should be no surprise. It is important to keep a note of changes which may turn out to be characteristic of new tendencies. One such, in tune with Katzenberg's rant against stars' levels of control, has paralleled the re-emergence of big-budget animated movies in the last decade.

The role of stars in animation, although important, is different. They can *voice* a character, and thus transfer to it some of the resonances of their established persona. But they cannot *own* it. When Tom Hanks speaks the words of Woody in *Toy Story*, Hanks' persona contributes to, but must not supplant, that of the animated character. When Robin Williams became the genie in Disney's *Aladdin* (1992, USA), he did more than supply his voice. He was allowed to riff his lines, in the way he had in *Good Morning, Vietnam* (1987, USA). Only then did the animators bring his character to visual life, matching both the pace and the dynamics of his recording. Yet Williams was paid actors' rates for his performance – plus a gift of a Picasso. Thereby no points, no rights in the character, no control.

What should we make of this shift? How might we 'name' the shift implied by this? We saw earlier the ways in which a crude, but still useful, history of the stages of stardom has been put together. I am suggesting that there is a seed in here of a new kind of star relationship, in which the star becomes a *contracted semiotician*, i.e. a star in effect sub-contracts his/her accumulated star presence to a film, probably for a fixed fee, and without receiving in return much addition to his/her persona. Although it would surely be possible to find examples of such a relationship before the 1990s, it does seem to be a significantly new mode of using stars in the last period, as animation has become once more important. It is a *dependent* mode, in that it cannot occur on its own – stars still need to have established a sufficiently distinct persona that can then be traded upon.[8]

Something else may be implied here, about the partial separation of voice from persona. The use of actors' voices for advertisements (a closely related if not identical phenomenon) is widespread. One report on this noted the attractions for well-known figures – not just the money, but that they could 'voice' their support for a commodity without *directly* voicing support: 'A lot of people don't want to be seen endorsing something but are happy to have their voice used,' says Kate Stammers, a creative director at advertising agency, St Luke's ('Voice Recognition', *Guardian*, 12 June 1999). The split that this implies – 'I have not said I favour First Direct Insurance, even if my voice has added a dimension of humorous sexiness to it' – suggests an uneven flow between contracted semioticians and their 'parts'.

There are even fragments of evidence that this use of voiceovers is becoming a system. Now that it is evident that the 'revival of animation' has box office viability, Hollywood figures are orientating towards it, and seeing it as a solution to problems. UK Channel 5's *Movie Chart Show* ran a substantial item focused around *Ice Age* (2002, USA), suggesting that voiceovers have distinct advantages for actors. They provide a good out-of-body vehicle for stars who feel the need to reinvent themselves – perhaps because of die-back in their careers. They also provide an opportunity for actors who have not yet graduated to the A-list. From this category one actor talked about his admiration and gratitude to the animators: the silence he was asked to leave in his voicing became, through their skills, a moment pregnant with emotion, so that when his character sheds a tear and seems to choke on his words, 'I get the credit for that!'

But any discussion of voiceovers inevitably raises a second question: what do we say about the characters who are voiced? Can they be classed as 'stars' in their own right? This is a controversial issue. There are arguments that cartoon figures cannot be stars because they do not have a life outside the films in which they appear. This is an important point, but later in this book, Paul Wells makes a compelling case that they can indeed be stars. In common parlance, certainly, the characters are often so named. Witness the *Daily Mail*'s 'Weekend' supplement cover story (26 January 2002): 'The New Buzz about Town – Meet *Monsters Inc.*, Disney's Newest Superstars' – a feature article whose key component was its investigation of the ways in which 'the monsters are uncannily human'. For example:

> Any adult who has worked for a big company will recognise the intrigue and backstabbing [at *Monsters Inc.*]. They may have come across a boss like Henry J Waternoose (voiced by James Coburn), the factory's paternal, crab-like chief executive. . . . Randall, who will stop at nothing to beat Sulley's scare record, may seem like the incarnation of evil in children's eyes. But from an adult perspective, he's not so far from everyone's most loathed and competitive colleague.

If we take this at face value, it seems that these animated figures may indeed have life outside their film vehicles – but of a very different kind from one we are used to considering.

My discussion of this is honestly tentative. If a case might be made that the voice of Whoopi Goldberg in *The Lion King* (1994, USA) provides an apologia for the narrative racism attached to her hyena character, does it begin to look thin when extended? A straight-to-video 'borrow' on this smash hit – *The Lion of Oz* (2000, USA) – proudly announced its 'starring the voices of' among others Tim Curry, Lynne Redgrave and Jane Horrocks. The fact that the last was completely unrecognisable, because of the disappearance of her northern accent and ditzy screen-personality, surely gives off the smell of yet further marketing ploys. The rhetorical functions of references to stars must never be forgotten.

VOLUME OF INFORMATION

If one recent change in Hollywood stardom has to be nominated above all others, it would surely be the multiplication of kinds of images, information and stories about stars. In the course of writing this Introduction, apart from a range of resources that I have specially assembled for my own research and teaching, I have had recourse to the following, all easily available to me: a host of websites, including the Internet Movie Database, which offer vast, searchable archives; an array of publications that routinely accompany many films' releases (for instance, free booklets produced by cinema chains as part of their bid for 'loyal' audiences); newspaper supplements about particular films, given away presumably to prove that this newspaper is 'in touch' with a major leisure event; *The Making Of* books, which promote their films by telling a thousand background facts and stories about them; a parade of star biographies, written and televisual, celebrating and dishing the dirt in equal proportions; gossip columns, DVD commentaries, press previews, and a host of other materials which do little more than recirculate what others have already said. Of course all these have existed to a degree before – they are a condition of existence of stardom. But perhaps we need to attend, as never before, both to their sheer quantity, and to the manner of their organisation and availability.

In 1985, the screenwriter William Goldman made his famous pronouncement: in Hollywood 'Nobody knows anything' (Goldman, 1985: 39). Nobody can predict with any reliability what makes a film succeed or fail, therefore each next decision to 'go' is an act of risk and of faith. But perhaps in the light of the last few years his slogan needs modification, to say that '*Everybody knows* that nobody knows anything.' The paradox is surely undeniable. More and more is seen and known, yet the glut of information amounts to so little understanding. Stardom is visible as never before – down to each stitch in actresses' dresses, and every inch of skin exposed or not exposed by them. More and more, we seem to be able to see whatever we want, in the Oscars, and the annual hoopla of the Academy Awards Ceremony (and increasingly, it feels, in months of preparation from Cannes, the BAFTA Awards, and the Directors' Guild Awards); in celebrity gala events of various kinds (after the terrorist attacks of September 11th, any number of stars felt the need to go walkabout in New York); in the routines of gossip. We can offer grand theorisations of this if we wish – the debates about the 'information society' and the domination of 'simulations' are enticing, to say the least. But if at the very least this book improves in a small way our abilities to sift through the garbage bins of journalism, to find the joins in the shredded paperwork of publicity machines, then not only film studies will be the better for it.

---

1 Although this essay was largely written by Martin Barker, it owes a great deal to discussions with and the critical commentary of Thomas Austin.

2 We are not alone in wanting to see this reawakening. See for instance Paul McDonald (1999) and Ndalianis (2002) as illustrations of this reawakening.

3 Actually, the figures are interesting – commonly seen as a failure, *Dick Tracy* in fact gained a US box office gross of $103 million, on a budget of $47 million. This tells an interesting story about Disney's investment expectations.

4 The story of the debacle is well recounted in Base (1994).

5 See also the excellent essay on this phenomenon by Timothy Corrigan (1998) which in particular argues that recent developments in the role of the 'auteur' have produced a series of stresses and conflicts that have 'evacuated it of most of its expressive power and textual coherency' (1998: 60). In the other direction it is of course important to remember that there are precursors, perhaps most obviously Alfred Hitchcock. Hitchcock worked in both film and television, and his name became associated with crowd-pleasing popular films and with films celebrated by 'auteur' critics such as Truffaut. See in particular Kapsis (1992), who explores the construction of a 'reputation' for Hitchcock both during and after his life.

6 Among them, a one-year fall in cinema audiences in both the US and Britain; head-to-head competition with *Batman Returns*; and generally weak reviews of the film.

7   Recently, though, there have been signs that this very reticence about investment of self in his performances might turn against him. Reviewing *K-Pax* (2002, USA), the *Guardian* for instance commented unkindly on the comparison between Spacey's performance there, and his earlier, more 'dangerous' outings in, for instance, *Swimming With Sharks*. The enigma is, for some, taking on the dimensions of an over-reproduced Mona Lisa smile.

8   Exaggerated claims are sometimes made to the contrary. In a 1998 BBC documentary, *The Computer That Ate Hollywood*, one insider suggested that the move to develop entirely virtual stars was directly driven by the studios' desire to control, if not dispense with, their dependence on this expensive, often unreliable resource.

Section 1

Star systems

Thomas Austin

That film stardom is always an intertextual and multi-media phenomenon has become a truism of star studies. This commonplace is re-examined from a range of different perspectives in this section, which addresses the overlapping political economic, technological and discursive dimensions of contemporary Hollywood stardom. These interrelating fields of activity can be termed *star systems*, in that they each play a part in the production and circulation of star images and narratives. This is best thought of as a shared, but never fully equal, venture involving film-makers, marketers, reviewers and commentators, fans, and stars themselves, as active players within such economic and discursive machinery. The work gathered in this section traces ongoing developments in the intertextual networks, technological apparatuses and commercial logics that frame and constitute stardom. How have such processes been organised and reconfigured during a period that has witnessed Hollywood's continuing appetite for cross-market synergies and tie-ins, the popularisation of 'new media' applications such as the internet, and the increasing use of computer-generated imagery?

During the 1990s, the internet developed into an important new means for film marketing and the dissemination of 'official' star images, as well as the circulation of gossip and unauthorised images beyond the control of studios and agents. Hollywood's initial rush to exploit the internet as a promotional window has been followed by increasing caution and retrenchment. Bob Levin, of MGM Distribution Co., recently commented, 'We were all had in the beginning' (*Screen International*, 5 April 2002: 5). However, sexual and pornographic images have proved hugely popular on the net. Pornographers deployed the new technology 'farther and faster than legitimate [*sic*] providers', as Chuck Kleinhans (2002: 293) notes in his discussion of the internet-based circulation of Pamela Anderson and Tommy Lee's now notorious home video of sexual activity.

Sexualised and nude celebrity images (including fakes) are among the materials considered by Paul McDonald in his investigation of official and unofficial websites devoted to

Hollywood film stars. He traces important continuities between modes of star discourse on the net and earlier regimes of knowledge about stars, from the construction of the picture personality's professional identity to the revelation of the 'hidden truths' of star bodies. But his work also leads to a reconsideration of some established paradigms, notably those used to think about fan activity. McDonald argues that the radicalism of fan discourses should not be taken for granted: 'While authored outside institutional conditions of production, fan sites emulate rather than criticise commercial popular culture.'

The internet is one of the media outlets trawled by Barry King in his ambitious exploration of proliferating popular constructions of stardom in the 1990s. King considers journalistic writing about stars, and the procedures of 'persona management' deployed by studios, and stars themselves acting as 'stakeholders' in their own careers. He suggests that, while older modes of persona construction have persisted, new ones have also emerged. Focusing on Sharon Stone, he argues that exhaustive public scrutiny is managed by the production of an 'elastic persona' constructed via 'a process of constant re-writing in order to accommodate the fact that past and present personae all occupy a common discursive space'.

What are the commercial benefits to be achieved from realising inter-media synergies around the figure of a successful star? And, perhaps even more importantly, in an industry susceptible to its own hype about new markets and business opportunities, what are the limits to such strategies?[1] Geoff King's chapter considers such issues via an investigation of Will Smith's 'crossover' career as a successful film star and recording artist. King focuses in particular on *Men In Black* (1997, USA) and *Wild Wild West* (1999, USA), in order to determine whether or not these film 'brands' delivered on the promise of a cross-promotional bonanza effectively embodied in the figure of Smith himself.

In recent years, the deployment of computer-generated imagery (CGI) in Hollywood films such as *Terminator 2* (1991, USA), *Jurassic Park* (1993, USA) and *Titanic* (1997, USA) has been scrutinised by academics (see Darley, 2000; Pierson, 1999; Prince, 1996). But little consideration has been given to the implications that such uses of 'impossible photography' (Darley's phrase) might carry for star studies. Is it now possible to talk not just of 'synthespians' and computer-generated extras, but of 'post-human' stars, realised via CGI? Or is the notion of a 'cyber-star' effectively a contradiction in terms? These questions are raised, among others, by the final two chapters in this section: Matt Hills' investigation of discourses of fan loathing towards Jar Jar Binks, the often derided source of comic relief in *Star Wars Episode I: The Phantom Menace* (1999, USA); and Paul Wells' consideration of the affective investments simultaneously invited and interrogated by Woody and Buzz Lightyear, the 'stars' of *Toy Story* (1996, USA).

How useful is it to bring such computer-generated characters under the heading of film stardom? At the very least, thinking about 'virtual stardom' throws into relief some of the prevalent assumptions (some obvious, others more tacit) at work in approaches to Hollywood stars. If 'virtual' stars are not 'true' stars, then the terms of their failure to gain admission to that category should help clarify what 'real' stardom is. The obvious, but nonetheless useful, place to start here is with the notion of stars' humanity, which can be elaborated by thinking in particular about two terms: attractiveness and agency.

Ideals of human attractiveness, grounded in the body and in particular the face that provides the referent for an indexical representation (albeit one often 'improved' via make-up or surgery, not to mention airbrushing or digital 'retouching'), are a common component of stardom. The conventions of 'handsome' appearance clearly inform the constructions of Woody and Buzz, but these CGI heroes remain distinct from indexical images of male beauty. Equally, human stars are endowed with an agency (often celebrated in star discourses) that entails both the living of an extra-filmic 'private life' (always liable to partial 'revelation' and rewriting via the operations of journalism, biography, promotion and gossip); the deployment of performance techniques and decisions; and a series of lived experiences, contingencies and outcomes which are understood and narrativised as a 'career'.[2] By contrast, such manifestations of agency are absent from the personae of cyberstars. Instead, ideas of self-determination and creativity are often displaced onto popular auteurist discourses, which connect George Lucas to Jar Jar, and John Lasseter to Woody and Buzz.

The move to thinking about 'virtual stardom' also demands a return to the notion of stardom as constituted partly via 'subsidiary forms' in circulation around and beyond film appearances (Ellis, 1984: 91). Clearly, promotional images of Jar Jar, Woody and Buzz perform a familiar commercial function, but the nature of such appearances also differs intriguingly from those of human stars. These computer-generated characters function as visually distinct, recognisable and readily transferable film-related images, much like, say, images of human stars 'in character' as Rocky or Spider-Man. However, 'post-human' stars promote their respective films without demanding the stellar fees, royalties, perks and entourages typically associated with human stars. In addition, appearances by Jar Jar *et al.* in advertising campaigns and on merchandising, foreground not only new technological capabilities but also stars' status as commodity forms, a function partly concealed by the presence of a unique, embodied individual human agent. Thus, 'virtual stars' become reminders of the often uneasy mix of elements – the commercially motivated exploitation of film components, star-actors' career management decisions, connotations of professional ability and glamour – that underlie the mediated appearances of human stars.

Finally, 'virtual stars' raise some important issues that require further study. For example, how has CGI impacted on film financing, budgeting and conditions of production? How is the labour market for screen 'blood actors' (not just the star elite) in the USA and elsewhere being shaped by new technology?[3] Are screen performers having to adjust their acting techniques to incorporate 'virtual' co-stars?

Another area still in need of more research is the (contractual and self-managed) labour expected of human stars, and the related roles of agents and studio staff. Stars' work needs to be conceived as a series of tasks that include publicity tours and press junkets, as well as the performance of diegetic screen roles. For instance, the strike threatened by the Screen Actors' Guild in spring 2001 concerned distributors and producers because of the possible withdrawal of star labour from promotional duties, as well as from shooting schedules.[4] Such work has been the object of intermittent critical curiosity but, perhaps inevitably given the reluctance of Hollywood insiders to reveal too much about present operating practices, this particular terrain remains relatively opaque to academic scrutiny. Hopefully, future research agendas will continue to work at opening up this sector of the star system to further inquiry.

---

1   AOL Time Warner's announcement in April 2002 of the biggest quarterly loss in US corporate history prompted some commentators to question whether media mergers and convergence could deliver the trumpeted benefits of synergy. For example, a *Screen International* editorial noted: 'no matter how logical or visionary such mishmashes can look on paper, too often they end up turning what was once golden into something much more leaden' (3 May 2002: 6).

2   For an informative account of the part played by contingency in the careers of Hollywood stars, see Base (1994).

3   For an initial inquiry, see Magder and Burston (2001: 226–9).

4   More recently, the Hungarian director Istvan Szabo has talked about the difference between American stars and their European counterparts in terms of the labour that the former are prepared to put into film promotion (*Screen International*, 29 March 2002: 9).

Chapter One

STARS IN THE ONLINE ☐ UNIVERSE: PROMOTION, NUDITY, REVERENCE

Paul McDonald

Exploring the early years of the film star system in America, Richard DeCordova (1990) identifies the emergence of the system with how the press and other media circulated different categories of knowledge or discourse about stars. After an initial period during which performers had remained anonymous, from 1909 onwards American cinema witnessed the first publicising of performer names. Making the names of performers publicly known was central to creating the identity of what DeCordova calls the 'picture personality'. Naming had the discursive function of individuating performers, and constructed a performer's identity across a series of film performances and published inter-texts. With the personality discourse, DeCordova observes, knowledge of the performer was restricted to his or her on-screen existence. This had the effect of constructing the identity of a performer in the entirely professional terms of his or her public role as a film actor.

As the names of performers came to be used for the purposes of promoting films, the American film industry saw a change from what Eileen Bowser (1990) observes as the previous system of selling films through the brand names of studios. Naming performers therefore provided the developing industry with a fresh marketing mechanism. Henceforth, the names of performers would play a significant part in the commercial existence of American films. Naming also provided the foundation from which the identities of film performers would eventually be integrated more widely into commercial culture.

This development can be seen as having two significant effects on the film business in America: naming performed the symbolic function of individuating performers as identities to be circulated in public discourse, while the commercial purposes of the film industry were served by a new category of branded resource to be used in the marketing of films. Through the personality discourse, the American film industry was able to recognise simultaneously the cultural and economic values of performers, for the personality was created as an image, and could equally be deployed as capital. The picture personality therefore made performers into commodified identities.

For DeCordova, star discourse only fully developed after 1914 with the first reporting of film performers' off-screen lives. During this period, knowledge about the private side of stardom was controlled and represented in ways that suggested a performer's off-screen life was a reflection of his or her on-screen roles. In this way, star discourse achieved moral closure around the identities of performers. By achieving this closure, the star system amplified the marketable value of the star's identity, and the off-screen lifestyles of stars became a focus for the consumer aspirations of the age. This closure was disrupted, however, when a series of high-profile scandals in the early 1920s created a fissure between the public and private sides of stardom. Destroying the marketability of stars like Roscoe 'Fatty' Arbuckle, scandals drew attention to the fact that in the off-screen lives of stars, degrees of privacy existed, divided between a publicly promoted sense of the private – a public-privacy – and an intimate hidden life – the private side of privacy.

Star discourses were distributed in public life through a range of media channels: the press, book publishing, photography, radio, television and – one of the most effective channels of all – gossip. From its earliest days, the film star system in America has therefore always operated as a multiple media system. More recently the popularisation of computer-mediated communications has made the internet a new universe for the circulation of star discourse. This chapter sets out to look at the ways in which the internet has contributed to the distribution of discourse relating to Hollywood stars. Influenced by the significant work of Richard Dyer (1998), reading the meaning of star images has become an established feature of the film studies agenda. What DeCordova's study explores, however, is how knowledge about stars circulated in the earliest years of the film industry in America, and also the forms of insight provided by that distribution of knowledge. It is by engaging with this systematic distribution of meaning that this chapter examines the ways in which the internet has contributed to the circulation of star discourse. What is involved in such a line of enquiry is a reflection on the online contexts in which the meanings of stars are circulated, instead of the actual meanings of stars. The chapter is therefore investigating the collision between the star system as the organised distribution of star discourse and the internet as a system for the relay of text and image. What follows is a look at how the cultural and economic values of star discourse are distributed in the online universe.

References to film stars now appear on thousands of sites across the internet. These sites see the identities of stars situated in a range of contexts. This chapter considers star discourse in several contexts: film promotions; entertainment news; celebrity nudes; fake celebrity nudes; fan sites; and clubs (see Table 1.1, p. 31). While the distribution of star discourse is evident in other contexts (for example, databases and archival sites), these will not be addressed here. Each of the categories discussed will be considered for the types of knowledge or discourse made available, the various ways in which sites create a

Table 1.1: **Star websites**

Film promotions	*Meet Joe Black* http://www.meetjoeblack.com
	My Best Friend's Wedding
	http://www.spe.sony.com/movies/mybestfriendswedding
	Seven http://www.sevenmovie.com
	There's Something About Mary
	http://www.aboutmary.com
Entertainment news	E! Online http://www.eonline.com
	Hollywood.com http://www.hollywood.com
Celebrity nudes	100% Nude Celebrity Pics http://www.nudecelebpics.net
	CelebsXposed http://www.celebsxposed.com
	True Male Celebs http://www.truemalecelebs.com
Fake celebrity nudes	Absolute Fake Celebs http://www.celebfakes.com
	Celebbondage http://www.celebbondage.com
	Scott's Fake Celebrity Nudes Galleries
	http://www.scottss.com
Fan sites	Adonis of the XX Century: Brad Pitt
	http://bradpitt.arteonline.net/
	Dream World of Brad Pitt
	http://members.tripod.com/~bradnval/bradnval.html
	JC's Brad Pitt Links and Photos
	http://www.angelfire.com/ut/LovesBrad2/BradPitt.html
	Like an Angel: Cameron Diaz
	http://likeanangel.homestead.com
Fan clubs	Brad Pitt the Sexiest Man Alive
	http://clubs.yahoo.com/clubs/bradpittthesexiestmanalive
	The Ultimate Brad Pitt Fan Club
	http://clubs.yahoo.com/clubs/theultimatebradpittfanclub
	All Cameron Diaz
	http://clubs.yahoo.com/clubs/allcamerondiaz
	The Real Cameron Diaz Fan Club
	http://clubs.yahoo.com/clubs/therealcamerondiazfanclub
Databases/indexes	Internet Movie Database http://www.imdb.com
	Silent-movies.com http://silent-movies.com
	The Silent Artists Index
	http://www.mdle.com/ClassicFilms/FeaturedStar

relationship between the computer user and the star, and how they are positioning star discourse as part of a commercial cultural economy.

There is a need for a point of specification here. With the exception of the online fan clubs, each of these categories is a form of publishing on the World Wide Web (www). Only with the clubs is the chapter moving tentatively towards an exploration of the interactive potential of online communications. The chapter therefore only addresses star presence on a part of the internet – the web. What is excluded by this emphasis is the realm of inter-personal communications served by the internet, comprising asynchronous (e-mail, news groups, and mailing lists) and synchronous systems (chat rooms and messaging applications). While there is much talk about stars conducted through these systems, in the limited context of this study it is not possible to deal adequately with the discursive complexity of this activity.

With the presence of stars so widely distributed over the internet, there is also a need to find a practical point of focus from which to start. Throughout this chapter references to the presence of Brad Pitt and Cameron Diaz will regularly appear. The selection of these stars was not made by any calculated method but simply by observing frequent references to them – more than many other stars – in researching star-related sites. In choosing Pitt and Diaz, the chapter is not making any special claims about these two performers (although youth appeal and attractiveness certainly accounts for their widespread presence on the web); instead, it is using these names as examples with which to address the various contexts in which star discourse is present in the online universe.

FILM PROMOTIONS

Through publicity and promotion, marketing channels have constructed the meanings of stars as part of the routine business of the film industry. Online communications provide a further addition to the marketing mix. Movie promotional websites are commonly used by film distributors in conjunction with trailers and poster campaigns. In this context, stars' images are used to develop the meaning of a film and build expectation. Like the trailer, sites work to create interest in a film by constructing what John Ellis (1982) has called a 'narrative image'. To differentiate films, sites must use their style and content to create a distinctive image. While all sites are therefore theoretically different, any glance at recent and current promotional sites will reveal a common structure and set of contents. On the home page, links usually carry the visitor to separate pages providing profiles of cast and crew. Other links go to pages with streamed video trailers and galleries of stills. Additional features may include links to merchandise shops, interactive games, chat rooms and voting forums.

On the site for *There's Something About Mary* (1998, USA), the names of stars (Cameron Diaz, Matt Dillon and Ben Stiller) are foregrounded on the home page as a key part of the film's narrative image. The link, 'Who's Behind All This?', recounts the story of the film and offers behind-the-scenes insights into the production history, the film-makers and separate cast members. For Cameron Diaz, the site constructs a short biographical account of her life, picking out what are regarded as key professional moments. Likewise, in another example, the site for *My Best Friend's Wedding* (1997, USA), publishes a biography as the Diaz profile. In both cases these sites are published by the respective distributors for the two films: Twentieth Century Fox and Sony Pictures Entertainment.

Both profiles select nearly identical moments in Diaz's life: Long Beach childhood, modelling career, film stardom, the awarding of the Sho West Star of Tomorrow title by the National Association of Theater Owners (NATO). Other details relate to the star's film roles. *The Mask* (1994, USA) is identified as Diaz's debut film appearance, followed by roles in *The Last Supper* (1995, USA), *She's the One* (1996, USA) and *Feeling Minnesota* (1996, USA). She is variously described as 'captivating', 'flamboyant' and a versatile performer. What emerges from this information is a version of Diaz's life consistent with the discourse of the picture personality, the construction of what DeCordova describes as 'a professional existence – a history of appearances in films and plays and a personality gleaned from those appearances' (1990: 92).

Although the use of the internet for promotional purposes is relatively new, the content of these sites remains very traditional. Promotional sites have not significantly altered established methods of marketing practices. Stars are still used as a key marketing hook. Promotional sites are continuing in the online universe many of the functions already performed by the medium of posters in outdoor advertising. Like posters, star names feature prominently on the front pages of sites. Alongside posters, press books are one of the oldest marketing tools in the business, containing star profiles, cast lists and stills provided by distributors (Sennett, 1998). Electronic press kits have expanded these capabilities by circulating audio or video recordings of star interviews and stories for use by journalists. Promotional sites do not appear to offer anything significantly different, but simply synthesise these various materials into a single electronic resource. If the internet has done anything to transform marketing practices in the film industry, it has been to make this information more directly available to the movie-going public and so to lessen the importance of the press as a mediating agency. What has not changed, however, is the basic function of using the star name and identity to sell films. Stars still emerge from promotional sites as fundamentally commodified identities.

ENTERTAINMENT NEWS

Up-to-date news and gossip about film is now available daily through dedicated entertainment sites. Two leading sites in this category are E! Online and Hollywood.com. As part of their main menus, both sites carry 'Celebrities' links. In the case of Hollywood.com, the link leads to a name search facility which takes the visitor to biographical information on stars, together with news stories, film credits and links for streamed trailers. With E! Online, film stars are grouped in the celebrities section with celebrity names from other sectors of the entertainment business, including music performers and television personalities. Mainly, but not entirely, the forms of knowledge which circulate in these contexts remain restricted to the realm of the picture personality, focusing on the star's previous and forthcoming roles.

What is significant about these sites is how stars are situated in a context which integrates their images into the broader commercial infrastructure of the film and entertainment industries. E! Online, a wholly owned subsidiary of the US cable service E! Networks, offers news, features, reviews and gossip concerning movies, music and television, together with an E!-branded merchandise shop. Since the site's launch in August 1996, E! Online has built its presence on the web, claiming to attract users from over 100 countries and forming partnerships with America Online (AOL), Microsoft Network (MSN), Yahoo!, Excite, NBCi, MSNBC and RealNetworks.

Founded in 1992, Hollywood Media Corporation operates Hollywood.com, which boasts over one million pages of movie-related information, including news, reviews and links to various entertainment services. In the 'Marketplace' area, CDs, DVDs and posters can be purchased. In partnership with CinemaSource, the site offers comprehensive movie listings for approximately 36,000 screens across the United States and Canada. When buying tickets through this channel, transactions are directed to the virtual ticket office, MovieTicket.com, a joint venture between Hollywood Media Corp (30 per cent) and leading theatre chains, including AMC Entertainment, Famous Players, Hoyts and National Amusements. Streamed feature films and shorts can be viewed over the Unlimited Cinema subscription service, while **www.Baseline.Hollywood.com** performs as a research resource for the industry. These sites therefore combine news and information publishing with a range of entertainment-related commercial services.

Film promotional sites use the identities of stars in a direct manner to advertise individual films, and the inclusion of streamed trailers or merchandising links for DVD sales on the star pages carried by entertainment sites also use stars to promote specific films. However, on these sites the real impact of the stars comes from their collective weight: the phenomenon of film stardom is integrated into these sites towards promoting a general culture of fame and celebrity. E! Online and Hollywood.com recognise the value of film stars in the media marketplace, using news and gossip about stars as an important draw to sustain the attractiveness of commercial culture. Stars are used in this context to create a general 'buzz' about the world of entertainment.

CELEBRITY NUDES

Mass market pornography has a history of appropriating technologies of image reproduction and distribution. From photography to 16mm film and home video, the adult entertainment industry has always quickly adopted new media technologies, and the internet has proved no exception. Pornography has become one of the most prevalent forms of electronic commerce and a channel for sexual entrepreneurship (Lane, 2000). Possibly more than any other type of entertainment content, porn seems most appropriate for taking advantage of the distribution channels offered by the internet. Images can be easily distributed across borders in ways that escape national censorial frameworks, and, without the linguistic barriers of television or film, pornography is not subject to the same cultural discount as these media. Popular adoption of the computer as a domestic technology has allowed direct access to porn in the private confines of the home. With an over-abundance of images and easy access, the internet is close to representing what Laurence O'Toole describes as the pornutopian fantasy of 'sex now and without complication or issue . . . no headache, no limitations of size, stamina, performance or desirability' (1998: 23).

Similar to the segmentation of the market for printed pornography, commercial porn sites provide hundreds if not thousands of titles, catering from broad to narrowcast tastes. Amongst the range of erotic sites on the internet, celebrity nude sites have formed connections between the porn business and popular fame. Celebrity nude sites carry galleries of naked public personalities, with images of film stars posted alongside those of music stars, television and sports personalities, and other well-known figures, including models and politicians. In keeping with the representational economy of pornography in general, the volume of female celebrity images far exceeds the number of naked male images. Celebrity nude sites carry images of stars in various contexts; stills from intimate scenes in films, or from porn films made before the performer was famous, are part of the familiar repertory; paparazzi photos catch stars in states of undress while on holiday or relaxing in their private lives. For example, a naked image of Brad Pitt sunbathing is one of the main promotional windows for True Male Celebs, which also carries images of George Clooney, Matt Damon, Leonardo DiCaprio, and Mark Wahlberg. On 100% Nude Celebrity Pics, images of female film stars are collected under various headings: 'Oops – Upskirt Pics' catches stars exposing more than they had intended; 'Paparazzi Shots' includes images of Cameron Diaz nearly naked on the beach, along with shots of Uma Thurman, Drew Barrymore and Gwyneth Paltrow, while Neve Campbell, Heather Graham and Reese Witherspoon appear under 'Young Nude Celebrities'; 'Rare XXX Celebrities Movies' uses film clips to isolate Jennifer Lopez, Demi Moore, Sharon Stone and Barbara Streisand, amongst others, performing sexual acts.

To satisfy legal conditions, a number of disclaimers are made by these sites. The small print at the bottom of the front page for True Male Celebs, states 'Please note that all the images contained herein are for newsworthy purposes only. Any fees payable for this site are exclusively for bandwidth charges associated with the internet.' It is also affirmed that all the subjects were aged over 18 years at the time that the sexual depictions were created. CelebsXposed and 100% Nude Celebrity Pics cover issues of intellectual property by declaring that the operators believe all images carried by the site are public domain. However both offer to remove any material for which it is proved that rights are held. Wary of the many panics which have surrounded concerns over child pornography on the internet, True Male Celebs carries the logo of ASACP – Adult Sites Against Child Pornography.

Sites vary in their methods of access. After a three-day trial subscription of $2.95, a monthly subscription charge is made for access to True Male Celebs ($36.19) and CelebsXposed ($25.95). For 100% Nude Celebrity Pics, access is restricted by the Adult Check age verification system run by Cybernet Ventures Inc. For $19.95 per month, the system's Gold Service operates as a central gateway to access a vast number of premium sites which, at the time of writing, totalled 14,126.

After recognising that these payment systems further locate the identities of stars in the context of commercial exploitation, the question remains, what are they selling? It would be easy to view these sites as further evidence of how pornography has colonised the internet, regarding celebrity nudes as images intended to cause sexual arousal. However, this would provide only a partial explanation of the phenomenon. When the first star scandals appeared in the early 1920s, stories revealed a side of stars hidden from public view. As DeCordova suggests, the personality, star and scandal discourses incrementally deepened a star's identity. Together these discourses constructed a series of layers in which a 'set of secrets was introduced beneath a set of secrets' (1990: 140). 'First, fans "discovered" the secret of the star's real, bodily, existence outside of films, later the secret of the star's married life, and later still, in the twenties, the secret of the star's sexual affairs and transgressions' (1990: 142). Through these secrets, the discourses of stardom promised to reveal the truth of a star's identity. Taking a Foucauldian line, DeCordova suggests that scandal stories served to make sexuality the ultimate truth of a star's identity: 'The sexual scandal is the primal scene of all star discourse, the only scenario that offers the promise of a full and satisfying disclosure of the star's identity' (1990: 141).

Celebrity nudes may not contradict the on-screen images of stars, but they do function in the same way as the scandal discourse to reveal a hidden truth. While so far arguing for seeing celebrity nudes as a form of pornography, there may be a problem with such a conclusion. Celebrity nudes may or may not be judged erotic; the caught-off-guard moments of many paparazzi images lack the sexualised aesthetics of porn. Rather than the eroticism of the image, what is potentially more significant about celebrity nudes is the curiosity they evoke. Like the scandal discourse, the nude image uncovers the secret, hidden star. Regardless of who the star is, celebrity nudes all articulate a similar appeal: this is what a star looks like naked. The intimate transgressions reported in scandal discourse were not interesting, however, for making sex in general known, but for how they made the sexuality of particular stars known. Like the whole star system, celebrity nudes acclaim the exceptional individuality of stars, for their promise is to show not just anybody naked but *this star* naked. Seeing stars naked makes a direct voyeuristic appeal to internet users, catching the star in his or her intimate private state.

FAKE CELEBRITY NUDES

The internet has also seen the publication of fake celebrity nude sites. In their organisation and structure, these sites closely resemble conventional celebrity nude sites, and similar subscription systems also apply. What differentiates fake sites is their content. Images of stars are digitally manipulated to create naked images or construct scenarios displaying stars in erotic contexts. Star faces are grafted on to naked bodies, and the faker's best efforts are made to hide the join. O'Toole's description of these images is very apt – they are 'pseudo-photos' (1998: 279). Celebrity nudes construct the voyeuristic attraction of seeing a star in a situation he or she is aware of, but oblivious to the photograph. Fake nudes double the voyeuristic effects of the image: not only is the star unaware the photograph has happened, but is also pictured in situations in which he or she has never even participated.

In this respect, the fake promises visitors a voyeuristic fantasy more intense than that of conventional nude sites, exposing the subject in a situation beyond his or her control. But it would appear too simple to see these sites as just a means of exposing a hidden aspect of the star. Fake sites do not attempt to deceive visitors into believing what they see is real. The counterfeit status of images is declared in the names of sites: 'Absolute Fake Celebs'; 'Scottss.com Fake Nudes Gallery'. In the case of the former, a disclaimer distances the content of the site from the real star, placing the images entirely in the realm of fantasy:

> I understand that the pictures displayed on this site are digitally retouched
> and altered photos (fakes) of well-known people and are not intended to be a
> true representation of the celebrities or the activities they engage in, nor
> should they reflect the character or reputation of the persons involved. These
> images are intended as parody of the celebs portrayed and are not to be
> taken seriously. The pictures merely depict the fantasies of the fakes'
> creators.

As if to emphasise the constructedness of fake nudes, Scottss.com includes an online tutorial on how to use Adobe Photoshop to make a fake Winona Ryder nude. Visitors are therefore fully aware of the reality behind the image. Celebrity nudes may promise the truth, exposing the star in his or her real natural state, but fake nudes reveal their digital lie. Celebrity nudes work to represent a sense of authenticity; fake nudes display their artifice. In so doing, fake nudes show that they expose nothing. Instead of undoing a layer of secrets to arrive at the truth of a star, fake nudes declare that there remains a secret that is as yet unseen and remains to be unmasked.

But there seems to be an alternative way of reading the motivation behind the fakes. Stars are manipulated into ridiculous situations: Sandra Bullock arrives naked at an awards ceremony; Audrey Hepburn sits naked on a piano; Gillian Anderson is penetrated by an alien. While the majority of fakes feature female stars, all the male stars previously mentioned in connection with authentic nude sites are featured, together with Tom Cruise, Val Kilmer and Keanu Reeves. What appears to be at work here is the mocking and humiliation of the star. Stars are taken down from their lofty plane and ridiculed. If the fakes ultimately leave the real nudity of the star a secret, then the act of mocking the star suggests the attempt to try and break apart that secret. Compared to the wealth and power associated with stardom, the faked body of the star is rendered vulnerable to the actions of the image creator. Fake nudes see members of the audience using technology to take control over the stars.

FAN SITES AND ONLINE CLUBS

Fan magazines represented a significant development in the distribution of star discourse. The first fan magazine, *Motion Picture Story Magazine*, appeared in 1911, carrying photos, interviews and a correspondence column (Grieveson, 1999). Other titles soon followed, such as *Photoplay*, *Picture Play* and *Motion Picture Classic*. Fan magazines included stars offering advice to readers about romance and etiquette, positioning stars as what Lee Grieveson calls 'ethical exemplars', embodying 'ideal selves that would in turn enable audiences and readers to shape their own conduct and identity in line with prevailing norms of morality' (1999: 26).

Through this moralistic discourse, fan publications offered an institutionally authored address to audiences, positioning the film and media industries as talking to fans rather than fans talking between themselves. Outside institutionally produced media, fan cultures have formed their own networks of communication to circumvent media organisations and engage in the direct discussion of popular pleasures. With the internet, this form of fan discourse has proliferated. In her study of the online presence of fans of the television series *Xena: Warrior Princess*, Kirsten Pullen suggests that on 'the internet, it seems as though nearly everyone is a fan, and nearly everything is worthy of fan adulation' (2000: 56). Pullen argues that the internet has 'mainstreamed fandom, allowing more viewers to participate in activities usually reserved for alternate communities' (2000: 56).

Sites dedicated to individual stars are just one of the forms of fan authorship found on the web. Unlike the mocking snipes of the fake nude sites, fan sites assume a respectful attitude towards the stars they admire. Titles like 'Dream World of Brad Pitt', 'Adonis of the XX Century: Brad Pitt', 'Abandon Yourself to Cameron Diaz', and 'Like an Angel – Cameron Diaz', emphasise the reverence in which stars are held by fan authors. These sites are not produced for profit, but appear online as labours of love.

Although created outside institutionally controlled media channels, fan sites vary in the degrees to which they declare their conditions of production. Some sites proudly announce the origins of their authorship: 'JC's Brad Pitt Links and Photos'; 'Tim Ree's Cameron Diaz Page'. These sites read as shrines of personal devotion to stars. Others hide the traces of authorship, taking names such as the 'World of Brad Pitt' or 'Cameron Diaz UK'. By choosing this anonymity, fan sites remove the presence of the fan in the online discourse, masking their subjective origin, and giving a greater sense of their published content as authoritative objective information. The reverence with which stars are treated is therefore given more force, for sites do not appear to be the creation of one person's admiration, but the impartial recognition of a star's divine status.

A further context in which fans and casual admirers can voice and share their views about stars is in the interactive forum of online fan clubs. Providing a one-stop site for a range of services, including e-mail, clubs and chat rooms, the Yahoo.com portal runs a vast collection of clubs that can be searched by category. Visitors may join existing clubs or form their own. Film star clubs deal either with stars in general or specific stars. Sites carry a common set of features: a message board, galleries for uploading and downloading photos, a chat room and a list of members. Members join for free and are identified to the club by profiles created at the point of registering.

'Brad Pitt the Sexiest Man Alive' was established in 1999. At the start of 2001 the club had 144 members: 91 female, 50 male and 3 who did not identify their sex. Membership was predominantly concentrated in the United States, but also included fans from Canada, Israel, the Netherlands, Philippines, Singapore, Turkey and England. The age of members spread from teenage years to mid-thirties. Message boards offer a space for fans to articulate their thoughts and feelings about stars. At the time the club opened, early messages were concerned with forming a consensus around the desirability of the star:

> 'brad is soo hot!' *(11 February 1999)*
> 'Yes I agree also that Brad Pitt is very very sexy and HOT!!!!!' *(11 February 1999)*
> 'I would just like to say I loved Brad with the long hair. Not that I have hated his other styles but the long hair was dead sexy.' *(6 October 1999)*
> 'Hi, I'm Ms Curls and I'm also new to Brad's fan club, and I think Brad is so sexy. I love his eyes, and his sexy smile. Write back to me. And let's talk some more about Brad! Ms Curls' *(1 October 1999)*
> 'Are there any other gay men out there who love Brad?' *(30 December 1999)*

For one member, discussing Brad became the occasion for emphasising the ordinariness of her life:

'Hey everyone! I've been a Brad Pitt fan ever since Interview came out. I was pregnant with my second child and he thinks it is a really cool movie to quote me 3 yr old. I have quite a few of his older movies but have not had to operutnity to see any of his more recent ones.

I'm 31, married, 2 kids and a dog. I live in Pearland Tx (just south of Houston) and lead a pretty normal life.

I have to say that I hope that he and Jennifer A will get married. He deserves to be happy and I think that she makes him happy.

Well enough for now, I got to go save the 3 yr old from the 10 yr old.'
(13 February 1999)

The private life of the star was another key area of discussion:

'Has anyone heard of it is true or not that Brad bought jennifer A a 2 million dollar place in Ireland? I heard it on the radio the other morning when the station I listen to had their "hot hollywood gossup". I was just wondering.' *(20 February 1999)*

'no but i heard about the ring he got her that was 500,000' *(23 February 1999)*

'Did Brad and Jennifer get married? I thought that I saw on the cover of one of those cheap mags that they did. If they did I hope theya re truly happy' *(2 March 1999)*

Reading through messages posted in clubs, what becomes evident very quickly is the mundane manner in which stars are talked about. Messages express very ordinary and familiar concerns: stars are sexy, they lead interesting private lives and are glamorous.

What is interesting about this mundaneness is how it does not sit easily with presumptions made in opposing perspectives on fan culture. Scholarly analysis of fandom is divided between negatively pathologising fans, and the more recent trend for seeing fandom as an emancipatory culture. Traditionally, as Joli Jensen (1992) has shown, many academics and medical professionals have taken the strength of identification between fans and the stars they adore as the basis for representing fans as isolated, socially dysfunctional individuals, or as members of an irrational, hysterical crowd. These representations, Jensen argues, emerge from anxieties over the effects of modernity: the lonely fan is the effect of alienation and social atomisation, while the hysterical crowd is seen as an irrational force swayed by agencies of mass persuasion. In both cases, fandom is regarded as a form of deviancy, a modern madness.

More recent work on stardom has countered this view, regarding fans as active agents who do not simply consume media but engage in textual productivity to create their own media artefacts (Fiske, 1992). Henry Jenkins (1992), for example, regards fans as active cultural producers who, rather than passively accepting the output of the cultural industries, are demanding critics who actively argue and express their opinions about what they see and hear. He argues that the textual productivity of fans involves the appropriation of mass commercial culture to create a distinctive folk culture (1992: 279). For Jenkins, the critical activity and textual production of fans has political consequences: fandom 'constitutes a base for consumer activism ... a response to the relative powerlessness of the consumer in relation to the powerful institutions of cultural production and circulation' (1992: 278). Jenkins views fans as engaged in producing their own culture, forming not-for-profit networks that escape the institutional control of the media industries. For this reason, he argues that fans form alternative social communities, empowering individuals by involving them in active resistance to consumer culture.

Film stardom is only one point of focus for fan cultures, and fandom does take many other forms. However, fan sites and clubs relating to film stars appear to display no evidence of the alienated loneliness or cultural resistance proclaimed by either critical position. Despite the anonymity of some fan sites, many unintentionally reveal conditions of production through their rough style of presentation. However, there are numerous fan sites with qualities of presentation equalling the design aesthetics of commercially produced sites. As John Fiske notes, the textual productivity of fans can often result in works that imitate the production values of commercial culture, but on a reduced budget (1992: 39). Similarly, the content of these sites tends to reproduce the forms of star discourse found on film promotion and entertainment news sites. Fan discourse is consistent with the types of knowledge that formed the picture personality as a commodified identity: stars are known for a collection of roles, with gossip circulating excitedly about a star's appearance in forthcoming films.

Following Pullen's (2000) suggestion that the internet has mainstreamed fandom, the appeal could be made that sites and clubs are failing to articulate an authentic expression of subcultural identity. However, the decentralised infrastructure of the internet would appear to be the ideal environment for forming the very types of alternative media networks which Jenkins suggests are the domain of fan cultures. If fan cultures produced the form of active critical debate which Jenkins suggests, then it could be presumed that fan authorship on the web would demonstrate a confrontation between fans and media institutions. However, browsing across fan sites, it is difficult to distinguish their content from sites produced for the purposes of film marketing and entertainment news. So, while authored outside institutional conditions of production, fan sites emulate rather than criticise commercial popular culture.

On the one hand, the online clubs operated through Yahoo can be seen as offering a democratic space in which individuals may voice their opinions about an aspect of public culture. However, portals have influenced the structure of the internet. By providing services linked to a search engine, portals become some of the most visited sites on the internet, forming what Vincent Miller (2000) suggests is a 'hub and spoke' model, as users return to a single point from which to conduct searches and access services. These hubs have therefore become prime sites for online advertising. So while the clubs provided by Yahoo are accessible for free, they operate under conditions of indirect sponsorship. Clubs on Yahoo may decentre the means for the mass distribution of fan discourse but these channels operate through a structure of centralised economic power on the internet.

Although this argument would identify the online traffic of fan discourse remaining under the control of corporate capitalism, it would be presumptuous to believe that the substance of that discourse is determined by those economic conditions. Because portals or internet service providers do not undertake any systematic monitoring of the content of fan sites and clubs, then fan authors and members remain largely at liberty to express whatever they wish. However, rather than break with convention, fan sites provide straightforward information on star biographies and film roles that stay firmly within the parameters of the picture personality discourse. Fan writing on message boards is preoccupied with simply praising the star in terms already set by film marketing. Based on the sites studied here, when discussing fandom and the film star system, it would appear mistaken to presume that alternative media channels create oppositional cultures.

CONCLUSION

Jay David Bolter and Richard Grusin (1999) argue that all innovations in communication technology draw upon previous media forms in a process of remediation. New media borrow from old media, with their newness arising from how they integrate and adapt those past forms. For Bolter and Grusin, the world wide web has provided an eclectic space for combining and reworking many old media, with text, graphics, photos and video variously combined to form a heterogeneous screen.

When looking at the presence of film stars in the online universe, the internet can not only be seen to remediate other media forms – the news story, the press kit, the pornographic image – but also the types of discourse distributed by old media. The categories of star discourse that emerged in the earliest years of the star system still structure the terms in which knowledge about stars circulates on the internet. Naming stars created the picture personality, forming an identity across various sources of meaning. On the internet, the star name becomes the hyperlink, connecting the many and various contexts of star presence. In film promotions and entertainment news sites, the discourse of the picture personality is still visible as published profiles construct the image of the star around his or her on-screen roles. Stars are then used as a form of capital to advertise films directly, or indirectly to promote commercial entertainment in general. Celebrity nudes recreate the types of revealing images found previously in print with magazines like *Celebrity Skin*.

Images of naked stars may offer a different type of content to that of star scandals, but both have the same effect of making public the private side of privacy. Star scandals exposed the stars, nude sites show the stars exposed.

Fan sites and clubs have provided new contexts for the textual productivity previously witnessed in fan cultures. Looking at current fan activity on the internet, there seems to be neither deviant madness nor challenging activism. In fact, fan activity on the internet seems less exciting than either of these perspectives would suggest. Individuals express a strong engagement with certain star images, which in some cases is expressed as desire, but while the language used may be intense in some cases, it seems a long way from crazed obsession. Internet access may encourage a more participatory relationship vis-à-vis the cultural forms of mass communication, but fan sites suggest that it is mistaken to assume that participation necessarily means critical activism. Fans or visitors actively express their attraction to stars in ways that celebrate, rather than challenge, commercial culture.

Faced with the newness of the internet, there is the temptation to be seduced into believing that the technology is determining change wherever it is used. Here the emphasis has been on seeing the internet as continuing rather than changing the circulation of the discourses of stardom. Although stars may be thought of as a phenomenon of the old media world, the presence of stars on the internet represents the extension of the star system into the new media universe. Online communications have provided new channels for distributing star discourse, but these have not transformed film stardom in any significant way. Rather than displace the importance of stars in the cultural imaginary, the internet appears to have continued and maintained the star phenomenon. Star discourse on the internet displays a continuing engagement with the stars as revered others and commercial identities. In the collision of the star system with the internet, what is demonstrated is a new media channel maintaining and perpetuating an old media realm of discourse.

However, this sense of continuity has to be situated against the changing nature of the online universe. While the internet has existed in some form for several decades, the period in which it has been used as an accessible domain of public communication is still, at this moment, relatively short. The extent of the internet's reach, and the intensity with which it has been used in regular interactions, has changed dramatically in a few years. If a similar speed of change were to be witnessed in even just the short-term future, then the internet will be significantly transformed over the next decade. In the period of time during which this chapter was researched, transformations occurred as sites were redesigned or disappeared. DeCordova's work explored a particular phase in American cinema history which relied on returning to archives in order to trace the changes he describes. But what is the historian of the internet left with? In this transitory landscape, where forms of discourse can be available everywhere and then just disappear completely, how is it possible for media or cultural history to recover the past? Mindful of this escaping history, the various contexts of star discourse identified here can at best be seen as only a provisional account of how the film star system is engaging with the internet. While this chapter has made a series of critical points about the phenomenon of film stardom on the internet, its main purpose has been to simply describe what the online discourses of film stardom looked like at one particular time.

My thanks to Tamar Jeffers and Marcus Leaning for useful suggestions during the preparation of this chapter.

Chapter Two

EMBODYING AN ELASTIC ☐ SELF: THE PARAMETRICS OF CONTEMPORARY STARDOM

Barry King

Recent inquiry into audience perceptions of stars has uncovered a new configuration in the existential parameters of stardom (Gamson, 1994). Today's stars – Madonna is the favourite example – epitomise the postmodern self, a de-centred subject, deeply reflexive and disdainful of the claims of identity. How rigorously the notion of textual dissemination can be applied to human identity or, more to the point, to a commercially valuable persona is an important question begged by such musings.

However, it is true that contemporary star interviews about self or craft are marked by a certain indeterminacy in identity reference. In many interviews there seems to be a constant circulation through all modes of actorly identity – character, persona, personality and person. Stars today seem like Rameau's nieces and nephews, prepared to be anything as the occasion demands (Diderot, 1976). Such vacillations of *being in public* encourage speculation that there is no 'reality' outside of a performance (Butler, 1990). Emboldened by signs of a new stellar plasticity, fans and general readers can be viewed as exercising 'semiotic power' over stellar texts, becoming in a sense the stars of their own interpretations (Sigelow, 1993).

I do not dispute the appearance of increased plasticity, but question whether this is a symptom of postmodern liberation. Taking another tack, I suggest that the contemporary representation of stardom is a narrow occupational response to the new conditions of production in the post-Hollywood era. This response is ideological because it is designed to resonate with popular themes of the self as orphaned from the collective process of identity formation. The case has been made that we have all been abandoned to the task of forging our identities in an increasingly hostile and indifferent social cosmos (Giddens, 1991). The stars have identity problems too. Scanning the lavish pastures where the stars forge their life course, the obscure may find consolation, not to mention valuable advice on identity triage (see Evans and Wilson, 1999).

PERSONA AS PROCESS

As a figure of identity, the actor has always posed the question of authenticity – of who speaks here, under what capacity of the self and with what moral authority[1] (Barish, 1981). Thomas Hobbes, for example, denied that the actor could be a real person since real persons were the authors of their own words (Hobbes, 1975). The anti-theatrical prejudice has deep roots in moral and religious controversy, but its historical reproduction probably draws on a simple fact of occupation – actors are pretenders, which raises recurrent questions about the fit between who they seem to be and what they are. This is obvious when an actor changes character many times, but even individuals who seem to play themselves are pretending.

The character portrayed by any actor has only a nominal existence and is only a flaccid designator of person (Kripke, 1980). The character could be played by a large (but not infinite) number of actors. The actual performance, especially when recorded, has the potential to create a rigid designator – this performance of a character is in some sense definitive. After the fact of a great performance on film, the character can never resolutely return to a state of flaccidity.[2] Anthony Perkins (*Psycho*, 1960, USA) *is* Norman Bates, and Vince Vaughn's recreation (*Psycho*, 1998, USA) is at best, homage, at worst, a parasitic reactivation. Perkins *is* Bates; Vaughn *played* Bates.

Naturally, there is room for debate about the definitiveness of a character rendition. From a craft point of view, a performance may be regarded as weak, even if it is regarded amongst the film-going public (or film reviewers) as definitive, and vice versa. In Hollywood, at least, performances are regarded as definitive if they entail a projection of a rich interior, and box office success. These dimensions do not always jell with craft or critical standards, and remain contentious. However, institutionally, they are the *essence* of stardom.

In the performance of the Hollywood star, the projection of a rich inner self by external means is at its fullest remove from the impression of interiority that the actor could accomplish unaided, or with a passive use of cinematography. Appearance, demeanour, vocal and physical behaviour are not only given a new semantic importance in film signification, but the possibilities for fabricating these qualities are vastly increased compared to live performance. The strategy of *concerted cynosure* – the use of close-ups and framing to create a spectacle of the actor inside the narrative process – only deepens the perception that the actor and character are intimately connected.[3]

In addition to the apparent fusion of star and character on screen, the publicity machine works to maintain this impression off-screen. In general, the public is invited to suppose that what is seen on screen, if aided cinematically, is nonetheless the 'natural' fruit of the star's personal agency – creative vision, personality, etc. – that inheres before and after filming. Even for the ordinary actor, the nominal husk of a character has the potential to become a persona. But the star can also rely on a history of past projections of persona, which in confronting a new role, functions as a personal intellectual property, emblematised by name and likeness (Gaines, 1991).[4] The melding of on-screen performance and off-screen publicity – both *kinds* of performance – imparts an *existential* portability to a fictional character which is wrapped around the *being in public* of the star. It would be too crude to say that the star just plays her persona in every role; rather, the persona is differentially activated in successive roles with the supposed qualities of the star inserted into a character. Some roles are more rigidly designated than others and this may have a bearing on 'customer' satisfaction and perception of efficacy. The persona, in other words, serves in Hollywood as a *grammar of characterisation*. The coherence of this grammar relies to an extent on *elaborative ignorance*. The less that is known about the tricks of moviemaking as applied to the star, the more coherent and serviceable is the persona. Conversely, the less that is known about the private person of the star, the more the persona can bind together the inter-text of performances that sustain 'presence'. Overexposure, in the sense of revealing the underpinnings of presence, is an exigent sociological factor today.

Therefore, contrary to the view that the screen image constitutes the supreme moment of presence of the star, it is necessary to recognise that such a presence, the presence of persona, is reliant on the circulation of meaning through acts of viewing, and the consumption of texts and images in secondary circulation (Ellis, 1982). The act of viewing may be a potent source of discrepancies between what is expected from the star's persona and what is seen. But what is expected is conditioned by frameworks established by publicity and promotion, which in themselves draw on general notions of type and the spectator's past experiences of the star (Austin, 1999). I am in the presence of George Clooney when prior understandings and present performance are roughly consonant. In the empirical case, it can turn out that the encounter leads to re-realisation or de-realisation of persona, but it is the expectation of constancy that underwrites the entire interaction.[5]

If this is accepted, then the difference between postmodern stars and 'traditional' stars needs to be rethought as a function of the expectation of constancy. The difference between traditional stars and contemporary stars lies not in the denial of reference, but rather in a re-articulation and pluralisation of the referring relationship between the star's persona and what the star would seem to be as a person – a value always related to a social category or type. To understand this, we need to recall what the actor does.

THE DECLINE OF METONYMIC SERVITUDE

Acting is a personal service, inalienably vested in the person of the actor. Even though this person is variously modified by training, professional experience, cosmetic alteration, performance techniques and technologies, its ground remains deeply proprietorial, legally protected by the actor's name and likeness. Of course, there are definite limits on each actor's personal input into the process of portrayal.

The majority of actors – walk-ons, supporting players – are destined to serve as *obtuse indices* of the ordinary existence conjured up in a particular narrative setting, and beyond that a particular studio tradition of the real. A minority of actors – character actors, leading players and stars – function as subjectively differentiated agents of narrative. This crucial threshold of professional development is for the most part ensured by the casting process.

For those who can show 'personality' as stars or leading players, there is a further distinction in the reference which they make to the audience sphere. Here it is useful to distinguish between metaphorical and metonymic servitude. Metaphorical servitude proper is the domain of the leading character actor who subordinates person as far as possible (technically and genetically) to the purposes of narrative, becoming a narrative function.[6] Metonymic servitude by contrast rests on analogy; the actor as a 'natural' being is already a pre-given servant of narrative, with a minimal reliance on make-up, dramatic techniques and vocal control in the performance of character. Here, the *as if* of metaphor is replaced by *I am*.[7]

Metonymic servitude has two poles of articulation: narrative servants without personality (human objects) and narrative 'guests' whose narrative agency or 'character' rests on an extra-digetically preserved persona. The latter are stars.[8]

Stars of the studio period undertook metonymic servitude. Their personae were fabricated in recognition of the need to stand for some principles of collective organisation, and to that extent they seemed real outside of any narrative engagement. We now recognise that this 'realism' followed the norms of white, Anglo-Saxon patriarchy (Jarvie, 1991). Yet, this ideological gearing acknowledged, traditional stars at least sustained a dialogue between the general and particular, seeming to speak as personal samples of pre-existent social types (Klapp, 1972).

Contemporary stardom no longer attempts to fabricate an unambiguous connection with a collective definition of normality. On one hand, it is difficult to rest 'naturally' inside a persona, given the immense ramification of promotion and publicity by the logics of branding (Klein, 2000; Wernick, 1999). On the other, the very notion of normality has been radically undermined by identity politics. One way to surmount the obstacles to metonymic servitude is to become a servant of metaphor, with the not inconsiderable advantage of claiming the status of 'creator'. Some stars (such as Bruce Willis and Brad Pitt) have ventured into the metaphorics of character portrayal, but this is only a temporary and usually temporising departure from stardom.

More likely is a retreat to a more abstract level of identity affirmation that, in contrast to traditional conceptions of the persona as an extension of the self, seems positively post-modern. In such a circumstance, there is likely to emerge in fact or by design a projection of a persona that is *present but absent* in each of its manifestations – persona in other words becomes meta-textual:

> Madonna still has an identity. It is located where it has always been located. At the point where the postmodernist audience finds meaning – not in the manifest content of the surface, not in the historical discourses beneath the surface, but above the surface, in the area of exchange and wager in the pursuit of privilege and power.
>
> *(Tetzlaff, 1993: 259)*

THE INSTITUTIONAL COORDINATES OF THE META-TEXTUAL PERSONA

But it is not just a textual matter. Certain trends in the commercial husbandry of movie stardom are rendering the projection of persona a risky enterprise. Compared to former times, today's stars are *discursively challenged* in their efforts to meld all the practices under-taken in their name into a coherent commercial identity. The new trial of persona goes beyond the usual complaints of lack of privacy and wears away at the notion of authenticity itself. The following developments, all dynamically interrelated, are relevant.

1. Persona management has become a multi-staged industrial system. New Hollywood resembles a Fordist assembly line, with specialist departments managing different aspects of the star's likeness as an asset, ranging from care of the star's psychological and corpo-real well-being through to legal and fiscal management. Stars now have a 'wardrobe of identities' connected to a product stream. As the star becomes a brand, the notion of a per-sonal centre becomes problematic and requires extensive rationalisation (Mitroff and Bennis, 1989).

2. Stars are no longer employees (on a freelance, let alone fixed-term, basis), but stake-holders in the enterprise that manages their career (Baker and Faulkner, 1991). Within any product cycle the star has a direct commercial interest in claiming a deep existential commitment to a given role. Yet, the star as entrepreneur must be ready to switch roles as business opportunities arise. Hence the paradoxical desire to be protean and yet quintessential in every role. The globalisation of the market for the star's services exacer-bates this process, because claims of existential commitment multiply as films and product open in different markets and address different cultural constituencies. 'Big in Japan' is not the same semantically as 'Big in America'. This can require a higher level of abstraction from the star's private person. Stars, such as Sylvester Stallone, may speak less and behave more, but this simply aggravates the range of identity claims that can be applied to silence.

3. All efforts at persona projection obey the imperative of box office. But even where an actor is a success, a consistently high level of performance in craft standards or box office is hard to maintain – indeed, success in one might highlight the need for success in the other. To compensate, the discourse of stardom may become subject to its own hyperbole. No performance in public or private, on-screen or off, can be less than great, and no failure less than cataclysmic. A process of *inauthentication by perfection* begins, in which there is no space to be the self as ordinary – ordinariness becomes a perfectible performance amongst others (Gergen, 1991: 205).

4. The old formula of embedding the shifts of identity implied by casting in a 'real time' community of stars (Hollywood) has become problematic. In the package deal environment, interactions between stars are strictly by engagement and discontinuous in respect of time and place. In old Hollywood, there was a reality (however fragile) to the notion of a film-making community. With the end of fixed-term contracts, the referential economy of persona cannot be nurtured by a corporate studio image. To sustain persona, the star as a self-contained 'auteur' pursuing a personal vision is evoked, which refocuses the search for meaning on the private person of the star as the 'abode' of genius. The emphasis on the star as an autonomous agent goes hand in hand with the tendency for publicity to evoke a virtual space called show business, in which all kinds of public figures apparently interact. This evocation opens the door to the phenomenon of absolute fame – in which individuals are well known for being well known – even as stars claim artistic status based on specific professional service (Boorstin, 1963).

5. The sheer increase in the number of media outlets creates a global market for celebrity gossip. This in turn creates a need to 'break through the clutter'. Being sensational in word and deed emerges as a high-risk but potentially effective means of burying rivals. As sensation becomes a general market value, publicity sources close to the star compete with unofficial sources whose purposes range from the mildly mocking to the heartily scatological.

6. The universe of available product has grown exponentially with the development of cable and satellite television. The past and recent product available means that the stars are literally on show more than ever before. Video recorders have vastly augmented this presence at the cost of adding immeasurable depth to the forensics of fame. The public today has the opportunity, once only available to critics, film buffs and academics, to review and compare extensively past and present performances. Stars seen once in the time-bound context of theatrical release can now be seen repeatedly, their performance analysed and sifted for 'essence'. Especially with the development of the internet, star images and texts become a common resource available to anyone who wants to comment publicly. The poaching activity of fans is not exclusively driven by adulation. Homage websites, corporate or individual, compete with hate sites. If the former can effectively neutralise the latter, they still contribute to the dissipation of persona. As a result, persona promotion is decreasingly a *negotiated celebration* between journalists and stars. (Gamson, 1994).

7. The media, whether internet, print or broadcast based, are mindful of the increase in textual curiosity, and exploit it through the promulgation of insider gossip and perspectives. In a paradoxical development, the multiplication of public and private information about the stars reinforces the notion of true meaning and authenticity. Somewhere in the hypertext of celebrity, a morsel of the star's activities will unlock the enigma of identity.

8. Inside celebrity journalism, an acceleration in the perception of biographical time follows from the tying of the persona – as compensation for the intermittency of professional engagements – more closely to the private lives of the stars. The milestones of private existence (romance, infidelity, marriage, divorce, illness, parenting) are treated as profound existential transformations. The *spatialisation* of biography, native to the obituary, becomes the normal mode, with every interview setting itself out as an occasion for self-transformation. As written or as interviewed, the stars become characters in the drama of their own biographies. Each life transition seems like assuming a new role. A new present centredness enters the interview form, which becomes essentially photographic (the photo opportunity) or verbal-indexical as typified by the pre-scripted question and answer session. Despite the defensive value of a minimalist presence, it increases the intensity of the regime of observation. Attention-grabbing poses and statements out of context are still sutured together by writers (who may never actually meet the star) in order to simulate *presence*. Candid photography revealing stars with sweat-stained garments becomes meaningful.

9. The spatialisation of biography is redoubled by the spatialisation of fictional identity, as special effects and spectacular action scenes privilege the spectacle of the star as a corporeal signifier. Computer-generated spectacle is matched by a sharp emphasis on appearance. Stars off-screen strive to appear as an independent source of spectacle, implicitly denying that they are merely passive recipients of cinematic prostheses. Further, since anything said or done will invite comment, looking good is serviceable. The physiognomic rule disarms criticism: nice-looking people are nice.

Wracked by these developments, the *being-in-public* of stars becomes a polycentric process in which the mechanisms of pretence are subjected to exhaustive public scrutiny. The reported unease of the stars in the glare of publicity, despite the fact that they enjoy historically unprecedented rewards and long-term financial security, is an expression of the fact that their names *no longer turn into an essence or nominate a certain quality of personality*. It is not just a matter of morally suspect reporting. Even positive achievements are subject to a relentless interrogation, which ranges across private and public life without regard to the different standards that apply to these realms. What adults consent to in private without reproach becomes a public gesture. Nor is it any good to claim that the actor only owes the public a good performance. There are many performances that are relevant, and all are thrust into the public sphere without respect for time and place. As Nicolas Cage put it: 'When you start acting at 17 you say things sometimes like a 17-year-old and those things come back to haunt you when you're 32. People have to be allowed to grow' (*Movieline*, May 1996: 83).

In the realm of fiction, the old problem of reassuring the public that the actor is not a morally suspect character has been surpassed by the necessity to stand aloof from persona construction itself. Even in authorised biography, it is no longer possible to present stardom as a condition of relaxed integrity. The possibility of the disintegration of persona is endemic, even if one sets aside false rumours that link stars with bizarre events and practices, such as Richard Gere's deep-tissue encounter with a gerbil.

One response is 'licensed withdraw' – of being visible and yet absent in public since the real feelings of the star are forever outside the terms of their fame (Goffman, 1979). An article on Mary Tyler Moore is typical: 'it isn't easy to accept, that she's an insecure, talented person trapped in the aura of an icon, struggling to find her way out' (*New York Times*, Magazine, 26 November 1995: 39–41). Withdraw is also evident in 'bon mots' collections that regale the public with celebrity one-liners (Berlin, 1996). With their rich provender of wisdom, these collections signal the seriousness of stars as enduring public intellectuals (Winokaur, 1992). Seeking political involvement, even if sincere, accomplishes the same effect.

In summary, today's stars are less fiends of postmodernity than individuals engaged in constantly re-negotiating the terms of their engagement with public life. It is, of course, their commercially driven choice as to the *rate* of re-negotiation. As the commercial value of persona has been vastly enhanced, its nurturance has become a process of constant re-writing to accommodate the fact that past and present personae all occupy a common discursive space. The digital reactivation of dead stars such as James Cagney or Humphrey Bogart compounds the confusion of tense and kinds of stardom. The old stars, of course, actually had very little connection with the parameters of mundane existence, but they were presented as though they did. Stars today seem permanently resettling the terms of their representation, and this equivocation becomes *their* story. I term this phase of stardom *autographic*: I write me.[9]

WRITING SHARON

Sharon Stone appears to be renegotiating her image: one minute she's a dangerous blonde in a jet-black jeep, the next she's a stately, politically concerned vision in tweed. Lloyd Grove gets several takes as Stone basks in the praise for her Oscar-caliber Casino performance and buffs up her credentials as a serious *artiste*.

(*Vanity Fair, March 1996: 156*)

The *being-in-public* of Sharon Stone offers a good example of the new configuration of stardom. It is useful to begin with authorised biography – if an assured sense of identity is not accomplished here, where could it be (Munn, 1997)? Regarded as exceptionally beautiful, Stone has claimed lineage with Jean Harlow and Marilyn Monroe. But the 'dumb blonde' stereotype is immediately qualified. As her press cuttings unfailingly remind us, Stone has an IQ of 153 and is very intelligent. In casting herself as the clever blonde, Stone can be read as attempting to sustain the cultural capital of a traditional motion picture star when Hollywood itself is a kind of quotation. Her efforts reveal the troubles that afflict the linear equation of place, activity and being that underwrote 'old' movie stardom, when overexposure and the excessive ramification of the realm of the 'personal' are pervasive realities.

Stone's persona is intimately connected with the contradictions of gender. No surprise here, but it is important to understand what this means in terms of her public biography. Stone, who began her professional career as a fashion model, has cultivated the look and appearance of a 'human Barbie doll', the better to manipulate men. As she put it, 'If you have a vagina and a point of view, that's a deadly combination' (*Guardian Weekend*, 5 December 1998: 25, 31).

Of course, the persona implied here of a sexually attractive but dangerous woman, is intimately connected with Stone's character in the erotic thriller *Basic Instinct* (1992, USA), the role that made her a star. As Catherine Tramell, a successful novelist who carries out murders based on the plots of her best-sellers, Stone's performance with star Michael Douglas stretched the limits of explicitness in the mainstream cinema. Scenes in which an underwear-free Stone 'flashed' a group of interrogating police officers, or the opening sequence in which a naked blonde (later revealed to be Tramell) takes herself and a trussed-up male to orgasm then kills him with an ice pick, have a legendary status. Indeed, the ice pick, with its overtones of seizing the phallic initiative, might well be regarded as Stone's trademark. With three female leads who are either lesbian or bisexual, *Basic Instinct* only served to deepen the association between Stone's physiognomic capital and alternative (media conventions imply deviant) sexual practices and psychopathology. Protests by

53

lesbian and gay groups during filming only served, inadvertently, to cement this association and generate spin and controversy.

Serviceably equivocal, the plot of *Basic Instinct* does not actually condemn Tramell for her behaviour. No extenuating circumstances such as a history of childhood abuse are offered. Tramell delights in manipulating others, shows evident enjoyment in 'perverse' sexual practices and at the end, apparently appeased by the sexual prowess of Detective Nick Curran (Douglas), is unpunished for the murders (Cohan, 1998). Despite the evocation of Monroe, Stone entered the public domain as a sexually aggressive *femme fatale* or 'bitch goddess'. Her breakthrough role in *Total Recall* (1990, USA) as a kick-boxing assassin disguised as the wife of Arnold Schwarzenegger, seemed retrospectively to affirm that these qualities were resident in Stone. The mixture of aggression, sexual explicitness and latent misogyny served to align her with sex, rather than film, stardom.

As a starlet supporting an established star, it can be argued that Stone had no choice but to accept the moral and psychological content of Tramell's character as central to her persona – and to play this content for all it was worth on-screen and at press junkets. She subsequently voiced concerns about being typecast and sought to make amends for the negative aspects of her breakthrough role. One tack was to deny the realism of *Basic Instinct*. Thus her stated intention in accepting the lead in the erotic thriller *Sliver* (1993, USA) – again written by Joe Eszterhas – was to use her sex appeal to correct the erroneous view of female sexuality projected in her first hit:

> *Basic Instinct* was about fantasy. I mean who, who makes love like that? All
> back-bends and an orgasm every second! And who has such confidence to
> rip off all their clothes? . . . This time, my character is more real, and
> women will recognise all her insecurities. She has spent most of her life with
> one man and she is frightened about making a new relationship. She is shy
> and scared about making love with someone else. I have tried to do it in a
> way women go about their private lives – me included.
>
> *(Munn, 1997: 100)*

But the character of Carly Norris in *Sliver* – 'vulnerable, insecure about sex' – still replays elements of Tramell's bitch goddess persona. In one scene, set in a posh restaurant, Carly exposes her breasts and removes her panties, which she passes to her lover (played by William Baldwin). Other scenes involving nudity, masturbation, covert surveillance of sexual activities, and sexual dialogue, although less explicit for Stone, draw on the graphic scenography of *Basic Instinct*. Carly Norris may not have, like Catherine Tramell, 'deep psychological and sexual defects, which affect her mental stability', but she is nonetheless placed by design at the centre of a game of voyeurism and pathological desire. The main difference is that we are invited to see her as victim rather than a predator.

This commercially driven tweaking of persona (ultimately unsuccessful at the US box office) was soon followed by a *star as auteur* policy of casting in and out of type – for example, *Intersection* (1994, USA), *The Quick and The Dead* (1995, USA), *Last Dance* (1996, USA), *Diabolique* (1996, USA), *The Mighty* (1998, USA) and *Gloria* (1999, USA).[10] This policy – involving *inter alia* playing a wronged spouse, a prisoner on death row, a revenging cowgirl, the simple mother of a gifted child – is meant to prove that she is capable of characterisation in depth. As she freely admits, she needs to develop her range in order to accommodate the ageing process. These efforts have been uneven in terms of acting quality and box office. It may be as she said, that her one critical acting success to date (her Oscar-nominated role in Scorsese's *Casino* (1995, USA)) has wiped out the Tramell legacy. But her performance as Ginger, a coke-snorting hooker, still draws on elements of the bitch goddess persona (*Hollywood Online*, 1998).

Rather than examine the critical reception of these efforts (or Stone's actual performances which are seldom less than striking), I would suggest that they serve notice on the general public and Stone fans, in particular, of an interactive rule. All concerned must recognise a gulf between the 'real' Sharon Stone and the characters which she portrays. Such an existential bracketing signals the value 'actor', not 'sex symbol'.

Although she has insisted on an unbridgeable gulf between what she feels and how she is required to act, on-screen and in promotional settings, the Tramell legacy is often deployed for purposes of ingratiation. It may be a 'stupid objectification' but it has a solidarity value with women in late modern capitalist societies.

> You just cannot be a blonde with a good body and pretty looks and have any options in Hollywood. . . . To the boys who run things, you're just a dumb blonde, so you better know your place.
>
> *(Munn, 1997: 24)*

Such stereotyping is part of the symbolic annihilation of women:

> Even though women are not a minority, we are treated like one. So many female characters are written the way men experience women or would like to experience women, and that's not the way women really are.
>
> *(Munn, 1997: 71)*

55

Far from being a *winner*, Stone is a victim of patriarchy and proof of its pervasiveness. Her decision, after *Total Recall*, to do a centrefold for *Playboy* magazine, rather than contradicting her femininism was part of a larger career strategy forced upon her by her 'Barbie doll' image and a history of insubstantial parts:

> I'd have liked to have been Meryl Streep or Glenn Close and be accepted on
> the integrity of my work, to have been able to do a performance like *Basic
> Instinct* without taking my clothes off. But Hollywood wouldn't let me do
> that so I had to make a decision. Was I willing to strip to save my career?
> Ultimately I decided I was.
>
> *(Munn, 1997: 57)*

Or:

> Women my age do not get leading roles and you need to be sexually
> appealing for parts in movies you might be right for. It's a man's world, and
> when you look like I look, that's what it is. I'd taken my top off in three
> movies and nobody noticed. I felt I was reclaiming my femininity.
>
> *(Munn, 1997: 57, 84)*

The perspicacious (and seemingly valid) thrust of these observations sets the real Sharon Stone at an existential distance from her persona. It is not difficult to discern, and this may be intended, the notion of femininity as a masquerade – a decorative layer which conceals a non-identity (Doane, 1988). Stone has embodied, on-screen and in auditions, the script of masculine desire, the better to gain control of her career and, it is tempting to assume, her personal life. 'Being a blonde is a great excuse when you're having a bad day' – even if as she subsequently admitted, she is definitely not a natural blonde.

Such observations do not stand alone. It is not difficult to find others that threaten the *cordon sanitaire* between person and persona. A persistent theme is that the persona of Tramell enables a certain kind of professionally and interpersonally efficacious role-playing:

> When I first got famous, the image of the movie [*Basic Instinct*] really
> protected me. Everyone thought I had so much bravado and was so wild. So
> I could continue to be that. It was a blast.
>
> *(Berlin, 1996: 43)*

Indeed, the depiction of a woman using her sexuality to manipulate might be seen as an empowerment metaphor:

It is so rare that a female character is more than an appendage to some guy. But I never thought of Catherine as bisexual or even sexual. Sex is just the currency she uses to get what she wants.

(Munn, 1997: 69)

She has said that it is a tribute to her artistry if men believe (hope?) she is Tramell (Berlin, 1996: 204). But this artistry is not entirely a façade:

People who are sophisticated enough to know that I'm not Catherine are sophisticated enough to know that I could be, if I wanted to.

(Premiere magazine, May 1993: 65)

For the reader, of course, Stone's 'real' self is only what is available in the media. So assertions such as these may be taken as evidence of an out-of-sight primal bonding. Even if pre-release publicity had not played the ambiguity for what is worth, it is a small step from *appearing to be* to *being taken as being*, especially if playing a character is represented as a process of self-discovery and re-definition. Although publicity has countered that 'basic Sharon' is really more like a cuddly toy than a sexual tigress (*Premiere* magazine, May 1993: 65), the star's reported sexual affairs – probably far less extensive than rumoured – suggest that the image of a sexual predator is not entirely undeserved. Even quotes in authorised materials failed to dispel this implication, discussing for example her very messy 'fling' with producer Bill MacDonald during the making of *Sliver*; or informing the reader that Stone's willingness to 'show all' in a *Playboy* centrefold surprised even a hardened photographer. Her reported musings that *Basic Instinct* did not go far enough since anal sex was not depicted, seem to hint at a greater sexual sophistication than Tramell's. Even her protest about being exploited by Paul Verhoeven in the 'flash' scene hints at inhibition, since the issue is respect rather than impropriety:

As a mature artist, I agree that shot was the best for the movie. I really disagree with the way he got it. Because it made me look incredibly stupid when I was very, very willing to do what it took to be that character.

(Guardian Editor, 12 December 1998: 10)

If Stone is prepared to 'go to the limit' in pretence and masquerade, readers may wonder how different is she from Tramell? Allowing that Tramell is a fictional construct, might the erotic energy and imaginativeness not arise from Stone herself? Certainly her fashionable adherence to 'method' underscores the rule that convincing characters spring from personal experiences.[11]

As a character actor, Stone's authenticity would not be an issue since the purpose of technique is precisely to impose a distance between each fictive incarnation and the person of the actor. But because she is a star, the commercial value of diminishing the social distance between herself and the public renders technique a means towards an epiphany. Stone's claims of deep bonding with successive characters might seem contradictory – she is apparently deeply in every role and yet outside of any role; a champion of authenticity and a smooth manipulator of appearances, including of course her own. There is another way to construe it, which has commercial efficacy – if acting is a process of self-development and self-discovery, then each role is a step on the road to actualising the real Sharon:

> I had certain rules. I'd have to be a better actor when I came out of each role and every other one had to be a potential hit.
>
> (Guardian Weekend, 5 December 1998: 25, 31)

But if this reasoning is applied, then surely the audience is entitled to suppose that her most successful 'hit' is the privileged site in which she succeeded in 'being' herself. It is a short step to conclude that the narrative existence of Catherine Tramell is simply an activation of qualities that Stone has in real life. Her authorised publicity may reassure interested male fans that this is not the case. Stone is really an ordinary, small-town girl who falls for guys who are 'regular' like her father. But she protests too much – if she is unlike Tramell, why is it necessary to fix her up with a non-threatening interest in the pipe and slippers brigade? Nor can her advanced physiognomic capital and professional determination be counted for nothing. The self-actualisation features of *Basic Instinct* are attested to by those who have observed first-hand: Paul Verhoeven has said on record that Stone is Catherine minus the killings; for Robert Evans, the producer of *Sliver*, she has 'Balls like Mike Tyson' (*Entertainment Weekly*, 21 May 1993: 16–21). If we step across the threshold of authorised biography, the threshold between the fictive and the real turns into a virtual freeway. The unauthorised biography, *Naked Instinct,* opens with an 'eye-witness' account of lesbian sex in the powder room of the Beverly Hills Hilton (Sanello, 1997). The action with Stone as predator and an unnamed, overwhelmed woman reads like a director's cut from *Basic Instinct*.[12] William Baldwin, who starred with Stone in *Sliver*, has referred to her as a 'paean to Lipstick Lesbianism' (Cagle, 'Sliver', *Entertainment Weekly*, 21 May 1993: 16–21). Stone herself fuels speculation: 'I have to straighten out my karma.... I've become a sex symbol, which is an absurd thing for me. Particularly since I symbolise the kind of sex I don't believe in' (*Premiere* magazine, May 1993: 59).

Ambiguous statements such as these, interfacing with proclamations of heterosexual desire, serve to reinforce the perception that Stone is bisexual. But if this is true then Tramell is, again, an apt extension of 'herself'.

In official literature, Stone is like a star in the sense that her on-screen performance is only weakly metaphorical, she relies on metonymic resources. For those who find her fascinating, this is good news despite her claim to be acting on metaphor. Her fans – or, at least, the journalists who stand as the nominal surrogates for them – want the person revealed in the husk of the role. The endorsement of 'method acting' easily spills over into imaginatively richer pastures (Naremore, 1988).

As an example, consider the scar theory website found on the Stone webring. This site is ostensively dedicated to solving the riddle of the cause of a scar on Stone's neck.[13] Interested surfers can log in to offer their 'theory' of its cause. It has been 'explained' by bizarre sexual practices involving overzealous asphyxiation, intercourse with or on a horse in a wire-fenced paddock, transsexual plastic surgery to remove an Adam's apple, surgery during alien abduction, and a poorly executed head transplant, for Stone is really a cyborg.

This is disturbing stuff, but it also reveals a deeper gloss on the Tramell persona with its 'queering' of categories. What is revealing about the scar theory site, apart from what it says about the intellectual level of e-mail, is that it constitutes an attempt to force Stone deeply into the Tramell persona. To this extent, this ever-expanding discourse becomes, under the rubric of free speech, a popular demand that Stone *be who she really is*. But such a demand is also problematic because it writes in the kinky overtones of that *persona* to *excess*. Intercourse with a horse indeed! At least the Tramell persona has the protective bracket of being a fictional performance, a nominalising site of selfhood where Stone can say she is or is not acting. Let her temporise, fans know better. *Basic Instinct 2*, if it ever happens, is the necessary eternal recurrence of what made her a star, of what she really is.[14]

CONCLUSION

On display through the optic of Stone is a sociological fact: in the post-studio context, the virtual private life of the stars cannot be discursively curtailed and comfortably equated with a character-inflected persona. Persona, once hardwired into a transparent public biography, now becomes an uncertain presence, dimly discernible behind a roster of successful characterisations. Of course, Stone's 'real' self as publicly known and her professionally valued persona, are both representations. But, as we have seen, she cannot simply treat them as separate and 'natural' values beyond question. Paradoxically, her fictive self can only be accorded the status of a performance by asserting that there is a real Sharon somewhere. Yet this 'private' self is another performance designed to be publicised, and only interesting because it plays on her persona.

From the perspective of the fan, the star's persona becomes a presence that is no longer available on-screen in all its desired-for comprehensiveness. It is, rather, an empirical totality that must be reconstituted from a multiplicity of texts and performances. Increasingly, though this may be difficult for fans to accept, persona no longer means a definite kind of individual. It is a mode of experiencing, a life force, the essential glue that holds together a series of approximating stabs at self-realisation. The fan's task, if he or she chooses to accept it, is to comprehend the object of desire by a means that denies closure. Should the desire for the object mutate into the desire for desire that, too, is good for business.

The overriding issue for the latest generation of stars is the control of the kind of personal knowledge that is claimed to be essential to understanding them as public figures. The fan or casual admirer can know more about a star (and for that matter stars of the past) than is consistent with this objective. Depending on what is known rests the marketability of the persona as a *guaranteed inherent property* that walks in the door with the star.

Responding to this situation, today's stars model the challenges of sustaining a viable self in a welter of interactions. As demands compete and have to be managed, persona work involves stretching an apparent core of personal qualities to cover all contingencies, and rationalising every shift and change as an aspect of constancy. In this process, persona is elastic rather than plastic, closer to a procedure for surviving, a heuristic of the self, than an essence. As a result, the norms of persona are now primarily indexical rather than iconic, of *being* rather than *of being like*.

A closing speculation: the public at large seems to perceive the star and the fan as sharing common existential burdens. Don't we all need to 'get our act together'? This bond of self-regard encourages the perception that the self is always on display and in need of diligence with regard to its image before others – an orientation that is fundamentally narcissistic (Abercrombie and Longhurst, 2000). In extreme cases, such as stalking and erotomania, the concept of a shared fate transmutes into the subordination of the star to the identity project of the fan (King, 1992).

There is a kind of empowerment here – the fan validates a possible self by bonding with millionaires. Yet the bond is fragile, constantly threatened by the prevarications of identity and, as in all peer relationships, rivalry. Perhaps here arises the pervasive interest in trashing stars. Their act is so much better than ours. How many superlative displays can fans take and not feel diminished?

---

1 I use the term 'actor' as gender neutral throughout this chapter.

2 Unless a succeeding performance is perceived as much better.

3 The appearance of on-screen completeness is, as modernist and psychoanalytically orientated criticism has shown, an illusion. It has no unitary origin; on the contrary it is the accomplishment of an origin.

4 Does the actor own his or her persona? The approval by the California Assembly in 1999 of a bill protecting the images of deceased performers as inheritable asserts a property right. On the other hand, George Wendt and John Ratzenberger failed to secure rights for the use of life-size statues of their on-screen likenesses in *Cheers* chain bars (*Equity Journal*, December 2000: 7).

5 The spectator's expectations may be entirely idiosyncratic. Where individuals are aware of the public text of a persona, but also know of alternative texts based on insider knowledge or gossip, the public or 'official' inter-text still serves as the foil for what is considered a more accurate account. The internet has, of course, introduced an alternative public sphere of stardom in this sense.

6 For a brilliant account of this process in theatre, see Sher (1996).

7 Metaphor rests on a subject/object relationship; analogy is a relationship of similarity between things.

8 The intermediate case of celebrities appearing as themselves is interesting, but I leave this aside here.

9 For an extensive discussion see my *Re-thinking Stardom* (forthcoming).

10 The formation of Stone's own production company, *Chaos*, is an important element in this. Between 1990 and 1999, Stone appeared in 15 movies with a total US gross of $582,300,745.

11 Compare: 'I like to get the chance as an actress to get under the skin of other kinds of personalities, to find out the way another person thinks without being bound by my own life experience and background. I've never killed anyone, but I had to know how Cindy (*Last Dance*) felt about it' (Munn, 1997: 175).

12 In relation to his accounts of Stone's sexual predatoriness, Sanello was sued by Stone. He was found not guilty of defamation and slander in October 1999.

13 There is no mystery because the scar is the result of a childhood riding accident.

14 Stone was keen to sign up for *Basic Instinct 2*, despite her earlier disavowals.

Chapter Three

STARDOM IN THE WILLENNIUM

Geoff King

Will Smith is a prime example of the 'crossover' star in Hollywood today, in two differ-ent dimensions. His persona – as a black, African-American performer – has been constructed to be essentially non-threatening to a mass white audience. This is the case in both aspects of a career that demonstrates crossover appeal of another kind, between different media: as a mainstream Hollywood star and a chart-topping rap performer (notable for his avoidance of explicit lyrics or anything likely to frighten white and/or middle-class listeners or their parents). The crossover star, of either variety, is a desirable quantity in Hollywood, carrying the potential to reach a range of audiences. Smith is one of a number of hip-hop artists to have crossed over into Hollywood stardom in the 1990s, including LL Cool J and Ice Cube, figures with large followings among a generally youth-ful music-buying public that represents an important audience demographic. This chapter will focus on two aspects of Smith's recent career: the cross-media dimension, particularly in the cases of *Men in Black* (1997, USA) and *Wild Wild West* (1999, USA), and how this is located in terms of the relationship between a star 'franchise' such as Smith and the con-temporary version of the Hollywood studio system.

Smith might appear to be the perfect Hollywood star for an era in which the major studios have become part of global multi-media corporations. A combination of success in blockbuster films and multi-million-selling records has, in some cases, made him an embodiment of corporate synergy: the much-touted ability of different media products to engage in a process of mutual promotion and reinforcement. Cross-media synergies have been actively pursued by the media corporations within which the Hollywood studios have become located. Few more clear-cut recent cases of mutual reinforcement by film and music can be found than the use of Smith's hit records to promote *Men in Black* and *Wild Wild West*, and vice versa. A performer such as Smith, with an ability to function in potentially complementary dimensions, is especially attractive to the indus-trial regime established in Hollywood since the demise of the 'classical' incarnation of the studio system from the 1950s. A number of developments (on which plenty has been written elsewhere) have heightened the desire of the industry to hedge its bets in search of the nearest possible thing to a pre-established guarantee of commercial success. Smith is one of a number of stars just below the very top in the current Hollywood hierarchy, his salary having risen from a reported $5 million for *Men in Black* to the elite $20 million bracket. He was ranked 14th in the 1999 'Star Power' survey by *The Hollywood Reporter*, one of only a dozen to have appeared in four or more films grossing more than $100 million in North America; he moved up to 13th place in the 2002 survey, based on a poll of more than 100 industry executives around the world (**http://hollywoodreporter.com/starpower**).

To what extent has Smith been secured as a synergistic property by the studios, and with what degree of sustained commercial success? If *Men in Black* was one of the biggest hits of the 1990s, what of his cross-media performance in *Wild Wild West*, a film that gained a strongly negative reputation? How are his manifestations in different media related? What kind of relationships have been established between Smith and the major studios, and what might this tell us about the broader industrial landscape of contemporary Hollywood stardom?

CROSSING OVER: THE APPEALS AND COMPLICATIONS OF FILM/MUSIC SYNERGIES

The release of *Men in Black* appeared to mark a perfect moment of corporate synergy, with Smith at its heart. The film, in which Smith starred alongside Tommy Lee Jones, was distributed by Columbia Pictures (it was produced by Steven Spielberg's Amblin Entertainment), part of the Sony Corporation. The music – a soundtrack album including the main theme, also released as the 'B-side' to the single 'Gettin' Jiggy With It' – was released by Columbia Records, another branch of the Sony empire (as was the Danny Elfman orchestral score, more of a niche-market product). Smith's image – cool, hip, but safe for family/white/middle-class consumption – appears to have been a defining component in each case. Sony was ideally placed to reap the proceeds in both dimensions (not to mention the broader benefits to its primary source of revenue: the production of electronic goods such as televisions, video recorders and CD players on which software such as films and music is played).[1]

The film earned $51 million at the box office over the opening '4th of July' weekend (a record for a non-sequel), ultimately grossing $250 million in the US and around $330 million worldwide. The 'Gettin' Jiggy With It'/'Men in Black' single was one of the hits of the summer, selling more than 500,000 copies; the soundtrack album sold three million. Sales of Smith's subsequent solo album, *Big Willie Style*, released in November 1997 and including the *Men in Black* theme, reached nine million in July 2000.[2] The hit records provided an ideal form of promotion for the film. Association with a major blockbuster film and its star, in return, would be expected to help to sell the music: a textbook example of cross-media synergy, in which total revenues promise to be greater than the sum of their parts. Radio play, record sales and airings of the music video offered hours of advertising that was not only free, but for which the corporation was paid. The soundtrack was released on 1 July, the day before the opening of the film, with the CD single following on 12 August, the main theme gaining considerable air-time in advance. The connection between theme and film was emphasised most clearly in the music video, the heavy rotation of which on MTV was credited with boosting the chart success of the soundtrack (*Los Angeles Times*, cited by the Internet Movie Database, Studio Briefing, 10 July 1997).

Equally significant, although less likely to gain the fanfare of recognition associated with the theatrical opening, was the simultaneous release by Sony/Columbia of *Big Willie Style* and the video of *Men in Black*, on 25 November 1997. This offered a fresh burst of Will Smith-ed synergy in arenas of high and more enduring revenue potential. Single-artist non-soundtrack albums have by far the largest long-term earnings scope in the music business, as demonstrated by the growth of sales of *Big Willie Style* in the years following its release. Video, likewise, has become the biggest single source of revenue for Hollywood films.[3] The video earned more than $100 million in rentals and sales in the US in its first six days.

A similar cross-media dimension surrounded the release of *Wild Wild West* in the summer of 1999. Smith sought to repeat two previous successes (*Independence Day*, 1996, USA, and *Men in Black*) as star of a '4th of July' hit (Smith's near monopoly of blockbuster success on that premium release date in the second half of the 1990s was a mark of his status in the industry). The film was another expensive and heavily promoted would-be blockbuster, accompanied by a single the lyrics of which, like those of 'Men in Black', revolve around an insistent repetition of the title, a particularly blatant form of cross-media promotion. Refrains such as 'here come the men-in-black' or simply 'wild-wild west' help to plant film titles into the public imagination, or at least those of pop-music-radio-listening or music-buying audiences. These are likely to overlap significantly with target audiences for the films, increasing the effectiveness of this kind of promotion. What is offered for the film is advance potential audience awareness of its existence, and a flavour of its style.

Cross-media patterns surrounding *Wild Wild West* were much the same as for its predecessor: film opening, 30 June 1999; 'Music Inspired by the Motion Picture' soundtrack, by various artists including Smith, released 15 July; CD single, 6 July. In the second phase, accompanied by a major marketing campaign, the *Willennium* solo album was released on 16 November, followed by a music video collection a week later (23 November) and the video release of the film a week after that (30 November).

Promotion of the kind offered by this strategy of coordinated film and film-related releases has long been attractive to Hollywood. A history of overlap between the sale of music and movies dates back to the start of the sound era. Figures such as Will Smith, with equally successful careers in film and music, were generally more common in the past than in contemporary Hollywood, as Paul McDonald suggests (2000: 87). One notable feature of the Smith music associated with *Men in Black* and *Wild Wild West* is that it does not feature in the body of the film text. It is reserved, instead, for opening or closing title sequences. It does not have the effect of disrupting or intruding on the narrative suggested in other cases, somewhat exaggeratedly in my opinion, by Justin Wyatt (1994). Much of the Smith persona is carried into the films, but not the music itself or its performance, a feature also of some of the other rap stars who developed Hollywood careers in the 1990s.

Synergy, of one variety or another, is far from new. But it takes on distinctive forms or implications according to the particular characteristics of one industrial regime or another. One significant development in recent decades is the pressure for films to perform well immediately on release, a pressure that increased during the 1990s. Hollywood has moved towards a strategy in which more and more films are opened on very large numbers of screens, and given only a few weeks, at best, to prove themselves at the box office. In this environment, advance recognition of the kind provided by music or other forms of crossover promotion is particularly desirable. *Jaws* (1975, USA) is generally credited with playing a key role in the establishment of this trend, although its opening on some 400 screens has been dwarfed by subsequent 'event movie' openings, including *Batman* (1989, USA) on 2,000, and the likes of *Men in Black* and *Wild Wild West*, which opened on 3,020 and 3,342 screens, respectively. By the late 1990s, an opening engagement on 3,000 screens had become the norm for prospective mass-audience films.

Wild Wild West performed healthily enough at first in this arena, appearing to demonstrate the imperviousness of mass-market filmgoers to critical opinion by taking a respectable $36.4 million during the four-day weekend, in the face of hostile reviews. Its first-week total was a blockbuster-worthy $49.7 million, with Smith earning the credit from the marketing head of one cinema chain for his ability to pull in 'all ages, all ethnic groups, all sexes' (*USA Today*, cited by Internet Movie Database, Studio Briefing, 6 July 1999). Smith contributes to particularly effective theatrical openings, a reflection of his appearance in productions of blockbuster scale in the latter half of the 1990s. He was rated joint-first with Jim Carrey, scoring an average North American opening of $34.7 million, in a table complied by *The Hollywood Reporter* as part of its 1999 'Star Power' survey. *Wild Wild West* suffered a rapid decline of attendance, however, as is typical of blockbusters that receive poor word-of-mouth, taking only $5.3 million on its fourth weekend, while still showing on more than 3,000 screens. Its final gross in the US was $113.7 million, a total of $217 million including the overseas market, compared with a total of $580 million for *Men in Black*; disappointing figures for a film for which the budget was estimated at between $105 million and $170–180 million (which may or may not include extensive promotional costs).

65

Despite its promising start, *Wild Wild West* was generally considered a failure at the box office. Revenue of $217 million would leave little in the way of net profits when all costs of release were included, even at the lower end of the budget estimates. Perhaps more than anything else, the difference between *Wild Wild West* and *Men in Black* was the 'buzz' produced in anticipation of, and during, the opening of the film; the amorphous and ephemeral sense of positive or negative associations. This is a quantity that exists in arenas – especially the internet – over which studio promotional efforts have only limited influence. *Wild Wild West* suffered from a strongly negative buzz, a factor that did not appear to undermine its opening performance, but which affected its value in subsequent release windows. I have not been able to obtain definitive US video figures,[4] but sales and rentals data for the UK show a marked disparity, even when allowance is made for the fact that *Men in Black* has been on the market for two years longer. By December 2000, *Men in Black* had achieved 3,396,856 rental transactions, compared to 1,121,994 for *Wild Wild West*; sales were even more divergent, at 1,224,000 and 84,000, respectively.[5] The television rights were sold for a mere $6 million, a fraction of the reported $70 million earned by *Men in Black* (Benjamin Svetkey in *Entertainment Weekly*, 9 July 1999, accessed at **http://www.ew.com/ew/archive** 1999).

What about the music sold primarily through Smith's presence in the film? To what extent does the success or failure of one affect the other (a crucial question in the analysis of cross-media synergy)? It is hard to be certain, as a number of variables are involved in the relationship between film and other media. In a case of clear-cut overall success, such as *Men in Black*, it is easy to assume a mutually positive reinforcement. The evidence provided by *Wild Wild West* is less conclusive. The performance of the film did not match studio expectations. Synergies via the figure of Smith did not quite perform their magic as far as the film was concerned, proving – if more proof were needed – that there is no such thing as a sure-fire sustained hit in Hollywood, and that even the most carefully orchestrated media corporation promotional campaigns are distinctly fallible.

The music, however, did not fare at all badly. The single sold more than 500,000 copies, in the same bracket as the combination of 'Getting' Jiggy With It' and 'Men in Black'. The soundtrack sold two million, which compares well with that of *Men in Black* (at three million), given *Men in Black*'s unusually high degree of success in all quarters. Smith's music video is reported to have been 'one of the few things that actually generated good buzz for the film' (Svetkey, 1999). The music products associated with *Wild Wild West* did not suffer as much, relatively, as the box office or video performance of the movie. This raises a number of questions. The two branches of the entertainment industry, often brought together within the giant media corporations, remain distinct in many respects. A considerable degree of insulation may exist, which complicates any simplistic picture of buzzing synergies between arenas such as film and popular music through the presence of figures such as Smith.

Smith's personae as movie star and rap artist are closely related in many respects. The former draws on the latter to a large extent (a generally 'cool' and 'stylish' image, elements of the 'funky' rap persona often blended with more authoritative or institutional roles; this is a process treated most explicitly in the transformation from not-so-plain-clothes cop to black-suited federal alien hunter in *Men in Black*). There may be considerable overlap between audiences for the mainstream films in which he has appeared and for his music, but the two are far from identical. The appeal of Smith-as-rapper – in movie-related single, contribution to a soundtrack, or free-standing solo album including a movie theme – need not be attached too closely to the positive or negative buzz attached to any film project.

Smith's music career was established long before he became a Hollywood star. In the late 1980s he achieved millionaire success as the Fresh Prince, half of a rap/hip-hop act with DJ 'Jazzy' Jeff Townes, which produced five albums on Jive Records. The last of these, *Code Red* (1993) performed disappointingly, and, along with the demands of his growing acting career and the imminent birth of his son, encouraged Smith to take a break from the music business that lasted until the release of *Men in Black* (Nickson, 1999: 81). Smith's reputation in the music business did not appear to suffer from any negative associations as a result of his participation in *Wild Wild West*. At the American Music Awards of January 2000, he won 'best male artist' in the pop/rock category and 'best soundtrack' for *Wild Wild West*. The single was named 'favourite song' and 'favourite song from a movie' in Nickelodeon's Kid's Choice Awards in April 2000, where Smith was voted 'favourite male singer' for the second year in a row, demonstrating his appeal to the youth audience ('Daily Music News', *Billboard* online, 12 January 1999; 18 January 2000; 17 April 2000). The continued faith of the exhibition sector in Smith's ability to draw crowds to the box office was indicated by awards presented at the ShoWest convention: he was named 'best actor' in 1999 and 'male star of the year' in 2002, following awards for 'male star of tomor-row' in 1995 and 'international box office achievement' in 1997 (*The Hollywood Reporter East*, 28 January 2002).

More research would be required to establish the nature of the relationship between audi-ences for the same performer in different media contexts. Conspicuous success in one arena may boost performance in another, to a greater extent than failure is necessarily translated across the media divide (although performers such as Smith remain wary about the potential implications 'unsuitable' roles might have for their image in the music busi-ness). Such a conclusion would no doubt be a comfort to the media corporations themselves, and a further justification for multi-media industrial strategies. Perhaps the performance of films at the box office is the particularly fragile and unstable element in the equation, theatrical release often being constrained by limited windows of opportunity and dependence on intangible advance impressions. Barry Sonnenfeld, director of *Men in Black* and *Wild Wild West*, reportedly blamed some of the problems of the latter on studio anxieties about unofficial pre-release comment on the internet, which, he suggests, led to a reduction in the number of test screenings permitted before release (Svetkey, 1999). In the music industry, by contrast, buyers have the opportunity to sample for themselves in advance, via radio and music television broadcasts, before deciding for or against any financial investment in the product. The two industries have been joined under the corporate umbrella, but they also remain very different enterprises with their own specific dynamics.

STAR BRANDS: THE SOMETIMES ELUSIVE FRANCHISE

The fate of film and music might have diverged to some extent in the case of *Wild Wild West*, but they remained linked as media products, sold at least partly in terms of the brand image established around the central figure of Will Smith. As with *Men in Black*, the distinctive Smith brand was a crucial ingredient in the selling of the product; it does not appear to have suffered much from the disappointing reputation of the film (*Wild Wild West* 'didn't hurt him. He's still a great investment,' as one 'top studio executive' is quoted as saying in a survey of star values in *Entertainment Weekly*, March 2000). The construction and ownership of identifiable brands and franchises is at the heart of the preferred industrial strategy of contemporary Hollywood. The ideal property for a studio is one over which it retains legal rights, for future exploitation in the shape of sequels or other spin-offs. *Men in Black* is a good example; a potent franchise developed by Amblin and Columbia which spawned a sequel in 2002, in which Smith reprised his role in return for a healthy slice of the gross. *Wild Wild West* is unlikely to follow suit in this respect, although it was exploited in other media, including books and a video game. A franchise is the clearly marked property of a studio, unlike a genre or cycle, for example, to which all have access (see Altman, 1999: 115).

Stars occupy a distinctive position in this industrial context. Stars such as Smith establish brand images of their own, based on the construction of an identifiable persona on-screen and off, effectively converting themselves into their own franchise properties, as Barry King (1991) suggests. These are not so easily 'owned' or controlled by the studios. In *Wild Wild West*, rights to the Will Smith brand were not secured by Sony/Columbia, the recipient of the synergistic benefits of *Men in Black*. For a moment, it seems, Sony/Columbia achieved the perfect combination of mutually reinforcing Smith-related in-house properties. Smith was at the fulcrum of an enormously successful collection of cross-media enterprises focused on his twin roles as film and music star. The coherence of this strategy did not last, however, a fact that highlights the difficulties the studios face in maintaining all-embracing relationships with such desirable star quantities. Smith's next film after *Men in Black*, *Enemy of the State* (1998, USA), was made under the aegis of Disney's Touchstone imprint. *Wild Wild West* came from Warner, part of the Time Warner empire (one of the largest of the corporate cross-media behemoths).

If the relative success of the music balanced to some extent the disappointing performance of *Wild Wild West* in the cinema, it did not, in this case, work to the benefit of the corporate parent of the film. The music associated with *Wild Wild West* was not released on any of the myriad labels in the Time Warner empire. If film/music synergy existed, it was not contained under any single corporate umbrella. Columbia maintained a large share of the Smith revenue stream, releasing both the single and *Willennium*. The Warner labels did not even have the movie soundtrack, which was released on Overbrook Records. And who controls Overbrook Records? Not one of the big conglomerates this time, but Smith himself, along with his partner and manager James Lassiter. Overbrook Records is part of Smith and Lassiter's Overbrook Entertainment, a company through which Smith, like many other Hollywood stars, has sought to gain his own stake at an industrial level.

Overbrook Entertainment is in some ways a typical example of the kind of company formed by Hollywood stars in recent decades, although most have been restricted to the arena of film (and, in some cases, television), rather than crossing over into the music business. Stars have gained a great deal more control over their destiny since the classical studio system – with its standard seven-year contracts – began to deconstruct during the 1950s. Big stars, as we know, have enormous industrial clout, seen as one of the most reliable sources of box office security. Many stars have established their own companies. In some cases, this is largely a matter of avoiding taxes; in others, however, it is an attempt to gain greater control over the kinds of projects with which the star is involved, whether *as* star or in the arena of producing or directing. The aspect of these companies on which I want to focus, through the example of Smith's Overbrook Entertainment, is the relationship established with the studios – not always an easy one.

Star-led production companies tend to exist within the orbit of particular studios, as do companies created by major producers or directors. They need access to studio resources: finance and access to the crucial networks of distribution and promotion. The studios, of course, are very keen to forge special relationships with stars, ideally tying them down in some way. Stars, with or without their own company infrastructures, are often given in-house or 'housekeeping' deals in an attempt to keep them attached. Overbrook Entertainment was created in 1997 in an arrangement with Universal Studios, part of the Seagram group (subsequently merged with Vivendi). Universal provided office and other facilities for Overbrook Entertainment at the Universal City complex in Los Angeles, along with finance for Overbrook to develop potential projects. In return, Overbrook was contractually obliged to offer Universal 'first look' at any projects developed, the first option to take any of them into production.

The system is designed to be of mutual benefit to star and studio. The studios are particularly keen to keep as much as possible of the film business within their compass, to maintain oligopoly power and hedge their bets, as demonstrated by their efforts to absorb the more profitable elements of the independent sector. In some cases, 'first look' or other such deals have led to stable and productive long-term relationships, such as that developed between Clint Eastwood's Malpaso and Warner since 1975. Elsewhere, however, and including the Overbrook–Universal arrangement, the benefits for the studio have been less tangible. A glance through the history of films in which Will Smith has appeared helps to demonstrate the difficulties involved for studios seeking privileged access to the star-image brand, one that is far more difficult to tie down than some other types of in-house franchise.

Smith is reported to have signed a two-picture deal with Twentieth Century Fox on the strength of the buzz created by his appearance in the pilot for the comedy television series, *The Fresh Prince of Bel Air* (1990–96), his first move into acting (Nickson, 1999: 49). What exactly became of that arrangement is unclear.[6] His initial foray into film was a small part in *Where the Day Takes You* (1992, USA), produced and distributed in the international/independent realm. *Made in America* (1993, USA), in which he had another minor role, was an independent production distributed by Warner. *Six Degrees of Separation* (1993, USA), an 'arty' film in which Smith played a central part, was distributed by MGM/UA. His association with Columbia came with his first major mainstream performance, in the buddy-action-comedy *Bad Boys* (1995, USA), although the studio initially resisted suggestions that he was suitable for the part ('Will power', *Entertainment Weekly*, 20 June 1997, accessed at **http://www.ew.com/ew/archive**; 'Will power', *The Hollywood Reporter*, 10 March 1999, accessed at **http://hollywoodreporter.com/archive/hollywood/archive**). His move into the ranks of major stardom began with *Independence Day* for Fox, followed by *Men in Black* (Columbia), *Enemy of the State* (Disney/Touchstone) and *Wild Wild West* (Warner). *The Legend of Bagger Vance* (2000, USA) was distributed by DreamWorks in the US and Canada, and principally by Twentieth Century Fox elsewhere. *Men in Black II* (2002, USA), another Amblin production, and *Ali* (2001, USA) were both distributed by Columbia/Sony.

Columbia appears, to date, to have gained by far the largest access to the career of Smith as a major star, although apparently through no formal multi-picture arrangement other than the studio's ownership of rights to the sequel to *Men in Black*. But what of Universal, with its privileged first-look deal? Very little was forthcoming, even allowing for the time many Hollywood features spend in 'development hell' before entering pre-production. Universal, along with Paramount, is one of the two major studios not to feature at all in the list of titles cited above. A number of projects are reported to have been in development, or under consideration, by Overbrook, involving Smith as star in some cases and as executive producer in others. Titles to which his name was strongly linked as star included *K-Pax* (2001, USA), a Universal film that eventually starred Kevin Spacey instead and was produced by Lawrence Gordon Productions, rather than Overbrook. *The Mark*, listed as a joint project with Roland Emmerich and Dean Devlin's production company, Centropolis, was reportedly to feature Smith as a con artist enlisted to save the world. He was also described as prospective star of *Love II Love*, a romantic comedy script bought by

Universal for Overbrook to produce ('Smith lands on "K-Pax" alien mystery for Uni', *The Hollywood Reporter*, 20 April 1998, accessed at **http://hollywoodreporter.com/archive/ hollywood/archive**). Other projects cited by the trade press or in various internet reports include the purchase of rights to remake *Diva* (1982, France), *Play Misty for Me* (1971, USA) and *Cat People* (1942/1982, USA). A number of film and television projects reportedly being developed by Overbrook during 2000 and 2001 were notable for the absence of any involvement of Universal.

A source to whom I was referred at Overbrook in December 2000 said 'a number of films are in development' but not one had reached a stage at which the company was prepared to confirm any details. Such reticence might have reflected embarrassment at the company's inability to deliver any of the high-profile projects with which Smith's name has been associated. A spokesman for Universal said: 'While they have projects they are developing, there is nothing currently in production or pre-production for Universal Pictures.' The arrangement eventually came to nothing, as far as features were concerned, and was put out of its misery when Overbrook signed a three-year first-look deal with Columbia in January 2002, a far more logical arrangement given the extent of Smith's previous and ongoing dealings with Columbia (the deal was announced within weeks of the US opening of *Ali*, which was produced by James Lassiter through Overbrook). In a statement that did not appear to reflect very happily on their time at Universal, Smith and Lassiter said:

> Home is a place where you feel completely comfortable and you get unconditional support, and Columbia Pictures has been that place to us for many years. Amy Pascal [Columbia chairman] has showed us through deeds, not words, how we can continue to grow Overbrook Entertainment, and you couldn't ask for a better partner than Columbia Pictures.
>
> ('Col inks Smith, Overbrook deal', The Hollywood Reporter, 31 January 2002 accessed at http://hollywoodreporter.com)

Overbrook Entertainment's deal with Universal was in no way an exclusive arrangement between star and studio. Its terms included nothing to prevent Smith from starring in or producing films elsewhere (especially at Columbia!). All it guaranteed for the studio was that it would receive first right of refusal on projects developed by the company. Big stars hold most of the power in this equation. The number of stars deemed to have the marquee value to 'open' a picture on their own, to gain finance for a project and to be considered close to a safe bet at the box office in the domestic and foreign markets, remains small, giving such individuals tremendous industrial power. For the studios, arrangements such as that between Overbrook and Universal can be expensive and somewhat uncertain investments. Exactly how much Universal spent facilitating the operations of Overbrook to no real avail, is not the kind of figure ever likely to be revealed by either party, but it must have been millions of dollars. What the studio was seeking to buy was not just the rights to a particular set of projects developed under the formal terms of the contract, but some additional sense of loyalty. Will Smith was under no great obligation to Universal, but, as my source at Overbrook intimated, 'loyalty is a different thing. [There] might be some kind of loyalty [involved in the relationship].' Or perhaps not, in this case.

Deals such as that involving Smith's company are often described negatively by industry analysts as 'vanity deals', designed to stroke a star performer's ego more than in the expectation of concrete production. That the studios should be tempted into offering such deals, in the hope of establishing some kind of moral commitment on the part of the star, is hardly surprising. It is a potentially nebulous business, however, reflective of wider tensions in the recent operations of the majors, which appear to be torn between contradictory desires: on the one hand, to meet the costs of various semi-independent in-house commitments, in an attempt to secure privileged access to potentially lucrative producer, director and star talent, and, on the other, to accede to demands to cut overhead costs. Periods of spending on this kind of arrangement appear to alternate with bouts of cost-cutting. Annual surveys by *Variety* over the five years to 2001 show an overall trend towards a reduction and tightening of in-house production deals, including those involving actors who produce (but not including deals with actors or directors who do not produce) ('Hollywood Filmers' Pact gets Whacked', *Variety*, 25 June 2001; 'Passion for Slashin'', *Variety*, 26 June 2000). Casualties during 2000 included Nicholas Cage's Saturn Films at Walt Disney, and deals involving Sigourney Weaver and Denzel Washington at Twentieth Century Fox. The number of producing deals at Universal dropped from 39 in 1997 to 21 in 2001.

It is safe to assume that what Universal wanted most of all from its arrangement with Smith was to secure his services as a star, rather than as a producer or executive producer. The latter is the 'vanity' part of the deal, whatever talents Smith might prove to possess in that direction, and may be a price worth paying for the former. But there was no guarantee that Smith's presence as star would be secured at all, let alone on a sustained basis. There were some other benefits for Universal, but of a less stellar variety. Overbrook has a television division that developed projects for Universal as well as for other studios, including Warner Brothers. There was also a music component to the deal, despite Smith's primary association with Columbia Records.

Releases from Overbrook's music arm were distributed by Interscope Records, one of numerous labels in the Universal Music Group, an arrangement launched with the release of the *Wild Wild West* soundtrack. Universal, in other words, managed through its relationship with Smith to tap into one of the better performing parts of the revenue stream of a project developed at a competitor studio. The existence of allied music divisions gives the studios another carrot with which to attract desirable talent within the film industry. Recent music and film deals have been offered by Universal to Danny DeVito's Jersey Films and to the director Tom Shadyac, figures with little or no experience in the music business who are seeking to benefit from the growing revenues earned by soundtrack recordings associated with their productions ('Disc Drive', *The Hollywood Reporter*, 1 June 1999, accessed at **http://hollywoodreporter.com/archive**). Smith also stars in the *Men in Black* ride, part of the Sony/Columbia franchise, which opened in April 2000 as the newest and biggest attraction at the Universal Studios theme park in Florida, although there was no suggestion that this was in any formal way related to the Overbrook/Universal association.

CONCLUSION

A dual-career performer such as Will Smith offers great potential in the cross-media corporate environment of contemporary Hollywood. Synergy remains a quality admiringly discussed in the trade press, and pursued where possible by the major studios. There is no guarantee, however, that success – or failure – translates automatically across media boundaries. The relationships between media such as film and music are more complex than they might sometimes seem. The same goes for the network of relationships that exists between stars, the studios and other divisions of the corporations within which the studios are located. If the positioning of Smith and Sony/Columbia in regard to *Men in Black* offers a portrait of intra-corporate synergy working at its most neat and tidy, the messier picture presented by both the performance of – and star-corporate allegiances surrounding – *Wild Wild West* is perhaps more typical of the vagaries of real-world stardom in contemporary Hollywood.

---

1   Of the company's $63 billion in sales and operating revenue in the year ended 31 March 2000, electronics accounted for $41.4 billion compared with $4.6 billion for Sony Pictures, $6.2 billion for music and $5.9 billion for video games (Sony Corporation, 'Annual Report 2000').

2   These and other music sales figures cited are from the Recording Industry Association of America (RIAA).

3   Some 46 per cent of the global revenue of the average blockbuster comes from video sales and rentals, compared with 26 per cent from the theatrical market, according to estimates supplied to the author by *Screen Digest*, January 2001. US video sales and rental accounted for $19.9 billion in 2000, nearly three times the $7.5 billion taken at the box office (Hettrick, 2001).

4   VideoScan, the industry research organisation that collates the figures, refused to supply data without a payment of $500.

5   UK rental figures from Media Research Information Bureau; sales figures from Chart Information Network.

6   Neither Fox nor Smith's publicist could supply any information on this.

Chapter Four

☐ PUTTING AWAY CHILDISH THINGS: JAR JAR BINKS AND THE 'VIRTUAL STAR' AS AN OBJECT OF FAN LOATHING[1]

Matt Hills

In this chapter I want to interrogate a number of assumptions which have structured prior work on stars in film theory. First, I want to consider how the term 'affect' has been restricted so that stars are typically discussed as objects of fan affect*ion*. Second, I want to consider how affect can be addressed pragmatically in star studies: can fans' 'discourses of affect' be analysed without considering what I will term 'affective discourses'? And finally, what is the place of the 'virtual star' within discussions of star-fan audience relationships? Each area of discussion will be linked to a case study of Jar Jar Binks (a 'star' of *The Phantom Menace* (1999, USA)), exploring the ways in which one faction of online *Star Wars*[2] fans responded to the character. Brooker (1999: 69) has emphasised the 'measured and entirely friendly' nature of online *Star Wars* fandom, but this observation was made prior to the release of *The Phantom Menace*. It seems likely that having the *Star Wars* franchise alive again through a contested but canonical film text presents its fans with new possibilities for communal in-fighting and factionalism, with one of the greatest dimensions of fan tension being generational.

STAR STUDIES AND MEDIA AFFECTS OF 'LOVE' AND 'HATE'

Unlike other areas of film and cultural studies, star studies has always reserved a conceptual space for affect. The fan's 'it just started from there' (Barker and Brooks, 1998: 67) has always been implied in star studies, even where 'empirical' audiences have not been investigated. Richard Dyer's seminal *Stars*, for example, suggests that 'particularly intense star–audience relationships occur amongst adolescents and women. ... These groups [Dyer also discusses 'gay ghetto culture'] all share a particularly intense degree of role/identity conflict and pressure, and an (albeit partial) exclusion from the dominant articulacy of, respectively, adult, male, heterosexual culture' (1979: 37). Dyer's later *Heavenly Bodies* again relates fan engagement, or 'love', to ideological concerns:

> We're fascinated by stars because they enact ways of making sense of the experience of being a person in a particular kind of social production . . ., with its particular organisation of life into public and private spheres. We love them because they represent how we think that experience is or how it would be lovely to feel that it is.
>
> *(Dyer, 1986: 17)*

But the audience's emotional attachment to stars is not simply related back to ideological concerns here. It also appears to form part of an ideological delusion or trap. Stars are loved because through this 'love', social experience can be idealised, and felt (temporarily) as this ideal. The 'love' for stars seemingly threatens to lead us all into temptation, and away from the path of 'good' analysis. This type of position restricts affect in at least two ways. First, audience emotion can be contrasted to the analyst's 'knowledge'. This renders the 'we' of the quote above highly unstable; Dyer is both 'inside' and 'outside' of the 'ideological investment' that he highlights. And second, the audience's 'intense relationship' with a star remains a matter of 'love'; stars are not important for Dyer because they may be intensely disliked, detested or denigrated by audiences.

I want to challenge both of these conceptions. Can devalued audience affect or 'love' simply form a counterpoint to superior analytical knowledge or 'cognition'? David Buckingham has recently suggested that this 'simple opposition between reason and pleasure, or cognition and affect' (2000: 112) requires rethinking. While cognitive film theory has partially broken down such an opposition, it has done so by rather rigidly subordinating affect to processes of cognition (Carroll, 1990; Smith, 1995; Grodal, 1999; Plantinga and Smith, 1999). Other recent attempts at escaping this subordination include Barker with Austin (2000). However, although avoiding the excesses of cognitive film theory, their account of audience affect seems to replay a 'folk theory' of audience reception at times. This is particularly evident in a speculative analysis of *The Lion King*. Here, the 'caring with' audience member is a child and the 'caring for' audience is allocated a parental role: 'you can imagine them [the 'caring with' viewer] turning to their parents and asking "Is he alright?" . . . To know like an adult while caring like a child . . . this combination is crucial.' (2000: 115–16) The imagined 'caring with' child is unaware of the codes and conventions of this type of film, and is therefore caught up in it, while the imagined 'caring for' adult is in 'a position of cognitive superiority' (2000: 115) and is hence insulated from the film's immediate content via an awareness of overall narrative structure. However Barker seeks to articulate or combine these positions, the argument remains reliant on a moment of child/adult splitting, and hence on an imagined scene of a vulnerable or affected child and a knowing adult/parent. But why should we assume that 'knowing' is experienced 'like an adult' and that caring is done 'like a child'? In fact, I will suggest later in this piece that the 'common sense' structural homology which Barker draws on (child is to adult as affect is to cognition) is also a central structuring premise in *Star Wars*' fans responses to Jar Jar Binks.

And if the affect/cognition opposition requires rethinking (and refeeling), so too does the assumption that audience–star affect can be equated with affection. Moving from Dyer's work to more recent star–audience studies, the restriction of affect to affection remains strangely consistent. McKenzie Wark (1999: 53) refers to 'the strange love of publics and celebrities for one another', while Stephen Hinerman (2001: 203) notes that 'stardom provides significant emotional connections for otherwise relatively disconnected individuals' without addressing the ambivalences and complexities of these 'emotional connections'. Jackie Stacey (1994) presents an analysis of audience–star relations which greatly complicates and reworks the troubled concept of 'identification', but again her work does not significantly touch upon audience–star dislike or revulsion. Of the major post-Dyer studies of stardom/celebrity (and I do not view these terms as marking a conceptual distinction), Gamson (1994) moves away from assuming audience–star 'love'. Instead he discusses the more prosaic and mundane 'gossip' which audience 'believing games' circulate without investing in celebrities as 'authentic' (1994: 173). This downplays the intensity of audience–star relations, viewing this connection as more rooted in everyday life and its evaluations (1994: 175). Gamson therefore also fails to address intense audience dislike for stars; his approach is more concerned with the cognitive-evaluative activities of 'producerly' and Fiskean audiences.

Marshall (1997) places affect at the heart of his analysis of *Celebrity and Power*, considering how 'the celebrity represents a site for the housing of affect in terms of both the audience and the institutions that have worked to produce the cultural forms that have allowed the celebrity to develop' (1997: 73–4). This 'housing' process means that a star/celebrity cannot be imposed on an audience, but can act as a focus for the binding together of an audience community. This is a suggestive notion, but even within this powerful framework, Marshall restricts his discussion of affect to affection. He limits the star's 'housing' of affect to matters of associative, admiring, sympathetic and cathartic identification, as well as referring to an 'ironic modality' which limits identification but is linked to 'modernist fiction and postmodern criticism' (1997: 69, drawing on the work of Hans Robert Jauss). While the first four options all involve a positive emotional link between audience–subject and star–text, the final option allows the possibility of non-identification but seems to rule out a lived experience of intense dislike, revolving instead around the modernist/postmodern generalisation of (distanced) aesthetic play over and above 'involved' referentiality.

Meanwhile, Geraghty (2000: 195) distinguishes usefully between cultural studies' work on fans' extratextual activity and audience appreciation of 'stars-as-performers'. Following but adapting Geraghty's corrective focus on star performance, I will argue in this piece that the 'fan position' necessarily encompasses both extratextual knowledge and (textual) arguments over 'performance'. However, despite usefully moving away from cultural studies' near-obsession with fandom, Geraghty's alternative 'position' remains focused on cultural value as this is produced through audience appreciation rather than through, say, audience–star distaste, disgust or dislike.

In the shadow of such structuring presuppositions, remarkably little work has been done on audience *dislike* for stars. This dislike may be assumed to hail from non- or anti-fans, but as I will show in the case of Jar Jar Binks, it can just as easily form part of a fannish cultural identity.

The work of Schulze, Barton White and Brown (1993) forms one honourable exception to the norms of star studies, being an excellent exploration of audience–star repulsion rather then fascination. Their work examined discourses drawn on by 'Madonna-haters', and identified how anti-Madonna audiences viewed the pop star Madonna as inauthentic along several axes (as low culture; via 'corruption' or 'disease' metaphors; as devalued or feared femininity). They concluded that:

> Madonna is not universally loved. She is, in fact, strongly disliked by many
> who share a vision of her as the low-Other – the symbolic center of much
> that is wrong with the culture aesthetically, socially, and/or morally. . . . To
> all of her critics, she is something to be reviled rather than revered.
>
> *(Schulze et al., 1993: 31)*

Exploring related territory, Thomas J. Roberts has noted the importance of analysing 'allergics', that is, readers who refuse to read certain material: 'We do not think of ourselves as having an allergic reaction, of course, but as truth seeing: this or that sort of story *is* obscenely violent, or viciously snobbish, or stupid, or grossly ignorant' (1990: 82).

In this instance, I want to focus on 'allergic' haters of Jar Jar Binks. What types of 'truth' do these *Star Wars* fans see in the character of Binks, and how is Binks discursively and affectively constructed as low-Other?

JAR JAR MUST DIE: CONSTRUCTING THE 'ADULT' *STAR WARS* FAN

Barker (2000) has argued that Jar Jar's racialised characteristics are insufficient to account for his unpopularity among *Star Wars* fans:

> John Sutherland discussed why the character Jar Jar Binks – ostensibly a
> cheerful alien ally – has become sufficiently controversial as to have a

77

> website dedicated to his death. . . . Sutherland argues that Jar Jar's
> problem is that he is 'miscegenated'. . . . Actually, a visit to the
> 'jarjarmustdie' website doesn't really support Sutherland's account – its
> objection to Binks is more that he just isn't funny.
>
> *(Barker with Austin, 2000: 202–3, n.11)*

Although I agree with Barker's argument that Jar Jar's 'racism' is relatively unimportant within fans' rejection of the character, I am less convinced by his alternative explanation. Although derogatory references to Jar Jar's 'toilet humour' are evident on jarjarmustdie.com, these criticisms are framed within a further opposition, that of child/adult:

> The only thing I didn't like about Jar Jar were the scenes of comic relief of
> toilet humor he encounters like: 'Youssa in big doodoo this time' or 'icky
> icky poo' and the farting beast of burden before the pod race. The
> underlying messages of the Star Wars fims [sic] are religious, hopeful, and
> full of love. How out of place would it have been if Luke asked Han on the
> Falcon in episode 4 in his extreme naïve nature 'Where's the toilet on this
> thing?'. I just think that the films are bigger than toilet humor. I really wish
> that they were cut out. But it's also for the kids and that must be what kids
> think is cool today because I feel like I'm getting older when I criticise it.
>
> *(JURMSON, 9/7/1999 2:17 am)*

The contributors to jarjarmustdie.com are clearly fans of *Star Wars*: 'First off, I am a huge Star Wars fan (of course) … (p.s. i'm 20)' (Overrun, 7/9/1999 10:05 am). In terms of a textual representation of fan cultural identity, the bracketed 'of course' is particularly telling. It indicates not only that *Star Wars* fandom can be asserted as a valued term, but also that this positively valued identity can be assumed by contributors. Detailed fan knowledge is frequently displayed by the Jar Jar haters, such as in these contributions to the list of 'Ways Jar Jar Binks Should Die!': 'Bantha stampede … [or] Tumbles into a Sarlacc pit' (**members.tripod.com/Freaky_Freya/diejarjar.html**).

But these *Star Wars* fans also appear to belong to a certain generation; or, at least, they discursively construct themselves – sometimes defensively and wearily, sometimes aggressively – as a generationally 'truth-seeing' section of *Star Wars* fandom. The fan identities at stake here are constantly juxtaposed to a low-Other which is not so much feminised as rendered 'childish' and hence low-cultural: 'Lucas insults his fans intelligence by doing cartoonish things like that' (JTPALADIN, 9/9/1999 11:07 am); 'Lucas created Jar Jar to sell toys to kids' (SAGRADA7, 7/26/1999 11:58 am).

These fans consistently devalue Jar Jar through articulated discourses: the character is childish and/or for kids, and is also simultaneously 'commercial', being a case of George Lucas 'selling out'. Such discourses position and utilise Jar Jar hatred as a form of communal legitimation. Detesting Jar Jar appears to act, in part, as a way of preserving the cultural values of a specific group of *Star Wars* fans, namely twenty- or, most likely, thirtysomethings (see Brooker, 1997: 102–3 on the '*Star Wars* generation') who saw the *Star Wars* trilogy on its first release:

> Star Wars and Empire were completely serious and well done sci-fi movies. The only real comic relief was provided by C3PO and R2D2. Even into Jedi it was still serious until they got to the Ewoks and then things went down hill. Why? Lucas knew he could make a fortune in marketing the Ewoks through videos and merchandising. And he was right. With incentive like that, is there any wonder he made Phantom Menace as basically a childrens movie?
>
> *(JTPALADIN, 8/19/1999 5:33 pm)*

But this 'discursive defence' argument raises a number of issues. First, if Jar Jar-bashing is a way of constructing lines of authenticity around a 'good' adult section of the *Star Wars* fan community, against which an imagined Other of 'next generation' *Phantom Menace* fan-children can be positioned, then to what extent is 'affect' a meaningful category of analysis here? Surely if jarjarmustdie and the Jar Jar Hate webring (founded 06/05/1999; 20 sites) are actually ways of socially and culturally defending a specific fan community, then their discussions of 'hate' for Jar Jar are somewhat beside the point? Second, if anti-Jar Jar fan activity is described as drawing on certain discourses, then does this not theoretically rule out a focus on affect in any case? Since discourses are cognitive and social constructions of meaning which rule out any 'affective' aspect, then such an interpretation seemingly opens the door to 'discourse determinism' (Lupton, 1998: 38) in which fan 'loathing' for Jar Jar is simply a performed series of signs.

These objections need to be addressed. I have already suggested that the notions of 'discourses of affect' and 'affective discourses' might be usefully deployed, and these terms could help to clarify matters here. By 'discourse of affect', I am referring to the notion that emotion can be performed without being experienced, and without this being a case of 'deliberate' dissimulation. As Claire Armon-Jones has observed:

> In the case of devotion, it can be argued that actions expressive of feelings of devotion have acquired a separate role in which they function independently of affect because they have, for moral and other social reasons, become institutionalised.
>
> *(Armon-Jones, 1991: 10)*

The establishment of jarjarmustdie.com as well as the Jar Jar Hate webring could be viewed as a certain 'institutionalisation' of anti-Jar Jar 'sentiment' operating for social reasons – the legitimation of *Star Wars* fan activities and identities. However, this argument is unpersuasive on two counts.

1. It neglects to consider that discourse is never solely cognitive/evaluative or linguistic. Such a 'discourse determinism' assumes that the communicability of affect must be premised on the non-existence of an affective ontology, whereas this is not in fact a logical consequence of accepting and examining 'discourses of affect'.

2. It neglects to consider that the social and cultural values that *Star Wars* fans are defending through their anti-Jar Jar stance are themselves open to further contestation. In this instance, then, even if a 'discourse of affect' is accepted, this discourse remains open to affective destabilisation. It has to defend itself, and not merely cognitively and logically but also *emotionally*, against the 'attacks' of counter-positions and counter-claims on cultural value. In short, my argument here is that 'heteroglossia' is not merely an 'abstract' philosophical question. It is also a lived, fraught experience which tends to discount and undermine the cognitive 'security' or rational 'fixity' of any given 'discourse'.

I would suggest that we need to view 'discourses of affect' as always-also 'affective discourses' – discourses which are themselves emotionally invested in and defended (see Hollway and Jefferson, 2000: 19; Lupton, 1998: 38; Williams, 2001: 135) and which often function to demarcate a sense of 'ownership' felt over specific texts or ideas. According to this perspective, the discourses of affect ('hate') drawn on and performed by anti-Jar Jar *Star Wars* fans are not spurious and 'false'; nor are they an epiphenomenal 'effect' of claims over cultural identity, or a case of nonserious 'humour' masking such claims. Instead, these discourses can be viewed as part of an affective discourse which works, emotionally as well as cognitively, to legitimate the fans' prior investments in the *Star Wars* universe. This process is similar to that uncovered by Julian Hoxter in his fascinating discussion of an *Exorcist* fan webring:

> The impression one gets from reading fan discourse is that of the centrality of ownership or perhaps more appositely, of possession and control of knowledge about the cult object which speaks to a sense of insecurity and anxiety regarding the status of the fan before his object.
>
> *(Hoxter, 2000: 178)*

However, Hoxter's psychoanalytic position ultimately depends on a splitting of affect and cognition/knowledge: he argues that the fans' knowledge acts as a defence against anxiety. On the other hand, I am suggesting that affect can remain *both* the 'subject matter' of fan discourse (which it is not for Hoxter's *Exorcist* fans) *and* the ontological underpinning of such discourse, rather than something which is to be wholly warded off through fan 'knowledge'. The 'Jar Jar hate' contributors do not ward off affect so much as translate their affective investment in *Star Wars* into a 'discourse of affect' which itself remains 'anxiously' open to further affective-discursive contestations.

By devaluing Jar Jar as a childish, cartoonish and commercial low-Other, these *Star Wars* fans construct a series of binary oppositions which work to legitimise their tastes. That this process is both culturally and emotionally important is testified to by the possibility that self-identifying 'adult' fans may otherwise be confronted by accusations that their fandom is childish or inappropriate:

> I HATE AHMED BEST ... I read on a webpage somewhere that when [Ahmed] Best was asked about what he thought of the cult following of Star Wars he said something along the lines of 'Some people are real fanatics and that's just nuts. Take a step back, get off the Internet.' Well I consider that to be pretty much aimed directly at people like me and I don't like his tone.

> *('The Jar Jar Hate Newsletter' Issue 4 at http://www.adamrulz.com/jj)*

Avoiding accusations of fan childishness seems to underpin much of the Jar Jar hate material; an effort which tends to defeat itself in a variety of ways (see the title of the webpage in the reference above). The possibility remains of self-identifying as 'adult' against Jar Jar's 'childishness' so virulently and excessively that the very status claimed is brought into question. The fragility of the fans' position is demonstrated in a number of ways. For example, immediately after a posting which defends *Star Wars* (1977, USA) and *The Empire Strikes Back* (1980, USA) 'as completely serious and well done sci-fi movies' while damning *The Phantom Menace* as a 'children's movie', there is a posting which reads: 'and what is Star Wars about may I ask? High drama?' (HEK4, 8/19/1999 5:33 pm). The Jar Jar haters are also forced to restate explicitly their own self-characterisation: 'Vast, grey, semi-intelligent masses? ... Jar Jar was CREATED for those "vast, grey, semi-intelligent masses", and the people that hate him ... ARE the intelligent people who wanted to see a Star Wars movie and ended up with something one step above "Barney's Great Sugar Adventure"' (IHATEJARJAR, 7/20/1999 11:43 am). One posting seems to reach the heart of the matter:

> I think the reason why people hate Jar Jar is because the people who hate him now are the people who are [*sic*] little kids anymore. Jar Jar is for kids and comic relief.

> *(JURMSON, 9/7/1999 2:17 am)*

This message, while arguing that Jar Jar haters are no longer 'little kids', playfully (or otherwise) omits the 'not' that its own logic requires. The Jar Jar haters therefore grammatically become 'little kids' while the implied meaning of the sentence requires the negation of this statement. Childishness is simultaneously projected out onto the 'Jar Jar lovers' (fans of Barney and Disney films, it is implied), and yet returns to haunt the 'discourse of affect' of Jar Jar hate. The discourse of 'lovers' versus 'haters' and 'us' versus 'them' is so strenuously asserted that these desired distinctions appear not to have been cognitively and securely achieved.

Identification as a 'fan' may be reinforced and yet also put into question by Jar Jar anti-commercial hate: 'If you DO think that Lucas is solely profit-driven, then why are you a fan at all? Why waste your time?' (JEDILAW001, 7/20/1999 3:10 pm). This specific counter-discourse works by making explicit the investment in the *Star Wars* universe that 'Jar Jar hate' seeks (covertly) to legitimate and defend. The Jar Jar haters' naturalisation of child/adult, authentic/commercial and intelligent/stupid 'truths' is challenged here. By containing and focusing their fan disappointment on a single element of *The Phantom Menace*, the Jar Jar haters defend their 'good' fandom and their 'good' fan object so extremely that they begin to appear as 'bad' or irrational fans. Their interpretive and affective fan activity leaves them open to the accusation that they are incapable of appreciating the very 'goodness' in *Star Wars* that they are so intent on preserving.

JAR JAR AS VIRTUAL STAR?

So far I have discussed star–audience relations and the role of Jar Jar 'hate' discourses in self-constituting 'good/intelligent/anti-commercial' *Star Wars* fandom. Although I have touched on the fragility of these claimed identities – a fragility which counter-postings and arguments keep reopening – I have yet to discuss the role of 'virtual stardom' within the 'Jar Jar hate' fan campaign.

Before considering how a fraction of *Star Wars* fandom read and responded to Binks as virtual, I want to return briefly to the matter of 'virtual stardom'. If I am describing Jar Jar Binks as a star, rather than a character, then how can this distinction be supported? Clearly Binks does not circulate in extratextual, official secondary texts, and thus a major aspect of stardom – where the star's 'authentic' lifestyle and persona are drawn on in publicity narratives – is seemingly absent. As Barbara Creed has noted, cyber-stars cannot endure or enjoy scandals in the way that embodied stars have done: 'unless, of course, the digital star is given an offscreen life in order to keep alive other areas of the industry such as fan magazines, merchandising and promotions' (2000: 80). Since Jar Jar has no off-screen life, then he cannot be thought of as a conventional star:[3] 'his' extratextual, publicity circulation is restricted (though not entirely blocked, since discourses of SFX technique and 'behind-the-scenes' insider knowledge can be mobilised to use Binks as a promotional element). As Thomas Austin suggested to me, Binks has no early career to reveal or conceal, no rise to fame to fuel gossip, and no new film to promote. Put like this, it seems patently obvious that Binks is definitively a character and not a star. However, I would argue that discussion of this sort fails to consider the qualifier 'virtual' in *virtual* stardom.

'Virtual stardom' is not and cannot be the same cultural phenomenon as embodied or conventional stardom. But neither is it exactly the same thing as characterisation or textual performance. By virtue of virtuality, the virtual star becomes both an effect and a textual performance: they are both something 'in' the text, and something that transcends their textual appearance, albeit without this transcendence being tied back to a real-world persona or identity. This lack of referentiality or indexicality distinguishes the virtual star from the embodied star; it is precisely this that defines them as virtual. And yet the virtual star – unlike the character – also exceeds the text just like the stars of old.

It could be said that virtual stars are akin to characters that take on an iconic status and thereby move through popular culture as mobile signifiers detached from their originating texts: Buffy the Vampire Slayer, James Bond, Batman, Dracula, and so on, would share this textual transcendence-without-embodiment. However, this misses the point that such media icons remain, in different incarnations and at different moments, realised through embodied stars/celebrities, whereas virtual stars are not significantly semiotically articulated to flesh-and-blood performers.[4]

This point, in turn, raises another likely candidate for the typological containment of virtual stars: they also closely resemble animated characters that take on iconic status, characters such as Mickey Mouse. But again the link between virtual stars and animated character-icons remains an incomplete metaphor, given the modality of animated characters versus the modality of digital/virtual stars. The integration of animation and live action depends on a virtuoso bringing together or matching of two 'worlds' already marked as distinctive. The use of digital images, however, aims to construct a coherent and consistently 'photo-realist' modality: 'a successful rendering of perceptual information ... can work to match live-action and computer environments and lend credence and a sense of reality to the composited image such that its computerised components *seem* to fulfill the indexicalised conditions of photographic realism' (Prince, 1996: 33). The realism of virtual stars is such that they can be 'referentially unreal' and yet simultaneously 'perceptually realistic' (1996: 35), and this is a combination which, as Prince has observed, 'exposes the enduring dichotomy in film theory as a false boundary. It is not as if cinema either indexically records the world or stylistically transfigures it. Cinema does both' (1996: 35). However, Prince's argument can be pursued further: by being akin to embodied stars (perceptual realism) but also resembling media icons (circulating outside the text) and animated characters (lacking an indexical referent), we are faced with a new cultural and textual phenomenon that does not only disrupt the realism/formalism dichotomy of film theory. It also, and for the same reasons, disrupts the common-sense categories of 'stardom'/'character' within film reception.

To gather together the argumentative threads of my position: Jar Jar Binks cannot be clearly thought of as a character, as an animation or as an embodied star, and we are therefore obliged to consider how such CGI creations – at this point in time and in relation to historical and cultural norms of realism – disrupt previous sense-making categories. Such CGI creations call for a new category or nomination, whether this is Barbara Creed's 'cyber-star' (2000) or my own 'virtual star'. Other theorists may prefer to discuss Binks as a 'virtual character' or as a 'cyber-character', stressing the links between such images and previous norms of character, but these theorists would still have to remain attentive to the cultural-textual fact that the likes of Binks do not quite fit previous dichotomies such as realism/formalism as well as star/character and live-action/animation.[5]

Having addressed the issue of 'virtual stardom', what, then, is the status of Jar Jar Binks within fans' loathing? The fans treat Binks as real, complaining about 'his' clumsiness, but they also treat 'him' as a CGI effect. The former type of comment shows how fans blur the distinctions between star 'performance' and 'extratextual knowledge' that Geraghty (2000) sets up; they both assess 'textual performance' and move through an extratextual array of *Star Wars* knowledge. The latter type of comment indicates that fans view Jar Jar as an (in)visible effect. As Barker and Brooks have noted:

> It is now common for films to be promoted for the novelty of their 'effects'. We are regularly encouraged to go and see films to see the 'new effects' in them. . . . And although such techniques are to be found in many kinds of films, their core, perhaps, is science fiction. What relation is proffered here, between experiencing and experiencing-as effects?
>
> (Barker and Brooks, 1998: 285)

Barker and Brooks' question is useful, but carries a certain limitation. They usefully point to the 'doubled attention' (1998: 283) that effects generate, and Barker has developed this approach to argue that the 'doubleness' of SFX must not be closed down in favour of hyper-realist or neo-immersive readings of SFX as 'more realist than realist' (Barker with Austin, 2000: 83). However, this emphasis on doubling is limited in so far as it assumes that SFX will be read by audiences in an 'as-effects' mode, as the type of effects which they are, textually and technologically. That is to say, CGI effects will be interpreted as CGI effects. And yet, against this implied argument (and despite the modality complications of Barker with Austin, 2000: 81), the Jar Jar haters consistently displace considerations of Jar Jar as a CGI or digital effect. Instead, their SFX discussions are reframed in, and subordinated to, a child/adult opposition. This has the effect of reworking CGI discussions so that the CGI Jar Jar becomes repeatedly either 'cartoonish' or 'Disneyesque'.

> It [the use of CGI] does make them look like cartoons and sometimes it feels like your watching 'Who Framed Roger Rabbit' but hopefully Lucas saw that and will change that with the later episodes.
>
> *(JURMSON, 9/9/1999 4:19 pm)*

> Needless to say, many us were offended by the cartoonish digital characters that were so heavily used in this film. Aside from Jar Jar, what about the two-headed pod race announcer? And what about all the extra silly looking aliens? Could Lucas not look at what was being done and say, 'Man, this is starting to look like a Disney film'?
>
> *(JTPALADIN, 9/9/1999 11:07 am)*

Some theorists have argued that CGI effects increasingly resemble animation in terms of production design, aesthetics and expertise: 'today, essentially everybody working in special effects is expected to understand techniques from the chase cartoon' (Klein, 1998: 210). However, this postulation of a production-led 'hybrid cinema' cannot be expected to translate automatically into the terms of audience reception. Promotional and marketing discourses surrounding the cinema of digital spectacle typically continue to emphasise the mimetic realism or 'impossible photography' of digital SFX. The infamous *Phantom Menace* trailer was certainly unremarkable in this respect. Covering similar ground to that of Stephen Prince (1996), Andrew Darley has discussed examples of the 'impossible photography' which is now promoted (although not always achieved) through CGI techniques:

> In films such as *Jurassic Park*, *Independence Day* and *Starship Troopers*, for example, such techniques are used in scenarios which, though involving high (if varying) degrees of fantasy, ... aim for a measure of classical realism in their overall affect. These films revolve around scenes of fantastic spectacle involving photographic mimesis ... these digitally rendered images seem real, they appear to have the same indexical qualities as the images of the live action characters and sets with which they are integrated.
>
> *(Darley, 2000: 110)*

'Integrated' CGI and live-action images formed the centrepieces of the promotional trailers for each of the films mentioned by Darley, and the same was true for *The Phantom Menace*. But in the face of such promotional discourses, the Jar Jar haters continually read Jar Jar not as dazzling, seamless CGI or 'impossible photography' but as cartoonish idiocy and childishness. Another of the recommended 'Ways Jar Jar Binks Should Die!', for example, is that he 'gets adopted by a Disney family (would drive him to suicide)' (**http://members.tripod.com/Freaky_Freya/diejarjar.html**). Jar Jar could, of course, be read by fans as an example of 'post-photographic' expertise, or even as an example of a particular 'slapstick' aesthetic. But for the Jar Jar haters this is a counter-factual reading. Although feasible, it does not meaningfully exist. We might expect some fans to defend Lucas's technique and SFX vision, given that Lucas is one of the few *auteurs* linked to 'digitally enabled spectacle cinema and the popular discourses that inform it' (Darley, 2000: 136).

And yet Jar Jar is not recuperated by auteurist reference to Lucas. Instead, given the dominant affective discourse which aims to build an 'adult' us versus a childish 'them', both Jar Jar and Lucas are condemned. A further aspect of this condemnation also falls under the topic of Lucas's assumed 'control' over the *Star Wars* universe. One exchange on jarjarmustdie.com deals with the issue of whether or not Lucas had control over the merchandising and marketing of *The Phantom Menace*: 'don't get the mistaken impression that Lucas orchestrated all of the nonsense you see out there. That's not how big business works, even when you are powerful like George' (JEDILAW001, 7/20/1999 4:19 pm). But against this dissenting position, the Jar Jar haters of the 'International Society for the Extermination of Jar Jar Binks' continue to view Lucas as solely 'responsible' for the childish and 'bad' object of Binks. It is worth noting that this specific discourse – Lucas as control freak – circulates widely beyond the Jar Jar haters, forming the lynchpin of *Newsweek*'s critique of *The Phantom Menace* (see 'The selling of *Star Wars*', *Newsweek*, 17 May 1999: 65–8). The Jar Jar haters, however, use this discourse in a specific and situated way. For them, Binks represents Lucas's controlling vision gone wrong, rather than operating as part of a global critique of Lucas and the *Star Wars* marketing machine. The question which remains is why Binks specifically should have attracted the fans' ire and acted as a focal point for fan disappointment with the first prequel, and as a way of regenerating a sense of 'good' fandom and 'good' *Star Wars*. Darth Maul could equally have been adopted as a focus for resentment, but survived this nomination. Boss Nass might also have soaked up fan frustration, indeed Slavoj Zizek discusses Jar Jar and Nass together:

> Jar Jar is a good hearted, charmingly ridiculous, cowardly prattling childish servant, while the ruler [Boss Nass] also displays the ridiculously pompous false dignity of the non-European master . . .; what is crucial here is that both figures are not played by real actors, but are pure digital creations – as such they do not merely refer to clichés; rather, they are directly presented, staged, as *nothing but* **animated clichés**. For that reason they are in some way 'flat', lacking the 'depth' of a true personality.
>
> *(Zizek, 2000: 7; my emphasis in bold)*

'Staged as animated clichés'; again the tainted term, the discursive marker of disgrace, is 'animation'. Digital creation is described as possessing a certain 'purity'. But when Zizek's account alights on the lack and flatness of these characters, it is their 'animation' which is condemned. So, the terms through which Binks is dismissed are, we could argue, far from specific to this one character.

WHY JAR JAR? DEFENDING TEXTUAL AUTHENTICITY

Why then the fan focus on Binks? I would argue that this occurs as a result of the screen time that the Gungan character 'enjoys', as well as the *specific narrative function that Jar Jar is required to perform*: it is his 'natural spontaneity' which defeats the machinery of the Trade Federation's war droids. This creates a powerful tension between the 'performance' discourses of *The Phantom Menace* as text and the extratextual discourses which these fans are drawing on. Some critics have viewed Jar Jar as an ideological trap, given that his construction as a technological special effect is translated into a textual effect of 'romantic authenticity':

> Jar Jar Binks . . . is by far the most 'human'-seeming figure in the film, given the one-dimensional portrayal of the Jedi principals and Queen Amidala. In other words a form of film-making heavily reliant on technology is subjected to the kind of separation that is often characteristic of ideological manoeuvres. One portion is condemned, righteously, for its cold rationality, while another is 'saved' by being pulled across the line around which textual oppositions revolve: in this case, the computer-generated Gungans, rendered with many of the qualities associated with a particular version of 'humanity' – quirky, comic and emotional. This may be important in terms of the debates surrounding a film like *The Phantom Menace*, in which accusations of over-reliance on the technological domain of special effects enter a public arena much broader than the confines of academic debate.
>
> (King and Krzywinska, 2000: 107)

This tension between Binks as techno-SFX and as a textual representation of 'humanity' is indeed important to the Jar Jar haters' debate. But their discourses contradict the 'ideological' and broadly structuralist interpretation offered by King and Krzywinska (2000). Instead, the Jar Jar haters side temporarily *with* narratives of 'Lucas as technological control freak' and *against* Jar Jar's performance of spontaneity, redrawing the 'line' around which moral oppositions revolve. This textual and extratextual clash between technological 'control' and human 'spontaneity' also allows fans to adopt a 'rebel' identification against the LucasFilm 'empire'. Barbara Creed has suggested that a 'digitised star is a studio's dream: capable of performing any task, continuously available, cost effective'

(Creed, 2000: 80). This possibility also feeds into the Jar Jar haters' opposition to Binks. Their readings continually emphasise that the digital star provides a space which marketing and merchandising concerns can swamp without, as it were, any indexical or 'real' resistance:

> Jar Jar was a ... ploy to get five year olds to come and watch the movie so Lucas would have another generation interested in his films because the average attention span of children is now limited to puny bits of CGI like that.
>
> *(LADYFIANNA, 7/10/1999 2:34 am)*

> well I hate Jar Jar because he is purely a money-making, kiddie pleasing character with no real depth of character
>
> *(TURNERJ1, 7/10/1999 6:51 am; compare Zizek quoted above)*

Star Wars: The Special Edition 'aimed at preserving the visual integrity of the original film' (Pierson, 1999: 159) and thus displayed a 'textual conservationist' ethic in line with the generation that grew up with the first trilogy. By contrast, *The Phantom Menace* exchanged this for an alien aesthetic of 'dazzling luminosity and playful plasticity' (1999: 159). But this aesthetic shift allowed established fans to construct a 'discourse of affect' which was also an 'affective discourse' by drawing on the notion of animation as 'an innocent medium, ostensibly for children' (Wells, 1998: 187) to support a child/adult split. In a recent edited collection dealing with morphing techniques, both Roger Warren Beebe and Angela Ndalianis cite Vivian Sobchack:

> As [Sobchack] writes in the section 'The Transformation of Special "Affect" into Special "Effect"' (a title that almost says it all), 'although special effects have always been a central feature of the SF film, they now carry a particularly new affective charge and value'.
>
> *(Beebe, 2000: 164; see also Ndalianis, 2000: 260)*

But the case of Jar Jar Binks reverses the terms of this specific 'morphing'. Special affects do not become effects. Rather, the special effects of CGI are transformed into, and read within, the 'special affects' of a fan community. This community is powerfully invested in defending its own sense of an 'adult' *Star Wars* against the encroaching interests and investments of 'another generation'. It thus relies on discourses of childishness, cartoonishness and low-cultural commercialism to construct Jar Jar Binks as a low-Other.

Although the Jar Jar haters continually seek to put away childish things, and hence to claim their adult fan ownership of the *Star Wars* universe, their imperial claim remains open to counter-discourses and to new rebel forces.

As Paul McDonald recently remarked: 'If the World Wide Web has done anything to change the star system, it is through decentring the production of star discourses . . . forms of online interactive communication can see writers publishing their most heartfelt love for a star but can also become the focus for some of the most vitriolic attacks on stars' (2000: 114–15). But we need to take care when assuming that 'love' or 'hate' are simply 'heart-felt'. For these performed discourses of affect are also affective discourses, that is, ways of marking out the fan-audience's sense of ownership over favoured stars and texts. 'Hating' the 'childish', 'cartoonish', 'commercial' Jar Jar Binks, in this instance, is one tactic aimed at preserving the fans' 'good' object of *Star Wars* as 'serious' and 'culturally significant'. The discourse of hate is taken up, however excessively, within fan struggles over cultural value.

---

1   I have placed 'virtual star' in scare quotes to indicate that Binks' status as a star – rather than a character – is something that must be asserted and defended. See more below.

2   Where I refer to '*Star Wars* fans' I am not typically referring to fans of *Star Wars* (1977, USA), but rather to fans of the franchise and its entire, associated intertextual network. Where the film *Star Wars* is meant specifically, then I will include the reference '(1977, USA)' to make this clear.

3   This sense of a star's 'ongoing life' outside textual performance is played with in the *Toy Story* films, where closing digital 'out-takes' portray characters 'as if' they are actors fluffing their lines or corpsing. However, this knowing play with the line between star and character remains embedded in the text rather than Woody *et al.* participating in promotional interviews. Interestingly, however, the 'star' and the 'character' remain conflated even in this textual play: Woody is Woody even when breaking the frame.

4   I use the phrase 'not *significantly* semiotically articulated', since Jar Jar Binks is linked to a flesh-and-blood per-former, the already mentioned Ahmed Best who provided a non-virtual presence for live actors to relate to, and for CGI compositors to work with. However, as I show here, the vast majority of fan 'haters' do not invoke the figure of Best, instead treating Binks as if he were indexical/photo-real, or as if he were an anima-tion devoid of any referentiality whatsoever.

5   That Binks does not fit previous cultural categories makes it all the more interesting when specific cultural groups (fans or academics) use these categories in an attempt to semiotically 'fix' or smooth over this viola-tion. As I argue later, the fact that a faction of fans views Binks as an 'animation' rather than a CGI effect needs to be analysed as part of these fans' performative claim to 'adult' status.

Chapter Five

☐ TO AFFINITY AND BEYOND: WOODY, BUZZ AND THE NEW AUTHENTICITY

Paul Wells

Toy Story (1995, USA) represents two highly significant moments in my life. First, it was the last film that I saw in the cinema with my then heavily pregnant wife, shortly before the birth of our son, Freddie. Second, it was the first full-length feature film that Freddie watched end-to-end on video, and demanded re-showing on some 45 occasions in the following six weeks. And yes, I was there with him for most of them, sharing the benefits of being a father watching his son interact with a film, and being an academic gainfully employed in conducting his research. Freddie has also benefited from my selfless inputs of the whole of the Oliver Postgate canon, Winsor McCay's *Gertie the Dinosaur* (1914, USA) and all things 'Jurassic' thereafter, and, most recently, *Thunderbirds*, which incidentally, 'are go!'.

So, what of this? Unsurprisingly, the scenario I have just presented has proved important for a number of reasons. I first engaged with *Toy Story* because of my investment in academic research about animation. It represents a major achievement in the field as being the first full-length computer-generated film, though as I will explore later, this is perhaps one of the least significant of its credentials. Further, it embodies the first major pinnacle in the work of PIXAR, and director, John Lasseter, who in CGI works from *Luxo Jnr* (1986, USA) onwards, defined the terrain where animators impacted upon the new resources made available through computers. *Tin Toy* (1988, USA) and *Knick Knack* (1989, USA) to name but two, explore the interaction between cartoonal aesthetics and the new potentialities of CGI, in a way that fully exploits the material nature of the objects which serve as characters in the films, and work best within the geometric space and synthetic gloss of the graphic environment. *Toy Story* was also a culmination of 'toys-come-to-life' stories, both in children's literature and animated films, and a storehouse of popular culture reference points, which further stimulated my engagement with the terms and conditions of its thematic and conceptual playfulness; this engagement has continued with *Toy Story 2* (2000, USA).

Significantly, though, as well as pursuing what one might regard as the traditional aspects of analysis for these films – their status and impact as 'texts'; their modes of production and technological enhancement within 'institutional' frameworks; and the cultural work necessary for the 'implied audience', child and adult, to understand the film – I have constantly returned to the role of Woody, the pullstring cowboy, and Buzz, the gadget-laden electronic astronaut, as the film's 'stars'. This is mainly because I noted that for my son, Freddie, then nearly three, these characters represented a mode of interaction to which he immediately related. In his sometimes surprising, and increasingly sophisticated, observations as showing passed into re-showing, he noted the apparently contradictory and sometimes complex behaviour which underpinned the idea of 'friendship'. One of the only scenes that he insisted should be 'fast-forwarded' in some of the early repeat viewings was Woody and Buzz's apparent despair that they could not help each other in the face of the imminent brutality of Sid, child maniac, one-boy crimewave and toy-mutilator. Freddie had signalled some *fear of* Sid and his newly hybridised toys, but nevertheless, endured the anxiety, and this was replaced by a much more affecting *fear for* the fate of Woody and Buzz. For him, the fact that two friends were isolated, marginalised and under threat was often too much, even though he knew that they escaped the predicament. This concentrated my mind further on what Woody and Buzz had come to represent. I realised that the two major agendas that characterised my own investment in them were not privileged within 'star' studies, and in a certain sense marginalised in favour of ideological and quasi-ethnographic concerns. These are namely Woody and Buzz's status as 'animated' characters within the critically neglected terrain of animated films and, relatedly, the conditions of 'authenticity' that underpinned their possible meanings and affects. Why had the 'emotional' conduct of two 'non-human' forms translated so vividly into a child's imagination and, further, how might they operate not merely as affecting characters, but as bonafide 'stars', within a meaningful definition of 'stardom'? The following discussion offers some tentative answers to these questions.

QUESTIONING PARADIGMS OF STARDOM

Christine Gledhill suggests,

> The star challenges analysis in the way it crosses disciplinary boundaries: a product of mass culture, but retaining theatrical concerns with acting, performance and art; an industrial marketing device, but a signifying element in films; a social sign, carrying cultural meanings and ideological values, which expresses the intimacies of individual personality, inviting desire and identification; an emblem of national celebrity, founded on body, fashion and personal style; a product of capitalism and the ideology of individualism, yet a site of contest by marginalised groups; a figure

consumed for his or her personal life, who competes for allegiance with statesman and politicians.

(Gledhill, 1991: xiii)

This useful summary merely points up the problems presented by Woody and Buzz. Though clearly a product of mass culture, and raising issues concerning acting, performance and art, the disciplinary boundary that they cross (existing as 'animated' rather than live-action figures) changes the nature of how the idea of acting, performance and art may be reconfigured. Their modes of signification and social identity are intrinsically bound up with this aesthetic terrain and its distinctive industrial and commercial context. While carrying cultural meanings and values, and provoking emotional reactions, Woody and Buzz operate in a different 'fictional' category wherein their complete 'artifice' challenges the nature of the extratextual connotations associated with the character, and the idea of 'individualism' as an ideological currency. Consequently, I am arguing that Woody and Buzz in being animated characters intrinsically interrogate the boundaries of 'star' paradigms predicated on codes and conventions which do not embrace them.

I will not be the first to cite Richard Dyer's classic paradigm as a starting point in addressing some of these issues (Dyer, 1979). Dyer's categorisation of stars as 'social phenomenon', 'images' and 'signs' plays out a mode of integration which usefully organises analytical approaches. His discussion is predicated on live-action stars and the phenomenology that underpins their construction and consumption, suggesting along the way that stars embody a performative typology of meanings and affects. The terrain which Dyer defined and explored remains an aspect taken for granted for this discussion, as I wish to prioritise Dyer's specific work on 'authenticity' as one of the central planks of the following remarks. As Dyer suggests:

Authenticity is both a quality necessary to the star phenomenon to make it work, and also the quality that guarantees the authenticity of the other particular values the star embodies ... [I]t is this effect of authenticating authenticity that gives the star charisma.

(Dyer, 1991: 133)

The initial question which arises here is whether Dyer's observation remains pertinent for animated characters and, further, how do comparatively new forms of extratextual discourse and dissemination affect this hypothesis and potentially alter any coherent evaluation of 'stardom' *per se*.

The agenda that underpins 'stars' and 'stardom' might usefully be allied to definitions of 'celebrity' in the contemporary era – one seamlessly eliding into the other in many media contexts. Consequently, I would like to offer the following definition of contemporary celebrity in support of the following discussion. A celebrity is:

- a person whose personal, social and occupational identity is a cross-platform, mass-mediated phenomenon, generated through publicity, promotion and presence
- a person who, whatever they do or have achieved, is constructed through varying degrees of public relations strategies, into being perceived as a figure within the 'entertainment' industry
- a person whose role, function and image is intrinsically related to market requirements and consumer culture
- a person who is known within the public sphere by reason of (a) talent, expertise, status and achievement in a particular profession; (b) notoriety through social and cultural transgression; or (c) affiliation to already established popular personalities, contexts and trends

This broad definition has a clear relationship to the 'star' paradigms established by Dyer and Gledhill, but seeks to stress more of the simulated and overly constructed aspects of establishing a figure in the public domain. Rein, Kotler and Stoller have identified eight industries that are instrumental in achieving this: the representation industry (agents, public relations etc.); the endorsement industry (advertisers); the publicity industry (promoters); the communications industry (new and information providers); the entertainment industry (mediated performance contexts); the training industry (producers, educators, coaches etc.); the legal industry (rights, copyright, identity etc.) and the appearance industry (presence in mediated cultural contexts) (Rein *et al.*, 1997). The interface between these industries in the creation of 'celebrity' is effectively a process of 'authenticating authenticity', defining and simulating 'specificity', without any necessary recourse to a pre-defined model of value or particularity, the fullest determination of the 'phenomena of production' suggested by Dyer (Dyer 1979: 10). Crucially, then, if we are to identify 'stardom' in the contemporary moment, this phenomenology of 'celebrity' may prove a useful tool in recognising the phenomenology of production, fully and literally embodied in Woody and Buzz.

Crudely, Woody and Buzz in the *Toy Story* films may be seen as an even more literal 'phenomenon of production' than their live-action counterparts (Dyer, 1979: 10). The production process of an animated film and, in this case, a post-photographic, computer-generated film, becomes of clear significance in addressing this 'difference'. For example, Woody and Buzz are a consequence of the elision of the physical presence of the 'actor' with the animated construction of the character. The implicit 'frame-by-frame' construction of the characters means that, as Will Eisner has noted apropos of comics, that the

93

frame itself is 'part of a creative process, rather than the result of the technology' (Eisner, 1985: 38). While the vocal performances of Tom Hanks (Woody) and Tim Allen (Buzz) may carry with them aural signifiers of their pre-established film and television personae (a point to be addressed later), this is significantly counterpointed by the graphic signifiers of the moving, visualised figures; figures which in turn embody traditional conceptions of the comic-book 'cowboy' and 'astronaut' while being rendered in animated form within a computer-generated aesthetic. In many senses, there is no 'actor' here who significantly impacts upon the iconography. The nature of the design of Woody and Buzz, and the manufacture of their motion calls into question their status as 'actors', in the sense that not merely should they be viewed as 'cartoonal' forms which re-define the body and its iden-tificatory principles, but as representations of 'toys'; material objects which they actually become in the extratextual 'real-world' environment. Woody and Buzz are predicated *only* through modes of artifice; they exist *as* their iconic form. Tom Hanks and Tim Allen dressed as Woody and Buzz would be exactly that, and categorically *not* the characters who are ultimately played out through the 'phenomena of consumption' (Dyer, 1979: 39). It may be useful to remind ourselves of veteran Warner Bros animator Chuck Jones' anec-dote, which recounts that, when introduced to a little boy as 'the man who drew Bugs Bunny', he found himself corrected as 'the man who drew pictures of Bugs Bunny' (Cholodenko, 1991: 59). Bugs had transcended his status as a cartoon character, and in doing so, made invisible both his author and the production process that had created him.

ANIMATION AND 'SPECIAL EFFECTS'

This remains an ongoing issue in animation. It has taken an inordinate amount of time to suggest and evidence the view that animation works as a singular and distinctive vocabu-lary outside the parameters of live-action film-making. When acknowledged, 'animation' has largely been viewed as 'cartoonal' at its most populist, and 'avant-garde' at its most experimental; a schedule filler; children's entertainment; and most significantly, in the context of this discussion, a form which has time and again been absorbed into an 'Effects' tradition, a pre- and post-production phenomenon made invisible within the remit of live-action cinema. Martin Barker, for example, regards DreamWorks SKG's *Antz* (1998, USA) as a 'special effects movie', 'one long special effect'; a film which has 'special effects within an effects film' (Barker, 2000: 79). Consequently, its whole vocabulary, intrinsically drawn from the 2D graphic and 3D stop-motion modes of animation is marginalised as the film's overwhelming signifier in preference to reading its extratextual reference points – its self-conscious, cinematic, storytelling conventions, star-voice casting, quotation from live-action film etc. – when its currencies lie in the history and aesthetics of the Disney, Warner Bros and Fleischer Bros cartoons, which manipulate graphic space, perspective, scale and representational style at will. Further, the film is grounded in a tradition of 'insect' animation which includes Starewich's *The Cameraman's Revenge* (1911, Russia); Disney's *Pinocchio* (1940, USA); the Fleischers' *Mr Bug Goes to Town* (1941, USA); Reiniger's *The Grasshopper and the Ant* (1953, USA); and De Patie-Freleng's series, *The Ant and the Aardvark* (1969, USA) of the early 1960s. These aspects of production make a significant difference in the ways that the film has been created, and also make a difference to the way in which the phenomenon of the animated 'star' must be understood. Crudely, these figures and forms should not be wholly construed as, or absorbed within the paradigm of 'stardom' played out in live-action cinema for human actors.

Barker also suggests that instances of 'extra special effects' in *Antz* offer shifts in modality, taking the narrative and thematic concerns to another level (Barker, 2000: 170–2). This may be so, but this is a characteristic of *most* animated cartoons, and *not* a consequence of heightened manipulations of CGI. What has led to this misconception, I think, are the prominence of sequences in traditional 2D animated features, which have foregrounded the new 3D wonder – the ballroom dance sequence in *Beauty and the Beast* (1989, USA), for example, or the magic carpet ride in *Aladdin* (1992, USA) – where the effect is conspicuous, yet ultimately undermines the *particularity* of animation as a versatile and variable language which depicts figures and forms on its own terms and conditions, and *in its own right*. Instead of being viewed as another 'pencil', these technologies and techniques are somehow viewed as different – an 'effect'. This has done a great deal to discredit the specificities of animation and, consequently, has seen the form consistently ignored, or drawn into comparative discussions about live-action cinema, instead of critical debates which reinforce its distinctiveness. So preoccupied, for example, are Byrne and McQuillan in their highly illuminating deconstruction of Disney's late-1990s canon, that no consideration is given to their status as animated films, nor why the ideological insensitivities and brutalities which they suggest characterise Disney films seem to go unnoticed by the millions of viewers worldwide who enjoy them (see Byrne and McQuillan, 1999). But that is another chapter.

How does this digression inform this discussion? First, one consequence of this conception of animation as an effect negates significant authorial figures like Willis O'Brien, Ray Harryhausen and Dennis Muerhen. Second, and crucially in this analysis, the substantive work that they undertake operates within the site and space nominally taken up by 'stars'. What is *King Kong* (1933, USA) without Kong? Fay Wray and an air show. What is *Jason and the Argonauts* (1963, USA) without the skeleton fight? Big lads in togas. What is *Jurassic Park* (1993, USA) without the dinosaurs? A lot of people frightened by wind. When animated 'figures' constitute the main claims to narrative imperative and modes of spectacle, they in essence become 'stars' because of their fundamental relationship to the new graphic terrain of late twentieth- and early twenty-first-century visual cultures. These are prosthetic phenomena that embrace all the credentials of performance, persona and proto-meaning, and *transcend* the context which produced them, operating in a comparatively new cultural space which allies them with the virtual automata of computer games and cyber-worlds. Woody and Buzz must be aligned *not* with a phenomenology of 'Hanks' or 'Allen', or what may be termed the traditional mode of 'star' defined by the economic, artistic and socio-cultural factors discussed by Dyer and Gledhill, but to the phenomenology of Lara Croft and the burgeoning conception of the 'cyborg'.

I have written elsewhere that:

> . . . the prominence of the 'Croft' aesthetic and identity has moved computer games beyond the realm of the 'toy' or a mode of 'technology', and created an impactive 'lifestyle' agenda which insists upon the relationship between the intrinsic physicality of the 'character'; the character's 'experience' of their environment; and the ways in which the inter-active simulation of this physicality and experienciality prompts feelings and reactions in the games players and their companions . . . the nature of the engagement with the computer game speaks to the codes and conventions of verisimilitude but from a more invested position of the simulated experience.
>
> *(Wells, 2001: 8)*

I include this extended observation here because it provides a context by which I wish to enhance my definition of Woody and Buzz as 'stars', and recall Dyer's discussion of 'authenticity'. The films themselves constitute an extended discussion of these issues.

Toy Story and *Toy Story 2* are interrogations of what it is to be a 'toy', played out by toys in a way that invests them with an understanding of their own mechanism, market and mortality. Further, the self-conscious recognition of the materiality of 'toys' is allied to the self-reflexive understanding of the 'technology' as a space by which to acknowledge the current place of animation as *the* intrinsic language not merely of film, but of all contemporary visual cultures. Woody and Buzz speak to new modes of visual literacy, and most importantly, *interactivity*. For adults and children, the films foreground the notion of 'play'; issues of ownership and control; and, most significantly, the *emotional* investment in bringing identity to the technological *difference* that now underpins notions of creativity, whether in the realm of 'play' within the text, interacting with a text, or in the act of constructing texts. These factors amount to a version of stars as 'post-human' reconstructions which speak to the generational orthodoxies of a star persona, but more importantly relate to the interactive accessibilities of new communications and entertainment technologies. Simultaneously, adults can have a virtual engagement with the 'toys of their youth' and children can engage with the 'youth of their toys'.

Animated characters becoming 'stars' is not a new phenomenon, of course. In the pre-war era of cartooning, Felix the Cat, Mickey Mouse, Donald Duck, Betty Boop, Bugs Bunny and Popeye all transcended their status as animated drawings to become bona fide cultural figures. As now, this was considerably enhanced by the proliferation of merchandising associated with the characters, and the increasing presence of the characters at film premieres, social functions etc. as live personae – people dressed up in character costumes. In the public imagination, the characters represented a curious mix between 'fantasy' and 'reality', in which the people could recognise human traits in what for the most part were *drawn* animal figures, but which were nevertheless recognisable as fictional constructs performing acts outside the human capacity. These included 'gags' that could only be performed as graphic phenomena; 'titillatory' imagery which challenged the parameters of the body and social behaviour; and interaction which had no parallel in cultural contexts. The 'symbolic' identity of the characters was well understood – Mickey as 'John Doe', Donald as 'the average irascible American'; Betty as the sexually harassed 'flapper', Bugs as a 'wise-ass victor' – and this, in effect, was part of their currency as 'stars'. Their dominant traits represented something clear and meaningful in their own fictional context, and this transposed to the broader cultural realm – perhaps best evidenced during the war when their propaganda value was pronounced because of their already established identities. Donald Duck was Disney's most popular character, and featured in much of the studio's wartime output on the basis that the American public would more identify with his anxiety, irritability, and defiance as necessary requirements in the fight against the axis powers (Holliss and Sibley, 1988: 46–54). Bugs Bunny was similarly employed by Warner Bros as he was already established as a character who would only respond when provoked, and then humiliate always inferior opposition (Dalton, 1980: 158–62). Betty Boop, of course, had to clean up her act much earlier. The Hays Code significantly curtailed her raunchy reputation, and her re-design – no garter, no cleavage, longer skirts, no innuendous songs – changed her cultural coding, and reduced her commercial and social significance (Cabarga, 1988: 53–81).

'THREE-DIMENSIONALITY' AND TOYS

In recent years, the phenomenology of characters has increased with the two-fold development of theme parks and studio stores specialising in any number of toys and costume paraphenalia which enhances the 'three-dimensionality' of two-dimensional figures. While 'dolls' have always been a significant part of a child's play environment, their specificity in relation to other media texts is an escalating aspect of their production. What becomes interesting here, however, is the contemporary status of the 'toy' amidst the competing attractions of other mediated forms. It is becoming increasingly difficult for toy manufacturers and retailers to secure profitable margins purely in the market of traditional toys, which are being significantly challenged by the impact of computer games and PC applications. Major retailers FAO Schwarz and Toys 'R' Us have seen a rapid decline in 'toy' earnings, and have had to embrace the well-known phenomenon in the industry of 'Kids getting older younger', and the consequent abandonment of toys by children at a much younger age (*Livewire*, October–November 2000, London: Artisan Press: 22–6). Industry figures assume that any child over the age of eight years, will have already moved into the competing arenas of fashion, personal accessorising and new media entertainments, only to re-activate an interest in their childhood interests at 17 years old, and sometimes enduringly throughout adulthood. Consequently, producers, manufacturers and marketers have an invested interest in creating artefacts which both move across platforms and have an appeal which reaches across ages and interests.

It is this phenomenon which characterises Woody and Buzz, and is so self-consciously interrogated in the *Toy Story* films. Woody and Buzz stretch across the digital divide into reality, embracing the computer game aesthetic and sensibility, and the substantiveness of an enduring identity predicated on the sense of a 'historicised' emotional investment addressed by the films. Jimmy Hunter, Chairman of the British Toy and Hobby Association, suggests:

> As an industry we've never been very good at standing up and shouting
> about what an important role toys play in a child's life. It's by playing with
> toys that children learn how to do things, how to build things, how to
> cooperate. It helps them find their place in society. Computers can't help
> them do that.

> *(Quoted in* Livewire, *2000: 23)*

Demonstrably, through figures like Woody and Buzz, they can. The characters use their post-human status to recall the values and purpose of their representative forms as toys, while promoting the aesthetic and interactive aspects of their role as animated action figures in the new entertainment environment. Their prominence and claim to 'stardom' is the fact that they carry traditional values into the virtual 'modernity' of the new graphic space, and represent the vanguard of a perception of 'toys' as material *and* conceptual phenomena. This is what makes Woody and Buzz intrinsically different from all other toy/game/film tie-ins. They embody an interrogation of their own 'reality' and the 'experience' which gives them their identity, from the multiple point of view of those who create them, market them, watch them, play with them and invest in them. Barry King has described this 'cyborg'-like identity as 'a state of self-sufficient knowing or textuality', arguing that such figures operate at 'a new level of representation in which textuality [i]s triumphantly divorced from context' (King, 1989: 122).

Crucially, Woody and Buzz only partially embrace this definition. Woody and Buzz always retain a sense of context because they have re-defined modes of authenticity. Dyer argues that authenticity is predicated on a notion of truthfulness, and points out that the central tenets of Marxism, behaviourism, psychoanalysis, liguistics and modernism have been to expose the contexts in which they operate as intrinsically masking and disguising their essential but invisible 'truths' (Dyer, 1991: 134). He continues that 'stars' may be perceived as the embodiment of a 'genuine' meaning because they expose their points of reference within and outside of 'texts', thus simultaneously speaking to the textual, sub-textual and extratextual agendas which they carry at all times – essentially this multiplicity of authentications carries with it a guarantor of a discursive but perpetually anchored discourse. He notes, 'The basic paradigm is just this – that what is behind or below the surface is, unquestionably and virtually by definition, the truth' (Dyer, 1991: 136). But what of Woody and Buzz? There can be no pictures of Woody's wedding in *Hello!* magazine; no off-limits exposés of Buzz *sans* spacesuit. Arguably, they are only 'surface', and embody their own truth as 'textual events', transcribed into their status as iconic phenomena *and* toys. Dyer, of course, recognises the instability of his paradigm, and addresses the 'rhetoric of authenticity' in which the tensions between the manufactured aspects of the 'star' *persona* and the revelatory modes which expose the real, uninhibited, unpoliceable aspects of *being* define the 'authentic' and 'truthful'. A considerable irony arises for me here. Woody and Buzz in *not* being characterised by these tensions, and being wholly defined by their 'manufacture', are invested with a sincerity, genuineness and clarity that speaks to a contemporary sensibility which embraces the needs of the *text*, and not the pursuit of the *subtext*; the requirements of the *narrative* above the invisible premises of its implications.

EMOTIONAL WORK

Woody and Buzz are essentially 'stars' because their functions prompt a form of 'emotional work' which is about versions of preservation and conservation, yet embodies an understanding of new modes of investment intrinsically related to mediated cultural knowledge and new media applications. This is crucial to the understanding of Woody and Buzz, because they simultaneously operate as a meta-narrative about the impact of new information and entertainment technologies, but embody deeply primal imperatives about survival and reproduction. *Toy Story* and *Toy Story 2* are effectively stories about toys resisting their own obsolescence. In *Toy Story*, the toys are consumed with anxiety every birthday and Christmas in fear of being replaced by newer, more up-to-date toys. Woody, his owner's erstwhile favourite toy, desperately tries not to be usurped by the claims of Buzz to Andy's affections, having to conquer his jealousy and sense of inadequacy along the way. The toys mobilise to protect themselves from destruction and the extremist wing of creative play in the hands of Andy's neighbour, Sid. Woody's whole imperative is to save Buzz from the fate of living outside the safety of the domestic bedroom. As film director, Rowan Woods has noted:

> . . . the whole premise of the central characters is that they are toys with no power beyond the fact that they are toys. In a sense they're like real people as opposed to action heroes, or ordinary toys as opposed to action toys which can do anything, perform any function.
>
> (Sight and Sound 9(1) (NS) January, 1999: 62)

In *Toy Story 2*, some toys are 'shelved' and sold in a yard sale because they are broken or not used any more – Woody's attempt to save the 'voiceless' Weezy the penguin results in his own abduction by the villainous Al, owner of the 'Toybarn' who recognises Woody as a 'collectible'. This clever conceit adds another dimension to the idea of the 'shelf-life' of toys, and their contemporary status as collectible items, or cultural artefacts: their value ironically rests in the idea that they have never been used as playthings. The central tension in both films is the 'meaning' of a toy. Both films address the value of a 'toy' for its owner, as a plaything, companion and harbinger of joy, an object defined outside the parameters of economy or longevity, while also showing that if toys had a degree of consciousness, *their* preoccupations would be entirely about those parameters. In *Toy Story 2*, Woody is given the dilemma of remaining Andy's long cherished toy, or joining up with Jessie, Bullseye and Stinky Pete the prospector, other toy characters from Woody's 1950s children's television show, *Woody's Roundup*, and going on display in a Japanese Toy Museum. This is effectively a choice between the temporary pleasures of being loved, played with and ultimately abandoned by a child – a story heart-rendingly played out through Jessie's song, 'When you loved me' – and the immortality of preservation without use. Woody is seduced by his previously unknown identity as a national icon who features on the cover of *Time* magazine, and on all manner of collectible merchandising from yo-yos to record players, but he ultimately refuses to relinquish his real function and identity as Andy's toy. This is a neat reversal of Buzz's narrative in *Toy Story*, in which he has to come to terms with the 'artifice' of his role as a 'space ranger' and accept that he is a toy, essentially given meaning by his owner – a revelation he is forced to come to terms with when cast as 'Mrs Nesbit' at a play tea party by Sid's sister. All delusions of heroic grandeur are absent here, reinforcing Buzz's function as a toy; they are however partially recovered in the stunning 'computer game' opening of *Toy Story 2*, and indeed, in the spin-off 2D animated television series, *Buzz Lightyear of Star Command*, where Buzz is given back his role as a space ranger battling it out across the universe with Emperor Zurg (all self-reflexive 'toying' with different levels of reality and identity is removed). Woody and Buzz move seamlessly across platforms, taking with them their range of narrative, aesthetic and integrated meanings. Most importantly, though, there is nothing reductive about these transitions – they merely add to the ongoing re-construction of 'context', and another level of emotional work which is related both to their non-human fate as 'technologies' and their human fate as carriers of explicit feelings.

If Buzz has to learn that he cannot really fly but can engineer 'falling with style', then Woody must transcend his own nightmare of being ripped, thrown away, stolen, sold or lost. In *Toy Story 2*, his self-consciousness about this leads him to counsel Buzz in the need to rotate the toys at the bottom of the chest so that as many get remembered and played with as possible; that new batteries are placed in toys; and that toy parts must not be misplaced. Both films show the material culture of the toys as it is experienced, and in doing so demonstrate to the children watching aspects of their own behaviour, the value they place on things, and the emotional investment they bring to the objects of play and amusement. Woody and Buzz implicitly encourage the child, and indeed the adult, in the emotional work that preserves their status as visual icons and physical artefacts by virtue of presenting what those visual icons and physical artefacts mean and represent to them. It is this construction of 'affinity' which most underpins Woody and Buzz's claim to stardom.

For adults, this is played out in a number of ways. The vocal performances of Tom Hanks, a less contradictory latter-day James Stewart in films as diverse as *Forrest Gump* (1997, USA) and *Saving Private Ryan* (1999, USA); and Tim Allen, with his bluff machismo persona from the sit-com *Home Improvement*, may have some resonance, but this is merely in support of the personae of the American 'cowboy' and 'astronaut', each potent symbols of the construction of the 'frontier'. As the embittered Stinky Pete, 'in the box that has never been opened', he remarks in *Toy Story 2*, with the launch of Sputnik, 'children only wanted to play with space toys' to which Woody ruefully replies, 'I know how that feels.' The tension between Woody and Buzz is ultimately a recognition, however, that the frontier is no longer about an implied communality or consensuality in pursuit of the way west, or the conquering of the universe, but the management of identity and purpose in a world fragmented by the proliferation of new communications technologies. Progress cannot be measured in a grand narrative, but only in the transience of the local, and the success in sustaining individual purpose and achievement. Both children and adults recognise that Woody and Buzz transcend their 'post-human' agendas as toys, as a cowboy and an astronaut, as animated characters, to re-engage the viewer with the necessity of human bonding and affection in the light of this unstable and fluid context. Adults recognise that their toys carry with them memories of the relationships with them, and the largely unconditional affection accorded to them. This is more than 'nostalgia'; it is an intrinsic landmark in personal development. The *Toy Story* films feature Mr Potato Head (1952), Slinky (1953), Barbie (1959) and GI Joe (1964) as poignant reminders of that emotional work and its longevity and affect. This 'encultures' the space in which Woody and Buzz take their place, and contributes to what Mike Featherstone has called the process of 'instantiation' (Featherstone, 1991), in which pleasure arises immediately from the artefacts or virtual objects which are subject to contemplation.

This immediacy of cultural immersion also characterises children in the contemporary era, as their playthings in being predicated on transience, technology and modes of interactive practice are configured in a way that provokes short-term intimacies. Again, Woody and Buzz transcend this temporal function and identity by virtue of their iconic value as embodiments of the technologies and socio-cultural infrastructures that produced them. Their theme tune – 'You've got a friend in me' – moves beyond the 'buddy' sensibility, and offers itself as an anthem for the emotional work and symbolic maintenance of 'affinity' in the pairing of Woody and Buzz; and crucially, their 'mediation' of the space between character and animated CGI forms, character and toy, character and historically determined icon, and character and sense memory. They are 'stars' because they anchor and represent the highest-quality representation of the transition from the culture of the camera to the dynamics of the digital, and the machinations of the mercantile, while encompassing the most important characteristics of each.

CONCLUSION

The post-photographic film may become the dominant mode of image production in the future, but at present is intrinsically bound up with the free-play of animated forms, which in themselves have never been entirely free of childhood associations. At any one stage in the development of the moving image, the emergence of new technology has always prompted fears of technological determinism; that, somehow, the purposes and outcomes of creativity would be overwhelmed by the impact of technological capability in itself. An allied issue has always been the idea that such technological capability is intrinsically bound up with the principles of display and spectacle in its own right, beyond the import of narrative – a cinema of attractions (Gunning, 1990: 57) – which privileges visual effects and relationships. Interestingly, computer-generated imagery, especially in relation to *Toy Story* and its sequel, has embraced its 'determinism' in relation to what may be viewed as a 'technological instrumentalism' which maintains, reveals and enhances the generic potentialities of animation as a distinctive aesthetic and cultural form. Woody and Buzz are associated, therefore, with a range of contemporary cultural resources that at the level of character and technical achievement promote identification and progress, and that signify a mode of resolution and affirmation in emotional work as the cornerstone of human values and continuum. Woody and Buzz allay the age-old anxiety concerning technological and social change because they embody an 'authenticity' which is *about* this very change, and the powerful feelings that are associated with it. Woody and Buzz may constitute a downsizing of what it is to be 'a star', but also an upgrading of their value and effect in a contemporary era where visual and social communication is in transition, and subject to new forms of understanding. So then, 'To affinity . . . and beyond!'.

Section 2
Star performances

Thomas Austin

The previous section concentrated on some of the discursive, technological and economic structures within and through which stars are produced and circulated. The following chapters address a facet of screen stardom that has been somewhat neglected until relatively recently – the profession of acting. Crucially, they do so not by considering star acting in a vacuum, but by locating performances within prevailing institutional systems.

Screen acting plays a central role in the productive labour demanded of stars, and in their popular appeal. The inclusion of analyses of stars' work as actors within a book focused on this Hollywood 'elite' runs the risk of reproducing a common division between the star echelon and 'lower ranks' of the profession. (Connections between star-actors and the labour pool of less well-known and rewarded professionals include shared performance techniques and the logic of the economic system in which they work. See Peters and Cantor, 1982; Clark, 1995; Lovell and Krämer, 1999.) But the studies here do not simply detail and applaud 'great acting' by celebrated exponents. Instead, each takes care to link performance with something of the wider commercial and cultural machinery of Hollywood.

Thus, Christine Geraghty's chapter examines not only performances by Emma Thompson, Kate Winslet and Gwyneth Paltrow, but also 'the national discourses which help to shape how acting is understood as a sign of status, class and skill'. Geraghty focuses on heritage films, and traces how each actress deploys voice and body to meet the requirements of role and genre. She argues that Thompson's acting in *Sense and Sensibility* (1995, USA) is marked by an irony and restraint that fit the norms of the heritage genre as well as notions of English middle-class behaviour. By contrast, Winslet occupies a 'crossover position' between British 'lady' and a more glamorous 'dame' in films like *Sense and Sensibility* and *Titanic* (1997, USA). Rather like Winslet, Paltrow's performances in *Emma* (1996, UK) and *Sliding Doors* (1997, UK/USA) combine elements of Hollywood glamour with a restraint that is coded as English. Ultimately, Geraghty argues, the

heritage genre has provided the opportunity for such actresses to showcase their performance skills, much as gangster films have for male actors often trained in the techniques of
the Method.

A critical engagement with the Method is central to Sharon Carnicke's chapter, which
explores acting guru Lee Strasberg's late-blooming screen career. Carnicke plots how
Strasberg's work in films such as *The Godfather, Part II* (1974, USA) raises questions about
his public persona as 'teacher of the stars' and provides a fascinating test case for his
influential theories of acting. She examines how Strasberg's casting and performance as
gang boss Hyman Roth, playing opposite Al Pacino's Michael Corleone, drew on his
off-screen relationship with Pacino, one of his famous pupils. Carnicke also traces how
Strasberg responded to the task of putting the Method into practice, and how he dealt with
the shift from enjoying the reflected glory of a 'star-maker' to becoming a performer
celebrated and denigrated in his own right.

Finally, I consider attempts made in promotional and journalistic discourses to align
different star-actors (Michael Keaton, Val Kilmer and George Clooney) with the role of
Batman. I then examine the performances of Kilmer and Jim Carrey in *Batman Forever*
(1995, USA), an example of the 'high concept' blockbuster that is 'frequently regarded as
a hostile environment in which to attempt, or look for, "real" acting'. These star-actors'
contrasting performances in portraying different types of masculinity are contextualised in
terms of the economic and aesthetic imperatives of the Batman franchise. I argue that the
film's 'multiple address as that generic hybrid known as the family adventure film is rendered somatically by the bodies, voices and acting styles of its two major stars'. In this
setting, the Batsuit costume is simultaneously a physical constraint on the actor's freedom
of movement, a resource for the identification and characterisation of Batman, and a
distinctive element of iconography that facilitates licensed merchandising and spin-offs.

Chapter Six

PERFORMING AS A LADY AND ☐ A DAME: REFLECTIONS ON ACTING AND GENRE

Christine Geraghty

In her (2000) essay on the British film star Margaret Lockwood, Sarah Street quotes from *Picturegoer*, a popular British film magazine in the 1940s. Defending criticisms of British actresses, the commentator distinguishes between British 'ladies' and American 'dames', protesting that 'we may lack glamour and we may be old-fashioned but our actresses play the parts of ladies – not dames' (10 May 1945). I start with this quotation because much of what it expresses still rings true – the rivalry between the two cinemas, the use of class terms to describe the differences, the feeling that American cinema 'wins' in terms of glamour and that British performers therefore have to do something else to obtain approval. But 'Dame' of course has other connotations in the British honours system, and ironically the British actresses who have done best recently in terms of Oscars and awards are Dames, such as Judi Dench and Maggie Smith, or those who will surely be Dames in due course, such as Emma Thompson. When *Sense and Sensibility* (1995, USA) was nominated for Oscars, the British contribution centred on script (Thompson) and performance (Winslet). In this paper, I want to look at the way in which a study of performance (including the speaking of the script) can assist our work on contemporary stardom.

This essay is in many ways a companion piece to one which I wrote for Gledhill and Williams' collection *Reinventing Film Studies* (1999). In it I expressed some dissatisfaction with the theoretical model of film stardom which emphasises the polysemy, contradiction and instability of the star-image and treats extra-filmic discourses such as advertising and the press as an important basis for the star-image. In this, I share Lovell and Krämer's contention that an emphasis on the star as text has directed interest away from performance and acting (1999). In this essay, I want to look at some specifics of performance and characterisation in relation to two contemporary British stars, Emma Thompson and Kate Winslet, and at the rather different emphases brought into play when the same terms are applied to the American actress Gwyneth Paltrow. I have chosen Winslet and Paltrow in particular because I think of them as crossover stars – that is to say, their work reveals something about the national discourses which help to shape how acting is understood as sign of status, class and skill. To adopt *Picturegoer*'s terms, Paltrow, despite being an American, is clearly a lady, while Winslet shows the potential at least to be a US rather than a British Dame.

EMMA THOMPSON: A VERY BRITISH STAR

Emma Thompson is representative in many respects of the way in which acting by a British female star is positioned within wider cultural contexts. Directed by Ang Lee from an adaptation by Thompson herself of Jane Austen's classic novel, *Sense and Sensibility* is a costume or historical drama, a genre which, in the 1980s/90s, was characterised as heritage cinema and strongly associated with British reworkings of the past. Without entering the debates which have surrounded the genre, it is worth noting that adaptations of classics present actors in a particular way. Acting in cinema, particularly by stars, tends to be driven by the narrative and is associated with physical grace and psychological realism so that the best performance is regarded as invisible. What Naremore calls a 'representational rhetoric' (1988: 36) encourages a 'restrained, intimate style' (1988: 43), the Hollywood studio style in which as Dyer suggested the actor appears to be playing him/herself. This is reinforced by the fact that in cinema there is only one performance, that which is on the screen. Unlike the theatre, there is no variation on different nights with different audiences, no possibilities for comparison between different actors in the same roles, and no moment at the end when the actors come out of role and take a bow.

Writings about adaptations have been wary of the concept of fidelity to the original text as unhelpfully setting up a value system in which the film almost inevitably fails. Nevertheless, the notion of faithfulness nearly always remains a critical issue in adaptations of well-known novels, and the pervasiveness of the theme indicates that the notion of something being performed in a different version is at the heart of such films. It is not uncommon for classic novels to be filmed more than once, or for television and film versions to both be available, so that the sense of there being more than one account of the central story is part of the enjoyment of such films. In adaptations, it is clearer than usual that the actors are giving performances in particular roles which involve an interpretation of a pre-defined character. A gap is thus opened up between character and performer which is reinforced by the historical dimension, since the costume and setting make it explicit that we are being invited to a performance in which characters are dressed up in elaborate and sometimes uncomfortable-looking costumes which often limit their physical movements. The gap between past and present can result in the nostalgia for which the heritage genre has been criticised, but it also allows for the use of irony as contemporary values are brought to bear on stories set in the past. The adaptation thus makes more obvious the process of transferring the story to the screen and of acting as part of that process.

Sense and Sensibility is a good example of this. It offers a wide range of acting styles, from Hugh Grant's reprise of his loveable self, to the comic overplaying of Imelda Staunton.

Thompson's sensible Elinor Dashwood is at the heart of the film, and just as the narrative is organised through her, so her performance becomes the norm for good acting in the film.[1] The film's irony also centres on Elinor, since in *Sense and Sensibility* it is the contrast between the manners and assumptions of the past and the 'contemporary, liberal, feminist sensibility' (Pidduck, 1998: 383) of the heroine which provides the gap into which Elinor's ironic comments are inserted. This in turn reinforces the emphasis on acting since the script's ironic moments remind us of the modern woman (Thompson) who is here playing the perfect Austen heroine (Elinor).

In thinking about Thompson's performance, it is helpful to reflect on the use of her body and of her voice. In physical appearance, Thompson is by no means glamorous. Her hair has been lightened and she adopts the feminine hairstyles and pretty, flimsy dresses of the period, but the style does not suit her. The empire-line dresses have the effect of making her look slightly stout without the distractions of a full cleavage. The necklines of her dresses, including her wedding dress, are often filled in with a shawl effect and, at Barton Cottage, she frequently wears an apron (for example, towards the end of the film Elinor is at work in an apron while Marianne plays the piano in an elegant black dress). Thompson's relative plainness is reinforced by Ang's direction. This is a historical film which places relatively little emphasis on sensuous materials, elaborate costume and fine décor, so Thompson's rather plain looks are unadorned by a more sensual *mise-en-scène*. In addition, the lighting serves to underline her rather drawn features, and she is often lit rather harshly. Key conversations with Brandon and Edward, for instance, take place in daylight with bright light coming from the side; in the stilted conversation with Edward in Lucy Steele's presence, white light shines on Thompson's forehead and the side of her face. In another example, a cut from Marianne in candlelight making a silhouette of Willoughby to Elinor in daylight in the kitchen, points to a contrast in treatment of the two actresses. Thompson's body is thus not presented as a glamorous object to be looked at, but is instead used to express control. Thompson uses few gestures and she is often seen in long shot, with her arms and body in a formal position. Rather than claiming space or expressing emotion through the body, it is Thompson's gaze which becomes an indicator of Elinor's control. Thus, Elinor observes both Brandon's first sight of Marianne and Marianne's immediate absorption with Willoughby after the rescue. Her looks are often ironic or warning, particularly with her mother and sisters. These movements of her eyes and head mean that Thompson's body is one of the ways in which the story is laid out intelligibly for us.

Even more crucial in maintaining Thompson's role at the heart of the film are her voice and use of words. Naremore suggests that naturalist acting styles in cinema have 'made the language of players seem less elitist, closer to speech on the street' (1988: 47), and that the voices of actors have become 'relatively transparent, less expressive instruments' (1988: 48). By contrast, the classic adaptation, because of its origins, always tends to bring language to the fore, and Thompson in *Sense and Sensibility* demonstrates how she controls a situation through language with the use of witty conceits and ironic summaries. In a throwaway comment, Elinor can sum up Mrs Jennings or mock Marianne's view of Brandon as aged and infirm. She deflates Marianne's romantic notions ('What care I for colds when there is such a man?' 'You will care very much when your nose swells up.') and uses long and complicated phrasing even at the height of emotion ('Believe me, Marianne, had I not been bound to silence I could have produced proof enough of a broken heart even for you.'). In using language in this way, Thompson achieves an effect of certainty and control by appearing to under-emphasise nuances and phrasing; her tone is rather flat and unexpressive, words are spoken quietly and quickly through a narrow mouth and the audience is expected to follow the irony of quite complicated constructions without the help of facial expression. Most characteristic though is the use of the word 'Dearest'; normally a term of endearment, as Thompson uses it the word becomes an ironic warning to characters on the verge of misbehaviour.

Thompson's work in *Sense and Sensibility* is an example of how middle-class British actresses have succeeded as ladies, rather than dames, in contemporary cinema. In some sense, this heritage mode is the equivalent for female stars of the recognition that the Method acting route brings to male stars, but it relies on very different values.[2] Thompson's work draws attention to the process of acting, but acting here is a matter of control, of making ideas and emotions intelligible rather than felt. It makes a virtue of restraint, but can easily become mannered because it relies on a relatively narrow range of gestures signifying more than appears. It is a style marked by irony which demonstrates the heroine's superior understanding and, in stories which give a moral value to manners and class, the emphasis on restraint and hidden meaning in the acting style makes for a particular fit between star and genre which has proved highly successful.[3]

KATE WINSLET: FROM BRITAIN TO AMERICA

I would suggest that this mode of acting has been adopted by a number of British actresses, and in a modest way has made them unlikely stars. While there are individual differences, the work of Judi Dench, Maggie Smith and Helena Bonham Carter, for instance, could be studied from this angle. I want now though to turn to Kate Winslet, who was nominated for an Oscar for her role as supporting actress in *Sense and Sensibility*, to see what this model might tell us about her work. While in Thompson's performance voice and body work together in a consistent approach, in Winslet's case the two registers of voice and body often work in contradiction. Where voice is concerned, Winslet frequently adopts the manner I have described in Thompson's work. Early in the film, Marianne imitates Elinor's subdued description of her feeling for Edward ('I greatly esteem him, I like him'), and Winslet adopts the characteristically flat tones at other points. Like Elinor, Marianne has control of language and is one of the few characters who can respond to Elinor's irony; Winslet uses a flat tone for these retorts, often expressed in a curt way – 'You are right,' she self-mockingly replies to Elinor's comments about colds in the exchange quoted above. Even at high points of emotion, such as when she reads Willoughby's letter of rejection, Winslet speaks quickly and softly, without the expected inflections. Thus, although in narrative terms Marianne is the opposite of Elinor, Winslet is restrained in how she uses her voice, and even the declamatory voice she uses for reciting poetry is relatively hushed and quick, operating within the vocal range established by Thompson.

The use of the body though is very different. Her appearance is initially like Thompson's – light hair styled in the same way, the similar pale, floating dresses. Winslet though gives the impression of needing to escape from the restrictions of the historical costumes and manners. The empire-line emphasises her full bosom, and her strong body is clear under the thin material of the dresses. Her hair is frequently dishevelled, escaping from ribbons or hats that attempt to restrain it. Her white skin colours easily, and Marianne is seen biting her lip and pinching her own cheeks to deliberately bring up the colour. More often though the blushing is the 'natural' product of physical exertions or the pressures of emotion. Thus, her flushed face is caught in close-up on a number of occasions: under a straw hat when cutting reeds with Brandon, with Willoughby at the picnic or with Brandon in the garden at the end. The lighting, often by candle light, reinforces Winslet's different skin tones and softens her face. This difference is reinforced by camerawork. While Elinor looks, Marianne is looked at and she is filmed in such a way as to bring out Winslet's beauty.

Winslet's strong physical presence in the film is used to create her character and to forward the narrative. It is she who is first to enter the Dashwood's new home, breaking into the idyllic picture of the cottage exterior to explore what is inside. Her relationship with Willoughby is expressed through physical gestures when, for instance, he swings her round at a picnic or drives her recklessly in his carriage; on such occasions, words fail her and she screams in delight. But the story also emphasises the dangers of relying too much on the body. The only embraces of the film are given to Marianne, but they occur when she is picked up and carried, first by Willoughby and then by Brandon, after she has tested out the limits of her strength and been found wanting. In thus exposing the limitations on Winslet's physical presence, the film accords with the values of restraint which are strong both in the genre and in Lee's direction. But while Thompson's body is used with restraint to reinforce her verbal control, Winslet's, in opposition to the use of her voice, is used not only to give the conventional pleasures of looking at the female body but also the pleasures of a sensual challenge to the British female acting style. While clearly being a lady, Winslet also offers the glamorous pleasures of the dame.

We can see how this develops in two later costume films in which Winslet starred after *Sense and Sensibility* – *Jude* (1996, UK) and *Titanic* (1997, USA). It is no accident that

Winslet has appeared in these historical/literary dramas since they offer the opportunity to repeat the contradictory acting style and narrative positioning she deploys in *Sense and Sensibility*. Hardy's relentlessly depressing tale gave Winslet and the director little room for manoeuvre, but we can nevertheless see some of the elements here. The narrative positions Sue as the rebellious women who is destroyed by the narrow conventions of society and accepts her punishment. This is done conventionally through *mise-en-scène* in which Winslet's blonde hair, light blouses and bright dresses consistently stand out from the dark background and her association in Jude's mind with the carved angel stands as a metaphor for the loving relationship they could have had. The defining moment for Winslet's performance though occurs early in the film. The previous scene has indicated a political source for Sue's rebellion when she attends a socialist meeting, but in this scene she sits still and silent, filmed in long shot. Afterwards she joins Jude and his friends in the pub and is caught by the camera in movement, drinking and smoking. This lively, vital moment allows Winslet to express the character's rebellion physically, through her body, and it is through her naked body that Sue offers herself to Jude when the two set up house together despite their unmarried state. These two motifs reappear in *Titanic*.

In terms of budget and production, *Titanic* is in a different league from the other films discussed here. Nevertheless, it does have some of the characteristics of a classic adaptation. It has a double story, stressed this time by the use of the voiceover which identifies and tries to bridge past and present, as the elderly Rose tells the story of her youth. *Titanic* is of course telling a story with a basis in historical fact and other filmed versions, so it shares with classic adaptations that sense of being a different version of the same story.[4] Like the heritage texts discussed by Pidduck (1998), it is informed by a feminist sensibility, mainly through its strong identification with Rose's viewpoint; this is explicitly articulated in the script when Rose makes a bitter joke about the men behaving as if they were 'Masters of the Universe' or when her mother points to the limitations on women's choices. In addition, of course, the film's strong moral message is rooted in a debate about the value of class and manners. In a strong binary drive, the British who run the ship are associated with the East Coast aristocracy, while Jack Dawson represents the freedom of America and the west. It is into this binary that Winslet steps.

I want to look at moments in Winslet's performance to illustrate why as an actress she was so suited to the part. Once again, body and voice are key features here, but this time rather differently articulated. When she first appears, Winslet is hidden under a wide-brimmed hat. A camera movement allows us to see that her face is heavily made up, her red hair neatly tucked away, and her black and white coat firmly buttoned up to the neck. The voiceover tells us, 'Inside I was screaming.' This image is soon contrasted with another, that of Winslet running along the deck, hair wild, arms and bosom on show in a skimpy, delicate dress. While Winslet never returns to the buttoned-up state of her first appearance, throughout the first part of the film she oscillates between the controlled and organised body demanded by the East Coast (at one point her mother laces her into her corset), and the freer, looser movements allowed when she can let go with Jack. This is linked to questions of manners and different forms of socially acceptable behaviour. Thus, at the dinner table in first-class section, Winslet is relatively immobile, using eyes and face to warn Jack of potential solecisms, and leaving the more expansive gestures (leaning sideways for more champagne, throwing a lighter) to Jack who is taking control. At the party downstairs, however, her beautiful outfit is transformed, her bare back turned more often to camera, her shoes shaken off and skirt lifted. Winslet's body is continuously moving as she drinks, smokes, laughs, spins and dances, finally transforming the feminine skills of ballet into a competition of bodily strength. Such a demonstration prepares us for the second half of the film when the romantic commitment has been made but the couple have to battle to stay together. It is striking that, amid the competing spectacle of the ship sinking, it is Winslet's body, rather than teen idol Leonardo DiCaprio's, which is on display; draped by wet fabric, her shoulders and arms are strongly revealed as she works her way along the flooded corridors.

In some senses, Winslet's voice works, as it does in *Sense and Sensibility*, against the sensuality which her body displays. Her accent is now American but her voice is still high and light, she speaks formally and is prone to anglicisms; 'goodness gracious' she exclaims when her fiancé Cal presents her with the fabulous diamond, and Jack's drawings are deemed 'rather good, very good actually'. Nevertheless, *Titanic*'s screenplay has few of the long speeches of the classic adaptation, and Winslet's speaking voice becomes less important than the nervous laughter, breaths and sighs which accompany her bodily movements. Thus, at the party below deck, her first sound is a nervous laugh as she looks around the crowd; when Jack pulls her to him to dance, she responds with an apparently instinctive exhalation of breath, and her dancing is accompanied by little shrieks and laughs. When Cal hits her as a warning against her running around with Jack, she tries to pull herself together but sinks to the floor, moans and holds her stomach. Similarly, when she and Jack run around the ship to escape Cal's manservant, the Irish music on the soundtrack is accompanied by Winslet's exclamations and giggles. By contrast, it is significant that the voiceover which gives coherence to the narrative and measures the significance of each event is performed by a different actress.

Given all this, it is hardly surprising that *Titanic* uses Winslet's body for some of its set-piece moments, loading it with narrative significance. Thus, the high spot of the romance is the moment when Winslet's body supported by DiCaprio becomes the live figurehead of the modernist ship, caught up in the sensation of flying and moving towards the west and the sunset. And the nude scene, which seems initially to be a further demonstration of Rose's love and Winslet's authenticity, has a narrative purpose in that the sketch becomes Rose's act of defiance to her fiancé, a symbol of her refusal to have her living body locked up like the picture. And finally, as they wait to be rescued, Rose complains

'I can't feel my body' and it takes a conscious act of will, inspired by her promise to Jack, to reanimate her freezing body to seek to return to life. But in some senses, these set-pieces are less important than the living, breathing bodily presence with which Winslet suffuses the stilted script and special effects of the blockbuster.

In *Titanic* it seems to me that Winslet makes the move that was promised in earlier films, and establishes a crossover position between the British heritage picture and the Hollywood star vehicle. She remains a lady, still able to use the class tones and the conscious performing style of the British adaptation, but her physical appearance and the use of her body for sensual appeal puts her into the more glamorous tradition associated with Hollywood. This is particularly important for *Titanic* given its message of the triumph of the American spirit of freedom over the class-bound and frigid British. Although in the narrative Rose is East Coast American, Winslet is a British actress. For a representative of the uptight heroines of British heritage dramas, the frumpy wearers of shawls and bonnets, to be won over to American film-making is a triumph indeed.

GWYNETH PALTROW: AN AMERICAN DOES BRITISH

I want to turn now from a British star moving westward to an American star moving east, Gwyneth Paltrow. Paltrow has a more extensive film career than either Thompson or Winslet, and here I concentrate on two of what might be called her British films (in setting if not production terms) to look at how costume films have allowed her performance style to develop in a particular way. Paltrow's first leading role was in *Emma* (1996, UK), an adaptation of another Austen novel which was released a year after *Sense and Sensibility*. The film's credits emphasise the distance between audience and drama in the historical film, taking us literally to a different world which is presented first through a spinning globe on which the settings of Britain, London and Highbury are identified and then, in a series of painted miniatures, the buildings and people of the forthcoming drama. This sense of a different, more orderly world is continued in the film which is organised around a series of dinners and parties, and the *mise-en-scène* presents the internal and external décor as highly composed, decorative and elegant. A voiceover positions Emma within the society she seeks to organise, and at various points Emma's voice, motivated by diaries and letters, provides a commentary on events. The picturesque nature of the setting and use of the voiceover opens up the possibilities for irony, while the casting of an American actress as the English heroine of a revered classic foregrounds even more the question of performance.

As Emma, Paltrow conforms to but also softens the model exemplified by Thompson, using her voice and body in a similar way. Emma seeks to control scenes and people through her use of language. Thus, she manoeuvres through delicate irony ('If you prefer . . .; if you think . . .') Harriet's rejection of Robert Martin, and rebukes Knightley by lightly mocking his declarations of moral postion ('How fascinating . . .'). Emma's speeches are marked, even at times of emotion, by elaborate grammar and complicated phrasing which Paltrow delivers in a light, often almost whispered tone: 'my astonishment is beyond anything I can express', she whispers rapidly to Mr Elton in response to his unwelcome marriage proposal. Although Paltrow more consistently than Thompson stresses particular words, the speed with which she speaks is comparable and at times, particularly in voiceovers, her voice flattens and deepens to adopt Thompson's more consistently ironic tone. Thus, when she believes Frank Churchill to be in love with her, she tells herself, 'I felt listless after and had some sort of headache' and, continuing with a lowered, harder tone, 'so I must be in love as well'. Later, as she picks off the daisy petals while determinedly not thinking of Mr Knightley (whom she now knows she really loves), she comments in sardonic tones, 'We should not have daisies in the garden. They really are drab little flowers.' Like Thompson, Paltrow often speaks through a narrow, closed mouth, and her conversations with Harriet and Mrs Weston provide a contrast between her still face and their relatively more open expressions, particularly using the mouth, of humour or astonishment.

Paltrow thus adopts the accent of the English middle classes with the favoured ironic and mannered restraint of the classic adaptation. In body and movement, she also fits this style. Her hair is fair and pulled back into the styles of period, exposing her face though the back of her head is often decorated with curls, ribbons or flowers, thereby softening the effect. The empire-line dresses, mainly in white and soft pastels, fall from the bust without revealing her figure; she frequently wears shawls over her shoulders and, though the necklines are low, her cleavage is minimal. Indeed, one of the points of contrast between Emma and Harriet is size which, in the 1990s, perhaps stands as a better indication of vulgarity than low birth. The film frequently uses long shots, and the use of a relatively restrained camera allows for an emphasis on graceful movement. Emma's more pointed remarks are often disguised by a graceful gesture or a smiling nod and, as with Thompson, the body here becomes a vehicle for decorum and sometimes elegant dissimulation rather than the expression of feeling.

Paltrow in *Emma* therefore takes on the performance style of a British actress but there are differences from Thompson and Winslet. Paltrow performs being British with the appropriate emphasis on manners, restraint and control, but this is leavened by another kind of look connected to the kind of glamour which Thompson specifically lacks. Winslet gains glamour by giving the impression that she cannot be restrained by the genre, but *Emma* allows, indeed demands, that Paltrow while remaining controlled is also glamorous. This is particularly clear in the close-ups at key points which position Paltrow as the star of the romance narrative: the opening close-up of her smiling broadly at her friend's wedding, a wide smile, reinforced by red lipstick; a number of striking close-ups in an archery contest with Knightley when her glossy hair and perfect skin are emphasised; and the close-ups when she accepts Knightley's proposal, when he remains in shade but her face is highlighted by sun. The glamour of this rather different register is reinforced by the use of her body which, though not on display for sexual invitation, is revealed to be that of a contemporary model. The bones in the shoulders, the slight frame and the thin arms give her body a significance outside the conventions of acting and genre – as the desirable appearance of a modern young woman.

It is this emphasis on the modern young woman which I want to examine in another of Paltrow's British films, *Sliding Doors* (1997, UK/USA). Here she attempts to bring the acting style of *Emma* into a contemporary setting. *Sliding Doors* does have some connections to the adaptations we have looked at so far. The rendering of modern London owes much to the heritage approach in its use of landscape, its focus on dress and style as bearers of meaning, and its episodic narrative underpinned by the dynamics of romance. *Sliding Doors* takes an initial event – Helen leaving work after she has been sacked – and shows us what might happen in two stories which develop in parallel, in one of which she catches the train home, in the other she misses it. The narrative thus foregrounds performance in that Paltrow plays out different versions of the same character, and in the gap between the two stories allows for the possibility of irony.

Initially the film works hard to emphasise Paltrow's Englishness. Although smartly dressed, her long brown hair reduces her glamour and she wears minimal make-up. Her voice is deepened but has the middle-class accent and ironic tones which she used in *Emma*. Thus, when she is sacked by a group of young City men, she speaks quickly and quietly, congratulating them on finally getting rid of her; 'this is perfect . . . congratulations . . . very well done'. Shortly afterwards, in one version of the story when she finds her boyfriend Gerry in bed with the American Lydia, she announces that she has had 'a dreadful day' and offers 'a cup of tea' before she lays into him. Thus, the film establishes early on Paltrow's acting abilities in adopting an English accent and ironic tones, and does so with a knowingness indicated by a headline in the newspaper which Helen reads at one point: 'A Very English Oscar Triumph'.

But the film's double narrative provides us with two versions of this English Paltrow and the transformation is really the main point of the film, the point which it returns to again and again as if it cannot quite believe that a Hollywood actress (a dame) is appearing in a British film. The brown-haired Helen whom Lydia describes as 'quite pretty in a British, horsy sort of way' is thereafter the heroine of the version in which Helen does not find out about Gerry's betrayal. Kept in a state of unknowing, she takes a menial job to support him, dressing down in unflattering cardigans and childish plaits. But the Helen who finds out is literally transformed, washing the man out of her hair by getting a new haircut which turns her from a sexless, rather drab girl into a chic blonde in a smart polo-neck, an image which of course the audience is expected to recognise as Paltrow, the star. From this point, blonde Helen becomes more glamorous, displaying a series of cropped tops, well-cut trousers, shoestring-strap dresses and black leather coats.

In some senses, Paltrow's performance as the blonde Helen uses some of the traits of her Emma. In particular, in *Emma*, she had adopted two ways of looking; the first is a large-eyed, rather mournful but direct look to camera or character which seems to express frankness and openness, and which in *Emma* is used particularly when the character is apologising for her attempts to organise other people's affairs. The other is a much more indirect look in which the chin is tucked in and Paltrow looks up from under her brow; this look is particularly useful because it offers the appearance of restraint and modesty but is often flirtatious or calculating.[5] These looks reappear in *Sliding Doors* and are used particularly in the depiction of the relationship with James. Thus, at an early meeting with James over a milk-shake, Paltrow alternates direct looks at James with glances down or away from him, while later on at a meal with his friends a series of glances concludes with a direct exchange of looks, though Paltrow continues to cover her mouth with her hand. Significantly, the more modest look, the glance up with the chin tucked in, is used when the blonde Helen offers to organise the restaurant opening for one of James's friends. Certainly, Paltrow here lacks the controlling gaze which Thompson deployed in *Sense and Sensibility*. What is interesting though is that the looks, which in *Emma* indicated the heroine's engagement with the world she seeks to control, are in the more modern setting transformed into a 'little girl' defence against the world's difficulties.

This effect is reinforced by the lack of emphasis given to dialogue in *Sliding Doors*. Whereas the classic adaptation presents actresses with speeches and wordplay to demonstrate their skills, the film in a modern setting works to silence the heroine. From the relatively loqua-cious beginning when she is sacked, Helen grows more silent and the key scenes of transformation (the decoration of the office, the rowing sequence, the restaurant opening) are ones in which we are invited to look rather than listen. In these montage sequences, the emphasis is not so much on advancing the narrative but on looking at Paltrow. Thus, the decorating scenes involve three changes of clothes, with Paltrow, in effect, posing mutely, as if she were advertising fashionable 'lifestyle' women's wear. In addition, Helen's dialogue is often incoherent and inarticulate. There is a certain emphasis on her swearing (using a British term like 'wanker'), which surely creates a frisson in the gap between the coarse language and the classic image created by *Emma* and other roles. In addition, in the romantic scenes with James, part of the humour is generated by Helen being unable to express her feelings. This is part of a wider joke about British modes of expression, exem-plified by James's use of jokes and the Monty Python phrases which Helen adopts, but its effect is again to undermine Helen's control of her situation.

It is a long way from the elegances of *Sense and Sensibility* to the low-budget *Sliding Doors*, and Paltrow's status of a crossover star, with Hollywood glamour and British class, was confirmed much more securely with *Shakespeare in Love* (1998, UK), which returned her to a historical setting. But *Sliding Doors* works as a commutation test (Thompson, 1978). In it we can see features of the British female acting style which Paltrow takes into the modern setting but which are now disassociated from the literary script and the restrained setting of the adaptation. In analysing *Sliding Doors* in this way, we can see how important the generic features of the classic adaptation are in providing the space which is organised around both a particular character (the ironic feminist-before-her-time heroine) and a distinctive acting style.

CONCLUSION

In summary, I hope that my discussion of these particular performances has drawn attention to three main interlinked points. First, national identity is important in considering acting styles, and Winslet's and Paltrow's crossing the line between 'lady' and 'dame' illustrates that a star performance may involve an inflection of national position. Second, thinking about performance means paying attention to the different ways in which a particular acting style fits a particular genre. Third, and closely linked to this, we can note that acting and the values placed on it are heavily gendered. Certain kinds of genre/performance combinations direct attention to acting and give it value. A form of Method acting is commonly adopted by male stars to this effect, and the heritage film can serve a similar purpose for female ones. Just as gangster films such as *Reservoir Dogs* (1991, USA), *Heat* (1995, USA) and *GoodFellas* (1990, USA) have allowed male actors to indulge in 'putting on a show' (Naremore, 1988: 43), so classic adaptations have given actresses the opportunity to draw attention to their acting skills. Such a showcase has been particularly useful to British actresses because of the tradition of valuing acting as something which the British stars do differently from Hollywood. The tradition has continued with *Iris* (2002, UK) in which John Bayley's book is bought to the screen with Winslet and Judi Dench playing the young and old Iris respectively. Both were praised for their acting, with the *Guardian* critic Peter Bradshaw, for instance, commenting on the 'deeply intelligent acting' which marked the film. Dench's performance in particular is praised for its detailed restraint. The *Guardian* emphasised 'the enormous calm' which she brought to the role, while other critics commented on the way in which the actress could make her eyes go blank as Iris retreated into dementia (*Guardian* 2; 18 January 2002: 10–11). The Oscar nominations duly appeared – Dench for best actress in a leading role and Winslet in a supporting role, a category which also included nominations for Dame Maggie Smith and for Helen Mirren who, like Winslet, crosses the boundary between dame and lady. All these nominations were for performances in period films (*Gosford Park* (2001, UK/USA) as well as *Iris*), indicating that genre, gender and nationality continue to be crucial factors in the valuing of performance.

A fuller version of this article appears as 'Crossing Over: Performing as a Lady and a Dame' in Screen *43(1) 2002. I am grateful to Martin Barker and particularly Thomas Austin for encouraging the work that led to this chapter.*

1 In a television programme about the making of the film, Staunton and Hugh Laurie laughingly comment that Thompson as scriptwriter is able to write herself the best part. In a *Sight and Sound* interview with Graham Fuller, Ang Lee comments very interestingly on the different kind of work he did with various cast members to achieve performances which matched their character and their experience (Fuller, Graham (1996) 'Shtick, and Seduction', *Sight and Sound* 6(3): 24).

2 Naremore suggests that a film 'becomes a good showcase for professional acting if it provides moments when the characters are clearly shown to be wearing masks – in other words, exhibiting high degrees of expressive incoherence' (1988: 76) when, for example, actors portray the struggle to contain powerful feelings around loss, addiction or illness. I suggest that heritage films also show characters wearing masks and that they are thus good vehicles in which to showcase performance. Both kinds of films are good bets for best-acting Oscar nominations.

3 That this valuing of restraint is connected with genre as well as gender can be seen by comparing the moral sympathy demanded by the undemonstrative Brandon and Knightley, compared with the more expansive Willoughby and Churchill (the different acting styles would also repay examination).

4 In her discussion of Hitchcock's *Sabotage*, Speidel draws attention to Hollywood's liking for a story which has already 'proved itself in another medium' (2000: 133).

5 Despite my self-denying ordinance of sticking to the text, I am bound to record here the likeness to Princess Diana's famous shy but flirtatious look. Paltrow uses this look again at the end of *A Perfect Murder* (1998, USA) to indicate innocence, guilt and getting away with it. The film is an example of Paltrow taking her English (East Coast) mode back into an American genre.

Chapter Seven

☐ FROM ACTING GURU TO HOLLYWOOD STAR: LEE STRASBERG AS ACTOR

Sharon Marie Carnicke

Lee Strasberg's transformation from acting guru into movie star poses fascinating questions that have not been addressed in the press since his death in 1982, and have never been examined seriously by scholars. Despite a flurry of new articles, triggered in part by the 100th anniversary of his birth in 1901, his late-blooming career as an actor attracts little attention.

In the academy, where '"Method bashing" is in vogue', David Krasner of Yale University endeavours to rehabilitate Strasberg's reputation by correcting misinformation about the man and his method. Krasner's anthology explicitly 'seeks to set the record straight' (Krasner, 2000: 6, 3–4). In it, innovative scholars employ a range of current methodologies such as cognitive science, speech acts, feminisms and cultural politics to bring the twentieth-century Method into the postmodern world. No one, however, interrogates the link between his teaching and his practice.

In newspapers and magazines for professional actors and directors, Strasberg's centennial publicity includes recollections of him as a teacher (Karen Kondazian, 'A Personal Recollection of the Man and the Myths', *LA Stage* 7, March 2002: 11, 28–9), unpublished interviews (Griselda Steiner, 'Imagination's Tutor: A Personal Encounter with America's Most Influential Acting Teacher, Lee Strasberg', *American Theatre* 9(1), January 2002: 36–40; 108–12), and biographical articles that foreground the longevity of his influence (Jean Schiffman, 'Method Man', *Back Stage West*, 15 November 2001: 4–5).[1] Such articles bring the legendary master back to life for a generation of actors who never personally experienced the stormy passions of his criticisms, his awe-inspiring insights, or the stories he told about Stanislavsky and other great historical actors. These articles concentrate on his theories about acting. They deem him an 'icon' and 'an integral part of American actor-training' (Steiner, 2002: 36). They emphasise his recognition, nurturing and shaping of talent; they stress his uncanny success in making three generations of actors into stars, and their conclusions seem inevitable. 'Surely there's not an actor, teacher, or director alive in the Western world unaffected by the Method' (Schiffman, 2001: 4); he 'represents the ultimate teacher' (Kondazian, 2002: 11). In sharp contrast to his pedagogical reputation, recent publications mention Strasberg the actor in passing. He was a 'sometime actor' (2002: 4), who 'did a bit of acting himself' (2002: 28). Only *Variety* reports that the Egyptian Theater in Hollywood honoured his 100th birthday by screening Francis Ford Coppola's *Godfather, Part II* (1974, USA), the film in which Strasberg had made his acting debut at the age of 73 as the Jewish mafia boss, Hyman Roth.

In this essay, I focus on this undeservedly overlooked chapter in Strasberg's career. How did he value the stardom of his last few years? How did his persona as teacher and maker of stars feed his image as actor? Do Strasberg's performances on film illuminate what he taught?

LEE STRASBERG – A BRIEF BIOGRAPHY

Born in the Austro-Hungarian Empire on 17 November 1901, Strasberg arrived in the United States at the age of seven, speaking Yiddish. Manhattan offered the child more than the poverty of emigration – he found a vibrant theatrical culture in his native language. Famed Yiddish players like Jacob Adler and David Kessler (Strasberg's favourite), respected acting as art and brought the best of European theatre to émigré audiences. To this day, a walk of fame extends along Second Avenue (like the one along Hollywood Boulevard) where one can read the names of great Jewish actors in the pavement.

Strasberg first performed at ten years old for the Yiddish Progressive Dramatic Club, which had modelled itself on André Antoine's 'Théâtre Libre' (Paris) (Garfield, 1980: 3), the first theatre to advance realism as a style of production. Thus, Strasberg learned to value the illusion of reality from the beginning. At 16 years he stopped acting after what he called a 'traumatic experience'. The Club's actors rehearsed without props, and at one première Strasberg tried to light an old-fashioned oil lamp for the first time. Unfamiliar with the apparatus, he placed a lit match directly into the oil, causing an explosion. 'I blacked out,' he said, 'and didn't remember how I got off-stage' (Steve Hager, 'Lee Strasberg: The Acting Master Turns the Method on Himself', *Horizon*, January 1980). At about the same time (1918), he dropped out of school in order to earn money for his family.

Between 1917 and 1923 (when he first saw Konstantin Stanislavsky act), Strasberg read voraciously about theatrical art. When the famed Russian brought the Moscow Art Theatre (MAT) to the United States, Strasberg felt that he had finally seen in performance what he had envisioned as ideal through his reading, that 'acting is living on stage' (Garfield, 1980: 9). He promptly sold his business partnership in order to pursue theatre professionally. He enrolled at the newly created American Laboratory Theatre, where he studied for six months with Richard Boleslavsky and Maria Uspenskaya, both of whom had acted with Stanislavsky during the MAT tour. From them he learned about the operation of affective memory (both sensory and emotional). Later, he would develop this knowledge into the cornerstone of the Method. Strasberg's affective memory exercise trains the actor to recall the physical sensations connected with a past traumatic experience, in order to revive associated emotions. If the actor chooses an experience appropriately analogous to the play, the actor's resulting emotion reads as genuine for the character. Over the last five decades, Strasberg's advocates and critics have debated this technique more hotly than any other (Carnicke, 1998: 125–45).

In 1925, Strasberg took his talents to Broadway, where he played a number of small supporting roles for the Theatre Guild, a progressive production house that produced contemporary European drama. His last role was that of the pedlar in Lynn Rigg's *Green Grow the Lilacs* (1931) (Garfield, 1980: 19; Hirsch, 1984: 217–18). More significantly, while working with the Guild, Strasberg used a Yiddish amateur group, the Students of Art and Drama, as his personal laboratory. He directed for them in order to test techniques which he had learned from his teachers as well as his own theories about acting. He chose Heyerman's *The Good Hope* as his first project precisely because he knew his teachers had acted in it at The First Studio, a workshop which Stanislavsky had founded in 1911 to experiment systematically (Garfield, 1980: 18).

Strasberg's work in the Group Theatre (1931–41) has become American theatrical legend. In 1929, at the Theatre Guild he met director Harold Clurman (an assistant stage manager) and Cheryl Crawford (a casting secretary). They shared a similar vision: an art theatre that would address 'the truest preoccupation of an intelligent American audience' (Carnicke, 1998: 39), to quote Crawford. Together, the three formed a collective theatre that competed with commercial houses on Broadway and forever changed how America thought about acting (1998: 38–46).

With the exception of Jacob Adler's children, Stella and Luther, who were stars of the Yiddish stage, members of the Group were young and inexperienced. They needed not only direction but basic actor training to succeed in the ambitious productions planned by the Group. Thus, Strasberg first began to teach. He coined the term 'Method acting', when in 1934 Stella Adler challenged his emphasis on emotional memory. She had just returned from Paris, where she had spent six weeks studying with Stanislavsky. She shocked the Group by dramatically announcing that Strasberg had misinterpreted the Russian master. Imagination, she explained, not memory, was the true emotional springboard for the actor. Robert Lewis recalls that her words prompted Strasberg to respond defensively, avowing that 'he taught the Strasberg Method, not the Stanislavsky System' (Carnicke, 1998: 60). From that moment, the 'Method' took root in American theatre.

When the Group Theatre disbanded in 1941, many of its members sought careers in Hollywood, Strasberg among them. While former colleagues became famous, Strasberg's career stalled. Darryl Zanuck of Twentieth Century Fox may have praised him as an unusually successful coach of screen tests (Joan Barthel, 'The Master of the Method Plays a Role Himself', *New York Times*, 2 February 1975), but Strasberg felt that his idealistic view of acting rankled with the commercial realities of the entertainment industry. 'The studios used to hate me,' he said, 'because I taught that actors should be creative, should be allowed to think for themselves, and this challenged the studios' authority' ('Lee Strasberg: A Double Life in the Theatre', *Village Voice*, 26 June 1978).

In 1947 Kazan, Lewis and Crawford founded the Actors Studio in New York, as a special kind of club where members could perfect their craft without the pressures of production. The Studio became a unique force in American stage and film through the creation of a community of actors speaking a common working language. At the outset, the co-founders excluded Strasberg. Lewis explained that 'his manner of dealing with young people was light miles away from what we now planned'. Kazan more baldly said, 'what we were determined to get rid of forever was Strasberg's paternalism' (Carnicke, 1998: 49). Despite their best efforts, Strasberg began to teach at the Actors Studio in 1948. Lewis had quit over a professional quarrel with Kazan, who in turn had little time to teach as he tended a busy directing career. In 1951, Strasberg became Artistic Director and taught there until his death in 1982. Thus, the Actors Studio became Strasberg's bastion.

Internet subscription lists for actors and directors show that the Method and emotional memory remain as provocative as they were in 1934. Recent publications prove that Strasberg continues to draw contradictory responses – positive and negative, panegyric and dismissive, loyal and hostile. Through debate, a new kind of star had been born – the acting guru. While Strasberg's disciples did not literally call him 'star', they invented an array of metaphors, religious and familial, to describe his special status. He became rabbi, Talmudic scholar, guru, Zen master, cult leader, high priest, pope, fakir and saint. He became the great patriarch of the Actors Studio, the authoritarian 'Jewish papa'. 'We were Strasberg's children,' said Studio member Michael Wager. 'Many of us had a father/son, love/hate relationship with him' (Hirsch 1984: 166). Strasberg's images embody diametrically opposed traits. In turn 'volatile and aloof' (Schiffman, 2001: 4), nurturing and cruel, supportive and judgmental, he functioned as 'father and judge'. He 'could make grown men weep' and reward those he favoured with 'the sought-after privilege of becoming a member of that exclusive club called the Actors Studio' (Kondazian, 2002: 11). His charismatic personality combined pathologically shy, introverted behaviour in social situations with angry, sometimes cruel, always extroverted outbursts in the classroom. With a perspective on acting as art that demands respect, he wedded idealistic passion to intolerant rejection of differing points of view.

The more he incited debate, the more controversial became his ideas, and the more his disciples saw extraordinary wisdom in him. Al Pacino said, 'what he tells, you hear for the first time and it's being told to you like nobody else could say it' (Suzanne O'Malley, 'Can the Method Survive the Madness?', *New York Times*, 7 October 1979). At the beginning of every session at the Actors Studio, members stood in silent respect as their mentor entered.

Most importantly, he became a star-acting teacher because he captured not only student attention but also that of the public. In 1956, Strasberg marvelled at the interest. 'Actors have been thought about in the past ... Duse versus Bernhardt ... But I think this is the first time in the history of theatre ... that general people – the barbershop and beauty parlor attendant – are discussing the work of the Actors Studio. ... I must say this is unusual' (Strasberg, 10 April 1956). The metaphors that his students had used to describe him travelled into the press, biographies and publicity surrounding the stars who sat at his feet.

Ironically, he developed his stardom by evading the public. During the 1930s at the Group Theatre, he rigorously excluded observers from acting classes and rehearsals. During the 1950s at the Actors Studio, he insisted upon utter privacy for actors to hone their craft. On one occasion, when a writer who had been invited to observe ventured an opinion, Strasberg exploded. 'You – on the outside – here your presence is a sufferance, it is an interruption to us, it is an interference in our work' (Strasberg, 26 February 1960). The more he excluded outsiders, the more he generated curiosity about a seeming cult of actors. Thus, the stars – these most public of personae – were born from one of the most secret of clubs. In Strasberg's domain, public and private merged as paradoxically as they do in one of his acting exercises, the private moment, in which an actor performs something in front of an audience that he or she would never do except in total privacy.

Unique among master teachers, Strasberg built fame through teaching. While he had acted during his youth and directed as a young professional, he devoted the majority of his 50 years in theatre to pedagogy. The trajectory of his career differs significantly from other acting gurus who turned to teaching only after establishing themselves as star actors and directors. Consider that Konstantin Stanislavsky began struggling with ways to teach acting only in 1906, several years after co-founding the Moscow Art Theatre (1897), nearly 15 years after first achieving acclaim as an actor (1888), and after directing his most famous Chekhovian productions (1898–1904). Notice that Stella Adler (Strasberg's major competitor) had found fame as a star of the Yiddish stage before meeting Strasberg (1931) and long before founding her school (1949). Remember that Elia Kazan and Robert Lewis had forged successful directing careers before creating the Actors Studio. Moreover, the era of American acting gurus developed in the shadow of Strasberg. The most famous – Stella Adler, Robert Lewis, Elia Kazan and Sanford Meisner – began as Strasberg's colleagues and ultimately defined their approaches to acting by distinguishing their techniques from his.

Against this backdrop, Strasberg made his film debut as an actor. He had not performed for over 40 years, and his unexpected change of direction represents an important reinvention of himself in the more traditional image of the screen star. The *Village Voice* (11 December 1974) called him 'Strasberg the reborn'. For his portrayal of Roth, he was nominated for an Oscar as Best Supporting Actor alongside his student Robert de Niro (who won). In two films, he performed opposite Studio member Al Pacino. Critical acclaim opened studio doors. 'Strasberg's recent film work has led industry sources to sit up and take notice' (*Hollywood Reporter*, 11 February 1980). He pursued his new career with vigour, admitting that his acting 'drastically altered' his teaching schedule (*Godfather, Part II*, PN 1974). In eight years, he played seven roles. Following his debut, he acted in two made-for-television films: *The Last Tenant* (1978, USA) and *Skokie* (1981, USA). He appeared in four features: *The Cassandra Crossing* (1977, USA) with Sophia Loren, ... *And Justice for All* (1978, USA), *Boardwalk* (1979, USA), and *Going In Style* (1979, USA) with George Burns and Art Carney. His ethnicity and age limited his roles to 'old Jews', as one critic put it (*Eastern Review*, February 1977): in *The Cassandra Crossing* he played a Holocaust survivor; in *Boardwalk* a Coney Island Jew, displaced by the growing African-American community; in *The Last Tenant* and ... *And Justice for All*, his characters live in nursing homes. He accepted his typecasting as a Jew with humour. 'I don't mind, so long as I'm left time to play Einstein and Freud' (*Eastern Review*, February 1977). He bridled, however, at weak portraits of the elderly, and consequently testified at a 1980 US Senate hearing on Hollywood's use of stereotypes (Jeff Young, 'Bumbling, Senile Old Fools – Last of Hollywood Stereotypes?' *Los Angeles Herald Examiner*, 27 April 1980).

HOW DID STRASBERG VALUE THE STARDOM OF HIS LAST YEARS?

The answer to this first question lies hidden in subtext. Strasberg usually called acting a 'relaxing' break from teaching, a mere 'diversion' (Philip K. Scheuer, 'Strasberg: A Man and His Method', *Los Angeles Times*, 25 June 1978; Hager, 1980). 'Don't call it a career,' he warned, 'I'm too old to start a career' (Hager, 1980):

> For me, acting is a relaxation from work I must do and want to do but which for me is physically exhausting ... You work so much harder when you are pushing someone else. Sometimes after a teaching session I can barely catch my breath.
>
> *(Michiko Kakutani, 'Ruth Gordon and Lee Strasberg: Two Old Troupers Who Age Like Fine Wine', New York Times, 23 November 1979)*

His words hide three interrelated messages. First, if little more than relaxation is at stake, then any failure to match fame as an actor to that of his reputation as a teacher becomes unimportant. Strasberg thus erects a tidy defence against potential criticism. Second, if acting is easy enough to serve as relaxation, then his skill must exceed that of his best students who consistently had told him how hard it is. Strasberg thus flaunts his mastery. 'I started ... in the movies with no experience', but 'it was much easier for me to do the things that I tell myself to do than to get other people to do what I tell them' (Scheuer, 1978). Columbia Pictures aggressively traded on his assumed superiority. 'Categorizing Strasberg as an "actor" is admittedly an understatement – like calling Leonard Bernstein a "musician" or Jacques Cousteau a "skin diver"' (... And Justice for All, PN 1979). Third, Strasberg implicitly reprimands students who had complained that technical aspects of cinema interfere with their creative work. He said, 'I had always told actors, who I thought were griping about things they shouldn't, that the griping came from the fact that they hadn't done their job' (Scheuer, 1978).

His words hide deeper truths. When negotiating the contract for *Godfather, Part II* (1974, USA), he delayed signing in order to force an increase in salary (Adams, 1980: 370). After his debut, he pursued roles with great energy. Such behaviour contradicts the studied casualness in his statements about his risky new career. In honest moods, Strasberg admitted difficulties which he generally preferred to deny. 'I had the tools, but I hadn't used them continuously, so some things didn't work,' he said (*Time Magazine*, 16 December 1974). Since film-makers 'gear everything for the lights and camera angles,' he also said, 'you hardly ever see scenes done over because of the acting. This makes it hard to do exciting work' (*Village Voice*, 11 December 1974).

If acting meant more to him than a holiday from teaching, stardom meant even more than acting – it carried special rewards. For one thing, Strasberg's screen appearances served as imprimatur for his teaching. Reviews of *Godfather, Part II* stressed that he 'practis[ed] what he preached to generations of actors' (Charles Champlin, '*Godfather II*: Expanding the epic,' *Los Angeles Times*, 7 December 1974; Gordon Gow, *Films and Filming*, August 1975). Critics emphasised that he had refuted an old adage. 'Anyone who still believes that those who can do, and those who can't teach should watch Lee Strasberg at work ... and repent' (*Time Magazine*, 16 December 1974). He showed Hollywood 'that he knows how to act even if he was an acting teacher' (Earl Wilson, 'The Prof Shows Them How', *Los Angeles Herald Examiner*, 4 January 1975). He had proven himself at last. At a dinner in June 1975, honouring him for 50 years of service, he betrayed a secret truth in the guise of a joke. 'I was surprised to hear about my testimonial. . . . I wonder if they're doing it because I became an actor and am now "respectable"' (Ron Pennington, 'NEA Rejects Strasberg Plan', *Hollywood Reporter*, 5 June 1975). A star on Hollywood Boulevard, planted in front of his private school (the Lee Strasberg Theatre Institute), on his 76th birthday, made that respect palpable.

For another thing, Strasberg had finally experienced the kind of stardom that he had long admired in others. As mentor to the stars, Strasberg had always shared in the glow of their fame. In analysing performances of Brando, Pacino and de Niro, Strasberg said royally of himself, 'Certainly, their talent is not due to us. ... But the particular character of it, the nature of it, the use of it, that I feel has been encouraged by us, to say the least' (*Godfather, Part II*, PN 1974). Until *Godfather, Part II*, the public knew Strasberg only through his protégés. 'He befriended Monroe, he scolded Pacino, he made Burstyn cry' (*People Magazine*, 13 December 1976). Strasberg recognised his fame as reflected glory. As actor Madeleine Thornton-Sherwood said, 'Lee knew his reputation was based on movie actors' (Hirsch, 1984: 160).

Despite such fame, the traditional kind had eluded and allured him. At least one critic speculated that 'he was tired of seeing pupils like Marlon Brando, Al Pacino, and Jane Fonda get all the credit' (*Time Magazine*, 16 December 1974). This speculation finds support in Strasberg's adulation of stars. His relationships were not strictly pedagogical; he stood in awe of celebrities as surely as any fan. He was, as Burgess Meredith avowed, 'star-struck' (*People Magazine*, 13 December 1976). 'Whenever a star called, Lee went running,' actor Carl Shaeffer recalled (Hirsch, 1984: 160). Far from endearing, his students found this trait maddening. They resented his deferential treatment of the famous. They bristled when he treated Anne Bancroft with more respect than beginners, when he praised Barbra Streisand's Juliet despite poor diction, when he suggested great classic roles for Marilyn Monroe even as he cautioned others to avoid such roles as beyond their grasp (1984: 161–2). What had been mild annoyance in earlier years became especially problematic in 1955 when Monroe became their guru's favourite. Strasberg allowed her to break Studio rules that remained otherwise hard and fast. She could observe sessions without becoming a member; she could choose membership whenever she wished and without the necessary audition (an option which she never exercised); she could live with him as if she were an adopted child. Strasberg's favouritism prodded Studio members into open criticism. They saw her presence at the Studio as 'a sign of Lee's lust for success', to borrow Jack Garfein's phrase (Hirsch, 1984: 161).

Strasberg's behaviour toward stars seemed to betray his loftiest and most cherished principles. Even as he cautioned actors against selling out to Hollywood and persuaded many to forego commercial work for fear of damaging their artistic instincts (Hirsch, 1984: 160), he bowed to those who had sold out. His film career seemed to furnish further proof of betrayal. During the late 1970s, he maintained his idealism by supporting the creation of a National Theatre, and appealing to the US National Endowment for the Arts for support. Next to news of his failed grant proposal, there appeared a photograph with words that stressed his commitment to art. 'Strasberg seems determined to preserve the integrity of his ideas at any cost – even if that means disassociating them from his star advertisements' (*Village Voice*, 11 December 1974). Despite such publicity, however, he sought commercial roles exclusively in films, fully aware that cinema promises fame. 'One movie,' he notes, 'is much more than many plays because of the exposure it gives you. You do one movie and the next week a lot of people will know you' (*Going in Style*, PN 1979). Moreover, Strasberg had such a finely honed sense of what it meant to behave like a star that he had criticised Pacino's humility during the filming of *Godfather, Part II*, saying that he 'hadn't learned to be a star yet' (Adams 1980: 372).

After he had appeared in *Boardwalk* and … *And Justice for All*, both of which received mixed reviews, one critic charged Strasberg with hypocrisy.

> The really pertinent point is that by appearing in these films, Strasberg has, first, denigrated the principles he has been teaching by separating principle from practice, and second, he has implicitly denigrated film. He implies that his friends and students will recognize that it's 'only a film', that one 'does if for the money'.
>
> *(New Republic, 24 November 1979)*

After *Going in Style*, another critic wrote, 'by now, Lee Strasberg ought to be able to dope out a script as well as anyone. Yet, in back-to-back films he has chosen movies with disheartening structural flaws' (Tom Allen, 'Benchwarmer', *Village Voice*, 17 January 1980). With the development of his film career, critics began to echo in public what had long been murmured in the halls of the Actors Studio.

Just three days before Strasberg died, he lent his talents to a benefit for the Actors Fund called The Night of One Hundred Stars, by appearing in a high-kicking chorus line at Radio City Music Hall. Wager wryly observed, 'He died dancing with celebrities. How ironic, and how appropriate in a ghastly sort of way' (Hirsch, 1984: 164–5). Had Strasberg's personal ambition conquered his idealism? Or had his students placed him on such a high pedestal that they could never fully accept that he, like they, had feet of clay? However judged, his behaviour proves that he valued his role as movie star enough to jeopardise his status as theatrical idealist.

HOW DID STRASBERG'S PERSONA AS TEACHER AND MAKER OF STARS FEED INTO HIS IMAGE AS ACTOR?

Of the metaphors used to describe Strasberg the teacher, that of patriarch finds clearest expression in his roles. In particular, Hyman Roth in *Godfather, Part II* and Grandpa Sam in … *And Justice for All* present Strasberg with opportunities to play out paternal aspects of his relationship with his real life protégé, Al Pacino.

Clearly the richer role, Roth successfully embodies contradictory aspects of Strasberg's pedagogical image. The Jewish mafia leader promotes and competes with a younger

Italian version of himself, in turn supporting, advising and threatening Michael Corleone. Coppola explains, 'I hope to give the impression that Michael has met his match in this wily old man who is a survivor' (*Godfather, Part II,* PN 1974).

Reviews called Strasberg's casting as Roth 'brilliant' and 'showmanly' (Pauline Kael, *New Yorker,* 23 December 1974; *Variety,* 11 December 1974). The public learned that Pacino, with the help of Strasberg's wife, tricked Coppola into meeting the famed guru and that the teacher asked for Pacino's reassurance that the film would have 'quality' worthy of his efforts (*Godfather, Part II,* PN 1974; Adams, 1980: 366–72). Such stories ensured that the public would view Strasberg's work through the prism of his pedagogical stardom and artistic idealism.

In short, Coppola typecast the role, not only paying attention to age and ethnicity, but to Strasberg's unique reputation. 'Like Roth, Strasberg was of New York, a Jew, a man with tremendous mystery that he's known for in his classes.' Moreover, by pairing Strasberg with Pacino, Coppola uses their off-screen relationship to sharpen on-screen 'competition between the mentor and the apprentice' (*Godfather, Part II,* PN 1974). When Pacino as Corleone says to Strasberg as Roth, 'You are a great man. There's much I can learn from you', the line between fiction and reality becomes especially thin. Coppola directed Strasberg to think of Roth as an old director with a young protégé in tow. 'And the old director loved the young director to come and listen to his stories. But at the same time, he hated the young director, because the young director was his ultimate replacement and therefore the symbol of his death' (*Godfather, Part II,* PN 1974).

The image of patriarch rang true in the final cut of the film. Strasberg 'sounds like a grand-father' giving advice about the importance of health and happiness. When Roth tells his associates what they will inherit at his death, Strasberg behaves 'as though he were handing out Kennedy half-dollars to the grandchildren for Hanukkah' (Barthel, 1975). Strasberg's problematic personality could also be read on the screen. He blends 'ordinariness and suggested evil' (Barthel, 1975); Roth is 'ruthless and durable' (*Hollywood Reporter,* 11 December 1974), 'wry and cynical' (Liz Smith, 'Encore', *Cosmopolitan,* March 1975), with 'deceptively folksy charm' (Charles Champlin, '*Godfather II*: Expanding the Epic,' *Los Angeles Times,* 7 December 1974). In short, as most expect from a Method per-formance, Strasberg seems to play himself. Historian of the Actors Studio, Foster Hirsch (1984: 292) explicitly makes the connection when he writes that Roth is 'paternalistic yet intimidating (like Strasberg at the Studio!)'.

By contrast, Grandpa Sam presents only one side of Strasberg's paternal image. Sam expresses unconditional love and pride in his grandson, Arthur Kirkland, a lawyer who struggles to maintain his integrity in a corrupt system. Yet, as 'a senior citizen who has outlived his memory' (*. . . And Justice for All,* PN 1979), love is distorted by senility. He forgets that Arthur practises law, assumes that he is still in school, and asks the same questions again and again. The role's pathos necessarily restricts Strasberg to 'an affecting cameo as Pacino's loving but senile grandfather' (Arthur Knight, *Westways*, November 1979). Consequently, Strasberg loses the edge of mystery and danger that had made Roth so complex. Sam misplaces his false teeth, drinks milk like a child from a cardboard container, and complains about a Thanksgiving meal that has been bought rather than prepared. He gives love without understanding. As Kirkland, Pacino tempers patient concern for the man who once put him through school, with impatient tolerance of Sam's forgetfulness. Love is still ambivalent, but sweetly and ironically so.

Advance publicity emphasised that casting Strasberg 'reunites Pacino with the distinguished acting coach who was one of his early teachers'. Director Norman Jewison points out that 'the warm relationship between the two actors [reflects] a bond that goes back many years [and] comes through on film' (. . . *And Justice for All*, PN 1979). Strasberg, however, expressed a more critical regard for Pacino than had appeared in publicity surrounding *Godfather, Part II*. On the one hand, Strasberg praises Pacino as 'one of the most complete actors I have ever known' (. . . *And Justice for All*, PN 1979). On the other hand, Strasberg criticises Pacino for 'taking his characters too much to heart. It's not right that he should continue to carry that identity around with him so long after the play or movie is over. It isn't healthy' (*Village Voice*, 11 December 1974). Strasberg thus uses interviews to remind the public of his powerful role as judgmental father, an aspect of his persona stolen from him by the film's conception of Sam.

DO STRASBERG'S PERFORMANCES ON FILM ILLUMINATE WHAT HE TAUGHT?

One reviewer directly asked the guru this question. '"Did you," I deadpanned, "think of applying the Method to yourself?" "Yes, of course," [Strasberg] returned. "The Method is nothing more than an analysis of what good actors have done when they have acted well"' (Scheuer, 1978). In this answer, Strasberg voices his persistent opinion that Method acting subsumes everything which successful actors do, and that any actor who rejects his teaching is in denial. From this point of view, Strasberg can be said to use Method techniques if we think he acts successfully. I invite you to approach the question more specifically, however. The Method tends to prefer realism as style, to teach that the director shapes performance (Carnicke, 1999), and to privilege certain acting techniques such as relaxation, objects of attention, and affective memory. Strasberg's film work can be viewed through the prism of these fundamental elements.

First, consider cinematic style. At the very least, Strasberg reveals his facility with psychological realism, a style often associated with Method acting. Despite Coppola's assertion that Roth was 'an amalgam of leading men from the syndicate' (*Godfather, Part II*, PN 1974) and Strasberg's disclaimer that he had done no research (*Los Angeles Herald Examiner*, 25

October 1988; Adams, 1980: 374), reviewers saw Roth as a truthful portrait of the famous Jewish mobster, Meyer Lansky. Anna Strasberg reported that her husband's portrayal had been so accurate that Lansky himself telephoned to 'praise' the likeness (*Los Angeles Herald Examiner*, 25 October 1988). Columnist James Bacon avowed the same. 'I used to know Meyer back in the days when he hung around the Flamingo in Las Vegas, and Strasberg's performance is so close to the real thing, it is eerie' ('Academy Award Caliber', *Los Angeles Herald Examiner*, 13 December 1974).

Rather than mimicry, however, the Method encourages an illusion of reality through the actors' ability to mask technique. In this regard, Strasberg successfully hides his acting, 'never for an instant seeming to act, yet acting truly: being, breathing, living the role he plays' (Gow, 1975). 'Lee Strasberg wears Hyman Roth snugly, like a first-hand skin. [. . . He] attains the classic objective: art that conceals art' (Barthel, 1975). His performance in *Going in Style* was praised as 'honest acting' (*Hollywood Reporter*, 19 December 1979). Strasberg accomplishes this feat in two ways: by building his characters through small details of everyday life and by internalising the character's thoughts and concerns.

Regarding details, Strasberg taught that the material world (furniture, hand props and objects on the set) provides a bridge to the imaginary world of the play. As he put it, 'A real thing will help to make an imaginary thing real. That's the basic thing in the Method – the way in which you turn on your imagination to believe in, to experience, to live through whatever it is the character's going through' (David Alexander, 'Lee Strasberg', *Season Ticket*, September 1980). Strasberg grounds Roth in the real world and expresses him through ordinary gestures. Roth watches television and eats a tuna fish sandwich for lunch. Although he celebrates his birthday with leading members of the underworld, he behaves simply, reacting in surprise at the appearance of the cake, cutting it with little ceremony, and joking about his age with his guests. Even in heightened moments, Strasberg uses everyday expressions. As he listens to Corleone's story about a Cuban rebel who commits suicide, Strasberg embodies Roth's edgy disagreement in subtle ways. 'Roth's fork poises over his cake, steady and still. His voice is level, there will be no problem. Then his eyes flicker upwards toward Michael, re-appraising' (Barthel, 1975). In the climactic scene when Roth confronts Corleone with his suspicions of betrayal, strange little clicks emerge from his throat, 'small nervous coughs' (Champlin, 1974), as tokens of his anger. Scholar Steve Vineberg describes these clicks as 'the imagined sound of a pacemaker as his burdened heart starts to race, but it's creepy, too, like a snake's rattle' (Vineberg, 1991: 110). Critic Pauline Kael relates this audible gesture to craft, noting that Strasberg's 'breath control is impeccable' (Kael, *New Yorker*, 23 December 1974). Yet, this eerie sound comes from Strasberg's private expressive arsenal. Burgess Meredith describes hearing this sound in his first session at the Actors Studio. 'Very occasionally he made a kind of click sound in the back of his throat. I learned later that this "tic" seemed to indicate his inner emotion or excitement' (Meredith, 1965: xii).

Internalising Roth's attitudes toward those around him served as Strasberg's primary means for preparation of the role, mirroring the Method's emphasis on creating a character's inner life. Speaking as if he were himself Roth, Strasberg explains, 'In the back of my mind was the feeling that all the people I've worked with – and even more the people I *haven't* worked with – would say, "Oh, he thinks he's somebody"' (Barthel, 1975). Strasberg's approach creates a performance that reviewers saw as 'subtly underplayed' (Barthel, 1975) and remarkable for its 'simplicity' (Donald Lyons, 'Screen Scene', *Interview*, January 1975). Indeed, critics marvelled at his ability to avoid the clichés of his own teachings. 'Those for whom the Studio and the Method are synonyms for indulgence will be surprised by Strasberg's thorough precise approach to his role' (*Time Magazine*, 16 December 1974).

Second, consider that film directors shape performances concretely through camerawork and editing; consequently, actors have much less autonomy than on stage. With an eye to this reality, Strasberg paid professional respect to his directors, despite the familiar stereotype that paints Method actors as difficult. Recall *Tootsie* (1982, USA) in which Dustin Hoffman, himself a Method actor, plays a Method actor who finds himself blacklisted for his unwillingness to cooperate with directors. In stark contrast, Strasberg taught that 'the performance is created by the director, rather than the actor' (Lee Strasberg, 'The Definition of Acting', *Footlights*, June 1978), and that the actor's primary job is to produce credible emotion and behaviour as requested by the director. In short, the good actor is 'capable of giving the director anything that he wants' (Strasberg, 5 December 1961). Strasberg strove to be just such an actor. As difficult as he had been as a director and teacher, he became a model of congeniality as an actor. Directors and co-stars alike testify to his cooperative spirit. Coppola said, 'I found Lee Strasberg to be warm and full of interesting ideas and incredibly patient' (*Godfather, Part II*, PN 1974). Tony Lo Bianco, his acting partner in *The Last Tenant*, agreed. 'I expected some problem, you know, not having been trained in the Method. But Lee was tremendous – very responsive – always wanting to get everything perfect' (*Godfather, Part II*, PN 1974). His last director, the 28-year-old newcomer, Martin Brest, added his voice to the echo. 'Because he is a philosopher of acting, one would think he'd be difficult to work with. ... But just the opposite is true. He's receptive to suggestions and very malleable' (Hager, 1980). In his working attitudes, clearly Strasberg practised what he preached.

Third, observe his performances for evidence of Method techniques. This task proves to be the most elusive as well as the most illustrative. While directors generally expect audiences to recognise cinematic style, specific acting techniques remain stubbornly illegible. The actor's work can be read only in the series of vocal and physical gestures recorded by the camera. Methods by which the actor produced these signs of character can only be inferred. However, Strasberg's teaching about the essential importance of relaxation, objects of attention and emotional memory suggests avenues for analysis.

The relaxed actor uses only the amount of energy necessary to accomplish the scenic action. In other words, relaxation means that the actor finds the level of tension appropriate to the character's emotional situation. During scenes in *Godfather, Part II*, Strasberg appears physically relaxed but vocally tense. He sprawls comfortably with his legs in open, vulnerable positions, suggesting that Roth feels at east and secure.

However, the rhythm of his speech belies his postures. He speaks slowly and deliberately in short phrases, stopping for breaths and pausing for thought. Perhaps Roth chooses his words carefully, guarding his thoughts. Or perhaps Strasberg takes care to pronounce his lines correctly, without the parenthetical verbal gestures ('you see', 'and so on and so forth') that characterised his personal speech. Critics saw this dissonance between posture and speech as appropriate to Roth, identifying Strasberg's acting as 'calculated casualness' (John Simon, 'Films', *Esquire*, March 1975; Paul Zimmerman, *Newsweek*, 23 December 1974), and his scenes as 'casual, but not careless' (Barthel, 1975). Yet this dissonance may also signal Strasberg's inexperience in acting. He admits that he felt 'uneasy' while filming *Godfather, Part II*: 'When I watch the movie, I can see in some of the scenes the uneasiness' (Alexander, 1980). To my mind, his careful speech most clearly suggests this tension.

The actor's focus on objects of attention directs the viewer's eye to the character's priorities. Usually one's partner becomes the most important point of concentration. Thus, the Method actor learns to listen actively, think about what is said, and react continuously. Estelle Parsons quotes Strasberg as saying. 'A good actor acts for the audience. A great actor acts with the other actors for the audience' ('A Teacher's Inspiration', *Horizon*, January 1980). *Godfather, Part II* reveals how masterfully Strasberg manages focus. In his first scene with Pacino, Strasberg controls the shape of the scene through his choice of objects of attention – television, Pacino and potato chip. When Corleone enters to discuss the recent murder of an old-timer in his family business, Strasberg as Roth lounges with one leg thrown across the arm of his easy chair. He watches a University of Southern California football game on television. 'His eyes never leave the TV screen' (Barthel, 1975). However, in the next moment Roth decides to deal directly with Corleone. Strasberg turns up the volume to mask the conversation and faces his guest. His posture becomes upright and alert. Strasberg now listens intently, looking into Pacino's eyes, responding with smiles and shrugs. Strasberg then signals the end of the scene by changing his object of attention. He looks away from Corleone to eat a potato chip, saying dismissively of the dead man, 'He's small potatoes.'

Affective memory, Strasberg explained, involves 'simply remembering how you felt during a similar experience in your life, and using this to create a living human being' (*Going in Style,* PN 1979). This technique attempts to turn uncontrollable aspects of the psyche into manageable material for the actor. 'We've always thought of emotion as irrational,' Strasberg says, but 'emotion can be treated logically' (Barthel, 1975). Two moments in Strasberg's films function as if they were emotional memories. The first occurs when Roth accuses Corleone of backing out of their Havana deal by relating a parable from the early days of Las Vegas about the mysterious murder of a young protégé. Telling the story revives the painful memory and reignites the anger which Roth felt at the murder. Strasberg then displays the way in which Roth characteristically represses emotion. 'This is the business we've chosen. . . . I let it go.' Strasberg said of Roth, 'I tried to create a facade of not showing emotion, the sense of a man for whom all things are business' (*Time Magazine*, 16 December 1974).

The second monologue occurs in *Going in Style*. Strasberg plays Willie, a retired cab driver who wakes up after a disturbing dream about his dead son. He tells how he once disbelieved and spanked the young boy, forever breaching their relationship. Willie remembers without reference to his acting partner. Strasberg directs his attention away from his concerned room-mate, looking out the window in order to better visualise the past. His friend stands by passively as if a surrogate audience, while Strasberg speaks with a thick voice on the verge of tears. As he proceeds with his story, his hand moves from his forehead, to his mouth, and finally to his heart. His lips tremble at the memory and his eyes fill with tears. While Roth's monologue clearly advances the relationship with Corleone, Willie's seems irrelevant to the narrative, a set piece. Brest has provided each of his stars with a moment that shows off his special talent: Art Carney dances to a steel band on a Manhattan street, exhibiting physical humour; George Burns ends the film with a dead-pan look of wry irony; and, true to the great debate over the Method's use of emotion, Strasberg emotes.

Both monologues narrate painful incidents from the past that call forth emotional responses; repressed anger in Roth, tears in Willie. Whether Strasberg used personal memories to create these moments remains a matter of speculation. However, both function as if they were affective memory exercises. While the Method values the use of real emotion, Strasberg ironically produced 'ice-cold' performances. Roth was 'cold-blooded' and Willie 'never elicits any emotional response more profound than curiosity', even though 'Mr Strasberg throws everything he knows about acting into the monologue' (Vincent Canby, 'Three Widowers Try "Going in Style"', *New York Times*, 25 December 1979). Sadly, 'one feels nothing' even when Willie dies (Frank Rich, 'Sunshine Boys', *Time Magazine*, 7 January 1980).

CONCLUSION

Overall, Strasberg's screen-acting projects careful technique, especially in regard to his ability to create focus through objects of attention, but remains emotionally aloof, much as he appeared to his students in the classroom. Steve Vineberg comments that 'if it's fair to offer Strasberg's own acting as evidence of his understanding of the role of emotion in acting, his portrayal of the mafioso Hyman Roth . . . is a remarkable example of "strong emotion curbed by ascetic control"' (Vineberg, 1991:109).

Assessment of Strasberg's acting, as of his teaching, swings from panegyric praise to dismissive disdain. Strasberg's Roth was seen as 'the dominant performance of the picture' (Vincent Canby, 'One Godfather too Many', *New York Times*, 22 December 1974), 'perfect' (Smith), 'a bull's eye performance' (Simon). As Grandpa Sam, Strasberg gives 'a beautiful interpretation of the hazards of time' (Robert Osborne, '... *And Justice for All*', *Variety*, 14 September 1979). 'The wisest critics have declined to dissect his performances,' writes one reviewer, 'relying instead on a catalogue of adjectives from "marvelous" to "marvelous"' (Barthel, 1975). Negative views saw his simplicity as flat and uninteresting. Of Roth, one spectator remarks, 'I don't know whether Strasberg is a boring actor or is simply doing an effective job of playing a boring character. I can't help wishing that instead of just sitting on that Havana terrace dolefully munching his birthday cake, Strasberg had really chewed up some of the scenery' (Hal Mark Arden, 'Letter to the Editor', *New York Times*, 23 February 1975). After the opening of *Boardwalk*, one reviewer mused that 'it may well be that Lee Strasberg is the master teacher of acting that many call him even though he is a platitudinous and unaffecting actor. ... What an example for his students! That he's a poor actor and doesn't know it, that he has the ego to want to act despite his limitations' (*New Republic*, 24 December 1975). Recent assessments follow the same contentious pattern. Strasberg's film appearances serve as 'the best promo anyone could ever have done for his approach to Method acting' (Vineberg, 1991: 110), or as proof of the Method's flaws: 'His performances are unrevealing. They certainly lack the emotional explosiveness of his finest students, but they also lack the introspection and self-indulgences of his worst. Straightforward, workmanlike, his acting has little to distinguish it from that of thousands of other Hollywood character actors' (Hornby, 1992: 174). Perhaps all these varying views prove only how subjective judgements about acting can be.

Ultimately, Strasberg's impact on film acting remains one of the most productive avenues for assessing his work, whether as teacher or actor. That Strasberg found fame as a guru for actors who excelled on screen rather than on stage speaks directly to his vision of acting that encodes the style of psychological realism, encourages an illusion of genuine life, and de-emphasises virtuosity in performance. Before his film debut he would have dismissed screen acting. Afterward, he said 'I am not one who thinks of movie acting as being less than stage action. Movie acting can be even more real; you don't have to worry about projection and sound' (Barthel, 1975). His words betray his underlying assumption – that good equals real, a belief that began with his theatrical reading, developed in the Group Theatre, and continued to condition critical assessment of acting at the Actors Studio. 'The basic thing in the Method is the way everybody tries to be real,' Strasberg notes (Alexander, 1980). This belief often underlies judgements about screen acting to this day, and in his acting Strasberg reflects this basic value. Coppola said of Strasberg, 'the sheer eccentricity of his being and of his voice and just how interesting he looked seemed to make [Roth] real' (*Godfather, Part II*, PN 1974). Moreover, Strasberg also taught actors to rely on directors as auteurs, a view sympathetic to cinematic art. Strasberg correctly sees the Method as an 'ideal means for an actor to summon up his best at a given moment. . . . That is why so many of our people have been so immediately successful in the movies, almost more than in the theatre' (*Going in Style*, PN 1979). Perhaps Strasberg did not sell out to Hollywood as his students insisted, but finally recognised the true value of his teaching to cinema.

---

1   Quotations from sources other than from books are mainly drawn from cuttings held in the Margaret Herrick Library, Academy of Motion Pictures, Los Angeles. This applies also to Production Notes (PN) relating to films discussed in this chapter. Specifically dated references to Strasberg refer to the Sound Recordings (1956–69) held in Wisconsin Center for Film and Theater Research, Madison, Wisconsin.

Chapter Eight

MEN IN SUITS: COSTUME, PERFORMANCE AND MASCULINITY IN THE BATMAN FILMS[1]

Thomas Austin

In the four live-action Batman features made by Warner Bros since 1989, the Caped Crusader has been played by three different star-actors:[2] Michael Keaton *(Batman*, 1989, USA, and *Batman Returns*, 1992, USA), Val Kilmer *(Batman Forever*, 1995, USA) and George Clooney *(Batman and Robin*, 1997, USA).[3] In each of the last two films, the opening sequence presents a new star-actor dressing for duty in the Batsuit, and so literally 'taking on' the role. These moments acknowledge that the familiar 63-year-old character of Batman precedes each filmic incarnation, and suggest that the role resides to a large extent in the costume – cowl and mask, suit emblazoned with logo, gauntlets and cape[4] – which is considered indispensable for the first appearance of a new player in the part.[5] Nevertheless, the precise way in which each star-actor inhabits the Batsuit depends upon a combination of the character-role, a star persona in process, and performance techniques grounded in the particular actor's body and voice – operating in conjunction with other cinematic codes, from script and *mise-en-scène* to cinematography and editing. In this chapter I set out to trace these inter-articulations while considering some of the masculinities variously embodied by this series of masked men, and the villains and victims which they encounter.

THE POLITICAL ECONOMY OF COSTUME

Such issues are shaped by, and need to be situated within, the political economy of contemporary Hollywood, in particular as it applies to family-oriented adventure films like the Batman series. A starting point for this contextualisation is provided by Robert Allen's discussion of licensed merchandising associated with the family film boom of the 1980s and 1990s. He argues that successfully branded franchises function as 'narrative and iconographic fields through which old licences are renewed and from which new licences can be harvested' (1999: 121). These commercial opportunities are facilitated by the 'toyetic' fantasy settings of many such films, from which action figures, video games, and transferable images can readily be derived. Allen suggests that the cultural and economic value of star-images appearing in this context should be reconsidered:

... with so much of the licencing and tie-in market directed at children, whose knowledge of or interest in any adult star might be non-existent, the value of a star's character likeness is based much less on star power than on preserving a coextensive identity between the licensable character in a film and its extra-filmic representation.[6]

(Allen, 1999: 120)

While Allen is largely concerned with the proliferation of Hollywood's merchandising strategies, and the consequent reorganisation of the boundaries of what might be termed 'the film' (1999: 119), I want to take the argument in a different direction, in order to consider the extensibility of film brands – notably the generation of sequels and television series derived from successful films.

Such operations rely upon a substantial degree of character likeness surviving the transfer from the initial property. But spin-offs usually attempt to retain recognisable components of the original film without incurring the expense of a returning star.[7] For example, the hit films *Stargate* (1994, USA) and *Ace Ventura: Pet Detective* (1994, USA) spawned successful television series that borrowed narrative premise, character, and – in the case of *Stargate* – iconography, while liberated from the financial obligations of star appearances.[8]

The inclusion of notably costumed – and masked – characters facilitates this uncoupling of character likeness from star presence, so enabling it to be re-deployed in commercial opportunities further down the product line.[9] Thus, commodities such as the animated television series derived from *The Mask* (1994, USA),[10] the comic book and television variations on *Robocop* (1987, USA)[11] and Warner Bros' three animated series, *Batman: The Animated Series* (1992), *Gotham Knights* (1997) and *Batman Beyond* (1999), have all proved reasonably successful without the film stars who played the eponymous lead roles. In these cases, star presence – in combination with other inputs, including script, distinctive costumes and iconography – has secured (or revived) cultural status and economic value for a character and concept which may then be detached from that presence and exploited in branded spin-offs.[12]

MATCHING STAR-ACTOR AND CHARACTER

The star/character interface also needs to be considered in relation to a second, discursive, project: the attempted alignment of these two. The fact that three different star-actors have played Batman in less than a decade foregrounds issues of casting, performance and the articulation of the role with distinct star personae.[13] In each instance, efforts have been made through promotion and publicity to blend star and character into a successful (that is, 'convincing') alloy. Such a strategy can be seen in part as an attempt to mitigate the centrifugal impact upon narrative that may be exerted by a star presence. As Miriam

Hansen has noted, star-actors not only invite audiences into film narratives by cueing investment in the characters they play. At times, star performance 'weakens the diegetic spell in favor of a string of spectacular moments that display the "essence" of the star' (1991: 246–7). I would suggest that the *mis*casting of a star threatens to unleash this intertextual dynamic in ways that can be particularly disruptive to mechanisms of narrative involvement.

Jack Nicholson's role as Jack Napier/the Joker in *Batman* has been cited by Justin Wyatt (1994) as a prime instance of how star and character are matched in 'high concept' Hollywood cinema.[14] Star persona and performance in character are mutually reinforcing, Wyatt argues, such that there is a 'close fit between Nicholson's star persona, the role of the Joker, and [his] ostentatious mode of acting' which contrasts with more naturalistic modes employed by the film's other actors (1994: 33). These three elements converge to produce Nicholson/the Joker as a madcap 'bad boy'. Not all star/character pairings are so 'self-evident', however. Sustained efforts frequently have to be made in promotional discourses to assert and secure such matches as 'natural' and 'inevitable'.[15] This is especially important with a role such as Batman. The character's multiple incarnations in comic books, television shows and merchandise precede his recent appearances on film. The familiar role will carry particular expectations, at least for many members of the prospective audience.[16] Casting Batman is thus a hazardous undertaking, as evidenced by reports of fan dissatisfaction and the vigorous attempts made to justify such decisions. Personnel interviews carried in satellite texts such as press packs and film magazines may operate in order to establish points of concordance between the star-actor and the role he or she plays. That said, the two are never entirely co-extensive. Moreover, the Batman role does afford a limited degree of elasticity, and allows for some rewriting of the character, the better to fit with a given star persona, as will become clear.

The casting of Michael Keaton in *Batman* became one focus for fan anxiety and discursive attempts to rebut such concerns (see Terry Minsky, *Premiere* (US), July 1989: 48–55). Keaton's public image in the late 1980s is better described as that of a 'picture personality'[17] rather than a fully fledged star. He was best known for his appearances in the comedies *Night Shift* (1982, USA), *Mr Mom* (1983, USA) and *Beetlejuice* (1988, USA, directed, like *Batman*, by Tim Burton). Keaton's (mis)casting in the title role led to well-publicised complaints from fans and commentators acting as would-be gatekeepers for the Batman canon.[18]

Particular grounds for disappointment about the casting of Keaton were provided by his perceived corporeal deficiency. For instance, science fiction writer Harlan Ellison commented: 'Michael Keaton truly contravenes the whole point of Batman. Here's the only prominent superhero without special powers; here's one of the very best detectives who ever lived, and he's being played by a scrawny comedian in plastic armor' (cited in Uricchio and Pearson, 1991: 183). The 'scrawny' physique derided here appears to be a long way from the 'musculinity' (Tasker, 1993b: 237) of male 'hard body' action stars such as Arnold Schwarzenegger and Sylvester Stallone (Jeffords, 1994). While the comparison is not made explicit, Ellison expresses contempt for the notion of a 'heroic' body that is reliant upon plastic armour in the absence of 'real' musculature. There is, however, a common element, in that both Keaton-as-Batman and the muscle stars rely upon significant inputs to produce their particular constructions of masculinity.

On the one hand, the Batsuit 'overwrites' the actor's own physique, covering up the naked body, even while gesturing at corporeal revelation by drawing attention to pectorals and abdomen (and, in *Batman Forever* and *Batman and Robin*, nipples, codpiece and, ultimately, buttocks).[19] On the other hand, the labour and self-presentation of body-building result in an 'enhanced' body shape that is no more natural. Thus, both dressing-up and bulking-up can be seen as performances of masculinity, in the sense that these notions of what it is to be male are fabricated and worked at, rather than occurring naturally. At this level, there is not so much difference between the Batsuit with its moulded body parts and the 'simulacra of exaggerated masculinity' (Creed, 1987, cited in Tasker, 1993b: 232) presented by muscle men such as Schwarzenegger and Stallone.

In all four Warner Bros films, the Batsuit has a crucial function in the attempt to secure a degree of what John O. Thompson (1985: 66) (following C.S. Peirce) calls 'iconic meaning', that is, a relationship of resemblance between actor and character role – even if the very presence of the costume may also foreground the 'inadequacy' of the body beneath it, as Ellison suggests. In the case of Batman or any other well-known role, whether factual or fictional, the requisite characteristics of the part will of course vary according to unevenly distributed viewer knowledges, repertoires and expectations. But, at the risk of generalisation, Batman's traits and attributes may be reasonably taken to include, for many viewers, 'wealth; physical prowess; deductive abilities and obsession' (Uricchio and Pearson 1991: 186). The whiteness of Batman (often taken for granted) should also be noted: his freedom of movement in urban and social space, and his ability to function beyond the law, yet with supra-legal authority, appear as raced entitlements. The familiar costume functions as an efficient short-hand for many of these characteristics.

The costume is not entirely sufficient in itself, however, as the controversy over Keaton demonstrates. So, rather than simply rely upon the Batsuit, promotional discourses stressed that key attributes were shared by star-actor and character, in order to align the two further. Thus, in the official press pack for the film, Keaton and Batman were ingeniously matched via their 'ordinary' American guy-ness:

[quoting Tim Burton:] 'It would have been very easy to go for a square-jawed hulk, but if some guy is 6'5" with gigantic muscles, and incredibly handsome, why does he need to put on an armored Batsuit with an arsenal of weapons and hightech gadgets? Why doesn't he just put on a ski mask and beat the daylights out of bad guys? In our film there's a mere mortal underneath that scary Batsuit.'

(Batman Production Information, 1989: 4)[20]

Burton's commentary is an attempt to engineer a match of types between Keaton and Batman, via the notion of the 'ordinary guy'.[21] The effort is not entirely successful, however, as the role of Batman is an aggregate of several character types – obsessive vigilante, thoughtful detective, energetic superhero, and (as Bruce Wayne) millionaire socialite and philanthropist – of which 'mere mortal' is only one, and not the most obvious one at that.[22] In other words, Keaton playing Batman can hardly be said to be an obvious example of type casting, despite the attempts made to establish similarities and affinities between actor and role.

Many discourses around star casting draw upon physiognomy in order to reckon the appropriateness of a decision. This is certainly true in the case of Batman: he is often expected to possess a reasonably athletic body,[23] and the lower portion of his face is rendered highly visible when he is masked for action. Moreover, as a character Batman carries a number of (somewhat variable, rather than entirely fixed) connotations about 'heroic' masculinity.[24] Not surprisingly then, many discussions of the casting of Keaton, and, later, Val Kilmer and George Clooney, judged 'character' and associated types of masculinity from physical appearance – not just body shape, but also the face. According to such logics, Keaton's deficit was not so much his comedic background,[25] but his lack of stature and his 'weak' chin. For example, the American film magazine *Premiere* stated:

The fact is, when Keaton isn't wearing his Batman paraphenalia, he doesn't look like the kind of person who would ever be in such an outfit. . . . Without the benefit of his Bat-biceps and his pointy Bat-ears, the 37-year-old Keaton could answer the call for an ordinary guy. He isn't physically imposing. His jaw doesn't jut and his voice doesn't boom, and his muscles, though well-defined, don't strain the fabric of his clothes. With the mask, he looks solemn and imperious; without it, his face has a friendly, playful quality, highlighted by Cupid's bow lips and a mischievous arch in his eyebrows.

(Minsky, 1989: 50)

The article noted that an on-set handyman failed to recognise Keaton as Batman, despite his half-suit (without mask, cape or insignia). The full costume is required to fix Keaton in character: 'The handyman is embarrassed by his gaffe. "S'pose I would've know that if you'd been wearing the mask and cape"' (Minsky, 1989: 50). By contrast, press commentary on subsequent star-actors playing the part (Kilmer in *Batman Forever* and Clooney in *Batman and Robin*) emphasised each actor's facial capital as an asset, freighted again with certain notions of masculinity.

Two key qualities which Kilmer was said to share with Batman were 'physicality and intellect' (Singer, 1995: 25). In addition, press commentary repeatedly emphasised his (hetero)sexual appeal to women, for which his pouting lips functioned as a synecdoche. For example, the British film magazine *Empire* commented:

> Kilmer cuts a fine, more regal figure as Bruce Wayne. He is slick and sexy, And as the caped crusader he leaps, loops and displays *those* lips. When your body is smothered by a jet-black rubber suit, leaving only the square jaw visible, the lips become real important. Just ask Nicole Kidman, who as love interest Chase Meridian, got to try them out for size. . . . 'He has the best lips I have ever seen,' she giggles. That's very important from a female perspective.
>
> *(Ian Nathan,* Empire, *August 1995: 113)*[26]

When Kilmer took the title role in *Batman Forever*, Batman's bare chest was revealed three times. The display of Kilmer/Batman's 'real' chest underneath the fabricated contours of the Batsuit may have been an attempt to guarantee the veracity of the costume, and thus to assert the 'authenticity' of Kilmer and/as Bruce Wayne/Batman: in contrast to Keaton's problematically covered-up body, neither the suit nor the man wearing it are (too) 'fake'.

After one film, Kilmer left the Batman franchise to play The Saint. He was replaced for *Batman and Robin* by George Clooney, a star-actor with a background as a heart-throb in the hospital-based television series *ER*, fresh from his first major film leads in the romantic comedy *One Fine Day* (1996, USA) and the vampire picture *From Dusk Til Dawn* (1996, USA). Like that of Kilmer, Clooney's face was judged in physiognomic terms to be well suited to Batman. However, the operative understanding of the character role expressed in press commentary and promotional discourses shifted slightly to accommodate his casting. For instance, director Joel Schumacher commented:

> The first three films had Batman brooding over the death of his parents. George is 36 years old, if you haven't gotten over it by then, well, you just want to shriek, 'Come on, lighten up, get with it.' So, we've matured him, he

is actually more interested in *other* people. And George has brought a real humanity, there is a wonderful relationship with Alfred, who finds he is ill.

(*Ian Nathan,* Empire, *July 1997: 107*)

Star and role are matched via a shared maturity, confidence, and interest in others, in addition to a notable jawline. On the latter, Batman's creator Bob Kane sanctioned Clooney's casting by commenting, 'I feel George is the best Batman of all. He's suave, elegant, has a great profile with a strong chin, like the features of Batman in the comic books' (Singer, 1997: 6). Clooney's bedside manner as Dr Ross in *ER* is recalled in the film when he is called upon to care for both the ailing butler Alfred, and Robin, incapacitated after losing a fight with Mr Freeze. As Uricchio and Pearson have noted, 'Robin's vulnerable reliance tends to reinforce [Batman's] more "human" dimensions' (1991: 197). Crucially, such dimensions accord with Clooney's star-persona, of which charm is a major part, sited to a large extent in his trademark grin.

Of course, the meanings of Batman's masculinity in any filmic incarnation are not only informed by intertextual factors such as star personae and the connotations accreted around the character role through its multi-media appearances. They are also constructed intratextually, in relation to the other characters that Batman encounters, from allies to villains and victims. In the following section, I develop this point with particular reference to *Batman Forever.* In doing so, I pay attention to (some) perform-ance practices in 'high concept' action cinema, a mode of film-making that is frequently regarded as a hostile environment in which to attempt, or look for, 'real' acting.

BODIES, VOICES AND IDENTITY IN *BATMAN FOREVER*

Actors' own statements and those of journalistic commentators tended to emphasise image styling and the physical labour of performance in the Batman films, rather than the emotional, psychological or oratorical demands of acting.[27] For instance, *Premiere* magazine's on-set report from *Batman* opened with this description of Keaton at work:

Oh, man, this mask is the worst. Your neck feels like it's in a vice, you've got no peripheral vision, and you can't really hear. . . . And the sweat – ten takes, eleven, twelve . . . you're fuckin' *dying* in this thing. . . . And the cape. Weighs a ton. Kills your shoulders every time you throw a punch.

(*Minsky, 1989: 48*)

For Kilmer, *Batman Forever* was a source of some contempt – at least in retrospect – because it prioritised visuals over acting. Discussing his disagreements with director Joel

Schumacher, who reportedly refused to let him view dailies of his own performance, Kilmer said: 'for Joel my work wasn't about acting. It was a modelling experience; he wanted to ritually sell an image. Once I realized that this movie was going to be a two-hour ad for the toys, that nothing I did mattered, I wasn't a pain in the ass' (Richard Corliss, *Time* 149(14), 7 April 1997: 73).

There is certainly an element of truth in Kilmer's remarks about the importance of the film's production design and its links to licensed merchandise. But his comments should not be taken entirely at face value. Batman's masculinity in *Batman Forever* is constructed in part via Kilmer's performance, including his bodily movements under the constraints of the Batsuit and the significance of the voice housed in the suited body. Both of these factors, in combination with script and direction, serve to distinguish Batman's particular masculinity from that of other key males in the film.[28]

Voice functions as an index of stability and authority in the film. While Batman possesses these attributes, the two villains with whom he battles, Two-Face (played by Tommy Lee Jones) and the Riddler (Jim Carrey), are unbalanced, literally and figuratively. This is signalled in part by their voices' much greater variances in volume and pitch.[29] They whisper, shriek, groan and give vent to their rapid moodswings vocally, and sometimes non-verbally. This general garrulousness signals a deficient masculinity.[30] By contrast, Batman often relies upon the taciturn masculine mode of 'strong silence' (Branston, 1995: 45). He is an embodiment of the cliché, a man of action and few words. What he says can be functional to the point of terseness: 'Give me your hand'; 'Hold on'. (These comments are addressed to a security guard bound and gagged by Two-Face. Overweight and sweaty, with a bald spot, glasses, a hearing aid and a relatively high-pitched voice, the guard is rather excessively marked as a site of inadequate masculinity, in contrast with the heroic masculinity of Batman.)

The way in which Batman speaks is also important. His voice is heard for the first time during the opening credits: in answer to Alfred's suggestion that he takes a sandwich with him he deadpans, 'I'll get drive-through.' Here and elsewhere the voice is husky, flat and somewhat thin – less sonorous than, for example, George Clooney's in *Batman and Robin*.[31] Kilmer/Batman sometimes talks rapidly, but is usually purposeful and unexcitable. This voice bespeaks authority. Batman has no need to shout or rage for people to listen to him.[32]

Use of the voice is thus a key part of Kilmer's performance as Batman, and those of his co-actors. Other important acting resources in quick-cut, fast-moving action cinema are gesture and carriage of the body, in conjunction with costume. Like his voice, Kilmer's deployment of his body as Batman is generally neat and well defined, controlled, focused and not 'excessive'. Unlike the guard writhing in a panic, and Two-Face throwing his head around and howling with rage or ecstasy, Batman's head and shoulders are a point of relative calm and stability. This is emphasised by the square and solid iconography of the suit and cowl, captured in a series of simple and graphic images. A small but important degree of embellishment is afforded by Batman's cape, however. Kilmer's movement of his body in this costume is crucial in establishing a point of distinction between Batman and Two-Face's thugs.

Batman's arrival at the Second Bank of Gotham in the film's initial action sequence is an energetic but perfectly measured swoop down by rope to the street, where a gawping crowd stand suitably impressed. Approaching the mumbling security guard, Kilmer/Batman makes a small leap into the walk-in safe where the victim lies, letting his cape flutter slightly around his calves in the process. Later, in a fight with Two-Face's gang, he skips over a dropped weapon and past two fallen heavies, and runs with surprisingly small steps down a corridor. His movements are limber and fluid.[33] The cumulative effect of costume and the movement of Kilmer in it is to emphasise the energy, mobility and athleticism of Batman, while maintaining a sense of power and strength. The former qualities stand in contrast to the relatively cumbersome, muscle-bound and block-headed masculinity of the gang members. Their blundering movements in turn serve to emphasise Batman's agility of body and, by implication, of mind too.

All these components play a part in constituting the physical, emotional and psychological authority of Batman. But it is important not to underestimate the spectacular impact and popular appeal of the melodramatic and 'unstable' villains confronting him. The villains provide both major star presences and degrees of novelty in a franchise built around a familiar and recurrent hero, setting and themes.[34] As George Clooney commented in the official *Batman and Robin* 'moviebook':

> The secret to Batman ... is that he's kind of the Johnny Carson of super heroes. ... [Carson] always made sure that the guest was the star. The truth of the matter is that the star of this movie is not Batman. The criminals are always the star, because they're so much bigger than life. Batman is the constant, the steady in this. ... My task is not to try and grab the attention all the time.
>
> *(Singer, 1997: 33)*

Clooney's analysis is borne out in the opening sequence of *Batman and Robin*, when Commissioner Gordon announces to Batman and the audience the latest 'guest appearance': 'a new villain has commandeered the Gotham Museum ... he's calling himself Mr Freeze'. The following scene shows Freeze (Arnold Schwarzenegger), spot-lit as he descends a staircase intent on stealing diamonds from the museum.

I will turn now to *Batman Forever*'s staging of the rivalry between Kilmer/Batman and the film's star villain, Jim Carrey as Edward ('E') Nygma, a disgruntled employee of Wayne Enterprises who transforms himself into the Riddler. While Batman is presented via body, voice and narrative function as purposeful, authoritative and heroic, Carrey's Riddler embodies a more open, fluid and insecure masculinity. Nygma is repeatedly presented as suffering from an identity crisis, as his name suggests. His booth at work is festooned with photos of Wayne; he mistakenly introduces himself as Wayne when he finally meets his glamorous boss; he tries out a list of possible 'superhero' identities on his computer (the Puzzler, the Gamester, Captain Kill) before settling on the Riddler; subsequently, he apes Wayne/Batman in both of his dual roles – slicked hair, wire-rimmed glasses and tuxedo as Edward Nygma, successful media inventor, and colourful comic book-style costume with matching accessory/weapon (the cane) as his alter ego the Riddler.[35]

Nygma's identity and his body seem more mobile, flexible, and ultimately vulnerable, than that of Batman. Nygma learns how to punch by copying Two-Face, dreams of usurping Wayne as Gotham's celebrity billionaire, and invents a device ('the box') which allows him to open up to other people's brainwaves, shown pouring into his head in a stream of lime green. On the other hand, Wayne/Batman inhabits a masculinity which is presented as secure, pre-existing, almost 'naturally' occurring.[36] He provides the enduring coordinates of an upright, heroic masculinity by which Nygma/the Riddler attempts to steer, and against which he falls short. Of course, any comparison of Batman and the Riddler has to acknowledge that Wayne/Batman also dresses up, and juggles two identities of his own. But this identity issue is familiar and routinised, rather than volatile and disorientating. As Batman asserts to the defeated Riddler, having overcome a moment of doubt, 'I'm both Bruce Wayne and Batman, not because I have to be, now because I choose to be.' By contrast, Nygma finally loses all sense of an identity of his own, and gives himself up to an overwhelming impersonation of Batman as he flaps theatrically in his cell at Arkham Asylum.

An exclusively narrative-centred analysis fails, however, to grasp the texture and – for this author at least – the pleasure of Carrey's performance as the manic Nygma/Riddler. In approaching Carrey and Kilmer as star-actors, and considering the strikingly different employment made of their bodies, it is tempting to recall Jerry Lewis's description of his comic double act with Dean Martin. This centred, Lewis recalled, on 'making a team out of the handsomest guy in the world and a monkey' (Bukatman, 1991: 190). *Batman Forever* toys with a similar pairing of the 'perfect man' with an uncontrollable, immature and 'imperfect' version. But Carrey's body in *Batman Forever* is not quite the belching, pissing, farting spectacle that it is in gross-out comedies like *Dumb and Dumber* (1994, USA) or *Me, Myself and Irene* (2000, USA). Sporting red hair and a lime green body suit as the Riddler, Carrey deploys a rapid succession of physical and vocal contortions, but his corporeal excesses are comparatively restrained. His body is more bendy than unruly.[37]

Nevertheless, the characters and masculinities of Batman and the Riddler are repeatedly counter-posed, with many of the contrasts written out across the star-actors' bodies, and realised by differing modes of performance. Carrey's movements in the part are exaggerated and expressive: cringing, dancing and gesticulating according to his shifting moods. This calculatedly frenetic and 'excessive' mode of (over-) acting contrasts with the more naturalistic performances of Kilmer, Kidman and most of the supporting cast. Clearly, a performance by a star comedian such as Carrey is not always securely integrated into narrative cinema's norms of character development and interaction. Carrey's playing of Nygma/the Riddler is largely motivated by and harnessed to these logics, but at times it threatens to exceed them.[38]

One example of this compromise between the comedian's routine and the demands of narrative progression is the scene where Nygma tries out his new invention on his boss, Fred Stickley. Staging, framing and editing of the sequence work to foreground Carrey's comic performance. As Fred sits strapped to a chair Nygma cavorts alongside, wearing the instantly recognisable costume of the 'mad scientist': a white coat with the breast pocket stuffed full of pens. Shot scale is adjusted throughout the scene to privilege the physical movements of Carrey's body: close-ups stress his bulging eyes and rapidly changing facial expressions of glee and anger; medium-long shots reveal more of his body, including wild hand gestures, such as those of mock dismay when Fred threatens disciplinary action; long shots reveal his rapid footwork as he dances on the spot while singing 'I'm sucking up your IQ' to the theme tune of the film *Top Hat* (1935, USA). But, in addition to showcasing the star comedian's skills, this performance has an important diegetic function. In conjunction with music, special effects and Ed Begley Jr's supporting role as Fred, it renders visible, audible and hence 'credible' the process whereby Nygma absorbs his boss's brain waves while the latter is entranced by the 3D television. The threat posed to Gotham's inhabitants by this device then becomes one of the film's subplots.

Compared to Nygma/the Riddler's ludic, manic masculinity, Batman may even seem stolid and dull to some viewers. The film effectively holds in balance these two contrasting masculinities, and the performance styles and genres with which they are commonly associated. Carrey/the Riddler's bendy body and mobile voice are those of the comedian comic, while Kilmer/Batman's upright, muscular frame and steady vocal delivery are those of the (glamorous) action hero. In this way, *Batman Forever*'s multiple address as that generic hybrid known as the family adventure film is rendered somatically by the bodies, voices and acting styles of its two major stars.[39]

The balancing act extends to the film's ambiguous presentation of Batman's sexuality. *Batman Forever* remains essentially uncommitted about this, or rather, it studiously plants cues which support conflicting interpretations. At the film's end, Bruce Wayne and Chase Meridian (Kidman) appear to be on the point of settling down – 'don't work too late,' she jokes – but it is Batman and Robin who run off together, dressed for duty in the emblematic slow-motion silhouette that closes the film. The clash between duty and a domestication associated with women is certainly a common device in American vigilante and superhero narratives (see Jewett and Lawrence, 1977). But the ending of *Batman Forever* can be seen as more than another instance of this convention, preceded as it is by several hints at the homosexual nature of the relationship between Batman and Robin. For instance, Manohla Dargis (*Sight and Sound*, August 1995: 41) notes Robin's reference to biker bars, and the 'bright red package' of his improved costume as cues to read the relationship as gay.[40] In effectively hedging its bets over which is the key sexual pairing (Batman with Robin or with Meridian) *Batman Forever* operates as an instance of what I have called the *dispersible text* – a film assembled with the aim of maximising its social reach and hence its commercial fortunes (Austin, 2002). If necessary, this goal is to be achieved at the expense of a degree of textual coherence. Thus, in contrast to the emphatically heterosexual celebration of Kilmer's good looks espoused in *Empire* magazine, Paul Burston (*Time Out*, 26 June 1995: 77) could equally lay claim to *Batman Forever* as a gay text: 'Short of changing the title to Batman and Robin Forever, it couldn't have been any more gay.'[41]

CONCLUSION

As a cultural product, Batman offers polysemic potential within any single film, in addition to dispersibility across multi-media forms. The character certainly has the mobility to accommodate some shifts in casting, along with possible future changes – much as Schumacher's two films have already incorporated gay readings.[42] Moreover, as I have demonstrated, the appearances and performances in the role of three different star-actors have had notable impacts upon the meanings of Batman, even while operating within the constraints presented by the commercial and aesthetic dimensions of this particular film franchise.

However, this is not to say that Batman is simply a tabula rasa, an empty vessel waiting to be filled in any way imaginable. For instance, in filmic manifestations at least, key continuities have persisted over and above the changes associated with different lead actors and production staff. Batman remains a wealthy vigilante with a battery of weapons and tools, who commands the authority of a 'natural' justice that sometimes chimes with, and sometimes takes precedence over, that of the written law. In addition, the character remains obviously and more or less unquestionably white (and male).[43] As a long-serving representation of the heroic, Batman is, for now at any rate, emblematic of not just the complexity and opportunistic flexibility of commercial popular culture, but also of some of the limits on that flexibility.

---

1   Thanks to Charlotte Adcock and Peter Kramer for insightful comments on drafts of this chapter.

2   This term encapsulates two important characteristics: that these are *professional actors* whose images circulate in, and are (re)constructed through, discourses of *celebrity*.

3 *Batman* grossed $413 million worldwide, *Batman Returns* $283 million, *Batman Forever* $333 million and *Batman and Robin* $237 million. Figures here and throughout are from imbd.com.

4 Bob Ringwood's redesigns of the Batsuit in *Batman Returns* and *Batman Forever* provided significant merchandising opportunities while remaining within this basic template.

5 Batman proved to be something of a star-making role in that it improved the status and earning power of Keaton and Kilmer, although neither fared particularly well at the box office in subsequent film roles. By contrast, George Clooney's career as a star-actor appears to have more potential for longevity. This success may have been shaped (although hardly guaranteed) by the fact that Clooney's face and 'charming' persona became quite securely established during his years as a star of the television drama *ER*. Thanks to Mike Hammond on this point.

6 Of course, given the multiple address of Hollywood's family films – to both adults and children – the casting of (adult) stars may still be deemed necessary.

7 The *Planet of the Apes* franchise, which encompassed five feature films and two television series from 1968 to 1975, is an early example of this trend. Original star Charlton Heston appeared only in the first film, and for a small cameo in the first sequel.

8 *Stargate* grossed $196 million worldwide on a budget of $55 million. The film was parlayed into a tele-movie, *Stargate SG-1: Children of the Gods* (1997), and then a television series, *Stargate SG-1* (MGM Worldwide Television), neither of which employed the film's lead actors Kurt Russell and James Spader. *Ace Ventura: Pet Detective* grossed $74 million in the US, on a budget of $12 million. It was followed by a sequel, *Ace Ventura: When Nature Calls* (1995, USA), again starring Jim Carrey, and in 1996 by an animated series.

9 The most recent example of this trend is *Spider-Man* (2002, USA). For commercial reasons, the star presence should not be overly obscured by costume. The marketing of *Judge Dredd* (1995, USA) presents a clash between star-image and comic book character, with the former winning out, to the extent that Sylvester Stallone appeared unhelmeted in American film posters (see imdb.com). The relative failure of *Judge Dredd*, which grossed less than $35 million in the US, also demonstrates that the presence of costumed and masked characters cannot guarantee a film's commercial success.

10 *The Mask*, derived from the comic book character of the same name, grossed $320 million worldwide on a budget of $18 million, and was followed by an animated series in 1995.

11 *Robocop* (1987, USA) grossed $53 million in the US on a budget of $13 million. The sequel *Robocop 2* (1990, USA) grossed $45 million in the US. Original star Peter Weller was replaced by Robert John Burke for *Robocop 3* (1993), which grossed only $10 million in the US on a budget of $22 million. However, the character was successfully redeployed on television throughout 1990s, in three live-action series (1991, 1994 and 1998) and an animated series (1994).

12 Of course, *Batman* (1989) boasted more than one star. Jack Nicholson's star presence as the Joker, in conspicuous make-up and costume, was a key component.

13 A full investigation of the mutual relationship between star persona and character is beyond the scope of this chapter. I concentrate on how each actor's star-image has been 'fitted' to the Batman role, which typically implies a certain narrative trajectory, but which may itself be rewritten slightly to accommodate a new star-actor. I have left to one side the question of how star personae may have been (re)constructed by the role, and by associated appearances in satellite texts such as fan magazines. I will note, however, an intriguing *Daily Mail* report that George Clooney vetoed a tie-in between *Batman and Robin* and Domestos lavatory cleaner, because it 'might hurt his image'. This suggests something of the power of major stars in negotiating tie-in deals, and shows that the process whereby stars act as 'proprietors' of their own image can apply to extra-filmic arrangements as well as to role choices. (It seems somewhat unlikely that Warner Bros would have wanted its character property linked with Domestos either.) ('Why all known germs are safe from Batman', *Daily Mail*, 3 April 1997: 19). Thanks to Charlotte Adcock for providing this reference. On stars as proprietors of their images, see King (1986).

14 For Wyatt, 'high concept cinema' describes a mode of textual organisation designed to facilitate the optimal marketing of films. He summarises its three key elements – production design, straightforward narratives, and pre-sold properties – as 'the look, the hook, and the book' (1994: 20–2).

15 A contrasting tactic is to emphasise the difference between star-actor and role, with the gap bridged by actorly expertise.

16 There will of course be a degree of diversity in these expectations. On how Burton's *Batman* was targeted not just at fans of the comic book, but at a wider, heterogeneous audience, see Bacon-Smith with Yarborough (1991: 90–1); Brooker (2000: 279–80, 293).

17 This site of interest is the personality as depicted in, and traceable intertextually across, film appearances. By contrast, discourses of stardom also encompass 'the player's existence outside his/her work in films' (DeCordova, 1991: 26).

18 As Brooker notes (2000: 279–80, 293), comic book fans lost 'ownership' of Batman once he was adapted to reach a larger film audience.

19 The Batsuit has not always been rendered as rubber musculature. In the 1960s television series, Adam West wore grey tights and matching top.

20 Thanks to Richard Allen for providing this reference.

21 The presentation of Bruce Wayne's class identity in *Batman* is ambiguous. The film places Wayne in an ostentatious mansion complete with suits of armour, but shows his down-to-earth nature when he shyly accepts Vicki Vale's gentle mocking of his inherited wealth. Keaton's lack of 'gigantic muscles' may match the notion of Wayne's aristocratic identity, to the extent that muscles still carry a connotation of working-class identity, via physical labour or sports such as boxing. Thanks to Sally Munt on this point. In later films, the terms of Wayne's wealthy identity shift from aristocrat (*Batman* and *Batman Returns*) to benign capitalist (*Batman Forever*) to celebrity (*Batman and Robin*).

22 As Brooker notes (2000: 59), the multiple manifestations of Batman have also oscillated between the two poles of 'dark loner' and 'benevolent father-figure' to Robin.

23 Adam West in the 1960s television series is an exception to this.

24 Debates over Batman's sexuality provide one indication of the character's synchronic and diachronic polysemy. Brooker (2000) has traced readings of Batman as gay (especially in his relationship with Robin) derived from comic books, television and film, along with homophobic attempts to 'defend' the character from such interpretations. Andy Medhurst (1991) has noted the camp pleasures of the 1960s television series, and the 'reheterosexualisation' of Batman in the graphic novels of the 1980s and the 1989 film.

25 On the clash between 'dark' and 'light' interpretations of Batman foregrounded by news of the employment of Burton and Keaton, see Brooker (2000: 281–2).

26 Kilmer was described as 'the man with the most instantly recognizable lips in the western world' in a review of *Batman and Robin* (*The Sunday Times*, 29 June 1997, Section 11: 4–5).

27 An exception is Arnold Schwarzenegger's employment of the language of the Method to discuss his part as Mr Freeze in *Batman and Robin*: 'Villains are fun to play, because you can dig as deep as you can inside of yourself to find whatever evil is there, and then play with it' (Singer, 1997: 28).

28 *Batman Forever* is very much a film about men. There is just one significant female character – Dr Chase Meridian, played by Nicole Kidman.

29 Two-Face's visual appearance (costume and make-up) is one indicator of his psychological instability, effectively summarising his split personality. On one side he wears the sober business suit of a professional lawyer; on the other, the gaudy clothes and purple skin of a deformed yet flamboyant gangster. His voice enhances this characterisation, oscillating violently from whisper to bellow and back again.

30 Gill Branston (1995: 42) makes a similar point about the loquacious 'old timer' in the western.

31 Kilmer makes a very different use of his voice as the tubercular Doc Holliday in *Tombstone* (1993, USA). Here he speaks with an effete, slightly lisping, 'educated' voice, which is apt to rise in pitch slightly when he is excited, but retains a strong 'frontier' twang. By comparison, Kilmer's vocal delivery as Batman is flat and

controlled. It is hardly lacking in connotations, but it is far less marked as a performance than the role of Holliday.

32 Decisions about vocal performance are not made by actors alone. As Branston notes (1995: 41), they are also shaped by the 'assumptions of sound technicians, script writers, and directors as to "appropriate" voices for men and women in particular roles and genres', as well as wider assumptions in society at large.

33 Such profilmic events of performance operate in conjunction with, and may be reorganised by, cinematic codes. In both instances here, the sense of Kilmer/Batman's agility is enhanced by the use of relatively low angle camera placements.

34 Some of the villains in the series (Arnold Schwarzenegger as Mr Freeze, Jack Nicholson as the Joker) have been played by bigger and better-paid stars than the title role itself.

35 Jim Carrey describes Nygma as a 'sycophantic stalker' in Singer (1997: 33). Manohla Dargis has suggested a possible gay subtext in Nygma/the Riddler's fixation with Wayne/Batman (*Sight and Sound*, August 1995: 41).

36 Although the formative events of his parents' murder and his discovery of the creature whose form he takes on are recalled, the tedious years of training and preparation are elided.

37 Carrey's performance as the Riddler also borrows gestures from Frank Gorshin's portrayal of the role in the 1960s television series. Thanks to David Dunn on this point.

38 On performance and narrative in comedian comedy, see also Seidman (1981); Krutnik (1995). Of course Carrey has played some 'straight' roles too, most notably in the critical and commercial success *The Truman Show* (1998, USA).

39 It should be remembered that both bodies – the muscular one and the bendy one – are the products of regimes of preparation, training and rehearsal.

40 For other considerations of a homoerotic/homosexual connection between Batman and Robin, see Brooker (2000); Medhurst (1991); Medhurst, *Sight and Sound*, August (1997: 40). The implication of a gay relationship in Schumacher's two films could be seen to mobilise a vestige of Wayne's aristocratic identity, in so far as some conceptions of homosexuality have been associated with the sexual practices of the aristocracy. Thanks to Sally Munt on this point.

41 Brooker suggests that Schumacher's two films, *Batman Forever* and *Batman and Robin*, have incorporated the 'queer reading' of Batman and Robin which previously had a more limited circulation (Brooker, 2000: 30, 126–70). From such a perspective, attention tended to focus more on Robin than on Batman, however. For instance, it was not Val Kilmer but Chris O'Donnell (who played Robin in both Schumacher films) who was cover star of the British gay magazine *Attitude* in 1995, and again in 1997 (2000: 164–5).

42 At the time of writing, Warner Bros is reported to be developing three new Batman-related films: *Batman Beyond* (based on the animated television series), *Catwoman* and *Batman Year One* (based on Frank Miller's graphic novel). The casting of Batman is at present undecided for all three films. Stars rumoured to be interested in the *Year One* project include George Clooney and Kurt Russell (see 'Batman. Forever', *Empire* September 2001: 41).

43 On the more radical proliferation of Batman incarnations, and the emergence of a 'team Batman' in comic books and television, see Brooker (2000: 244–8, 326–9).

Section 3
Stars and their audiences

Martin Barker

'There is a history of female cinematic spectatorship which has yet to be written,' wrote Jackie Stacey in 1994 (49). She was right, and unfortunately it is also true of every other possible categorisation of the audience we might make. In truth, the remarkable thing about our knowledge of cinema audiences, let alone our knowledge of audiences' relations to stars, is its paucity. With very few precursors, whatever work has been done has appeared in the last ten years – and that is a smattering.

Stacey's study remains among the few we have on audiences for stars. Stacey wrote as a 'friendly critic' from within feminist film scholarship, concerned to develop the critical trajectory that had moved feminist concerns with mainstream Hollywood from singular notions of a dominatory male gaze, to considering the ways in which women find spaces for participation and pleasure. What Stacey added to the debates was the richness which comes when the complex voices of real people are added to the melt. Stacey used archival materials, and letters from now-elderly women, to explore the meanings that their adoration of certain stars had had for their lives. This led Stacey to unpick certain concepts, notably 'identification', which textual approaches had made central to claims about stardom. She showed just how complicated and multiple are people's real relations with stars.

Stacey's work has rightly been quoted by many. It is now also possible to see certain limitations. For example, David Machin has recently looked critically at her somewhat exaggerated claims to have used 'ethnographic' methods (2002: Chapter 10). But perhaps this is more than methodological. Audience research does have persistent problems with how to determine how people's ways of characterising themselves need to be transcended, and with the relations between accounts by analysers and analysed. In Stacey, this surfaces in her insistence that the women's responses are best understood within a psychoanalytic framework – leading her to judge that their 'nostalgia' for a time when real stars were distant ideals indicates that specifically 'feminine identities [are] fragile and transient'

(1994: 226). It is hard to find evidence within her own account to substantiate anything like our ordinary meanings of 'fragility' or 'transience'. It seems more that this reading is required to reconcile what these women told her, while holding on to a broad psycho-analytic approach.

Perhaps the most important consequence of this tendency has been to narrow down the questions thought worth asking. Only those things currently under critical conceptual examination have tended to generate the energy necessary for the arduous pursuit of knowledge and understanding of audiences. This has meant that little attention has been paid to some very important issues. For instance, what happens when audiences are *disappointed* in stars that they are otherwise attracted to? The question has hardly been addressed because of an assumption that stars are, simply, successful in their attraction. Or, because stars have been primarily theorised in terms of the ways their intertextual meanings are inserted into films, little attention has been given to what else people may *do* with their star fascinations, other than just watch them. Finally, because stars have been understood for their 'fit' with wider systems of ideological, or discursive meanings, little attention has been given to the ways in which producers *research their audience* – because that assumes that they do not know what might work. Uncertainty and ideology are not obvious partners.

The chapters in this section tackle just these kinds of questions. Using case studies from a larger project, Ian Huffer examines the intersections between Sylvester Stallone's evolving star-persona, and the lives, needs and choices of three male fans. Huffer shows how different fans make selections from among Stallone's films – indeed, may go beyond the films to writings about him, or interviews with him. By editing out those films that contradict their requirements, they can find the 'real' Stallone who best meets the needs of their evolving identities. But this process, Huffer argues, may be 'inevitably fraught with tension – the force of audiences' socially formed desires and the force of Stallone's individual career choices resulting in a constantly evolving struggle to keep such categories meaningful for industry and the individual'. And in as much as these three individuals may be typical of wider responses, these very tensions may be integral to the 'instability that has so characterised Stallone's career'.

The majority of recent audience research has been determinedly qualitative – sometimes for pragmatic reasons (only limited time and small groups of people were available to the researcher, for instance), sometimes for philosophical reasons (the researcher was interested in patterns of meaning, for instance). Sometimes, however, it seems that a more generalised suspicion of quantitative methods lies behind this tendency. If this is so, then the essay by Máire Messenger Davies and Roberta Pearson will hopefully encourage people to look again at the potentialities of this approach. Using the opportunity offered by Patrick Stewart's movement between theatre and cinema, Davies and Pearson have conducted a series of studies on the cultural consequences of such a crossover. Here, they explore the ways in which a liking of Stewart combines with other wider taste preferences, and how far Stewart's attraction persuades different audiences to move into a different cultural environment. If Stewart was your major motive for seeing the film *X-Men*, does this increase the likelihood that you will want to see him in the theatre? And vice versa.

Their (inevitably complex) findings provide a significant empirical test for some of Pierre Bourdieu's claims about the relative separation of taste cultures in contemporary society, and his proposal of a 'correlation between class status and cultural consumption'. Their conclusion is that stars, and perhaps especially those who become visible through television, may have the ability to 'make viewers culturally "mobile", or "permeable" – that is, open to new cultural experiences'. The issues opened here are important, not least because they pass beyond concerns with the 'meanings' of stars, to what people may actually *do differently* as a result of their pleasures in them.

Joanne Lacey's essay takes us into another aspect of audience studies: she asks if there may not be different kinds of 'stardom' associated with a particular genre of films, the television movie. She examines one particular 'star', Melissa Gilbert, who first came to prominence as little Laura in *Little House on the Prairie*, but who graduated to being a prime player in a series of television movies. These differ from mainstream Hollywood output by being cheaply and speedily produced, and by having as their prime target a home audience of women aged 18–50. This leads, argues Lacey, to differences in the kinds of stars, and in the narratives within which their personae are revealed. Drawing on a mixture of her own research, and the industry's research into the audiences for these movies, Lacey brings into view a different kind of pleasure associated with a woman who does not embody Hollywood glamour.

Chapter Nine

'WHAT INTEREST DOES A FAT STALLONE HAVE FOR AN ACTION FAN?': MALE FILM AUDIENCES AND THE STRUCTURING OF STARDOM

Ian Huffer

> The promise of star studies . . . was that it might allow one to address the organization of the industry, the properties of individual texts, and the experiences of the audience, and to relate all three within a small and coherent focus.
>
> *(McDonald, 1995: 80)*

Paul McDonald stresses that this promise of star studies has been unfulfilled because existing studies have 'made reference to the audience but tended to ignore the industry' (1995: 80). I would add that although existing studies may have made reference to the audience, the majority have not spoken to them, leaving actual people's interest in stars largely assumed (Ellis, 1982; most of Dyer, 1987). A handful of recent studies (Stacey, 1994; Barker and Brooks, 1998; Austin, 1999; Lacey, 1999) have shown how an appreciation of actual film audiences seriously complicates accepted film studies orthodoxy. However, a great deal of work remains to be done if we are to understand how studying actual audiences can deepen our understanding of the phenomenon of stardom. Research on male audiences' interest in recent or contemporary stars remains particularly sparse. In response to this I am focusing on male audiences' enjoyment of Sylvester Stallone.

Writers such as King (1991), McDonald (1998) and Geraghty (2000) have begun to address the role that the categorisation of film stars plays in organising Hollywood for audiences' consumption. They derive their categories from the different modes of performance that actors employ, and the different modes of publicity that attach themselves to stars. While helping us to understand how such classification works to structure production and promotion, Geraghty goes further in hypothesising how this different labelling of stars might impact upon their reception (Geraghty, 2000: 189, 195). Here I interrogate this question of reception further, considering the way audiences may categorise stars as a means of negotiating the gap between their social identities and the film text, or other representations of the star.

STALLONE'S CAREER

Sylvester Stallone's career not only encompasses the last 25 years of Hollywood cinema, but also highlights the fragility of the fame that this industry can bring. From *Rocky* (1976, USA) onwards, Stallone's career has fluctuated between enormous success – *Rocky II* (1979, USA), *Rocky III* (1982, USA) – and spectacular failure *F.I.S.T.* (1978, USA), *Nighthawks* (1981, USA), *Rhinestone* (1984, USA). This pattern was at its clearest when Stallone's two most successful films – *Rambo: First Blood Part 2* (1985), USA and *Rocky IV* (1985, USA) – were closely followed by the box office disappointments of *Over the Top* (1986, USA), *Cobra* (1986, USA), *Rambo III* (1988, USA) and *Lock Up* (1989, USA). The run of failures continued into the 1990s with *Rocky V* (1990, USA) and Stallone's two comedies, *Oscar* (1991, USA) and *Stop Or My Mom Will Shoot!* (1992, USA). It took a return to action for Stallone to become successful again (*Cliffhanger*, *Demolition Man* (both 1993, USA)). Poor box office for the subsequent action films *Judge Dredd* (1995, USA), *Assassins* (1995, USA) and *Daylight* (1996, USA) led Stallone towards another change of direction into the ensemble drama *CopLand* (1997, USA). Despite positive reviews for Stallone's performance, its lack of financial success stalled Stallone's career in a state of limbo, only recently brought to an end by a new run of box office bombs (*Get Carter* (2000, USA), *Driven* (2001, USA) *D-Tox* (2002, USA)[1]).[2]

Such a career trajectory displays the stuttering, tentative nature of mass popularity, alerting us to potential tensions existing within audiences' understanding, and subsequent enjoyment, of a star. Through analysing audiences' specific relationships to Stallone, we can begin to gain an insight into the problems which stars face in maintaining a successful equilibrium that satisfies the competing desires conferred on them by audiences.[3]

FINDING AUDIENCES

For my research, I wrote letters to regional newspapers around the country and a range of national magazines, appealing for people to contact me for a questionnaire on Stallone. Many regional newspapers published my letter, as did the magazines *Gay Times*, *Attitude* and *Impact*, and I received approximately 100 responses. My qualitative questionnaire consisted of a combination of open, general questions and questions relating to key issues which I was addressing. I received 51 questionnaires (32 men, 19 women), from which I have chosen just three to form this paper. These were three men, Charlie, Paul, and Andy, all in their thirties and interested in Stallone since the 1980s. They are all white; Paul and Andy are heterosexual, while Charlie is gay.

CHARLIE

Charlie admits that, with regard to Stallone, 'to be honest I am probably more interested in him as a person than his films!' This declaration points towards his categorisation of Stallone as something akin to Geraghty's notion of the 'star-as-celebrity' in which 'the emphasis on the private sphere and the interaction with other forms of fame means that . . . the films are relatively unimportant' (Geraghty, 2000: 189). However, while Charlie may downplay the importance of Stallone's films to him, one particular film occupies a significant position in his relationship with Stallone:

> I think *Cobra* was the first film that made me really interested . . . I saw
> *Cobra* at the cinema and really enjoyed it. He was too cool for words! . . . I
> only have *Cobra* on video. . . . I still like *Cobra* because of the loner figure.

It is this 'loner figure' of Stallone which struck a chord with Charlie. Stallone's character, the renegade cop Marion Cobretti, is very much an individual, in outlook (clashing with authority in the form of his police chief and the media, who question his unforgiving treatment of criminals) and lifestyle (he lives on his own, eating cold pizza from its box as dinner). I would speculate that it is Stallone's omnipotence within this role that is so appealing, as it reveals strength in a quality that Charlie appears to perceive as a bit of a weakness in himself:

> Since I have been watching Stallone's films, I have always lived on my own
> and worked in factory jobs. Although I have six O-Levels, I've never had the
> confidence to push myself further. . . . Sometimes I've identified with
> Stallone both in his life and his films. I know what it's like to be a loner, to
> not fit in with people.

While Cobretti may not fit in with people, this does not affect his confidence. When he arrives at the scene of a hostage crisis, his superior says 'I don't agree with them bringing you in here.' However, Stallone's dress and demeanour suggest that Cobretti is impervious to such comments. He is firm and upright as he walks. His black jacket and T-shirt, blue jeans, black boots and reflective sunglasses are tightly fitted and coordinated. His face is impassive; he does not speak, even when spoken to. All of these elements indicate poise, confidence and control. He nonchalantly takes a sip from a beer can before throwing it in the direction of the armed hostage-taker as a distraction. As he confronts the killer, he begins to speak. However, he makes sure that he controls the conversation and their interaction, answering the killer with dry wit and, finally, a bullet. Stallone's performance within the narrative of the film seems to embody tensions existing within Charlie. Charlie's enjoyment appears to come from a sense that those tensions have been resolved in some way. Whether these tensions of not fitting in with people are formed out of his experiences as a gay man is a speculation tantalisingly out of reach. Nevertheless, a broad

157

understanding of Charlie's sense of alienation can still help to explain his deep emotional investment in *Cobra*, and the satisfaction he gains from watching Stallone fly in the face of adversity.

However, if Charlie's relationship with Stallone began in a cinema, it gained its greatest momentum outside of the texts of his films. Charlie's comments reveal that the connection he made with Stallone was a personal link, rooted very much in the 'real' of his life, if embodied in the fantasy of film. I would suggest that Charlie developed an interest in Stallone beyond the texts of his films in order to engage with the 'real' Stallone, and to forge a more intimate link, with greater echoes of personal contact. This interest might have been intensified by an increasing lack of engagement with the cinematic Stallone. He states that:

> I didn't like *Lock Up*, I find prison films depressing and predictable. I
> thought the *Rambo* films were a bit ridiculous, too flag-waving.

Barring *Over the Top*, these films were the next two Stallone vehicles after *Cobra* (*Rambo III* in 1988, *Lock Up* in 1989). In this light we could read Charlie's submergence in the celebrity of Stallone as a way of continuing a bond broken in the cinema.

The basis of Charlie's interest in the private life of Stallone is his 'autobiography which I really enjoyed':

> I know he has a great interest in art and he is quite a sensitive person with
> a great sense of humour. He is one of the few famous people I'd really like
> to meet, even now. I also know he takes romantic involvement very seriously
> and it affects him greatly when it goes wrong. I think reading his book kind
> of prepared me to see some of the humour in his films, and his own rags-to-
> riches story was in a way mirrored in the *Rocky* film. I still have the book
> somewhere.

The certainty of Charlie's language suggests a belief that the book represents the real Sylvester Stallone, a belief supported by the echo of its themes within interviews with Stallone in the media:

> I also like his taste in art and decor, etc. And I like the way he shows his
> vulnerable side in interviews. Years ago, *Hello!* magazine did a fantastic
> issue featuring his home and art collection.

These representations give Charlie an intimacy with Stallone as he is invited around his house and into his lovelife. However, it is interesting that Charlie chooses representations of

Stallone's private life in which Stallone would have had a large degree of autonomy, and were thus likely to show the star in a positive light. He appears reluctant to relinquish his idolatry of Stallone in *Cobra,* organising his consumption of Stallone as a celebrity into a form that mirrors his initial cinematic identification with the star: intimate and yet still awe-struck.

Charlie's comments on the autobiography and the *Hello!* interview also appear to be a response to attempts on Stallone's part to offer the reader a specific point of re-entry into his films. Charlie notes above that 'he is quite a sensitive person with a great sense of humour . . . I think reading the book prepared me to see some of the humour in his films.' The autobiography was published in 1991. Stallone moved into sensitive, comedy roles that year with *Oscar* and, the following year, *Stop Or My Mom Will Shoot!.* The representation of Stallone in his autobiography could, thus, be an attempt to re-formulate his image, preparing audiences for his change of direction through revealing the sensitive, humorous star as the real Stallone. Such a connection appears revealingly underlined when Charlie notes that 'I love *Stop Or My Mom Will Shoot!* . . . I like to see his sense of humour (there's a lot of it in his autobiography).'

Charlie's interest in Stallone is revealing in the way in which it takes a great deal of its power from his initial cinematic encounter with Cobretti. The fusion of Charlie's continuing needs, Stallone's subsequent performances and Stallone's representation in publicity has evolved such an identification into a close engagement with the star's private life, and a new interest in a different kind of Stallone performance. Charlie thus uses Stallone's celebrity status to keep alive an important strand in his life, while Hollywood uses Stallone's celebrity status to weave the star's audience back into his films.

PAUL

> I like action films and therefore action stars. Stallone was without doubt one of the biggest action stars of the 1980s, the era when I started to become interested in films. It is the action that makes his films enjoyable.

Paul's comment points towards Geraghty's notion of the star-as-professional, which 'makes sense through a combination of a particular star image with a particular film context. It arises when we check "whether an actor's presence in a film seems to correspond with his or her professional role" (Naremore, 1988: 262) and often involves the star's identification with a particular genre' (Geraghty, 2000: 189). Stallone's close association with the action film has helped make him representative of this genre to Paul, and Paul's enjoyment appears dependent on Stallone offering the particular pleasures of action. Looking at Paul's responses can help us to see, in greater detail, the way in which his understanding of Stallone works to form his enjoyment, and the precise nature of such 'pleasures of stability and repetition' (Geraghty, 2000: 191).

The spectacle of action is pivotal to Paul's pleasure in film:

> I think films have gotten worse recently. The reason for this I believe is that most films nowadays are running anywhere between two and three hours. ... Most people seem unable to make an action film last two hours so they fill it with story and drama. When films were an hour and a half you didn't have to wait too long between action sequences. The film effects are much better nowadays, but the films go on for so long there is too much of a gap between the action.

Paul's interest in stars is a by-product of this formal fascination with action, following stars who will offer him these pleasures repeatedly. However, the stars whom he enjoys do not offer him indiscriminate access to action but work to refine the pleasure in particular ways. For instance Stallone 'was better at being a more "realistic" and "believable" action star', 'Schwarzenegger was always able to take it a step further', into fantasy, as 'he is so big (physically)', and Jackie Chan 'has an unparalleled level of acrobatic ability that no western star could match'. The performance styles of these stars, and the subject matter of their films, introduce sub-genres for Paul, cueing particular expectations while still delivering the same ultimate promise of action. Paul's enjoyment of Stallone in action films is also formed from the qualities which Stallone brings to the film as an individual, hence his comment that 'if you'd had the combination of a good action film like *The Matrix* and a good action star like Schwarzenegger or Stallone then the film would have been even better'. However, while Paul may acknowledge the way that Stallone's performative skills can enrich action, he is not interested in those talents enough to see them exercised beyond this genre – signalling the primacy of generic content, however individualised. Paul is quite clear that 'I want to see him in action, not comedy or romance but action'. He comments that:

> If you want to watch a comedy you don't watch an action star trying to deliver it, you want a comedian. Would Jim Carey [*sic*] try to play Rambo? No, so why does Stallone try comedy?

The importance of Stallone's professional role, and that of other performers in Hollywood, as perceived by Paul, could not be clearer:

> Stallone's body is the prime reason for his success and therefore the main attraction to any of his films. We do not have, but we all want, a physique like his and so that is why we want to watch his films. He put on fat to appear in *CopLand*, to suit the character he was playing, and as such this was a film in which I have no interest. What interest does a fat Stallone have for an action fan?[4]

Stallone's sculpted body makes him an aspirational figure to Paul, lifting him in his iden-tification. He gains no pleasure in identifying with a 'fat Stallone' as he does not want this physique. Only action films properly expose/celebrate Stallone's body for Paul's enjoy-ment and, thus, he is careful to limit his consumption of Stallone to just this genre of films. Other genres compromise this pleasure – comedy downplaying and hiding it (e.g. *Oscar, Stop or My Mom Will Shoot!*); drama, in the case of *CopLand*, eroding it.[5] This interest in Stallone's physique extends into Paul's social life as:

> Stallone, and even more so Schwarzenegger, have certainly introduced me
> to what can be achieved by body-building/weight training and they inspired
> me to take up the sport. After all, who wouldn't want a body like that?
> However, more importantly they have shown that when you get to 50 years
> old you don't have to be fat, bald and unfit.

Stallone's aspirational status appears to have a meaning that extends beyond Paul's imag-ination into his everyday existence. I would speculate that this heightened model of masculinity has an acute appeal for Paul, due to particular events in his life:

> I got my first job in 1988 working in the office of a shipping company. I
> worked in shipping for five years with two different firms until I got laid off.
> While unemployed I joined a training scheme which led to me getting a job
> in the accounts department of a local Fish Factory. I learnt accounts there
> and have worked in accounts departments of another two companies since
> then. I have been forced to change jobs through redundancy and my lack of
> long periods of employment have meant that I have only recently been able
> to save enough money to buy my own house. I bought it last year and moved
> in with my fiancée.

Paul's active engagement with a type of masculinity that emphasises qualities of strength, power and control could be a coping strategy born out of the undermining effect of long periods of unemployment. Powerless in preventing redundancy and frustrated in his desire to buy a house with his fiancée, Paul's interest in Stallone, Schwarzenegger and body-building may represent an attempt to establish some control over his life and re-affirm a sense of pride in himself as a man (connecting to Walkerdine's observations on boxing as a 'counterpoint to the experience of oppression and powerlessness' for working-class men (1986: 172)). The representation of Stallone on film could, thus, be seen to form part of a wider chain of signification for Paul, impacting upon his social identity. As a result, the particular stability and repetition that comes from his selective consumption of Stallone does not just secure his enjoyment, it also works to keep his sense of self as solid as the bodies that he idolises.

His efforts to keep such a tight control over the meaning he gains from film stars, and Stallone in particular, are aided by the modes of categorising stars within the video industry – an industry relevant to his consumption of film:

> I prefer to watch films on video. For a start it's cheaper to rent a film than it is to go to the pictures and you don't have to pay £3.00 for a can of coke in your own house like you do at the pictures. Plus you get to see the whole screen, not part of the screen and the back of someone's head.

Geraghty notes that the connection of stars to particular genres is particularly prevalent in the video industry as 'the video shop offers the audience more films than even the multiplex, and linking the star to a genre gives a reliable indicator that a particular video will deliver what it seems to offer' (Geraghty 2000: 189). It is interesting to note that Paul's terminology of action, comedy, romance and drama films echoes that employed by video shops. Indeed, while there are substantial differences within the content and style of many of Stallone's films that Blockbuster Video, for example, categorises as action (the war of *Rambo*; the melodrama of *Lock Up*; the comedy of *Demolition Man*), such a categorisation stresses their homogeneity, and helps Paul with his personal project of retaining order and control in his life. Thus, the organisation of the video industry works, in part, to delineate the content and boundaries to Paul's categorisation of Stallone. Paul mentions that '*CopLand* was advertised as more of a drama than an action film and so I made the decision not to watch it' – the allocation of genre within publicity here warning certain audiences of stars' transgressions, in an effort to avoid potential disappointment, and retain this valuable pact between industry and individual.

ANDY

In contrast to Paul's rigid interpretation of Stallone, Andy actually changes his categorisation through the course of filling out the questionnaire. Near the beginning, Andy refers to Stallone as 'less of an actor and more of a character'. By the end, he admits that 'my perception of him now is more of an "actor" rather than a "character"'. Such a shift is indicative of the way in which Andy's categorisation of Stallone is an ongoing process, constructed in his language as he writes, and connected to a narrative of personal development as much as Stallone's performances.

For Andy this narrative begins in his adolescence:

> When you're a teenager trying to access films of a higher certificate than your age, films like *Rocky* and *Rambo* initially appealed purely for the attraction of action and the thrill of seeing a movie before you were supposed to. Most teenage boys would rather see an 18-certificate action movie than an 18-certificate art house movie, and as such Stallone fitted that bracket at the time.

For a teenage Andy looking for the 'attraction of action' and the illicit thrill of an 18-certificate film. Stallone 'fitted that bracket', acting as a guarantee of the fulfilment of particular pleasures (which appear closely tied to adolescent rites-of-passage and peer-group status (Austin, 1999: 154)). Andy's description of Stallone as 'more of a character' occurs as he is recollecting the success of the *Rocky* and *Rambo* films. Indeed, a large proportion of Stallone's 1980s output consisted of action films based around a common theme/character, that of 'a man down on his luck rising above adversity' as Andy puts it. Andy's categorisation of Stallone as a 'character' can be seen as a reflection of expectations encouraged by the tight repetition of performance/film content by Stallone, intensified by Andy's teenage fascination with the pleasure/status which this character delivered. However, between the period which Andy is recollecting and the present, a number of developments have caused Andy to adjust his categorisation of Stallone, in those same films of the past as well as those of today.

Stallone's growing age has made it difficult for Andy to enjoy Stallone as the character that he once enjoyed, as he no longer represents the same guarantee. While the nature of Stallone's action roles has not altered much, Andy's reception of them has:

> As he's got older he's less convincing in the action roles that I enjoy. If he was to pump himself up for another boxing film . . . I would find it hard to place any credibility against such pursuits as it would be misplaced largely because of his age.

This shows the way in which a category can still have meaning at a formal/industrial level, as these films are still organised and promoted around Stallone delivering particular pleasures that he has previously offered (Chris Heath, 'Don't Look Down', *Empire*, July 1993: 83), but that the same category can become redundant for the audience due to tensions they find within it. Andy mentions that Stallone's previous action roles made Stallone 'a larger than life character' (echoing the aspirational allure of Stallone to Paul). Stallone's age clearly compromises this promise for Andy.

Andy's mode of approaching Stallone seems not only to have been affected by Stallone's age but also by his own. For Andy, the very method of enjoying a film through a series of expectations generated by the star is one which he associates with his past:

> In my teenage years the star was the attraction, but for the last decade . . . I go for the experience and for the subject matter rather than the star – a natural progression of getting older!

Andy is keen to stress his maturity, much as he did as a teenager when attempting to access 18-certificate films. However, his desire is now articulated through an emphasis both on the new importance of subject matter to him, and on his appreciation of good acting. This is reflected most clearly in his enjoyment of the Stallone film *CopLand*:

> If he is able to expand his range into more adult roles like that of Freddy Heflin in *CopLand* then I'll continue to see his movies. [. . .] One of his most convincing uses of his size and stature was for his role in *CopLand* where he was required to add extra weight without being too muscular, giving him the air of a gentle giant to play Freddy Heflin convincingly. [. . .] *CopLand* has shown a new maturity for an actor who has had to diversify due to the ravages of time and he was critically applauded for it. The combination here of a strong cast and story brought the best out of Stallone and for me this is probably my favourite film of his.

As Andy has got older, his interest in film has grown to the extent that he sees 'an average of 85 a year at the cinema'. He is keen to stress his appreciation of the many facets to film, acknowledging, in contrast, 'that to the average cinema-goer the star is the main attraction'. Andy's interest in subject matter and the finer details of performance are thus a way of marking his distance from his own past and the 'average cinema-goer'.

Andy's interest in film has led him to the film magazine *Empire* and *The Sunday Times*' film reviews. Unlike Paul's video-based consumption of Stallone, Andy has become a cineaste, who seeks out information from sources which celebrate cinema as a form of entertainment requiring particular skill in its production – loaded with a value in itself rather than just its use-value to an audience. In an effort to underline this value, such publications reward films and performances which put this skill on display, in the form of such properties as story, dialogue, direction and performance (as clear examples, see Ian Nathan, review of *American Beauty*, *Empire*, February 2000: 12; and Adam Smith, review of *The Insider*, *Empire*, April 2000: 12). Hence, a star's performance that emphasises the skill of 'impersonation' (King, 1991: 176) is likely to be better received than that emphasising the continuity of their 'personification' of a particular star-image (see for instance Simon Braund, 'Stuck in the Middle With You', *Empire*, January 1997: 60–1). Andy's awareness of these discourses is underlined as he notes how Stallone's performance in *CopLand* was 'critically applauded' (albeit somewhat tokenistically by Ian Freer in his *Empire* review of *CopLand*, January 1998: 38). If we look at *The Sunday Times* review of the film we can clearly see the traces of such a discourse as well as a certain similarity to Andy's opinions:

> Stallone has gained more than just a belly in *CopLand* . . . his stature as an actor is established once and for all. . . . If asked to name one of the more moving sights in cinema this year, it has to be the sight of Freddy's

fumbling, furtive gaze, unable to make eye contact with the cops he so idolises. . . . Mangold's crisp eye for composition and magpie casting instincts make sure we have plenty to watch.

(Tom Shone, 'Heavyweight Hit', The Sunday Times, 7 December 1997: 4)

Such a discourse seems to appeal to Andy as it offers him the opportunity of utilising his immense consumption of film to form an exclusive knowledge, signalling a tangible property to be gained through the pursuit of a somewhat ephemeral hobby. Such a mode of engagement also intellectualises his interest, in contrast to the physically suggestive 'thrill' of cinema evident in his teenage recollections. These forces serve to underline to Andy the mature nature of such a relationship with film. This clearly pleases him. Just as his attempts to access high-certificate action films as a teenager can be read, in part, as a form of peer-influenced rites-of-passage, his current interest in quality discourses surrounding film appears to be part of a socio-culturally reflexive project of self-improvement and personal development.

Andy's new interest thus brings with it a new set of needs to be met by the cinema. As he observes above, Stallone's performance in *CopLand* meets these new criteria. Indeed, it is the gallery to which Stallone is playing (Faludi 1999: 580–90). In marked contrast to the introduction of Stallone in, for example, *Demolition Man* and *Cliffhanger*, which stress Stallone's physicality and activity, the introduction of Stallone in *CopLand* stresses his inactivity and inefficiency, heralding his versatility and impersonatory skills. After losing at pinball to the message 'You Have No Authority', we view Stallone standing alone at a bar. His posture is slouched, his clothes are baggy and ill-fitting. It takes him two attempts to get money out of his shirt-pocket to pay for his drink, and two attempts to hear the words of a nearby friend. His eyelids are almost closed and when he speaks his voice is higher, softer and, subsequently, more boyish than we are used to. As he brings some keys out of his pocket, the camera tilts down from his face to linger on his paunch. He is shambolic – the lack of authority in his presence a marked contrast to previous performances.

Stallone's fulfilment of Andy's new needs in *CopLand* seems to lead him to a re-categorisation of Stallone – 'my perception of him is now more of an "actor" rather than a "character"'. This has even led to a re-evaluation of Stallone's earlier films: 'I now have more appreciation of his acting ability in some of his early films such as *Rocky I* and *II*'. Andy's evolving understanding of Stallone displays the extent to which a star's performance can be made meaningful through extratextual discourses circulating within publicity/promotion. However, the significance of these discourses for Andy rests upon his interpretation of them – an interpretation formed, in part, out of a socially/culturally/historically reflexive desire for maturity as an individual.

CONCLUSION

Through a consideration of text, industry and audiences we can begin to gain a fuller understanding of the meaning which audiences get from stars, and a more nuanced appreciation of the way that meaning is organised (both by and for them). While King, McDonald and Geraghty may establish structures for the interpretation of film stars within Hollywood and wider media, Charlie, Paul and Andy show us some of the pleasures audiences may find in such structures. Their responses highlight the importance of their social identities in shaping that pleasure, while also forcing us to recognise their initiative in exploiting Stallone as a tool with which to mould those identities. However, while it may be their own specific desires that compel them to structure their consumption of Stallone, their close engagement with forms of publicity and promotion that work to organise their consumption into a form that benefits Hollywood (economically and culturally) points towards the film industry's ability to exploit this activity, shaping it somewhat (in direction, if not implication). Such a process seems inevitably fraught with tension – the force of audiences' desires and the force of Stallone's career choices resulting in a constantly evolving struggle to keep such categories meaningful for industry and the individual (these tensions possibly revealing themselves in the instability that has so characterised Stallone's career). Research from an integrative perspective is still needed into the extent to which developments in Hollywood and wider social/cultural history placate or intensify these tensions, as we try to discover why more people appear to choose Paul's method of categorising Stallone, despite the existing alternatives embodied by Charlie and Andy.

---

1   *D-Tox* has not, at the time of writing, been released at the US box office. It did gain an international release, but failed to make an immediate impact in the UK and disappeared from cinema screens quickly.

2   This pattern of success and failure is (bar *D-Tox*) specifically taken from Stallone's US box office record on **www.the-movie-times.com**.

3   While Susan Jeffords (1994) and Yvonne Tasker (1993a) thoroughly contextualise Stallone's career in the light of political and cultural developments in US and British society, the actual viewing processes of the men and women who have watched his films remain largely unexplored. Valerie Walkerdine (1986) and Martin Barker and Kate Brooks (1998) offer useful starting points for such research but limit their analysis to a single film from Stallone's career, and differ in their methodological aim from the work that I am undertaking.

4   This comment alerts our attention to the value of Stallone-as-body to Paul, but it is interesting to note that Charlie and Andy's investment in Stallone's physique differs from Paul's somewhat (Charlie eulogising a film which favours fashion over physique; Andy growing to respect this 'fat Stallone' which leaves Paul cold). Such differences complicate any notion of a monolithic masculinity, provoking questions that I am investigating as part of my doctoral research. I do not have the space to do justice to these debates here.

5   The necessity of action may be also be the result of a certain anxiety in gaining pleasure from the male form, the action giving it a purpose (Dyer, 1982: 66–7).

Chapter Ten

STARDOM AND DISTINCTION: ☐ PATRICK STEWART AS AN AGENT OF CULTURAL MOBILITY – A STUDY OF THEATRE AND FILM AUDIENCES IN NEW YORK CITY[1]

Máire Messenger Davies and Roberta Pearson

In summer 1986, television producer Robert Justman thought he had found the Captain of the new starship Enterprise, NCC-1701 D, but the Enterprise's originator, Gene Roddenberry, disagreed. Justman, a producer on the original *Star Trek* (1966–9), had been brought back aboard by Roddenberry, his former boss and colleague on the old show and executive producer of *Star Trek: The Next Generation* (referred to henceforth here as *TNG*) (1987–94). The new Enterprise desperately needed a new captain. Justman went to see Patrick Stewart, a British Shakespearean actor, giving a reading at the University of California, Los Angeles. 'He [Stewart] blew me away when he started speaking. And I said, I found our captain. There was no doubt in my mind. ... Gene didn't want him. Gene wanted a Frenchman.' For months Justman badgered Roddenberry in memos: '[Stewart's] repertoire, experience and classical background, coupled with his personal magnetism, would make him a valuable leading member of the Enterprise crew.' Justman described to us how 'Roddenberry was still so unsure that he turned to his assistant and asked her what she thought of Patrick Stewart ... She said Patrick Stewart has no sex appeal. I said, Patrick Stewart has no sex appeal? What would she know?!'[2] Five years after Roddenberry was finally persuaded to cast Stewart as Captain Picard, his unnamed assistant's judgement appeared even wider of the mark when Stewart was voted by the readership of America's *TV Guide* (the biggest-selling magazine in the US) as 'The Most Bodacious Man on TV'. Subsequently he was named as one of the 10 Sexiest Men by *Playgirl* (1995), and one of the 50 Most Beautiful People by *People Magazine* (1995).[3]

It is the public, not producers' assistants or even producers, who make stars. Now (spring 2002) that the tenth *Star Trek* movie *Nemesis* is in production, not only the public, but also, importantly for him, Paramount executives see Patrick Stewart as a star. He may not be in the A-list category of bankable stars who can single-handedly carry a film, but he has the financial pulling power and sufficient clout to make or break a *Star Trek* movie. Stewart is also a television star, not only for *Star Trek* but for a number of Hallmark dramas in which he has appeared, such as *Moby Dick* and *A Christmas Carol*, and, at least in the US, he is a highly bankable theatre star (although he feels that he is now less well known in the UK theatre).[4] Academic studies of stardom have tended to focus on 'the star system' as a component of the film industry's capitalist mode of production rather than upon the public's relationship to individual stars (McDonald, 2000). We propose that the audience's responses to stars must also be seen as part of this system, and that these should be studied systematically.

An early inspiration for the study reported here came from a comment that Patrick Stewart made when we first met him for an interview in 1999.

> It's a source of some puzzlement to me that you cannot guarantee a *Star Trek* audience. I know that *A Christmas Carol* on Broadway opened on the strength of the fan support. They bought out the theatre for the first week. That same body of fan support does not turn out for everything ... *Star Trek* fans are rather narrow in what they go to see.[5]

A few months later, we went to New York's Guggenheim Museum for a work-in-progress reading of Arthur Miller's *The Ride Down Mt Morgan*, which was to open shortly on Broadway. An amazing diversity of people had queued up for admission, from leather-clad bikers, to middle-aged ladies in furs and jewels – the former, at least, not the usual Guggenheim clientele. 'Who were these people?' we wondered, and particularly in the case of the young and the unconventionally dressed, were they *Star Trek* fans there for Patrick Stewart? An opportunity to test Stewart's hypothesis that *Star Trek* fans could not be guaranteed to watch him in different roles came when *The Ride Down Mt Morgan* opened. The final week of the play, in July 2000, coincided with the opening week of the summer blockbuster film, *The X-Men* (2000, USA), in which Stewart played Prof X. Would the *Star Trek* audience follow their Captain into the Broadway theatre and Manhattan cinemas? The question is specific neither to *Star Trek* nor to Stewart, but falls within the broad area of inquiry first mapped out by Pierre Bourdieu who, in *Distinction* (1984), proposed a correlation between class status and cultural consumption. Those at the top of the socio-economic scale consume products accorded high cultural value, while those at the bottom consume products accorded little value. Critics have pointed out that Bourdieu accounts well for stability but not for change. But even some who see cultural hierarchies now reconfiguring, assert that correlations between high/low social status and 'high/low' culture persist, if only at the 'bottom end'. Jostein Gripsrud states:

> While the audiences in the opera almost certainly go to movies and even watch television, the majority of movie and television audiences will never

go to the opera; or visit places like museums of contemporary art, certain theatres. The reception of high and low culture is still clearly linked to the social formations we call classes.

(Gripsrud, 1989: 199)

Richard Peterson and Roger Kern (1996) provide empirical support for Gripsrud's assertion, arguing that, in the United States, there is a historical shift among the higher social categories from highbrow snob (who does not participate in any lowbrow or middlebrow activity) to 'omnivore' (capable of appreciating them all). In contrast, argues John Frow, 'There is no longer a stable hierarchy of value running from "low" to "high" culture, and "high" and "low" culture can no longer be neatly correlated with a hierarchy of social classes' (1995: 1).

Our interest in this debate stems from a long-standing concern with television as a medium which challenges hierarchical definitions of cultural tastes in a number of ways; we hypothesised that one way was to make viewers culturally 'mobile', or 'permeable' – that is, open to new cultural experiences.[6] Further, television offers this cultural range freely to a huge number of undifferentiated people. Any television audience is a 'mass' audience in this sense. And all television audiences, no matter how 'small', include all sections of the population, though they may be skewed towards the higher or lower ends of the market.[7] This inclusiveness makes television audiences unlike theatre audiences or museum audiences, which is why, in addressing the question of cultural mobility, we became interested in theatre and museum audiences for plays and exhibitions which include elements imported from the popular 'mass' television product, *Star Trek*. In designing the audience research described here, we wanted to look at the extent to which this imported element might alter the demographic composition of these audiences for 'minority' cultural forms, to make them more like the television audience: more diverse, and more likely to include people who do not normally consume plays or museum exhibits. One agent for drawing in the television audience to these events, we hypothesised, would be the television star.

Certain stars, like Patrick Stewart, function not just as iconic and unattainable objects of desire to the readers of *TV Guide*, but in more culturally complex ways. One of these ways, we hypothesised, was as a kind of cultural 'magnet', drawing in audiences who would not normally enjoy 'serious' drama, or live theatre.[8] This magnetism could also work the other way, helping to persuade theatre audiences to take more seriously works of popular culture such as *Star Trek*, in which the admired stage actor also performs. This willingness we have labelled 'cultural mobility'.

Patrick Stewart seemed an ideal case study to test our hypothesis of cultural mobility since he crosses over the media of theatre, film and television as well as the barriers between taste boundaries ('serious' theatre, popular television, blockbuster films). Stewart was a member of the Royal Shakespeare Company for over 20 years prior to playing the role of Captain Jean-Luc Picard. His performance in the role, lauded both by critics and his fellow actors,[9] helped raise the quality of *TNG* to heights more usually associated with 'serious' canonical television drama such as 'Play for Today' in the UK, and the best of American series drama, such as *ER* and *The West Wing*. In the theatre Stewart has appeared in *The Tempest* (1995) on Broadway, *Othello* (1997) in Washington, DC, *Who's Afraid of Virginia Woolf?* (2001) in Minneapolis, and J.B. Priestley's *Johnson Over Jordan* (2001) in Yorkshire. In television, he has a continuing association with Hallmark Productions for whom he has starred in *The Canterville Ghost* (1995), *Moby Dick* (1997), *A Christmas Carol* (1999) and *King of Texas* (updated version of *King Lear*, 2002). At the same time, his continued association with the *Trek* television programme and films make him a central icon of a popular culture cult phenomenon.

THE AUDIENCE STUDY

In summer 2000 we carried out a survey of audiences for *The Ride Down Mt Morgan*, written by Arthur Miller, showing at the Ambassador Theater on Broadway, and for the summer blockbuster film, *The X-Men*, directed by Bryan Singer, produced by Fox Searchlight Pictures; both works starred Patrick Stewart. *The X-Men* premièred in New York on 14 July 2000, and *The Ride Down Mt Morgan* closed on 23 July 2000, so that the two productions played simultaneously in New York City for just over a week. By conducting research in New York during that week, we were uniquely able to reach audiences for two Stewart vehicles at the same time. In terms of their box office potential, both were successful vehicles for Stewart. *The Ride Down Mt Morgan* was moderately so, running from April to July 2000 in the 1,100-seat Ambassador Theater, and averaging about 50 per cent attendance.[10] *The X-Men*, produced for $75 million, opened on 3,025 screens in the US, took $54.5 million in its opening weekend and grossed $157,299,718 by the end of its first run in November 2000.

During this opportunistic week, we distributed questionnaires at five performances of the play and at four screenings of *The X-Men* at two different cinemas. One was the two-screen Park Cinema at 86th Street and Park Avenue (*X-Men* on both screens) on New York's Upper East Side; the other was the newly built AMC 25-screen multiplex at 42nd Street and 8th Avenue (*X-Men* playing on five screens) in a rapidly gentrifying neighbourhood around the formerly seedy Times Square. Despite its location on the classy Upper East Side, the Park Cinema, being just one subway stop from Spanish Harlem, draws an ethnically and economically diverse clientele. The clientele at the AMC cinema seemed similarly diverse. We received 1,192 completed questionnaires from the theatre audience and 951 completed questionnaires from the cinema audiences (the questionnaire is attached as Appendix A on pages 183–6). The box office figures for the shows at which we distributed questionnaires indicated that we achieved a response rate of roughly 50 per cent at both the theatre and the cinemas, remarkably good for a quantitative survey. We also compared our sample's demographic distribution with official data about the population of New York City as a whole and with New York theatre audiences in particular, to check the extent to which the sample diverged from, or conformed to, the characteristics of the populations from which it was drawn. These comparisons can be seen in Tables 10.1–10.7.

RESEARCH QUESTIONS

Our basic question can be summarised simply: why were people in the theatre? We hypothesised that many would be there because of Stewart and his star status – whether of theatre or of screen, and especially because of *Star Trek*. We also hypothesised that, in the case of the play, Miller would be a reason. For a certain age cohort (and our data bears this out) Miller was another kind of star: high profile for his liberal activities during and after the communist witchhunt, and associated with Hollywood both by virtue of writing screenplays and by his marriage to Marilyn Monroe. Even now, though he is perhaps more admired in Britain than in his native land, Miller is still revered in the US as the greatest living playwright.

Over 20 different reasons were given by the play audiences for being at the performance, including birthday outings, persuasion from friends, cheap tickets, bad weather and so on, but the most frequently given reasons were those pertaining to star and author. We wanted to compare those (nearly 20 per cent of the sample) who were solely attracted to the theatre by Stewart, the star of the cult television show, with those (17.5 per cent of the sample) who were attracted by Miller, 'the greatest living playwright'. Might the Stewart sample be more demographically diverse than the Miller sample? If popular television actors such as Stewart do indeed function as cultural 'magnets' to people who do not usually see themselves as theatregoers, would the Stewart group be more likely than the Miller group, or the sample as a whole, to consume texts from different 'rungs' on the cultural hierarchy, as measured by some of our questions about cultural tastes and behaviour in the questionnaire? Conversely, might the fans of the 'greatest living playwright' be more likely to be wealthier and more culturally conservative in their tastes? Our questionnaire also included sections on the audiences' other cultural tastes, including theatre and television consumption generally, and detailed questions about their familiarity with specific kinds of shows, whether 'upmarket' (serious Broadway theatre such as Eugene O'Neill's *Moon for the Misbegotten*) or popular television (such as *Buffy the Vampire Slayer*). How would the Stewart and Miller groups compare in these various kinds of cultural consumption, and would this, too, be related to demographic factors?[11]

PRIMARY REASONS FOR COMING TO THE SHOW

Among our New York theatre sample, 204 people (19.5 per cent of the sample) gave Stewart as their sole reason for coming to the show (the largest single reason); 143 (13.9

per cent) gave both Stewart and Arthur Miller combined as their reason, and 42 (4.1 per cent) mentioned Stewart plus another reason; the cumulative percentage of people mentioning Stewart was 37.5 per cent. By comparison, the merest fraction of the cinema audience cited Stewart as their reason for attendance: four said Stewart alone (0.7 per cent) while 12 (2 per cent) named him in combination with another reason, for a cumulative total of 2.7 per cent. Of course, the difference between the theatre and cinema samples can be partially accounted for by the different spatio-temporal nature of the two media. *The Ride Down Mt Morgan* could be seen only in New York City, and only for eight performances a week, while *The X-Men* opened on 3,025 screens (going even wider to 3,112 after the opening week), and played practically continuously on all these screens from late morning or early afternoon to night. If you wanted to see Patrick Stewart in the play you had to come to New York from other parts of the country (as many of our respondents did – see Table 10.6), but if you wanted to see him in the film, you could do so almost anywhere in the country, without the need to travel far. This suggests that 2.7 per cent of the whole vast audience for *The X-Men* came because of Patrick Stewart – this would be hundreds of thousands of people. A total of 29 (4.9 per cent) of our New York cinema sample said they came for the special effects. Interestingly, the highest percentage of people (162, 27.6 per cent) came because of prior exposure to the X-Men, through comics or cartoons. Here, it was the original text that had the star power.

Other reasons for attending were as follows: 17.5 per cent of the theatrical audience sample gave Arthur Miller alone as their reason for attendance; 13.9 per cent gave both Miller and Stewart, and 0.8 per cent gave Miller and another reason. This makes a cumulative percentage of 32.4 per cent, almost as many as named Stewart as a reason for attendance. Hence, in the case of the play, both star and writer were the most powerful single factors in drawing people to the theatre, but the Stewart group turned out to be different in interesting ways from the Miller group.

THE STAR-POWER FACTOR: AUDIENCE DEMOGRAPHICS

The following tables,[12] generated by our SPSS (Statistical Package for the Social Sciences) analysis, provide comparisons between the Stewart fans and the Miller fans in our sample audiences, and they also provide comparisons between the general Broadway audience and official demographic information about the New York population. We wanted to see whether there was a 'star-power factor' expressing itself in differences between the audience breakdowns in these groups, and whether the audience composition in the Stewart group differed from the general audience compositions and from the Miller groups. We were particularly interested to see whether the Stewart group was less elite than other groups, given the popularity of *Star Trek*.

Table 10.1: **Star power and audience age: age differences in the New York audience groups, including the Stewart and Miller groups**

NYC age groups	%	NYC Broadway audience age groups (source: Gabriel's Real Estate.Net)	NYC Broadway theatre audience, 1997 %	Study sample age groups	Whole sample (2,143 people) %	Theatre only group (1,192 people) %	Film only group (951 people) %	Reason: 'Patrick Stewart only' group (204 people) %	Reason: 'Arthur Miller only' group (182 people) %
Under 5	6.8	under 12	1.5	0–10	0.9	0.4	1.5	0	0.5
5–17	16.1	12–17	9.0	11–16	5.4	1.8	10.1	2.5	8.8
8–29	19.7	18–24	11.2	17–25	20.1	9.0	34.4	14.7	8.8
30–49	24.4	25–34	20	26–35	23.9	16.5	33.8	22.1	6.0
50–64	13.9	35–49	29.9	36–45	12.7	14.8	10.3	24.0	8.2
65 plus	13.0	65 plus	20	46–55	12.9	19.1	5.4	23.0	17.0
				55 plus	22.8	38.0	4.2	13.7	59.3

KEY FINDINGS

- There were more young adults (56.7 per cent of 17–45 year olds) both in our sample and the Broadway sample (51.1 per cent of 18–49 year olds) than in the population as a whole (44.1 per cent of 18–49 year olds).
- The proportion of young adults aged between 17 and 45 was even greater in the Stewart group – 61.8 per cent.
- Only 23 per cent of the Miller group was aged between 17 and 45, whereas 59.3 per cent of the Miller group was aged 46 and over.

This shows that the Stewart factor was associated with a much younger demographic than the usual theatre audience. It also sharply differentiates Stewart fans from Miller fans. The difference in age groups between the Stewart and Miller groups was highly statistically significant. This also tends to support the Gripsrud hypothesis that double-access audiences (i.e. Stewart fans attending a Broadway Miller play) are more likely to be aged under 50. When *Star Trek* viewing was controlled for, it emerged that 70 per cent of the 14–45-year-olds in the Stewart group were regular *Star Trek* viewers, suggesting that the star himself was mistaken in thinking that *Star Trek* fans would not want to see him in the theatre, at least on this occasion.

Table 10.2: **Gender differences in NYC population; general audiences; our sample and Stewart/Miller audience groups**

	NYC (source: Gabriel's Real Estate.Net)	NYC theatre audience	Whole sample (2,143 people)	Theatre only group (1,192 people)	Film only group (951 people)	Reason: 'Patrick Stewart only' group (204 people)	Reason: 'Arthur Miller only' group (182 people)
	%	%	%	%	%	%	%
Male	46.9	60.3	46.1	36.6	58.8	43.2	29.7
Female	53.1	39.7	47.6	57.0	36.7	56.8	70.3

KEY FINDINGS

- Gender was fairly equally split both in the whole sample – 46.1 per cent male, 47.6 per cent female (in contrast to the Broadway sample). It was also reasonably equally distributed in the Patrick Stewart group – 43.2 per cent male, 56.8 per cent female.

- There was a greater proportion of females (70.3 per cent) overall in the Miller group – but when age was controlled for, this was almost entirely accounted for by older women. A cross-tabulated comparison between the sex and age distribution in the Miller and the Stewart groups showed that in every age group between 17 and 55, there were more females than males in the Stewart group. However, in the 55-plus age group there was a really spectacular reversal, with 87.8 per cent of the females (72 people) in the Miller group and only 10 (12.2 per cent) in the Stewart group. Of the six people in the 11–16 age group who had given Stewart or Miller as a reason for coming, five of them came for Stewart: four boys and one girl.

Other data indicated more males than females among people who identified themselves as regular viewers of *Star Trek*. The more even gender balance in the Stewart group suggests that, in addition to the drawing power of his *Star Trek* role, Stewart is a factor in drawing women – at least women aged below 55 – both to the television show (and movies) and to other performances such as the Miller play. This provides more evidence of the failure of Gene Roddenberry's assistant to foresee the actor's appeal.

When *Star Trek* viewing was controlled for, within the 'never watch' and 'occasionally watch' groups, about two-thirds came from the Miller groups, of either sex. Within the 'regularly watch' viewing group, virtually all the respondents were in the Stewart group and only two were males (2.2 per cent). This suggests that the gender differences observed between Miller and Stewart fans, with a greater proportion of women in the Miller group, cannot be accounted for by the evidence that men are more regular viewers of *Star Trek* than are women. This detailed analysis of age and sex, accounting for the *Star Trek* factor, suggests that the Stewart star power is at work here, especially in his appeal to women.

Table 10.3: **Comparison of income between NYC, general audiences, our sample, and Stewart and Miller groups**

Annual income NYC	NYC (source: Gabriel's Real Estate.Net)	Annual income NYC theatre audience	New York theatre audience	Annual income: study sample	Whole sample (2,143 people)	Theatre only group (1,192 people)	Film only group (951 people)	Reason: 'Patrick Stewart only' group (204 people)	Reason: 'Arthur Miller only' group (182 people)
	%		%		%	%	%	%	%
$10–19,999	14.1	Under $25,000	10.2	$10–25,000	12.6	6.7	20.3	10.9	7.8
$20–39,999	27.2	$25–49,000	19.3	$26–50,000	26.8	21.9	33.3	29.0	27.5
$40–74,999	28.2	$50–74,000	20.4	$51–70,000	14.5	16.5	12.2	17.5	15.0
$75,000+	14.8	$75,000+	50.1	$71,000+	30.4	39.8	19.1	42.6	49.7

KEY FINDINGS

- Fewer (42.6 per cent) of the Stewart group were in the highest income bracket than the Miller group (49.7 per cent) although this was below the level of statistical significance.
- Slightly more of the Stewart group (10.9 per cent) than the Miller group (7.8 per cent) were in the lowest income bracket. This compared with 14.1 per cent in the lowest income group in the general New York population.
- All of the theatre groups included more high-income groups than the NYC demographic breakdown.
- All of the theatre groups included more high-income groups than the film group.

This generally supports the Bourdieu case that theatre will appeal more to high-income groups generally, and also more than a popular form such as blockbuster cinema. However, the people attracted to the theatre by Stewart included more lower-income groups and fewer higher-income groups – some slight evidence of a Stewart 'magnet' effect on less well-off groups in the population, who are less likely to attend live theatre. These differences were not statistically significant.

Table 10.4: **Ethnic groups in the general population, the Broadway theatre audience, our sample, and the Stewart and Miller samples**

Race/ ethnicity	NYC (source: Gabriel's Real Estate.Net)	Race NYC theatre audience	Race study sample	Whole sample (2,143 people)	Theatre only group (1,192 people)	Film only group (951 people)	Reason: 'Patrick Stewart only' group (204 people)	Reason: 'Arthur Miller only' group (182 people)
	%	%		%	%	%	%	%
White	52.3	87.1	Caucasian	64.0	6.2	37.2	86	91.5
Black	28.7	3.7	Afro-US	8.8	1.9	17.5	1.5	0.6
Hispanic	23.7	3.7	Hispanic	11.7	2.5	23.4	3.5	1.1
Asian/Pacific	6.9	3.3	Asian	4.8	3.1	6.9	3.0	1.7
American Indian	0.3	0	Native American	1.5	1.8	1.2	0.5	3.4
Other	11.6	2.2	Other	5.5	2.3	9.5	5.5	1.7

KEY FINDINGS

- The Stewart (86 per cent white) and Miller (91.5 per cent white) groups looked closest in terms of race. These proportions were similar to the Broadway audience survey (87.1 per cent white).
- 14 per cent of the Stewart group categorised themselves as non-white (including the 'other' category, which were usually people of mixed race), compared with 8.5 per cent of the Miller group. This difference was statistically significant.

- The largest minority group were the 23.4 per cent Hispanics in the Film Only group; 60 per cent of the cinema audience as a whole were non-white.

Proportionately, the theatre audience contained more white people than the general population of New York; in the census, 47.7 per cent of the population was classified as non-white. The cinema audience had a smaller proportion of white people, with nearly 60 per cent from other ethnic groups. Given the general whiteness of the theatre audience, the Stewart group was somewhat atypical, with a higher proportion of non-whites than in the Miller group, or the Broadway group. This again supports our hypothesis that Stewart might be encouraging cultural mobility/permeability in groups not usually associated with regular theatregoing to Broadway plays by elite white authors.

Table 10.5: **Education in the general population, the Broadway audience, our sample, and the Stewart and Miller groups**

Education NYC	NYC (source: Gabriel's Real Estate.Net)	Education NYC theatre audience	Education study sample	Whole sample (2,143 people)	Theatre only group (1,192 people)	Film only group (951 people)	Reason: 'Patrick Stewart only' group (204 people)	Reason: 'Arthur Miller only' group (182 people)
	%	%		%	%	%	%	%
High school (all)	57.8	20	high school	9.6	4.4	16.4	4.0	4.4
Some college	14.4	15.2	high school graduate	19.1	15.8	23.7	15.4	12.6
College degree	17.5	36.4	college graduate	36.4	36.7	36.6	42.8	36.3
Graduate degree	10.0	28.5	graduate school	30.8	41.4	17.9	37.8	46.7

KEY FINDINGS

- 80.6 per cent of the Stewart group and 83 per cent of the Miller group had a college education or higher – both clearly elite groups in terms of education, and very different from the general NYC population, of which 57.8 per cent had only a high school education.
- The cinema group (which included a high proportion of non-whites and was primarily youthful, with only 9.6 per cent aged over 45) was much more highly educated than the general population, with 54.5 per cent having a college degree or higher.

These findings provide little evidence that high-culture audiences (theatre) are more highly educated than 'low'-culture audiences (blockbuster cinema). They also indicated a small Stewart 'magnet' effect again, with slightly fewer highly educated people in the Stewart group than in the theatre group as a whole.

Table 10.6: **Home base of the theatre groups, the cinema groups, and the Stewart and Miller groups, compared to the general population and Broadway audience**

Home: NYC theatre audience	New York theatre audience	Home: study sample	Whole sample (2,143 people)	Theatre only group (1,192 people)	Film only group (951 people)	Reason: 'Patrick Stewart only' group (204 people)	Reason: 'Arthur Miller only' group (182 people)
	%		%	%	%	%	%
NYC	21.1	NYC	54.8	34.8	80.8	25.9	42.9
NYC suburbs	28.1		—	No figures for suburbs	—		
Other US	37.9	US, outside NYC	36.0	56.5	10.9	69.0	50.5
International	12.9	Outside USA	5.6	5.6	5.7	5.1	6.6

KEY FINDINGS

- Far more people in our cinema group (80.8 per cent) than in our theatre group (34.8 per cent) were based in New York. In the general Broadway audience survey, 49.2 per cent lived either in NYC or the New York suburbs.
- Given that theatre audiences usually travel further to shows generally, within our sample, Patrick Stewart was a more powerful factor in drawing them (74.1 per cent from outside NY) than was Arthur Miller (57.1 per cent from outside NY). According to a chi-square test, which measures the likelihood of unequal numerical distributions being due simply to chance, these differences were highly significant – i.e. much more likely to be due to star power than to chance.

The star factor – for both Stewart and, to a lesser extent, Miller – represented a 'magnet' in terms of drawing people in from other parts of the country. These figures help to explain the fact that the Stewart group was much more concentrated in the theatre than in the film audience; Stewart aficionados, whether fans, or those who gave him as a reason for coming but have other favourite actors, could see him in *The X-Men* all over the country. They could only see him in the flesh on this occasion in the Ambassador Theater in New York City – emphasising the enduring attraction of liveness (Auslander, 1999) which theatre has over film and television. This factor was obviously greater for Stewart than for Miller, since Stewart's physical presence must be an important factor in his star appeal.

THE STAR-POWER FACTOR: AUDIENCE TASTES

Our questionnaire (see Appendix A) was designed to operationalise the concept of cultural mobility in terms of both the consumption of media generally and the consumption of specific media products. With regard to the former, we asked how many times a year people went to the cinema and the theatre, and how many hours of television they watched a day. With regard to the latter, we asked about the consumption of texts that we assumed might be attractive to people across a range of demographic factors (e.g. *ER* or *Miss Saigon*) and other texts that might be attractive to those in specific demographic categories, e.g. *Masterpiece Theater* (anthology programme on the Public Broadcasting Service that airs British heritage television) or *Buffy the Vampire Slayer*. Those who exhibit diverse cultural tastes, enjoying cult as well as upmarket television, are those whom we would consider to be culturally mobile. Some of the more telling findings are detailed below.

COMPARISONS BETWEEN CULTURAL TASTES IN THE STEWART AND MILLER SAMPLES

Those in the Stewart sample were significantly more likely to watch *Star Trek* and *Buffy the Vampire Slayer* and significantly less likely to watch *Masterpiece Theater* or *60 Minutes* (a respected television news magazine programme) than the Miller sample, which is likely to reflect the comparative youth of the Stewart sample. In our whole sample, the former two shows were associated with younger viewers and the latter two with older viewers. These findings confirm standard predictions based on social distinctions in taste – the young cult viewers do not cross over to 'quality' television like *Masterpiece Theater*. However, there are different patterns of cultural consumption between the two groups, as outlined in Table 10.7 below.

Table 10.7: **Patterns of cultural consumption**

	Patrick Stewart group reason for coming	Arthur Miller group reason for coming	Whole sample (cinema plus theatre)
P. Stewart favourite actor	29%	4%	5.5%
Regular filmgoers	66.5%	70.7%	73.6%
Regular theatregoers	40.1%	63.7%	45.1%
Star Trek: regular/occasional viewer	83.9%	32.8%	57.2%
Buffy: regular/occasional viewer	23.5%	8.8%	33.7%
Masterpiece Theater: regular/occasional viewer	54%	79.3%	48.8%
60 Minutes: regular/occasional viewer	70%	86.9%	71.9%
Favourite television show	*Star Trek* (17.4%)	News (12.9%)	*Friends* (6.3%)
The X-Men (seen)	49%	6.6%	56.2%
Star Trek: Insurrection (seen)	67.6%	12.1%	34.3%
Galaxy Quest (seen)	40.7%	10.4%	29.7%
Insider (seen)	34.3%	45.1%	37.5%
Death of a Salesman (seen)	14.2%	39.6%	23.3%
View from the Bridge (seen)	10.3	35.2%	15.2%
Moon for the Misbegotten (seen)	6.4%	26.4%	9.5%

The relationship of star power (i.e. people giving the star individual as their sole reason for attendance) with cultural consumption can be seen in some detail in these frequencies. There is a 'Stewart effect' in the Stewart sample and a 'Miller effect' in the Miller sample, with the former being stronger overall:

- 29 per cent of those in the Stewart sample, as opposed to 4 per cent in the Miller sample and 5.5 per cent in the whole sample, named Stewart as their favourite actor
- 17.4 per cent named *Star Trek* as their favourite television show, as opposed to none in the Miller sample and 5.5 per cent in the whole sample
- 83.9 per cent watched *Star Trek* regularly or occasionally, as opposed to 32.8 per cent in the Miller sample and 57.2 per cent in the whole sample
- 67.6 per cent had seen the latest *Star Trek* film, *Insurrection* (1998, USA, starring Stewart), as opposed to 12.1 per cent in the Miller sample and 34.3 per cent in the whole sample; 49 per cent had seen *The X-Men* as opposed to 6.6 per cent in the Miller sample; these would seem to be people attracted to texts featuring Patrick Stewart
- this Stewart effect becomes even more pronounced among the Stewart sample at the theatre who had seen or intended to see *The X-Men*; 38.5 per cent of this group named Stewart as favourite actor, 85.3 per cent had seen *Insurrection,* 92.5 per cent watch Star *Trek* regularly or occasionally and 21.6 per cent named it as their favourite television programme.

The frequencies would seem to indicate that Stewart was drawing certain people to the theatre. But do these people exhibit cultural mobility more generally? A slightly larger percentage of them watched our bellwether 'upmarket' *Masterpiece Theater* than those in the whole sample (54 per cent as opposed to 48.8 per cent). But the figures for the 'high-quality' film *The Insider* (1999, USA), and the plays *Moon for the Misbegotten* (by Eugene O'Neill), *Death of a Salesman* and *A View from the Bridge* (other Arthur Miller plays recently on Broadway) revealed that the Stewart group was slightly less likely than those in either the Miller sample or the whole sample to consume these 'serious' or upmarket texts. In fact, there were fewer regular theatregoers among them than in the whole sample (40.1 per cent as opposed to 45.1 per cent) and far fewer than in the Miller sample (63.7 per cent). Might there be quite a few people in this sample who would not normally attend a serious Broadway play but are doing so because of Stewart? If this is the case, then we not only have evidence of cultural mobility but can attribute it to Patrick Stewart.

There was clearly a Miller effect in the Miller sample, 39.6 per cent of them as opposed to 23.3 per cent in the whole sample having seen *Death of a Salesman,* and 35.2 per cent as opposed to 15.2 per cent in the whole sample having seen *View from the Bridge.* But while there were slight indications of cultural mobility in the Stewart sample, the Miller sample seems more culturally immobile, primarily consuming texts that would normally be associated with those of their socio-economic status. They were more likely than the whole sample to watch *Masterpiece Theater* (79.3 per cent to 48.8 per cent), to have seen *The Insider* (45.1 per cent to 37.5 per cent) and to have seen *Moon for the Misbegotten* (26.4 to 9.5 per cent). And, as we have seen above, they were less likely than either the Stewart sample or the whole sample to consume texts that might generally be termed 'cult'.

So what provisional and tentative conclusions can we draw from the above concerning firstly the effect of stardom on cultural consumption and, secondly, cultural mobility? We are fairly confident that our data indicates both a Miller and a Stewart effect. Though we are less confident about this, our analyses might provide some indication of the relationship of the Stewart effect with cultural mobility in audiences – the willingness to try a new cultural experience, outside the normal range of cultural behaviour expected for one's particular demographic sub-group. In both the Stewart and the Miller samples, age was continually more significant than the other demographic variables – income, race, sex or education. The Stewart sample skewed younger than the whole sample with regard to theatregoing, watching *Masterpiece Theater* or attending *Mt Morgan*, and skewed older than the whole sample with regard to seeing *The X-Men*. These subjects were engaged in activities which, based upon the whole sample and conventional assumptions, were age-inappropriate.

It makes sense that cultural mobility or the lack thereof would be associated with age, if one assumes that one's tastes, while subject to change over the course of a lifetime, are primarily formed in youth. Almost 60 per cent of our Miller sample were aged 55 or older, meaning not only that many of them would have been young at the height of Miller's fame, but also that they would have grown up in a society which made firmer distinctions between high and low culture (though was also less obsessed with niche marketing). While the Stewart sample is older than the whole sample, it is younger than the whole-theatre sample and significantly younger than the Miller sample. These people may be Gripsrud's double-access audience, whom he hypothesises might be younger than 50. We can say that the people who identified Patrick Stewart as their reason for going to see *The Ride Down Mt Morgan* were more likely than the whole theatre audience, and more likely than the Arthur Miller group, to be younger; to include both sexes equally (except in the oldest age group); to include more people who are less well educated; to be more racially diverse and to include more people from lower-income groups. In all these ways, it seems as if Patrick Stewart drew people to the theatre who would not normally go to see a Broadway play.

We stress again that these are tentative conclusions, requiring testing through further analysis of the quantitative data as well as follow-up work of a qualitative nature. Our findings from the West Yorkshire Playhouse in autumn 2001, in which a significant number of first-time attenders went to the Priestley play because of Patrick Stewart, suggests that more follow-up is needed to see whether this 'magnetic' impact on cultural mobility is

181

something that can be sustained (with people returning to the theatre, after the magnet star has departed). It would also be important to see whether any reverse effects can be observed, with people who were attracted by writers, or by the appeal of theatregoing generally, being more likely to try out popular television such as *Star Trek*. This awaits further research.

---

1 Grateful thanks are due especially to Patrick Stewart for his help in arranging access to the venues for this research; to the managements of the Ambassador Theater in New York, and of the cinemas at Park/86th and on 42nd Street; to John Davies, David Black and Naisola Grimwood for help with surveying audiences; and to Obaid al Shaqsi and Nick Mosdell for help with data analysis.

2 Messenger Davies and Pearson, interview with Robert Justman, 11 January 2002.

3 See **http://www.primenet.com/~jbedford/PSEB/PS-FAQ.html** for more details of the statistics given here.

4 Personal communication to the authors.

5 Messenger Davies and Pearson, interview with Patrick Stewart, 16 March 1999. Stewart was filming *A Christmas Carol* at Ealing Studios, a Hallmark production shown on TNT in the United States and Channel Four in the UK.

6 This will be explored further in our forthcoming book, *Star Trek as Television*, to be published by the University of California Press.

7 Audience data provided for us by the head of television research at Paramount, Mike Mellon, indicates that *Star Trek* has more upmarket than downmarket viewers, but of course the overall audience for a popular show like *Star Trek* will always still include many millions of people from 'lower' groups.

8 An example of this effect was quoted in the *Guardian*, 15 February 2002, in which a spokesperson for the National Theatre pointed out that the soap star Martine McCutcheon, of *EastEnders* fame, had brought people to the theatre who had never visited it before, when she starred in *My Fair Lady*.

9 William Shatner, Stewart's predecessor, Captain Kirk in *Star Trek* (the original series), paid tribute to his quality: 'Patrick is . . . a marvellous actor, and he's essentially a character actor, who found this role that gave him international fame, but his beauty is his ability to play characters, so he's got a long, fertile life as an actor, as long as he wants, because he's this marvellous actor who can play any role'. Pearson and Messenger Davies, interview with William Shatner, 16 January 2002.

10 This compares to weekly grosses of around $400,000 for the long-running and very popular musical *Miss Saigon* and weekly grosses of almost $1 million for the mega-hit *The Lion King*. Although the disparities in revenue can be partially accounted for by the larger houses staging the musicals, they also accord with the conventional wisdom that musicals always perform better economically than drama.

11 We asked similar questions of the theatre audiences for J.B. Priestley's *Johnson over Jordan*, starring Patrick Stewart, at the West Yorkshire Playhouse, where we conducted a similar survey in the autumn of 2001. Here we were particularly interested in first-time visitors to the theatre. After interviewing the marketing manager, we were informed that the theatre promoted the Priestley season and *Johnson over Jordan* in particular, by emphasising Priestley as the major draw, rather than Patrick Stewart. Our analysis of people's reasons for coming to the play was able to test whether this had been a wise marketing strategy or not. (It was not.)

12 A note on the information in these tables: general demographic information about the New York population comes from a real estate analysis (Gabriel's Real Estate.Net), and the Broadway audience information comes from a study carried out on behalf of the Broadway theatres by the Theatre Development Fund and the League of American Theatres and Producers (**www.tdf.org**). These studies have slightly different categories from ours, as for instance in the income and education tables, but we wanted to include them as a means of comparison with our sample. We have organised the tables to make the categories as comparable as possible. Where our figures do not add up to 100 per cent, it is because there were a number of missing responses. Where the Gabriel's and Broadway figures do not add up, the inconsistency is in the source material.

APPENDIX A

THIS QUESTIONNAIRE HAS THE SUPPORT OF THE AMBASSADOR THEATER AND FOX PICTURES

We are media researchers from Cardiff University in Britain doing a comparative study of film and theater audiences in New York City. We would be grateful if you could spare a few minutes to answer the following questions. You do not have to answer any question that you do not want to answer or which does not apply to you. The information here will only be used for academic research.

A. ABOUT YOU:

Please **circle** the appropriate category, e.g. if you are 28 years old, circle 26–35:

1. **Age**
0–10 years   11–16   17–25   26–35   36–45   46–55   55+

2. **Sex**   Male   Female

3. **Race**   African-American   Asian   Caucasian   Hispanic   Native American   Other

4. **Occupation/parents' occupation (if under 16)** . . . .

5. **Annual income level:**
$10–25,000; $26,000–50,000; $51,000–70,000; $71,000 +

6. **Education:**
high school   high school graduate   college graduate   graduate school

7. **Home base:**   New York City   USA outside NYC   Outside US

B. LEISURE HABITS: Please check the appropriate boxes:

1. **I go to the theater:**

6–12 times a year	2–5 times a year	once a year	less than once a year	never

2. **I go to the movies:**

6–12 times a year	2–5 times a year	once a year	less than once a year	never

3. **Each day I watch television for:**

1 hour or less	1–2 hours	3–4 hours	5+ hours	never

4. **I have seen the following recent productions of plays**

The Lion King	
The Ride Down Mt Morgan	
Death of a Salesman	
Miss Saigon	
A Moon for the Misbegotten	
A View from the Bridge	

5. **I have seen/intend to see the following movies:**

Scary Movie	
The X-Men	
American Beauty	
Hamlet (Ethan Hawke version)	
Galaxy Quest	
The Insider	
Star Trek: Insurrection	

6. **I watch the following television shows:**

	Regularly	Occasionally	Never
Buffy the Vampire Slayer			
Masterpiece Theater			
Friends			
The X-Files			
Star Trek (any series)			
ER			
60 Minutes			

7. Do you belong to any groups such as Members of the Royal Shakespeare Company or Star Trek fan clubs? Please list below:

C. YOUR TASTES

1. **Please rank the following from 1 to 3 when choosing to see a movie:**

	1 very important	2 somewhat important	3 not important
The director			
The star			
The kind of story			
Friends' advice			
Critical reviews			
Trailers and ads			
Other (please specify)			

2. **Please rank the following from 1 to 3 when choosing to see a play:**

	1 very important	2 somewhat important	3 not important
The playwright			
The star(s)			
The kind of story			
Friends' advice			
Critical reviews			
Trailers and ads			
Other (please specify)			

3. **My favorite television program is:** . . . .

4. **My favorite actors/actresses are:** (name up to three)

5. **What was the main reason that you came to see this play/movie today?**

Any other comments?

Chapter Eleven

'A GALAXY OF STARS TO ☐ GUARANTEE RATINGS': MADE-FOR-TELEVISION MOVIES AND THE FEMALE STAR SYSTEM

Joanne Lacey

In this chapter I consider a female star of made-for-television movies, Melissa Gilbert. I explore Gilbert's star status in American made-for-television movies and the meanings she has for her female fans. I want to investigate the implications that the study of Gilbert and her fans might have for the analysis of the film star system.

·From the outset, this case study raises two points of debate in relation to the study of film stars. Made-for-television movies have been relegated to the dust heap of academic inquiry since the late 1980s. Studying made-for-television movies challenges the definition of film within film studies. Are they film, or are they television? Arguably most films made for theatrical release are also made for television eventually, in being bought up by television production and sales houses for television scheduling, and being transferred onto video or DVD for domestic consumption. But I am thinking here specifically about that peculiar and particular hybrid of film and various television dramas (documentary, drama, melo-drama, public service television, reality television, the mini-series) that emerged in the USA in the early 1970s as a 90-minute self-contained feature produced exclusively for tele-vision. There are detailed and developed studies of the history of this genre in America (Schulze, 1988; Gomery, 1983; Edgerton, 1985; Marill, 1980; Feuer, 1995). My intention is not to oversimplify or undervalue its history. I work with brevity with the knowledge that other scholars have worked on detailed histories that can be drawn on by those inter-ested in further reading.

The second point of issue here relates to Melissa Gilbert herself. Many readers will no doubt be thinking, Melissa who? If I said she used to be Laura Ingalls in *Little House on the Prairie*, you may well say, 'Oh her! I always wondered what happened to her.' Gilbert is now one of the most successful stars of the television movie, and also produces and directs. But, how do we measure the success of a star? How do we as scholars measure the significance of a star? How do we define a star? Can Melissa 'who?' be a star? Can a star of movies made for television be seen as a film star? Christine Gledhill argues: 'while other entertainment industries may manufacture stars, cinema still provides the ultimate confirmation of stardom' (Gledhill, 1991: xiii). Both David Lusted (1991) and John Ellis (1982) have argued that television does not produce stars but personalities. Lusted shows how television circulates and elaborates star personae which originate in other entertainment fields. The relationships between the very different forms of television and cinema and their star systems warrant detailed consideration. Does the television movie traffic in the production of television personalities and not stars? Or does the television movie circulate and elaborate star personae according to its own set of generic rules and conventions?

MADE-FOR-TELEVISION MOVIES AND THEIR FEMALE AUDIENCES

This chapter extracts ideas from a larger, developing research project, still in its early stages, about made-for-television movies and female audiences in Britain. The profile of made-for-television movies on British television does not mirror its status in the organisational culture of American television, where the television movie has consistently carved out a healthy market share of viewers, through dedicated television movie channels such as Lifetime. The television-movie format has fallen into decline in the UK where light entertainment shows dominate the prime-time schedules of Britain's free-television channels, and high-profile series and mini-series fill the gap; however the genre remains popular in UK sales and production houses (Carlton, Pearson, Granada, C4I). Television movie sales are booming in the cable and digital market.

In 1999 I became a regular viewer of the prime-time television movie screened at 9 pm, Monday to Thursday on the British cable and digital channel, LivingTV (part of Flextech television). I became interested in the scheduling of television movies on British television, and in particular the organisational culture of LivingTV. Changes to the political economy of television in Britain in the last ten years have been extensive: the realities that help to shape current television scheduling include an increased level of competition between terrestrial, cable and satellite companies, and an average adult weekly viewing figure of 27 hours that is unlikely to change. Programme executives are faced with an audience that is fragmenting under new competition pressures (Carson and Llewellyn-Jones, 2000: 2).

The researchers at LivingTV have conducted extensive research, using focus groups and viewing diaries, to improve their understanding of the audience for particular slots, and thus to target specific kinds of female viewers in programming decisions. The core of LivingTV's target audience is women, and it therefore provides programming to meet the needs of its female viewers. The made-for-television movie is a significant slot in the company's scheduling in terms both of viewing figures and of target demographics, and has become integral to LivingTV's recent marketing drive to turn around its image from a provider of talk show television (the Jerry Springer Channel) to a provider of quality drama for women. The kind of female viewers that LivingTV wants to target and recruit are (pre-family) modern women (the Bridget Jones type), modern women with children ('I am more than just a mum, I am an individual') and not so modern mums ('Mum first, but do not forget about me'). LivingTV does not want to recruit 'not modern mums'. The company does not want a woman whose motto is 'family and homemaking'.[1] LivingTV wants women who identify with Liza Tarbuck not Lorraine Kelly, *Cold Feet* not *Heartbeat*, Pizza Express not Pizza Hut and gym classes not Weightwatchers.

What is interesting from my point of view is the key positioning of the made-for-television movie in the channel's re-branding of its provision. These films are seen as a means of hooking 'persuaders' into an ongoing relationship with LivingTV (viewers who match one of the pen portraits may dip into the channel because a 'good film' is being screened, but are not regular attenders). The schedulers at LivingTV understand the potential draw of a made-for-television movie for female audiences; they also have little difficulty in categorising them as quality dramas. Television movies have been equated with 'trash TV' and with attendant assumptions about its target female audience.

According to Schulze, 'the TV movie, with its reliance on the family melodrama and the romance, its tendency to take up domestic issues, and its penchant for female protagonists and female stars may indeed lean toward what has come to be called a feminine narrative form' (1988: 26). This need not immediately equate, however, with a perception of the female audience as feeble-minded, masochistic and anti-feminist. Indeed, what is significant about LivingTV's pen portraits of target female viewers is their drive to link television movies with the modern independent-thinking woman, rather than the 'traditional' housewife figure that is implied in the popular and academic criticism of made-for-television movies. Academic feminist critiques of the 'dumb' female audience assumed for 'women's' television genres can be drawn upon to defend the female viewer for television movies (see, for example, Feuer, 1995; Byars and Meehan, 1998; Modleski, 1983).

In critical discourse, the made-for-television movie has been invariably compared to 'real' movies, and the comparison has resulted in a characterisation of television movies variously as 'non-movies', 'quasi-movies' or 'quickies'. There is an element of standardisation to the results of the television movie's mode of production, but the movies are not identical. Given that television movies are so often categorised as being 'the same', how do audiences differentiate those television movies that they like and those that they do not? What role does the central female protagonist play in the differentiation or popularity of the film? Do television movies have a star system? How might this be theorised through audience research? Would viewers like to see more television movies? Would viewers subscribe to a dedicated television movie channel? Out of this broad agenda, the relationship between television movies and female stars emerged as potentially the most interesting.

LIVINGTV

LivingTV works quantitatively with the star–audience relationship. Certain 'big names' of the genre such as Donna Mills and Melissa Gilbert guarantee ratings. I wanted to look qualitatively at why this should be, and what kinds of star/fan relationships circulate for British audiences. Chris Parr, head of UK drama at Pearson television has said that, 'names and packaging are clearly important as TV movies are the drama segment that has undergone the most fundamental changes. People do not make a date with a single drama without a very good reason for doing so' (*Screen International*, 14–17 April 2000: 15). Barbara Bellini-Witkonski, director of sales and rights investments at C4I maintains, 'highly recognisable names are the only way to promote a TV movie in the schedules' (2000: 16). LivingTV operates within this premise. Television movies are sold in packages, including some big-name films, and some ex-theatrical releases. LivingTV seems to understand from its research that audiences are attracted not simply to the genre, but to recognisable names. The company purchases from the back-catalogue on the basis of this, grouping films together in the schedules according to themes (for instance the wedding season (April 2001)), but marketing on the back of the name, the star. Laurie Schulze argues:

> While the mode of production and the institutional function assumed by TV texts works to establish a regular audience habituated to a particular programme, this does demand that programmes exhibit marks of similarity so that viewer familiarity will ensure repeated and predictable return to them, they must also exhibit marks of difference.
>
> *(Schulze, 1988: 29)*

To what extent is the central female actor a key mark of difference? To what extent is Melissa Gilbert a key mark of difference in the television movie? When did I start to see Gilbert as a mark of difference in my own viewing preferences?

I have an ongoing interest in mafia movies of all kinds, and am particularly compelled by the role of women in the representation of the Italian-American crime world. Melissa Gilbert starred in one of my favourite mafia movies, *Blood Vows: Story of a Mafia Wife* (1987, USA), in which Gilbert plays Marian, a clothes designer who unknowingly marries into the Mafia, slowly discovers the truth of her marriage and her 'family', and wants to turn them over to the FBI. Her husband, now the Don, finds out and shoots her through the heart under a pagoda in the garden, rather than let his family deliver a more gruesome death to his bride. I discovered the film and Gilbert some time ago, although in a sense I was re-discovering Gilbert, having already 'known' her as Laura Ingalls. I began to notice Gilbert more, and the regularity with which she appeared in television films shown in Britain after that. I went to America and spent some time bonding with Lifetime and a large-screen television; Gilbert was a prominent part of the scheduling, and also the subject of a Lifetime Intimate Portraits documentary. Here she was positioned as 'one of the most successful actresses of her time'. Her biography was given key melodramatic elements: adopted at birth, divorced twice, ex-brat packer in the 1980s (vague scents of drugs, sex and booze implied there), ex-girlfriend of Rob Lowe and (very briefly) Tom Cruise, now happily married to Bruce Boxleitner, mother of two, down-to-earth child star who stayed in touch with herself and decent morals, loves fried chicken and pork rinds, 'napping with the kids and reading'. I did not know that Melissa Gilbert was a star, but I was being told that she was. A prolific actress in a popular film genre. Could Melissa Gilbert be seen as a film star? Could she be seen as a star at all? I started to think about her relationship with her fans. If she was a star, then she would have fans. I began to look in more detail at Gilbert's fan relationships on the net. It is this research that I will examine here.

Before that, it seems necessary to establish a critical context for the examination of female stars of made-for-television movies. Paul McDonald's useful and timely theorisation of the star system as 'a visual, economic and industrial process of developing mechanisms for the production of popular identities' (2000:1) provides an interesting paradigm for the exploration of the production of popular identities in the television movie. We also need to pay particular attention to the reception of stars by audiences and fans. What are the visual, economic and industrial mechanisms by which television movies produce popular identities, and what meanings are made around these popular identities beyond the movie texts?

The economic and industrial mechanisms that surround the history, marketability and popularity of the made-for-television movie are often used cynically by critics to devalue the visual and aesthetic nature of television movies. Schulze argues that 'the history of the made-for-TV movie is largely the history of a television form that has been increasingly profitable for networks and that has taken on a significant role in competitive programming strategy' (1988: 32). In the 1950s, Hollywood's major motion picture companies released their pre-1948 feature films to local television stations for broadcast. In the 1960s, television successfully negotiated for recent feature films, and by the early 1970s the three networks were broadcasting ten prime-time movie nights each week. Ratings were high, and Hollywood features became, as Douglas Gomery puts it, 'one of the strongest weapons' the networks could deploy in the ratings wars (1983: 97). This programming practice rapidly led to a shortage of available and appropriate features: television broadcast them faster than Hollywood could produce them. By 1966, with the increasing costs of Hollywood features cutting away at their profits, the networks began to commission the production of films exclusively for television. For the next three seasons, movies made for television appeared intermittently in the network's prime-time programming. In 1969, ABC introduced its 'Movie of the Week'. From this date, the made-for-television movie has become a major part of network programming practice in the USA.

The job of a television movie, according to its negative commentators, is to deliver audiences to advertisers. The average three-week shooting schedule of the 'quickie' means that they are churned out to a captive target female audience aged 18–50. Significantly this audience also controls the majority of household spending. They are thus the proverbial ideological dupe, trapped like rats in a maze. The economic mode of production and institutional programming of television movies is undeniably tied into a relationship between commercial television and advertisers. LivingTV's drive to re-brand its audience is indicative of this relationship. But there is undeniably more to such a view than this, on at least three counts. First, the complexities of the relationships between audiences and advertising communication is left untheorised; simply delivering audiences to advertisers is not enough. Second, it ignores the life of television movies and their audiences beyond television scheduling in the video and DVD markets, as well as patterns of home recording, archiving and viewing. Third, this model ignores the television movie as a visual text that communicates meaning.

One of the key components of McDonald's theoretical paradigm for the analysis of the star system is a consideration of the textual markers, preferred codes and fictional contexts that produce a space for the star. Aaron Spelling claims that television movies are one of the few prime-time contexts in which women can be stars (Edgerton, 1985: 168). David Thorburn has analysed the 'segmented dramatic structure' (1987: 198) of the television movie, where narratives organised around commercial breaks have a mini-climax just before each interruption in a bid to keep viewers interested. Todd Gitlin (1983: 161–2) explores the narrative openings of TV movies: 'all salient (narrative) elements have to be established with breathtaking haste' and characters' traits must 'leap out of the screen'. Within these narrative conventions, the style of acting becomes centrally important, as the actors' performance needs an immediacy and style that viewers can recognise. 'Both the aesthetic of the close-up and narrative segmentation, as well as the reliance on melodrama, invest the TV movie heavily in the actor's performance, and the TV movie star is a significant aspect of the genre's popularity' (Schulze, 1988: 39). The visual style of the television movie differs in significant ways from theatrical releases. The television image is much smaller, it has a lower resolution, permits less detail than the cinematic image, the medium shot and the close-up dominate, focus is shallow, *mise-en-scène* stripped down (1988: 39). The particular skills and demands required of television movie acting within these narrative codes and conventions have produced an independent female star system with names that seldom appear in theatrical releases but which are almost guaranteed to win high ratings in 'made-fors': Lindsay Wagner, Veronica Bertinnelli, Tori Spelling, Elizabeth Montgomery, Mariette Hartley, Donna Mills and Melissa Gilbert.

The star system of the television movie is interesting because it opens up a particular window of opportunity for recycling the career of the 'fallen' female TV star, the has-been. Lyndsey Wagner used to be the Bionic Woman, Linda Carter used to be Wonderwoman, Meredith Baxter used to be the mum in *Family Ties*, the spectacular Donna Mills used to be Abby in *Knots Landing*, Farah Fawcett used to be Chris in *Charlie's Angels*. The recovery and recycling of the has-been, and the ageing has-been, is a significant part of the star discourse that surrounds this genre. Television movies deal regularly with the trauma-drama narrative of the woman who appears to have it all, loses it spectacularly, picks herself up and keeps going. They are about struggle and survival. The appeal, therefore, of an actress who has struggled and survived in 'real life' playing her part in a struggle and survival narrative is significant. Melissa Gilbert does not actually fit into this category. She has made over 40 films, beginning her film career with *Christmas Miracle in Caulfield* (1977, USA), at the tender age of 13. Her career has been consistently successful, both in the television movie genre, and in successful television shows such as *Superman* and *Babylon 5*. I did not know anybody who was a fan of Gilbert, so I decided to explore the internet. I began looking at the construction of Melissa through the official and unofficial websites.

GILBERT ON THE INTERNET

Thankfully, critical work has begun to emerge to give researchers a methodological framework for doing internet research, and more importantly for using data generated from websites and chat rooms (Mann and Stewart, 2000; Jones, 1999; Garton *et al.*, 1999; Baym, 2000). Steven Cohan's timely and useful (2001) article on Judy Garland net fandom has provided some degree of specific methodological examination of qualitative internet research to explore fandom, as indeed has Matt Hills' (2002) book on fandom. This emerging body of work is giving researchers a way of thinking about the internet as an object of study. If we are going to use internet data, then we must think carefully about the nature of the knowledge being transmitted, and what we can properly use it to say. Steve Jones argues: 'we can't simply apply existing theories and methods to study computer mediated communication, we need to build knowledge of the internet as a social medium . . . on-line experience is at all times tethered to off-line experience' (Jones, 1999: xii). The whole idea of the 'virtual community' must be questioned, argue McLaughlin, Ellison and Lucas:

> Researchers of the internet community have been forced to create new
> methodologies for studying computer mediated spaces. Even self reported
> characteristics such as gender, age and race as claimed by on line

participants must be subject to scrutiny, because many embrace cyberspace as an arena for experimentation with identity and communication.

(1999: 175)

There is an official Melissa Gilbert website – **melissagilbert.net**; there was also a large unofficial site, **geocities.com/tvcity/set/5958/melissa**, which shut down in January 2002. One of Melissa's fans runs a fascinating site at **www.smkfans.com**. She is a fan of Bruce Boxleitner, and became interested in Gilbert through him. I gathered data from the official website and the now defunct unofficial site. I analysed the content of the messages posted on the official and one unofficial site (the largest), and also posted a questionnaire to 21 people on the official site and 10 people on the unofficial site, asking them about their relationships to Melissa. (Many respondents were the same on both sites – identified by email addresses, hence the lower number taken from the second site.) The response rate was very high: 20 replies back from the official site, and eight from the unofficial site. The majority of respondents were American; the second largest group were from Germany and the rest drawn from various parts of the world, including Jordan, the Caribbean and Thailand. A total of 95 per cent of respondents were female, their ages ranging from 13–70. I asked for biographical information, age, gender, nationality, occupation, and all respondents filled this in. I introduced myself as an English university researcher and a fan of Melissa. I asked when they first became interested in Melissa. Did they think of themselves as a fan? Was being a fan of Melissa an important part of their life? How much did they know about her private life? Did they own a collection of her films? What is their favourite film? Does Melissa receive due respect as an actress? Would they like to see her in films at the cinema?

I wanted to see if recurrent themes on the message boards on the sites were in any way developed or contradicted in questionnaire responses. (Messages on the boards were collated over the course of two weeks, 15–30 March 2001.) Ostensibly (taking account of the play and performance of identity on the internet) the questionnaires allowed me to link meanings made of Melissa to age, gender and geography in a way that messages posted do not always permit. I want to focus on one particular theme from the research: the merging of Melissa Gilbert, movie star/actress with her character, Laura Ingalls, in the hugely successful American television show *Little House on the Prairie*. I want to think about the effect that this intertextuality might have on fan discourses surrounding Melissa Gilbert as a television movie star.

Nearly all messages posted said that they had first discovered Melissa through *Little House on the Prairie*. This is syndicated in America and Europe (not England) and thus respondents still watch it. Linked to this is the association of Melissa Gilbert with nostalgia. This is interesting, because not only is it the articulation of a nostalgia for the childhood of the fans themselves, and their memories of watching Laura and growing up with her, but relatedly a nostalgia that is heightened by the representation of American history and the nostalgic *mise-en-scène* of the nineteenth-century American rural represented in *Little House on the Prairie* (the television series and not the original Ingalls-Wilder books) itself. First screened in 1974 and continuing its run until 1984, *Little House on the Prairie* embodied the family and spiritual values of the solid God-fearing American Presbyterian mid-West (see also Feuer, 1995, for a discussion of the ideological anchoring of the show in the agrarian ideal). Pa Ingalls, played by Michael Landon, became an iconic figure, and a curious merging of Landon as Pa happened, so that they became a near-holy icon. This carried Landon through American television history to his role as the angel in the successful *Highway to Heaven*. Landon's sad death from cancer elevated his holy tragic status even further. My own memories of *Little House on the Prairie* are somehow resolutely Sunday and sacrilegious, even though it was scheduled mid-week for much of its life on British television.

Arguably, megastars such as Julia Roberts and Brad Pitt, no matter which character they play, are always Julia Roberts and Brad Pitt. This residual relationship to the pull of the star persona is an important part of their star quality. I would argue that Melissa Gilbert, no matter what character she plays, is always Laura Ingalls. Because of the intimacy with which fans first got to know Melissa as the red-haired, buck-toothed idealistic child Laura, and seeing her grow up into a woman, they feel that they already know her very well. The proximity of the visual codes of the small screen through which Laura/Melissa became familiar and the intimacy of the narratives of the life of the Ingalls family have arguably shortened the distance between Melissa/Laura and her fans. Many of the messages on the website are written in a personal, letter-like form, addressed to Melissa herself.

'Dear Melissa and fans. It took me a while to figure out what I could write. I love you. You have so many. You don't really need anymore. I love Laura. I have copied every episode onto video. I think Laura has magic. I think Melissa you are a very strong person. You have all my respect.' (Joanna, Germany)

'Hi Melissa. I grew up watching you on *Little House on the Prairie*. I've watched every movie and series that you've made since then. All that has to be mentioned is your name and I watch it. *Little House on the Prairie* is my favourite. I guess that is because I grew up as you grew up. I hope to see you on another series soon. Love (your biggest fan) Sharon.' (USA)

'Love the show *Little House on the Prairie*. When I someday have kids. I'd like them to watch it with me. The show and you have really touched me in a special way. Thank you.' (Barnaby, USA)

'Melissa, I've been watching reruns of *Little House on the Prairie* and would like to say how much I enjoyed growing up with the series. I have just bought the books for my daughter and want to go to Walnut Grove this summer.' (Mary, USA)

'Hi Melissa! I mean Laura, I always remember you as Laura.' (Ruba, Jordan)

This theme is developed in the questionnaires, and becomes once again the primary fan discourse through which Melissa is located. 'I used to watch her on *Little House on the Prairie*. She was such a spunky child star and she made the series all her own. I have watched her grow, get married, become a mother and remain drug free while other child stars could not make the transition' (Mark, USA, no biographical information supplied). 'I saw *Little House on the Prairie* and it touched my heart, and it still does' (Joanna, Germany, 32, artist). '*Little House* made me love her like a member of my family' (Rashid, 29, Morrocco). 'I grew up watching her on *Little House on the Prairie* so I always had a special place in my heart for her' (Gini Lea, 26, USA, marine biologist). Even those respondents who saw her in a film, contextualised her through a memory of Laura: 'I said to my husband, there's half pint off *Little House*, hasn't she got pretty?' (Shari, 27, USA, home-maker).

Melissa Gilbert has carried the moral rectitude and 'spunk' of her character, Laura, with her into the narratives of the television movies. Because of the moral certainties that become a part of the narratives of many television movies, Melissa Gilbert as Laura was made, intertextually, to succeed in television movie texts. Added to this are her qualities as an actress. Her fans say, 'she has grown up to be an intelligent fine actress with direction' (Debbie, Trinidad); 'Melissa I think you're a great actress, the greatest' (Christina); 'Hey, this is Maude from Holland and I think you're the greatest actress ever!!!!!' A critical analysis of Gilbert's performances in the television genre indicates an actress who understands and responds to the nuances, gestures and looks required of the style of acting for female protagonists in the television movie genre. The audience that grew up with Laura, generationally is a large part of the target audience for the television movie.

Melissa Gilbert is also not a great beauty, thus her status as a film star is tied to a narrative of the triumph of acting skill and personality over standards of beauty. She will always bear the marks of the plain, buck-toothed redhead. Her charisma on the small screen, the emotion that she carries across the not-beautiful, but attractive female face. She is the all-American girl-next-door, with good teeth, bad hair, dodgy skin, and the thin, but not compelling body – and she has red, not blonde hair. The female stars of made-for-television movies are rarely represented as great screen beauties. They need a degree of plainness in order to succeed, and they need to be reachable within the dramas that connect to the trials of everyday life. Gilbert evidently recognises her strengths and her limitations. She has not tried to become a star of the big screen, and this is an intelligent move. The majority of the fans that I contacted do not want to see her make the transition to large screen; they want her to be respected duly as an actress, but not to go out of their living rooms. 'The small screen creates a more personal level of fandom' (Emma, 26, USA, sales manager). 'I like that she only plays in movies for television because she isn't a star like any other famous actress, she is just an actress, she stays herself and that's what I like about her!!' (Maud, 14, Netherlands).

CONCLUSION

In the end, can Melissa Gilbert be seen as a star? This question brings me right back to the place that I started – what is a star? What makes a star? Some definitions of a film star are: someone who has successfully broken through the boundaries of television, can open a film at the box office, is visually compelling/beautiful, and always retains an aspect of their star persona in any character they play. To consider female stars of made-for-television movies as stars is to invent other categories. Gilbert is always Gilbert, and she guarantees ratings, she has not though broken through the boundaries of television – quite the opposite. She is a star to her fans, although a particular kind of star of the small screen and the 'real world'. She is not beautiful, although she is to many of them. She is not, ultimately, very well known.

McDonald's discussion of the star system producing popular identities is a more democratic means of figuring out the status of recognisable media names across a range of media forms. Gilbert is certainly a popular identity within the television movie genre, and within communities of viewers who have built and invested cultural capital both in Gilbert's career to date and in aspects of her private life in order to give her meaning beyond the screen. Stars are used by the film industry as a means to try to manage audience demand for films (McDonald, 2000: 5); Gilbert is used by television companies to market TV movies in the schedule. So, is she or isn't she?

As researchers we make a case for a star, and in some ways, given the range of possible definitions, this is arbitrary. Christine Gledhill argues that one of the enduring fascinations with academic star studies is the extent to which the star 'challenges analysis as it crosses disciplinary boundaries' (1991: xiii). The star is:

> . . . a product of mass culture, but retaining theatrical concerns with acting,
> performance and art; an industrial marketing device, but a signifying
> element in films; a social sign, carrying cultural meanings and ideological
> values, which express the intimacies of individual personality, inviting desire

and identification; an emblem of national celebrity, founded on the body, fashion and personal style, a product of capitalism and the ideology of individualism, yet a site of contest by marginalized groups; a figure consumed for his or her personal life.

(Gledhill, 1991: xiii)

I have attempted to make a case for Melissa Gilbert as a star who not only crosses disciplinary boundaries, but also the boundaries of film. I hope that my exploration of Melissa Gilbert has raised questions about the profile of an undervalued area of film studies, and also contributed to the ongoing debate about the categories through which we define and understand the meanings of film stars.

---

1   Pen portraits taken from market research analysis by LivingTV researchers carried out in 2000.

Section 4

Stars and gender, generation, cultural identity

Thomas Austin

The case studies in this section concentrate on how constructions of cultural identity, generation and gender have been foregrounded and inflected via stars' performances, career decisions, and their journalistic reception. Peter Krämer's investigation of Jodie Foster's career in the 1990s considers her 'a most unlikely, but very welcome figure to find in the male-dominated world of Hollywood'. Krämer traces Foster's breakthrough into the upper echelons of film stardom following her Oscar-winning performance in *The Silence of the Lambs* (1991, USA). He assesses how commentators drew correlations between her choice of roles in this and other films, and her private and professional life experiences as both 'victim' and, ultimately, powerful working woman. In the process, Krämer explores the generational constraints on women's professional opportunities in Hollywood, and Foster's emergence as a director and producer in her own right.

In conversation with Mike Figgis (1999: 42–3), Foster has suggested that 'a lot of male actors secretly feel very demeaned by [acting] – because they feel like it's a girl's job . . . thinking about emotions . . . [being] exploited for your looks'. A similar awareness informs Cynthia Baron's investigation of four different screen portrayals of the double role of Dr Jekyll and Mr Hyde. Baron compares the star-images and performances of John Barrymore, Fredric March, Spencer Tracy and John Malkovich. She argues that 'the stars' masterful and disturbing performances not only prove the true manliness of acting, an "intellectual" and therefore suspect profession, they also demonstrate the true manliness of "intellectual" Dr Jekyll [via] his shared identity and inner struggle with Hyde'. The four adaptations also offer insights into shifting popular ideals of masculinity from 1920 to 1996.

Julian Stringer focuses on issues of cultural and national identity in his wide-ranging examination of Asian stars and Asian American star cultures. Noting a common collapsing of

199

the categories 'Asian' and 'Asian American' in journalistic discussions of films and their stars, Stringer calls for a better understanding of 'basic separations . . . between Asian and Asian American screen cultures'. But he also argues that 'while "mainstream" media seldom promote this understanding and separation, the world of Asian American star culture scrambles such distinctions in a most suggestive fashion'.

Finally, Ewan Kirkland's chapter centres on the 'man-child' persona of Robin Williams, and argues that many of the star's performances of masculinity, in both comic and 'straight' dramatic roles, serve to symbolically reconcile conflicts between adult and child. Kirkland relates Williams' childish father roles to the emergence of a 'softer' but still authoritative masculinity in 1990s Hollywood. He also suggests that 'real' children are marginalised in many of Williams' vehicles, with the adult star embodying 'a more accept-able form' of childhood, so 'assuaging adult anxieties surrounding contemporary children'.

Chapter Twelve

'A WOMAN IN A MALE-
DOMINATED WORLD': JODIE
FOSTER, STARDOM AND 90s
HOLLYWOOD

Peter Krämer

In a pre-release article on *The Silence of the Lambs* (1991, USA), Katherine Dieckmann wrote that with her portrayal of FBI Trainee Clarice Starling, Jodie Foster 'provides us with our first genuine screen heroine for the 90s' ('Jodie Takes Hollywood', *Village Voice*, 1 January 1991: 31). As it turned out, the unexpected critical and commercial success of the film not only ensured that Starling became one of the 1990s' better-known screen characters,[1] but also turned Jodie Foster into one of the very few contemporary actresses who combine fairly consistent box office appeal with the power to make films, and largely according to her own designs. The film thus marked an important turning point in Foster's career. Furthermore, together with the previous year's surprise hit *Pretty Woman* (1990, USA), *Lambs* also marked a watershed in Hollywood as a whole, because it signalled a generational change in the pantheon of Hollywood's top female stars. According to Quigley's annual poll of American exhibitors and to *Premiere* magazine's power list – Hollywood's (semi-)official measurements of box office appeal and industry power – in the early 1990s the likes of Meryl Streep and Bette Midler gave way to a group of younger stars, including most notably Jodie Foster and Julia Roberts.

TWO GENERATIONS OF FEMALE STARS IN HOLLYWOOD

At the beginning of the 1980s, Quigley's top ten, which lists the stars considered by exhibitors as the biggest box office attractions of the year, included as many as four women, yet afterwards there were at most three, and usually only one or two; in 1983 there was none at all (Moser, 2000: 14). With the exception of Bo Derek, the female stars ranked in the top ten during the 1980s were in their thirties and forties: Jane Fonda (born in 1937), Barbra Streisand (1942), Goldie Hawn (1945), Bette Midler (1945), Sally Field (1946), Dolly Parton (1946), Cher (1946), Glenn Close (1947), Sissy Spacek (1949), Meryl Streep (1949), Whoopi Goldberg (1949). In 1989, 35-year-old Kathleen Turner (born in 1954) was the only woman in the top ten, at number ten.

In the 1990s, the frequency of female appearances in the annual top ten did not increase (at most three, typically one or two), yet the names and age range changed. Following the success of *Pretty Woman*, 23-year-old Julia Roberts was listed as the second-biggest box office attraction of 1990 – the only woman in the top ten. While Roberts slipped to number four in 1991, she was joined in the top ten by Jodie Foster (born in 1962) at number six, on the basis of her success in *Lambs*. With the exception of Whoopi Goldberg and Michelle Pfeiffer (1959), all subsequent top-ranked female stars were born in the 1960s and 1970s, on average two decades younger than the 80s stars: Meg Ryan (1961), Demi Moore (1962), Sandra Bullock (1965), Cameron Diaz (1972).

The shift towards a younger generation of actresses is also in evidence in *Premiere*'s annual list of the 100 most powerful people in Hollywood, which aims to measure the 'power over movies: the ability to get them made, to make them in a particular way, or to influence or manipulate those who make them with money, fear or simple persuasiveness' (Jonathan Hoefler, 'The Power List', *Premiere*, May 1993: 75).[2] For stars, such power depends largely on the commercial success of their most recent film(s). In most years, the list has included six or seven actresses, as compared to around 20 actors. In 1990 and 1991, the older generation of female stars was still dominant, with rankings for Cher, Midler, Streisand and Streep. With the exception of Streisand, all of them disappeared from the list after 1991, and the new generation took their place. Roberts was listed at number 38 in 1991, the highest ranking for any female star that year, and stayed in the top 100 for the rest of the decade. Foster made the list in 1992 and stayed on it; in 1993 and 1998 she achieved the highest ranking of all female stars (numbers 34 and 40 respectively).

The most obvious explanation for this generational shift in Hollywood's pantheon of female stars has to be age. Unlike male stars, with few exceptions women are unable to maintain their box office appeal when they enter their forties. This may be because they are not given lead roles in high-profile productions any more, or because of diminished audience interest; most likely it is a mixture of both.[3] On the other hand, it has to be noted that a certain age (of around 30) is usually required for an actress to have a chance to make it into the top ten. With only three exceptions (Roberts, Diaz and Derek), this has been the case throughout the 1980s and 1990s.[4] The reason is probably the same as for the over-40s: a shortage of lead roles in high-profile projects, combined with a lack of audience interest. Actresses (just like actors) need time to build up a reputation amongst critics, directors and executives, as well as a following amongst moviegoers through their appearance in a range of often medium- or low-budget films, before they can secure the choice parts.

Most contemporary actresses, then, have a comparatively small window of opportunity for making it into the top ranks of Hollywood stars and, not coincidentally, these ranks are completely dominated by men. As we have seen among the new generation of top female stars, Jodie Foster's success is only surpassed by that of Julia Roberts; and only Sandra Bullock matches Foster's track record (albeit for a shorter period, starting in 1995).[5] As is the case for most of the top female stars of the 1980s and 1990s, Foster's breakthrough came when she was aged around 30. At that point in her life, Foster's body of work was much more extensive and, at least in parts, much more highly esteemed than most of her peers', and her public profile was also considerable. Her film career already spanned almost two decades and included over 25 features and made-for-television movies as well as appearances on numerous television shows. The highlights of her career were her Academy Award nomination for Best Supporting Actress for *Taxi Driver* (1975, USA) and the Best Actress Award for *The Accused* (1988, USA). She had also gained notoriety for her unwitting association with the 1981 shooting of President Ronald Reagan by self-declared Foster fan John Hinckley Jr. While neither her notoriety nor the critical recognition of her acting talent translated into big box office success in the 1980s, *The Accused* was both a moderate hit (US gross $30 million) and a talking point.[6] This set Foster up for consideration for the lead role in the adaptation of Thomas Harris's best-selling thriller, *Lambs*.

As a medium-budget ($19 million) serial-killer movie by a director (Jonathan Demme) who had established his critical reputation with relatively small, off-beat films, *Lambs* was far from being a calculated blockbuster, especially when considering that *Manhunter* (1986, USA), Michael Mann's adaptation of Thomas Harris's previous novel about Hannibal Lecter, had been a major box office flop.[7] The actress had to contend with the fact that there were few successful precedents, apart from *Jagged Edge* (1985, USA), for a female-centred thriller containing graphic violence. There were, however, plenty of precedents in the much maligned low-budget cycle of slasher films. And while the story was clearly focused on the actions and experiences of the female protagonist, the showy part, which would allow an actor to display his skills in a most spectacular fashion, was that of Hannibal Lecter. It was to be expected, then, that the male lead would receive all the attention, especially if the part was given to an established Hollywood star. Crucially, however, the part went to Anthony Hopkins, who may have been a highly esteemed British actor, but was hardly a household name in the US.

THE SILENCE OF THE LAMBS AND THE RISE OF JODIE FOSTER

Sheila Benson's review of *Lambs* (1991) praised director Jonathan Demme for going beyond 'easy effects calculated to make an audience jump' so as to focus 'on the hypnotic duel between his two strong central characters, an FBI trainee and a brilliant sociopath' (*Los Angeles Times*, 13 February 1991: 1). For Benson, the duel between these characters was also a duel between the actors who portrayed them; while, in the film's story, Clarice Starling at best manages a draw with Hannibal Lecter, the clear winner in the acting stakes was Jodie Foster: 'Hopkins' performance may be the film's bravura showpiece, but

Foster's goes the whole distance, steadfast, controlled, heartbreakingly insightful, a fine addition to her gallery of characterizations.' Other reviewers tended to agree with Benson; while always highlighting the 'demonic' quality, 'quiet energy', 'pinched elegance' and 'vicious fun' of Hopkins' performance, they also noted the 'disciplined mix of reserve and revelation' through which Foster 'matches' Hopkins 'step by step', reaching 'the dizzying upper limits of acting' (David Denby, *New York*, 18 February 1991: 60; Jami Bernard, *New York Post*, 14 February 1991: 53; Jan Stuart, *Newsday*, 14 February 1991: 74; David Ansen, *Newsweek*, 18 February 1991: 64).

The most important quality of Foster's acting and Clarice Starling's character is, according to Benson, her intelligence, which mirrors the 'laser-keen intellect' of Hopkins' Lecter. Yet whereas Lecter uses this intelligence to satisfy his selfish urges, Foster's Starling applies hers in the service of an 'unspoken sympathy with the poor dead victims' of the film's second serial killer (nicknamed Buffalo Bill) and a 'most profound human concern' (Benson). Starling's concern for the victims derives partly, Benson argued, from the fact that like them she is 'a woman in a male dominated world'. Other reviewers drew similar parallels between Starling and the female victims. According to *New York Post* reviewer Jami Bernard, 'Buffalo Bill is just an exaggerated version of all the men in the movie, whose eyes pass inquisitively and acquisitively over Clarice.' And J. Hoberman wrote in the *Village Voice* that in the film 'all men have their hidden agendas' and cannot be trusted, while *Newsday*'s Jan Stuart noted that 'Clarice maintains distance from all of the men in the film . . . because they are all so creepy' (J. Hoberman, *Village Voice*, 19 February 1991: 61; Stuart, *Newsday*, 14 February 1991: 74).

Yet, while all the men are thus portrayed as potential victimisers, according to the reviewers, the women are by no means reduced to passive victimhood. Bernard pointed out that even Buffalo Bill's latest captive 'doesn't just lie there looking cute and helpless like most female victims in movies. Here is a victim who both whimpers and yells and has a plan of her own'. And Starling 'is one of the few realistic movie female heroes ever . . . a thoroughly capable woman who is straining all her mental and physical faculties to save other women'. In the light of Hollywood's general treatment of leading ladies, Bernard found Starling's characterisation and the fact that she was 'allowed' to take centre-stage in this film to be 'a miracle', which was of particular importance for female viewers: 'I hope women don't stay away just because there are some ugly scenes.' In a similar vein, *Newsweek*'s David Ansen declared Clarice Starling to be 'the strongest woman's action role since Sigourney Weaver in *Aliens*', five years earlier. And with reference to Foster's traumatic association with the Reagan assassination, J. Hoberman added: 'As the actress was a victim of American pathology, her character's mixture of beleaguered cool and intense isolation takes on additional resonance.'

Judging by these reviews, then, Foster won the performance contest to become the true centre and star of *Lambs*. Her success was also due in part to the associations she brought to the role, both from her previous films and her off-screen notoriety. Indeed, *Lambs* could be, and probably was, seen by critics and audiences as the culmination of her on-screen work and off-screen publicity during the preceding decade or so. Throughout the 1980s, Foster had become associated with the role of the victim. After it had become public knowledge that she had been pursued by John Hinckley Jr, and that she was traumatised by her association with Hinckley's attempt on Reagan's life,[8] journalists were inclined to see her subsequent film parts in the light of this trauma.

The fact that Foster continued to select roles which followed on from her portrayal of a child prostitute in *Taxi Driver*, rather than from her 1970s parts in Disney films, reinforced this tendency in the writing about her. After she had played, among other parts, a gang-rape victim in *The Hotel New Hampshire* (1984, USA) and young women manipulated by older men in two versions of the Svengali story (*Svengali*, 1983, USA, and *Mesmerized*, 1986, UK/USA), she then appeared as the object of the unwelcome attentions of a psychologically disturbed admirer in *Five Corners* (1988, UK), as a suicide in *Stealing Home* (1988, USA) and as another gang-rape victim in *The Accused*. The connection between such roles and the Hinckley incident was made explicit in an article in the *New York Post* from January 1988, which noted that *Five Corners* was 'eerily reminiscent' of her real-life experiences, and quoted Foster as saying that she 'never even thought of the script in terms of Hinckley until about three weeks into the shooting', and that she wanted to leave this incident behind her (Nina Darnton, 'Stranger Than Fiction', *New York Post*, 19 January 1988: 27).[9] At the same time, she insisted on her right, and perhaps even duty, to take parts such as the one in *Five Corners*: 'I can't stop playing a victim just because of Hinckley. Being a victim is unfortunately a big part of women's lives'. Similarly, in a *New York Times* article later that year, Foster played down her association with victim roles ('Well, I've played two, three victim parts in 22 years of acting'), yet also insisted on the importance of dealing with the victimisation of women: 'look at the statistics on sexual violence toward women – you're talking about one out of every four women in the United States' (Sonia Taitz, 'Jodie Foster: Tough Hero', *New York Times*, Section 2, 16 October 1988: 15).

While victimisation was thus a central theme in Foster's public statements and in the writing about her, journalists also emphasised her talent and maturity, and the strength of her characters. Thus, the *New York Daily News* declared in a pre-release article on *The Accused* that 'Jodie Foster has grown up to be serious and beautiful' and was 'widely regarded as one of her generation's most gifted actresses ... who brings both depth and quiet authority to every role' (Alan Mirabella, 'No Kidding', *New York Daily News*, 28 August 1988: 3). The film's reviewers tended to agree (despite the fact that many of them disliked the film intensely, for what they perceived to be its preachiness and exploitativeness), calling Foster 'a preternaturally gifted star', 'one of Hollywood's more undervalued assets', here giving her 'first full-scale, grown-up performance in the movies', characterised by 'blunt but marvellously controlled fury' (Sheila Benson, *Los*

Angeles Times, 14 October 1988: 4; David Denby, *New York*, 31 October 1988: 68; David Ansen, *Newsweek*, 24 October 1988: 74). Although the film's story initially revolves around the victimisation of her character (Sarah Tobias), Foster's performance was seen to emphasise Sarah's anger and her determination to fight back, in the process of which the victim becomes a hero. This combination of contradictory elements was also fore-grounded by Foster herself, when she described her role in *The Accused* as 'the sort of part where you get to do everything: be strong and be vulnerable, and be witty and humorous. And also be really frustrated and angry' (Matthew Flamm, 'Trials & Traumas', *New York Post*, 13 October 1988: 35). It was easy, for journalists and audiences alike, to relate Foster's choice of roles and her comments on the anger and strength of the victims she portrayed, to her own status as an actress fighting back against the vic-timisation she had experienced at the hands of an obsessive fan. With *Lambs*, this process was finally completed.[10] When Clarice Starling confronts and kills Buffalo Bill, it appeared that Foster confronted and finally overcame the Hinckley trauma. Indeed, an article on Foster in *Entertainment Weekly* published shortly after the release of *Lambs* declared it to be 'an artistic and perhaps psychic turning point for the actress', who was '(n)o longer playing the victim' (James Kaplan, 'Dark Victory', *Entertainment Weekly*, 1 March 1991: 24).[11]

A perhaps equally important factor was the perception that Foster's role in this film was a rarity (reviewers mentioned Ripley of the *Alien* films as the only other recent example of female heroism). The *Entertainment Weekly* article noted dryly that '(f)emale heroes haven't exactly been plentiful in Hollywood' and quoted Foster as saying that the film was 'about the making of a hero' (Kaplan). Furthermore, she was said to be a new kind of hero. Both Foster herself and journalists highlighted the distinctive qualities of Foster's brand of heroism, namely intelligence and empathy with victims. In an interview at the time of the film's release, Foster said, for example, that Starling 'isn't a version of Rambo. It's all about the brain' (John Horn, 'Jodie had a Little "Lamb"', *New York Daily News*, 17 February 1991: 5). *Entertainment Weekly*, on the other hand, revealed that director Jonathan Demme had been convinced that Foster was right for the role because, in his words, '(h)er identifica-tion was with a character who felt deeply for victims' (Kaplan). This emphasis on Foster's special relationship with victims, on and off the screen, was also emphasised by a press release from *Lambs*' distributor Orion which stated that Foster 'will appear in a series of public service announcements supporting the National Center for Missing and Exploited Children'.[12] And Foster herself explained the links between her earlier roles and Clarice Starling (who, apart from being a hero, it must be remembered, is also a 'white-trash' orphan) by saying that she tried to play '(w)omen who have survived', 'misfits . . . (p)eople who heretofore have been judged and been cast out as Other, not human, not valuable for our society' and that her performances were aimed at 'recognizing them and redeeming them in some ways' (Jami Bernard, 'Jodie on the "Lambs"', *New York Post*, 12 February 1991: 42).

This, then, was the 'first genuine screen heroine for the 90s' that Katherine Dieckmann had had in mind early in 1991: a woman who has overcome trauma, an actress who is dedicated to portraying and thus recognising and redeeming marginalised women, a female hero who is sympathetic to and acts on behalf of female victims. Yet Dieckmann also highlighted another dimension of Foster's heroism, namely her rise to a position of power in a male-dominated industry. She argued that, amongst many other things, *Lambs* was a parable of the professional lives of Foster and other women, 'commenting pointedly on the ongoing predicament of single career women in this decade' (Dieckmann). Indeed, after *Lambs*, Foster's public statements and much of the writing about her increasingly focused on the marginalisation of women in Hollywood and on Foster's exceptional status as a powerful Hollywood woman, thus to a large extent replacing the earlier theme of victimisation.

STAR, DIRECTOR, PRODUCER: JODIE FOSTER AFTER *LAMBS*

On 14 October 1991, eight months after the release of *Lambs*, *Time* magazine – which rarely puts film-makers on the cover and certainly not first-time film-makers – celebrated the release of Jodie Foster's directorial debut *Little Man Tate* (1991, USA) with a cover story: 'Jodie Foster: A Director is Born'. This unprecedented move for a leading news magazine indicates both the enormously high media profile Foster had achieved, and the somewhat exotic status of female movie directors in Hollywood. By this time, *Lambs* had already become a huge hit. With its $131 million revenues at the US box office, it was one of the ten top-grossing films of 1991, also earning another $142 million abroad. An even more astonishing success for this medium-budget thriller came at the Academy Awards ceremony the following spring: the film won the five major awards (for Best Picture, Director, Actor, Actress and Adapted Screenplay), a feat which had only been achieved twice before since the Oscars' inception in 1927, by *It Happened One Night* (1934, USA) and *One Flew Over the Cuckoo's Nest* (1975, USA).

At this time Foster was first ranked in Quigley's top ten, and she gained the number 52 position on *Premiere*'s 1992 power list. Her ranking in Quigley's top ten registered the fact that exhibitors did indeed consider Foster, rather than Anthony Hopkins, to be the key element in the success of *Lambs*. Her inclusion on the power list, on the other hand, registered her recent hit as well as her celebrity status, and also her willingness and ability to take control of the production process so as to shape the films in which she appeared.

Despite the *Time* cover, however, Foster's post-*Lambs* career had a slow start, when *Little Man Tate* was only a limited success upon its release in October 1991, grossing $24 million in the US. However, Foster did prove herself to be an undoubtedly competent and, perhaps more importantly, a fiscally responsible film-maker, bringing the film in under budget (she saved $1 million on the already small $10 million budget), which meant that the film produced a profit after all. This confirmed the trust that Orion Pictures had placed in Foster, not only by financing *Little Man Tate* (as well as *Lambs*), but also by entering into a production deal with her in August 1990 for two more films, which she would star in, direct and produce. This arrangement allowed her to set up her own production company, Egg Pictures, in December 1990. Unfortunately, Orion filed for bankruptcy in December 1991. Yet, on the basis of her recent work, Foster was soon able to make an even better deal with PolyGram in October 1992. The deal involved '$110 million in financing, and the authority to green-light six pictures over the next three years, three in the $12 million range, three in the $25million range. PolyGram would have no creative control (although each picture would be vetted with foreign sales agents . . .). Foster also had the unheard-of right to choose her own distributor. No other actress (and few actors) had ever been handed such ostensible power' (Abramowitz, 2000: 362–3).

The outcomes of the PolyGram deal were *Nell* (December 1994, USA) and *Home for the Holidays* (November 1995, USA). However, before these Egg Pictures, Foster appeared in *Sommersby* (February 1993, USA) and *Maverick* (May 1994, USA). While she acted neither as producer nor as director on these projects, she appeared to have a strong input; it was reported, for example, that she demanded script changes on *Sommersby* to make her character less hysterical and more realistic, and that she introduced slapstick comedy into *Maverick* (Kenneth M. Chanko, 'Leading Lady for the '90s', *New York Daily News*, City Lights Section, 31 January 1993: 14–15; Ian Spelling, 'The Soft Side of Jodie', *Upper West Side Resident*, 4 February 1993: 15; Michael Shnayerson, 'Jodie Rules', *Vanity Fair*, May 1994: 110–15, 167–72). With the exception of *Home for the Holidays*, in which Foster did not star, all of these films were moderate hits. Even though *Sommersby* and *Nell* performed disappointingly in the domestic market, their much higher foreign revenues ensured their overall success. Indeed, when *Screen International* (30 August 1996: 14) ranked Hollywood stars according to the performance of their last three films in foreign markets, Foster was the second most successful woman, at number 17 (after Whitney Houston, whose position at number 12 derived from a single hit, *The Bodyguard* (1992, USA), rather than from a solid track record). Furthermore, at the time of *Maverick*'s release, Foster was reported to be the third highest-paid actress in Hollywood, after Julia Roberts and Whoopi Goldberg.[13]

Foster achieved this extraordinary success by initially moving away from the portrayal of marginalised or victimised women. In *Sommersby* and *Maverick* she plays more conventional romantic leads – of the melodramatic variety in the former, and of the screwball variety in the latter. It is only with *Nell* that Foster returns, three and a half years after *Lambs*, to the thematic preoccupations that had made her a star. It is tempting to interpret Foster's turn towards conventional romantic roles as a response to her 'outing' as a lesbian, which occurred in the spring of 1991 in the wake of the controversy surrounding *Lambs*'s depiction of 'deviant' sexuality.[14] Foster herself refused to confirm or deny the statements made about her sexual orientation and indeed to discuss her current private life at all. But precisely because of this refusal, these aspects of her personality and life did not play a role in any of the press reporting about her that I have examined. References to Foster's sexual orientation only entered mainstream publications in a major way in 1997 when Foster's brother Buddy published a biography in which he claimed that she was bisexual.[15] Before that time, her sexual orientation was not a part of her star-image in mainstream media (although it was certainly discussed elsewhere and, among other things, provided the basis for a solid fan base amongst lesbians).[16] Hence, there was no need for Foster to confirm her heterosexuality with mainstream audiences by appearing in *Sommersby* and *Maverick*.

Instead, the two films might better be considered as an attempt to solidify her star status after the breakthrough with *Lambs*. Having appeared mostly in medium- or low-budget, often quite off-beat films for many years, Foster seems to have tried to prove that she could be successful in more conventional films, with big budgets and major male stars. In this respect, *Sommersby* was a kind of test run for *Maverick*, with her highest budget to date ($27 million) and a male star (Richard Gere) with an uneven commercial track record. *Maverick* cost $58 million and teamed her up with Mel Gibson, who for several years had consistently been one of Hollywood's top male stars. Critics did indeed understand these two films as crucial experiments for the actress. *Vanity Fair* noted that in *Sommersby* Foster was 'testing new ground as a romantic lead', and the *New York Daily News* asked her whether she had found it difficult to play a woman in love, to which she replied: 'The only thing I can't play well is a weak, ditzy woman' (Shnayerson; Chanko).

Similarly, reviewers found that *Maverick* broke new ground for the actress by revealing that she had 'a solid flair for comedy', while retaining her 'conviction and intensity' which blew 'her easy-going male counterparts off the screen in all the scenes they share' (David Sterritt, *Christian Science Monitor*, 20 May 1994: 10; Michael Medved, *New York Post*, 20 May 1994: 41). However, there was also some concern that this film was indeed primarily a commercial exercise for the actress. The *LA Times* noted that '(h)er performance has an only-kidding coyness' (Peter Rainer, 20 May 1994: 1), and *New York* magazine described her performance as being in 'her proficient, workmanlike I-can-do-this-commercial-shit mode', which was felt to be a great disappointment coming from 'a major actress with a talent for playing outsiders and losers who hold on to their will and integrity' (David Denby, 6 June 1994: 52).

Having consolidated her position as a Hollywood power player with *Sommersby* and *Maverick*, with *Nell* Foster then produced and starred in the kind of project that she had traditionally been most closely associated with: off-beat, without a major male star, concerned with the experiences of the ultimate female outsider, a woman having grown up in the woods, without any contact with other human beings except her mother (and, in her childhood, her twin sister). Again, women are shown to be subject to victimisation by males (the mother was raped, Nell is threatened on several occasions by predatory young men, a male doctor wants to lock her up in a mental institution), yet in the end she triumphs. As with the roles immediately preceding this one, journalists highlighted the fact that Foster was centrally involved in the making of this film (the screenplay was rewritten several times for her), and that the character of Nell was an extension of Foster's range of performances. Foster herself said: 'The one thing that I was most worried about is how I play a person whose emotions are so out there. I mean, I'm totally socialized and barricaded.' Previously, she 'didn't want to play vulnerable parts. But you change. I think the great lesson in this movie is vulnerability is Nell's greatest strength' (Bernard Weinraub, 'A Life on the Set, And That Says It All', *New York Times*, 12 December 1994: 15, 18). Yet, while there were new elements to her performance, on the whole *Nell* was received as a return to what Foster did best, namely, portraying the dignity and strength of marginalised women. The film was said to offer her 'a role worthy of her talents', and she was celebrated as 'an amazingly unselfconscious', 'a greatly compelling actress', giving 'a fearless, fierce, beautifully attuned performance' (David Sterritt, *Christian Science Monitor*, 16 December 1994: 11; Jack Mathews, *Newsday*, 14 December 1994: 2; Jack Kroll, *Newsweek*, 19 December 1994: 64; Richard Corliss, *Time*, 12 December 1994: 92). This praise is quite remarkable in the light of the fact that most critics did not actually like the film.

A closer look at the reception of *Nell* reveals the two main themes of most writing about Foster in the 1990s. Instead of dealing with her current private life (which Foster had declared a no-go area), journalists consistently focused on her past family life and her current professional activities. Thus, *Time* magazine characterised *Nell* as 'the worthiest kind of vanity production', suggesting that the film was all about Foster herself, with Nell as her alter ego (Corliss). J. Hoberman interpreted the film in very specific biographical terms, saying that *Nell* is 'Foster's own fantasy': 'Like Nell, Foster is misunderstood and unclassifiable, an innocent victim and a tenacious survivor, an intellectual and an autodidact, precocious yet backward' (J. Hoberman, *Village Voice*, 20 December 1994: 55). Hoberman also linked the film to her directorial debut: '*Nell* is a sometimes touching fairy tale that gives Foster a chance to be her own version of the child genius she directed in *Little Man Tate*.' Like *Nell*, *Little Man Tate* focused on an extraordinary child raised by a single mother. The parallels between *Little Man Tate* and Foster's life had been unavoidable. For example, Georgia Brown had written: 'There's reason to believe that Jodie Foster – raised by a single mother, child performer from age three, teenage movie star, Yale graduate – might have a special affinity for Scott Frank's screenplay' (*Village Voice*, 15 October 1991: 66).

In addition to regarding her films as autobiographical, critics also saw them as self-reflexive meditations on her present status as a movie star. This theme was already present, as we have seen, in the reception of *Lambs*, which could be understood as a film about the problematic status of career women such as Foster working in male dominated professions. A similar interpretation was proposed by David Denby for *Little Man Tate*, in which Foster's working-class mother fights with a lonely and repressed female career psychologist over the fate of her son, in the process 'suggesting that the career woman is hopelessly inadequate because she hasn't given birth. ... Could Foster be ambivalent about her stardom?' (*New York*, 21 October 1991: 95). And J. Hoberman interpreted Foster's explanation of *Nell*'s theme as a statement about her own difficulties with being a different kind of female star in Hollywood: 'This movie is about defying description, about not being put in a box, and not being labeled and marketed.'

More generally, both journalists and Foster herself throughout the 1990s placed her work in the context of an industry which did not give women enough adequate roles and did not cater adequately to female audiences. In its review of *Little Man Tate*, the *LA Times* noted that Foster 'would have thrived in the 30s and 40s, when Hollywood wasn't terri-fied of women with smarts and mettle', whereas today 'Foster's unwillingness to play demure damsels may have contributed to a shortage of good roles for her' (Peter Rainer, 9 October 1991: 1). The reviews of *Nell* included references to 'the shortage of substantial female roles' in contemporary Hollywood, which actresses like Foster were 'combating' often by becoming producers so as to make movies which Hollywood otherwise would not produce anymore (Sterritt; Corliss).

Foster firmly established her own, explicit concern for these issues through a series of high-profile pronouncements, including speeches at the Golden Globe and Academy Award ceremonies in 1992. At the Golden Globes in January, she used her press confer-ence to talk about the fact that women were usually denied, in Hollywood and elsewhere, the role of the hero in modern versions of the mythical journey outlined by myth scholar Joseph Campbell, and that Starling in *Lambs* was exactly such a hero. When she received the Best Actress Oscar a few months later, her speech referred specifically to the prob-lematic status of women in Hollywood: 'I'd like to dedicate this award to all the women who came before, who never had the chances I've had, and the survivors, and the pio-neers, and the outcasts. ... Thanks to the Academy for embracing such an incredibly strong and beautiful feminist hero that I'm so proud of' (Chunovic, 1995: 140).

CONCLUSION

In the context of Jodie Foster's ongoing critique of Hollywood's male bias, her last two films of the 1990s, *Contact* (1997, USA) and *Anna and the King* (1999, USA), took on special significance. They were both big-budget epics[17] – one a philosophical science fiction movie, the other a proto-feminist costume drama – which deal with the plight, adventures and triumphs of women in a male-dominated profession (*Contact*) or society (*Anna and the King*). Furthermore, *Contact* deals with yet another gifted child (or rather, the woman that this child grows into), and *Anna and the King* with yet another single mother. At the same time, the first of the two films, following the lead of the *Alien* and *Terminator* films, tried to reclaim one of Hollywood's most important genres, science fiction, for women; the other, coming in the wake of *Titanic* (1997, USA), aimed to revive the romantic historical epic, which together with the equally female-orientated and female-centred big-budget musical and with biblical epics, had been at the centre of Hollywood's operations in the 1950s and for most of the 1960s, before Hollywood's marketing strategies shifted towards young males and their preferred genres.[18]

In the late 1990s, then, Foster moved her campaign against Hollywood's male bias to the very centre of the industry. Without the support of major male stars, she played the lead in big-budget movies, with mixed results: a hit (*Contact*) and a huge flop (*Anna and the King*).[19] With her $15 million fee for *Anna and the King*, she, together with Meg Ryan ($15 million) and Julia Roberts ($17 million), began to close the salary gap between the top male and female stars (Bernard Weinraub, 'Reaching for a Glass Ceiling', *New York Times*, 8 January 1999: 9). And with a new production deal in 1998, she moved Egg Pictures away from its previous association with the comparatively small company PolyGram into an alliance with one of Hollywood's biggest players, Paramount.

At the same time, she became a single mother (in July 1998), leaving the identity of the father unknown. Pointing out that her own mother has given her a lot of support, and that she first thought about motherhood when playing a mother in *Little Man Tate*, she calmly stated: 'Single parenting is something I know a lot about' (Bert Mills, 'Jodie Foster Delivers', *New York Daily News*, Now section, 23 July 1998: 45–6). In her private life, then, as well as in many of her films, Foster went it alone, and if there were strong personal bonds, they were more likely to be with other women than with men. Thus, the actress that Katherine Dieckmann declared to be 'our first genuine screen heroine for the 90s' entered the new millennium as a single mom superstar, largely independent and in control of both her private and her professional life, her on-screen performances and even her off-screen publicity. She was a most unlikely, but very welcome figure to find in the male-dominated world of Hollywood.

At the same time, as Rachel Abramowitz argues, Foster's achievements were limited, and her position fragile: Foster's 'much-hyped PolyGram deal fell far short of its initial agenda of producing a slate of pictures. She executive-produced only one effort in which she did not star or direct, the cable movie *The Baby Dance* (1998, USA)' (Abramowitz, 2000: 443). Foster's more conventional Paramount deal could therefore be seen as a retreat from her ambition to become a major producer of other people's work. Furthermore, while Foster had been able to set the terms for much of the writing about her, she was overwhelmed by the media's strong response to her willingness finally to talk about John Hinckley Jr. Abramowitz reports her angry response: 'This fascination that people have with celebrity is plain gross. . . . It's grotesque. It makes me feel like I'm being used, which of course I am, and I should be used to it, but I like to have some good feeling about humanity instead of being a misanthrope.' Similarly, the tabloid press focused its attention on her during and after her pregnancy, and according to Abramowitz, '(t)o escape scrutiny, she temporarily moved out of her home when the baby was born' (Abramowitz, 2000: 443). Finally, and perhaps most importantly, Foster's 40th birthday on 19 November 2002 loomed large. As we have seen, in Hollywood turning 40 usually means that an actress's days as a major star are over.

POST-SCRIPT APRIL 2002

After an absence of three years, Jodie Foster returned to the big screen with a splash when David Fincher's thriller *Panic Room* (2002, USA), in which she stars as a single mother, grossed $30 million during its opening weekend. By this time, however, her long-standing plan to make a film about German film-maker Leni Riefenstahl had become mired in controversy (Amy Wallace, 'Will Jodie Whitewash Leni? Hitler's Filmmaker is Foster's Fixation', *The Nation*, 2 April 2001: 37–9), and the deal between Egg Pictures and Paramount had been discontinued, without a single film going into production. The films that Egg did produce were all for other distributors: *Waking the Dead* (2000, USA; US box office gross less than $1 million), *The Dangerous Lives of Altar Boys* (scheduled for a 2002 release, with Foster in a supporting role) and *Flora Plum* (directed by Foster for release in 2004). After the discontinuation of her Paramount deal, Foster folded Egg Pictures altogether, because, she told *Premiere* magazine, '(p)roducing other people's movies is just hard on your soul' (Sean M. Smith, 'Jodie's Choice', *Premiere*, March 2002: 48). In the light of the renewed media attention attracted by the birth of her second child in September 2001, *Premiere* marvelled at her continuing ability to protect her privacy: 'We cannot name a single person she has ever dated' (Smith: 86). And the article's subtitle confirmed Foster's exceptional status as a female icon: 'In *Panic Room* – as in life – Jodie Foster has become the kind of hero she believes in.'

Research for this essay in American archives was funded by the British Arts and Humanities Research Board.

---

1 For a discussion of the return of Clarice Starling in *Hannibal* (2001, USA) and the reasons for Foster's withdrawal from the project, see Jill Bernstein ('But Dino, I don't want to make a film about elephants ...', *Guardian*, Review, 9 February 2001: 2–4).

2 In the following paragraph, I am drawing on the research of Sultan Sahin Gencer, University of Nottingham.

3 There is also the distinct possibility that in the few cases in which an actress aged over 40 stars in a box office hit – an example would be Meryl Streep in *The Bridges of Madison County* (1995, USA) – she is not given credit for the film's success, and thus not ranked highly by exhibitors in Quigley's poll.

4 According to Emanuel Levy's study of the careers of all stars listed in Quigley's annual top ten between 1932 and 1984, the median age for making it onto the list was 27 for women and 36 for men. A total of 60 per cent of the female stars first made the list between the ages of 25 and 34, whereas 60 per cent of male stars were over 34 when they were first listed (Levy, 1990: 252).

5 On this, see Krämer (forthcoming b).

6 *The Accused* was just outside the list of the top 30 hits of 1988. Box office information – and also information about budgets which I use below – is taken from the German magazine *steadycam*, which derives its figures from the American trade press.

7 As Bernstein puts it: 'it grossed $8.6 million, less than the cost of its print ads'.

8 See, especially, her article in the December 1982 issue of *Esquire* entitled 'Why Me?', which is discussed together with her earlier public statements about the impact of the assassination attempt on her in Chunovic (1995: 59–60). A key section of Foster's *Esquire* article is the following (quoted in Abramowitz, 2000: 182): 'I was crying for myself. Me, the unwilling victim. The one who would pay in the end. The one who paid all along, and, yes, keeps paying.'

9 Some time after this interview, Foster began categorically to refuse to answer any questions about Hinckley Jr; her silence lasted until the late 1990s.

10 Between *The Accused* and *Lambs* Foster only appeared in *Backtrack* (also known as *Catchfire*), a troubled production in which she plays the witness to a mob killing who is abducted by a hitman. *Backtrack* was shot by Dennis Hopper (who also co-starred) in 1988, and after Hopper had withdrawn his name from the film, it was released straight to video in 1991. See Abramowitz (2000: 270) and Elley (2000: 139).

11 Several critics related her performance as Clarice Starling to Foster's earlier roles and her real-life experiences, emphasising both continuity and change. Dieckmann, for example, wrote that '(t)he part dovetails neatly into Foster's repertoire of child women imperiled by deranged men', yet the film 'puts a choice spin on Foster's afflicted history'.

12 Orion press release, Jodie Foster clippings file, Billy Rose Theatre Collection, New York Public Library.

13 Foster's $5 million salary for *Maverick* was dwarfed by the $20 million that male stars could command ('Superstar Salaries', *Film Review*, December 1995: 9). By the time this article appeared, Foster had been overtaken by several actresses in the salary stakes.

14 The circumstances surrounding the claims made by gay and lesbian activists and publications about Foster's homosexuality are discussed in Staiger (1993: 142–54). For a general discussion of the media's treatment of homosexuality in Hollywood, including numerous references to Foster, see Ehrenstein (2000).

15 See, for example, Dana Kennedy, 'Sib Story', *Entertainment Weekly*, 16 May 1997: 105–6. In an early announcement of the book, it was falsely reported that her brother claimed she had had no homosexual relationships (George Rush and Joanna Molloy, *New York Daily News*, 5 July 1995: 19). In January 1995, it had been reported that she was having a relationship and indeed lived with a male casting director, but this was felt to be a plant intended 'to make the hard-core bachelerette more simpatico to Oscar voters' (Richard Johnson, *New York Post*, 17 January 1995: 6).

16 There is considerable academic interest in this issue. See, for example, Whatling (1997: 134–59) and Lane (1995).

17 *Contact* cost $90 million, and thus had by far the highest budget for any Jodie Foster film up to this point. For a discussion of *Contact* see Krämer (forthcoming a).

18 For a more extensive discussion of production trends in contemporary Hollywood, especially the role of epic romances and action-adventure, see Krämer (1999a) and Krämer (1999b).

19 With $101 million, *Contact* was the 12th highest-grossing film of 1997 in the US. *Anna and the King* grossed only $25 million in 1999.

Chapter Thirteen

FROM TORMENTED GENIUS TO ☐ SEXUAL ADVENTURER: STARS AND MASCULINITY IN THE JEKYLL AND HYDE FILMS

Cynthia Baron

The continuous adaptation of Robert Louis Stevenson's 1886 allegorical shilling shocker, *Strange Case of Dr. Jekyll and Mr. Hyde*, can, as Brian Rose suggests, 'serve as a "tracer" of shifts in attitudes' (1996: 1). Analysis of even a small sampling of Jekyll and Hyde adaptations reveals that the films' representations of two passages in Stevenson's novella are especially pertinent to inquiries into shifting constructions of masculinity. The first concerns the secret pleasures that led the doctor to see the duality of his identity long before the invention of Hyde; in recounting his tale, Jekyll explains:

> And indeed the worst of my faults was a certain impatient gaiety of
> disposition, such as has made the happiness of many, but such as I found it
> hard to reconcile with my imperious desire to carry my head high, and wear
> a more than commonly grave countenance before the public. Hence it came
> about that I concealed my pleasures.

> (*Geduld, 1983: 43–4*)

The second passage makes Hyde's horrific cruelty into a spectacle by having a woman witness Carew's murder. Stevenson's narrator sets the scene by telling the reader that 'a maid servant living alone . . . had gone upstairs to bed'. The narrator continues:

> It seems she was romantically given, for she sat down upon her box, which
> stood immediately under the window, and fell into a dream of musing. And
> as she sat she became aware of an aged and beautiful gentleman . . . and
> advancing to meet him, another and very small gentleman . . . next moment,
> with ape-like fury, he was trampling his victim under foot and hailing down
> a storm of blows, under which the bones audibly shattered and the body

jumped upon the roadway. At the horror of these sights and sounds, the maid fainted.

(Geduld, 1983: 25–6)

These moments of revelation that establish Jekyll's inherent duality and the necessity of a female witness to establish Hyde's potency, are defining features of the four films I will discuss. These are all films that have been shaped by the picture personalities[1] and performances of their stars John Barrymore, Fredric March, Spencer Tracy and John Malkovich. Studying them, I have been struck by the ways in which the productions have mobilised their leading actors' star-images to flesh out narratives that have, over the course of a century, increasingly *suppressed* the idea that Jekyll's secret pleasures might have something to do with 'a certain impatient gaiety of disposition', and increasingly *developed* the idea that seeing the effects of Hyde's 'ape-like fury' causes women – figuratively vulnerable because alone at night or literally vulnerable because a servant, daughter or prostitute economically dependent on men – to faint. Moving from narratives that centre on the ethical anguish of Victorian gentlemen to films that focus on the psychic problems of tough guys and new age men, the four films increasingly equate 'true' masculine identity with potential and/or actual violence against women in particular.

While analyses of the films' narrative trajectories have led audiences to discuss Christian, Darwinian and Freudian allegories in the texts, using insights from star studies reminds one that these Jekyll and Hyde productions have consistently invited their audiences to experience *performances* of masculinity.[2] Studying the ways that Barrymore, March, Tracy and Malkovich have portrayed the connection between the doctor and his transgressive self can be deeply troubling, for audiences from various eras have been invited to enjoy permutations on a central, abiding vision of masculinity; namely, that unlicensed sexual activity and violence against 'strangers' is the most conclusive sign of hard masculinity. The actors' performances can also provide a great deal of information about star performances, for in the films I have considered their performances resonate on more than one register. The stars' masterful and disturbing performances not only prove the true manliness of acting, an 'intellectual' and therefore suspect profession, they also demonstrate the true manliness of 'intellectual' Dr Jekyll, a character whose masculinity is confirmed by the flamboyant display of his shared identity and inner struggle with Hyde.

ANTECEDENTS

There have been wildly diverse adaptations of Stevenson's novella from the moment it was published. These include: the burlesque piece entitled *The Strange Case of a Hyde and a Seekyl* produced five months after the novella was in print; the competing film productions released by Selig and Kalem in 1908; the 1963 Jerry Lewis comedy entitled *The Nutty*

Professor; the 1973 NBC television musical that starred Kirk Douglas; the numerous cartoon and pornographic versions of the story; more recent treatments such as the Classics Illustrated adaptation by John K. Snyder; the New York theme restaurant called the Jekyll and Hyde Club which opened in 1996; and the Broadway musical that debuted in 1997.[3] The adaptations at the centre of my study all draw on the Stevenson novella and the theatrical adaptation commissioned in 1887 by actor Richard Mansfield (1854–1907). The play, written by Thomas Russell Sullivan, debuted in Boston on 9 May 1887. It had a highly successful run at New York's Madison Square Garden Theatre in 1887 and another at the Lyceum Theatre in London in 1888. It continued to be played by Mansfield in repertory until his death in 1907.

Mansfield's memorable portrayal introduced the dual role into a select bravura repertory that offered unique opportunities for leading actors who were prepared to engage publicly in a supreme test of their professional skill.[4] Mansfield's productions also codified the characterisations. He not only 'depicted, with horrible animal vigor and with intense and reckless force of internal malignity, the exultant wickedness of the bestial and frenzied Hyde, [he] was able, in the concurrent, associate impersonation of Dr Jekyll, to interblend the angel and the demon' (quoted in Geduld, 1983: 164). Actors who followed Mansfield were required to contend with his powerful originating performance. March and Tracy would build on Mansfield's portrayal of Hyde's 'horrible animal vigor'. Barrymore and Malkovich would challenge that model by choosing almost languid gestures in Hyde's most threatening moments.

The script that Mansfield commissioned also established the narrative blueprint for the ensuing film adaptations.[5] Sullivan's stage adaptation compressed the story's events and replaced Stevenson's series of retrospective accounts with a linear narrative that used Hyde's powerful actions to propel the story, included scenes centred on the actor's transformations from one character to another, vividly portrayed Jekyll's inner struggle as he prepared finally to kill himself, and expanded the maid's role to create the character of Carew's daughter who is desired by both Jekyll and Hyde and who, in the final moments of the play, discovers the poisoned Hyde.

The place of Jekyll and Hyde's love interest has become increasingly expanded as the film adaptations move from 1920 to 1931 to 1941 to 1996. The love interest becomes especially important in the film based on Valerie Martin's 1990 novel, *Mary Reilly* (1996, USA), starring John Malkovich. Based on Martin's re-visioning of Stevenson's text, Mary is a composite character who represents the original novella's maid, the delicate love of Dr Jekyll, the poverty-ridden deflowered woman who is Hyde's object of desire, Dr Lanyon who is witness to Jekyll and Hyde's physical transformations and Mr Utterson whose 'approved tolerance for others' often led to him being 'the last good influence in the lives of down-going men' (1990: 17).[6]

The films' developing emphasis on Hyde's sexual sadism parallels the emerging emphasis on Jekyll/Hyde's love interest. It also reflects a process of accretion that has shaped the novella's adaptations ever since Mansfield's London productions were linked to the coincident outbreak of the Jack-the-Ripper mutilation-murders in London's East End.[7] By conflating Stevenson's story of a discontented, middle-aged bachelor ashamed of his 'impatient gaiety of disposition' with the lurid accounts of prostitutes murdered by someone with a knowledge of surgery, the film adaptations have been able to mask the effeminate or homosocial or homosexual implications of Dr Jekyll's secret pleasures and, at the same time, give expression to the troubling connections between violence (especially against women) and prevailing constructions of masculinity.

FROM BARRYMORE TO MALKOVICH

The four productions examined here reveal distinct intersections between the star-images of their leading actors, the textual emphases of the specific productions, and the horizons of expectation that helped to shape audience interpretations. The 1920 film was released a few weeks after the première of Barrymore's theatrical production of *Richard III*. This is an important conjunction, for as theatre scholar Michael Morrison points out, 'Barrymore's *Richard III* and *Hamlet* are generally acknowledged to be two of the most significant Shakespearean events in the history of the modern stage' (Morrison, 1997: x).[8]

Variety understood that 'to the theatre-going public the appearance of John Barrymore in any production [was] an event' (2 April 1920), and the 1920 Paramount film was seen as an opportunity to witness a performance by the century's greatest tragic actor. In his mid-thirties and having made his reputation on Broadway as a matinée idol in productions such as *The Fortune Hunter* (1909, USA) and *The Affairs of Anatol* (1912, USA), Barrymore's collaboration with playwright Edward Sheldon, director Arthur Hopkins and designer Robert Edmund Jones contributed to the creation of a new star-image for Barrymore: a gifted dramatic actor whose family lineage had been finally proved by his becoming 'the legitimate successor to Richard Mansfield in the American theatre' (Morrison, 1997: 63).[9]

Barrymore designed his portrayal of Hyde while developing Richard III. With the image of a tarantula at the foundation of both portrayals, Barrymore created two characters whose hunched posture and crabbed movement were visual indices of their deformed psyches.[10] Theatre audiences would be able to see literal and figurative connections between Barrymore's interpretation of Jekyll and Hyde and his portrayal of Richard III, which presented the character as a tragic figure whose physical and psychic deformity had caused the callow youth to devolve over time into a tyrant. Audiences of the time could also interpret the actor's portrayal of Jekyll and Hyde through and in terms of his performances in *Peter Ibbetson* (1917) and *The Jest* (1921, USA). Both dramas featured a 'soft and feminized [man who is] recuperated into hegemonic ideals of masculinity' by uncharacteristic assertions of violence (Studlar, 1996: 122).

In the 1920 film, Barrymore's Dr Jekyll is graceful, elegant, refined and handsome in his ruffled shirts and tailored waistcoats. When compared to the other male characters in the film, he is also younger, more innocent, more emotional, a man whose worst fault might be 'a certain impatient gaiety of disposition'. While Hyde's exploits suggest that Jekyll has a darker side, it is only in the final sequence of the film, alone in the laboratory with Millicent Carew (Marsha Mansfield), that the young doctor's masculinity is finally and convincingly proved. In much the same way that Barrymore's highly reported exploits of drunken escapades counter-balanced the suspect masculinity that came with being an actor and, worse, a foppish matinée idol, Barrymore's bravura performance in the 1920 film assured audiences that even weaklings possessed a darker, more masculine private self. Moreover, the tragic effect of Hyde's deformed desire could be counted on to resonate with Euro-American audiences whose current understanding of humanity had been shaped by the carnage of the First World War. Driven by the demands of Victorian patriarchy to prove his manhood through violent aggression, Barrymore's Dr Jekyll provided a melancholy expression of the life-denying limitations of a patriarchal society that conferred value only on a man's (failed) attempt to control that aggression.

With Universal's *Dracula* (1931, USA) and *Frankenstein* (1931, USA) enjoying box office success, Paramount elected to remake *Dr Jekyll and Mr Hyde* as a sound film. At director Rouben Mamoulian's insistence, the studio awarded the dual role to Fredric March who was a John Barrymore stand-in by virtue of his matinée-idol good looks, his Barrymore-like profile, and his stage and screen impersonations of Barrymore. March's lively portrayal of Barrymore in the 1928 West Coast productions of *The Royal Family* had led Paramount to sign March to a contract. When he reprised the role for Paramount's film, *The Royal Family of Broadway* (1930, USA), March received his first Oscar nomination. March was Mamoulian's first and only choice, for Mamoulian had seen the actor's performance in the screwball comedy *Laughter* (1930, USA), which showed March's ability to portray a character whose scintillating expressivity could also reveal a 'darker, repressed, and perhaps self-destructive energy' (Palmer, 1996: 763). March's romantic comedy image also made it possible for the film to soft-pedal the narrative's salacious underpinnings. March's performance, for which he won an Academy Award, suggested that Dr Jekyll's fate could be attributed to a tragic flaw, namely 'a certain impatient gaiety of disposition'. It suggested that Jekyll was an exuberant youth whose masculinity remained in doubt until, by an act of atonement, he conquered the violent force that had overtaken him.

The 1931 film has consistently been the most critically acclaimed Jekyll and Hyde film adaptation.[11] Its respected status indicates a match between vehicle and star-image. By presenting the tragic downfall of the noble, albeit sometimes giddy, young doctor, the film used established associations with its star's image to communicate with and appeal to audiences for whom economic crisis had caused a crisis in gender roles as well. The film banked on March's physical beauty, romantic picture personality and public biography as a thoughtful husband and 'firm defender of the spoken drama' to assure audiences that even a gentleman could be overwhelmed by unforeseen circumstance ('Who's Who in the Pictures', *New York Times*, 26 November 1933).[12]

March's highly expressive portrayal of the tormented young doctor provided a safe, handsomely packaged illustration of the era's perceived threat to American manhood. Given that the film was produced at a moment when economic crisis had left many men feeling out of control, March's sterling image gave credence to the doctor's valiant attempt to control a manmade terror. The actor's public image sustained the impression that Jekyll's ethical struggle was a powerful demonstration of his manhood. Considering that the film was released at a time when women could have felt increasingly vulnerable to the vagaries of dislocated men, March's matinée idol image perhaps also mollified the significance of Hyde's brutality toward women.

In retrospect, the 1931 film represents the beginning of a transitional moment in star images, film performance, and notions of masculinity. A handsome, young romantic star, March relied on a 'classical' acting style (larger, more theatrical than 'naturalistic' acting) to convey the idea that Jekyll was forcibly overtaken by the 'jagged toothed simian' Hyde (Nash and Ross, 1985: 676). Ten years later, Spencer Tracy, a rugged-looking, 40-year-old biopic star would present what began as a 'naturalistic' performance of a hypermasculine, inherently 'simian' character. Building on Tracy's physicality and star-image, which fleshed out the conflicted middle-aged bachelor in Stevenson's novella, the 1941 film was designed as a challenging vehicle for one of the era's most respected actors. Stepping up the latent violence suggested by his Academy Award-winning performances in *Captains Courageous* (1937, USA) and *Boys Town* (1938, USA), Tracy's performance ushered in a time when tough guys made the best psychopaths (see Cohan, 1997: Chapter 3). In contrast to the Barrymore, March, and even Malkovich films, the 1941 film emphasised 'Harry' Jekyll's friendship with bachelor buddy John Lanyon, his contemporary in age and sensibility. In marked contrast to the Barrymore and March films, Jekyll's earthy desire for fiancée Beatrix Emery (Lana Turner), a sweet little sex kitten half his age, made moral and/or sexual deviancy an inherent feature of the 'good' doctor's character.

Tracy's performance overturns the image of the dandy created by Barrymore and March, for by 1941 the stylishness of that figure would be a sure sign of effeminacy. While the 1931 and 1941 films cover very similar narrative ground, Tracy's performance differs sharply from March's. For example, in the scene that follows Jekyll's last normal, or conscious, encounter with his fiancée, March shows audiences that Hyde forcibly overtakes the earnest young doctor as he wistfully peers through Muriel's window to have one last look. By comparison, Tracy uses a casual, even gait as he strolls back to ravish his sobbing fiancée in her garden. Tracy's performance shows audiences that Hyde has emerged directly and naturally from Jekyll. It suggests that the transition from one persona to another is a process needing no external catalyst. His portrayal presents masculinity as no longer being founded on a virile, 'muscular', ethical struggle with base desire. Instead, embodied by Tracy, 'true' masculinity is a latent potential that is released by the expression of violent, sexual assault.

Markedly different from the characters portrayed by both Barrymore and March, Tracy's Dr Jekyll personified an ideal of masculinity that solidified during the years of the Great Depression. Tough times called for tough men: men who could take on and take down the 'effetes' whose failures had led to worldwide economic depression, the 'aliens' whose ethnic minority status and/or allegiance to foreign regimes threatened the security of (White) Americans; and the demagogues whose clever use of modern military and communication systems threatened to control ever increasing numbers of people. Tracy's 1941 performance in many ways encapsulates the transition from wartime to post-war and Cold War visions of masculinity. It moves Jekyll from the safe world of male bonding (with Lanyon) to his frustration with the restraining world of domestic duty (with Beatrix) and from there to his sublime pleasure in the satiated world of the social deviant (with Ingrid Bergman's Ivy).

Blending Tracy's stoic and ultimately violent masculinity with the 'effeminate' theatricality displayed by Barrymore and March, the 1996 production of *Mary Reilly* with John Malkovich used his stolid physicality and mobilised his multivalent star-image to convey a vision of masculinity that depended on displays of actual or threatened violence. Christopher Hampton, who wrote the screenplay for the 1988 adaptation of *Dangerous Liaisons* (1988, USA), co-authored the adaptation of *Mary Reilly* directed by Stephen Frears. The film's sympathetic rendering of the dual character builds on the image which Malkovich established in his performance as the wicked but finally tender Vicomte de Valmont in *Dangerous Liaisons*. Malkovich's portrayal of Jekyll as a doomed but engaging figure whose profligate sexual adventures prove his potent masculinity also creates associations with his performance as the driven but fated assassin Mitch Leary in *In the Line of Fire* (1993, USA).[13]

TriStar Pictures may have envisioned *Mary Reilly* as a sequel to films such as *Bram Stoker's Dracula* (1992, USA), *Interview with the Vampire* (1994, USA) and *Mary Shelley's Frankenstein* (1994, USA), for these films also depict masculinity as a descent into the primitive. But *Mary Reilly* did not meet expectations. With a $47 million budget but gross domestic box office receipts of only $5 million, the film was a financial disaster. It was also a critical failure.[14] Yet Malkovich's career was not affected by the film's bad press or dismal box office figures. In 1998 he was given a lifetime achievement award at the San Sebastian Film Festival for his work in film and theatre. In 1999 he became an icon of contemporary popular culture with the release of *Being John Malkovich* (1999, USA), a film that played on Malkovich's status as one of the era's most unlikely but most interesting screen villains.[15]

Described in the popular press of the 1990s as a 'non-standard hunk', Malkovich became a star whose contradictory soft and hard physicality played into contemporary explorations of ambiguous sexualities and gender identities. Representative of the new age man with a receding hairline, wide waistline and nondescript biceps, Malkovich could also portray and embody compulsory hypermasculine aggressiveness. That combination made Malkovich a phastasmagoric figure that could be easily tailored to audience desires. His ambiguous public image gave form to a vision of masculinity that invites and perhaps sustains homosexual, heterosexual, and bisexual desires and fantasies. With his soft, formless body portraying characters whose hard masculinity is proved by their cold-blooded cerebral vengeance, the Malkovich image has kept oppositions between 'hard' and 'soft', 'masculine' and 'feminine' in play.

While flamboyant actors such as Barrymore and March began their careers as matinée idols, and tough American types such as Tracy consistently played biopic heroes, Malkovich's 'non-standard' physical appearance ensured that audiences would never consider him a handsome matinée idol or rugged man's man. Articles about Malkovich in the popular press invariably note that his physical appearance does not reflect conventional notions of beauty. Chris Chang summarises Malkovich's unattractive physical features by calling attention to his 'gangling frame, thick legs, receding hair, buttony eyes, blank look [and] hallucinated voice' (1999: 2). In a publicity piece in *Cosmopolitan*, David Gritten describes the actor's 'off-center looks' and explains that Malkovich is 'far from conventionally handsome [because] his receding hairline accentuates a high forehead; he is barrel-chested and walks with a pigeon-toed gait; his deep-set eyes border on beadiness [and] you could apply the adjective "reptilian" to Malkovich and stay well within the bounds of libel law' ('What is John Malkovich – A Man or a Louse?', *Cosmopolitan*, November 1992: 247). With Malkovich's physical features falling outside conventional norms of beauty, commentators find themselves pressed to explain the actor's audience appeal.

Seeming to use the actor's highbrow biography as a touchstone, critics often suggest that if audiences find physically unattractive Malkovich appealing, it must be because they are drawn to his intelligence. Their discussions sustain the 'common sense' mind–body opposition that has led generations to believe that intelligence and beauty cannot reside in the same human being. Even today that supposition frequently leaves both smart and beautiful women out in the cold. Yet when the 'common sense' opposition between mind and body is refracted through patriarchy's equation between masculinity and reason, Malkovich's unattractive physical appearance can, with the right support from his public biography, become a sign of his intelligence.

Because Malkovich's public image is also coloured by the cruelty of the characters he often portrays, his presumed intelligence becomes a sign of his powerful masculinity. Publicity pieces that link Malkovich's intelligence, intensity and hard masculinity sometimes tacitly appeal to the nineteenth-century paradigm that equated primal masculinity with 'powerful, raw, explosive energy' (Rosen, 1993: 218). Following that line of discussion, commentators locate Malkovich's unique sexual appeal in what they see as his 'electrifying' intensity. Writing about the actor's 'combustible talent', Gritten argues that Malkovich's 'high-voltage intensity frightens some, seduces others' (1992: 246–7). Synthesising some of the most common reasons given for Malkovich's success, Gritten explains that his 'ability to smolder and mesmerize, combined with shrewd intelligence, has put Malkovich in the category of the thinking-woman's hunk' (1992: 247).

Malkovich's career has kept clear definitions about his identity at bay and in play. Working in theatre, film and television, and shuttling between 'high-art foreign language roles [and] lazy overplaying in commercial fare such as *Rounders*' (Jonathan Romney, *Sight & Sound*, March 2000: 2) has made Malkovich's star-image difficult to pin down. Malkovich's indefinite public persona is further complicated by the fact that Malkovich's picture personality is also deeply contradictory. Portraying the selection of characters with which audiences are now familiar, the actor has, as Chang notes, 'made a career out of an unnerving balance between quasi-reprehensibleness and enigmatic sexual attraction' (1999: 2).

Malkovich's portrayals in films such as *Places in the Heart* (1984, USA) have presented audiences with characters who are not quite men but who nonetheless possess the power to represent a potential (sexual) threat to women. His rather different performances in films such as *In the Line of Fire* flesh out an image of compulsory and mercenary masculinity that somehow still leaves the character's sexual orientation in play. Malkovich received an Academy Award nomination for best supporting actor for his performance as Mitch Leary in *In the Line of Fire*. The recognition for his portrayal of the 'twisted genius [who was a] rogue warrior with dead eyes' (Richard Corliss, *Time*, 17 July 2000: 62) seems especially significant because Malkovich's only other Oscar nomination was for his performance as the vulnerable but intense blind boarder in *Places in the Heart*.

There, Malkovich portrayed the film's most feminised man who was, at the same time, the only man to engage even tacitly in 'masculine', sexually aggressive behavior. By comparison, Malkovich's characterisation in *In the Line of Fire* began at the opposite end of the spectrum, for Mitch Leary was ostensibly the film's most 'masculine' figure. He was the most ruthless, aggressive, driven character in the story. Yet *In the Line of Fire* played Malkovich's psychotic, flamboyant masculinity off Eastwood's unremittingly hard masculinity so that over the course of the narrative Malkovich's character took on 'feminine' traits. When the film was released, one reviewer saw in Malkovich's character 'a multiple, feminised foil to Eastwood's monolithic male ... glacial one minute, on the edge of histrionics the next' (Jonathan Romney, *New Statesman and Society*, 3 September 1993: 35).

Another critic called attention to the characters' 'mano a mano duel, their love bouts (mostly phone sex, though at one point Mitch takes Frank's gun in his mouth) that are the heart of the movie' (Georgia Brown, *Village Voice*, 13 July 1993: 49).

Malkovich and Eastman's contest of will and strategy keeps them spatially distant throughout most of the film. The capricious, hysteric and finally 'feminine' qualities that make Mitch Leary dangerous but 'less of a man' than Secret Service agent Frank Horrigan are, however, given full expression in their final confrontation in the glass elevator at the hotel where Leary had hoped to make his hit. This carefully orchestrated sequence finally brings the two adversaries into direct contact. Locked together in the confined but exposed space of the glass elevator, Malkovich's gestures are consistently larger and more staccato than Eastwood's. His body is more off-balance and akimbo than Eastwood's; his line readings are more erratic and highly pitched than Eastwood's. In sum, Leary and Malkovich can embody mercenary masculinity and still fail to sustain the image of the ultimate hard masculinity that makes characters such as Horrigan and stars such as Eastwood 'real men'.

Even a cursory look at Malkovich's characterisations indicates that the composite Malkovich image embodies contradictory visions of masculinity.[16] At times, the actor's public image seems to anchor connections between masculinity and rational intelligence. His portrayals of Mr Will in *Places in the Heart* and Valmont in *Dangerous Liaisons* invite audiences to see the characters' (and the actor's) shrewd intelligence as a sign of 'masculine' power. In films such as *In the Line of Fire*, Malkovich's portrayal underscores connections between masculinity and instinctual destructive violence. That part of Malkovich's image and of contemporary visions of masculinity is sustained by his performance in *Mary Reilly*, which gives full expression to the idea that masculinity finds its true manifestation in threatening, destructive behaviour.[17]

Malkovich's characterisation of Jekyll and Hyde was very much a part of 1990s American culture. With the Women's Movement creating some shift in cultural norms, the 1996 film eliminated most on-screen displays of rape, battery and murder. For example, in *Mary Reilly*, audiences never meet the prostitutes that Hyde murders. They meet Carew only once, briefly, and the film justifies his murder by showing Carew select a very young and vulnerable-looking girl at Mrs Farrady's brothel. Yet, following the pattern set by Tracy's 1941 film, *Mary Reilly* presents even Dr Jekyll as a threatening character. In the opening passages of the film we learn that the middle-aged doctor is in the habit of staying out all night and is known by his servants to frequent brothels. Moreover, as revealed by the bloody handkerchief tucked in his bed linen, the film establishes that Jekyll is party to violence even before he discovers the formula that allows him to transform into Hyde.

Malkovich's portrayal seems to embody the contradictory elements wedged into constructions of masculinity at the end of the century. The film gives expression to the idea that men in power should also be seen as victims, as individuals who have been suffering from the oppression of responsibility. As if patterned after the stories of today's weekend warriors who long to escape the wives, mothers and children who make them listless and lifeless, Jekyll explains to Mary (Julia Roberts) that the only solution to his 'malady' is to seek escape. *Mary Reilly* invites audiences to pity the sensitive but troubled doctor, to be sympathetic to the master of house who suffers more than any of his servants ever could.

Given the shifting qualities of the dual character at the centre of its narrative, the film mobilises other, contradictory, features of Malkovich's composite picture personality. *Mary Reilly*'s unfailingly sympathetic portrayal of a character who, until the final moment of the film, commits a string of horrible acts, seems to have a great deal in common with *Dangerous Liaisons*' earlier presentation of Malkovich's philandering but finally repentant lover. In both films, Malkovich's ambiguous image made it possible for audiences to imagine that his character embodied contradictory impulses. His physical appearance, which perhaps typified the cliché image of the sensitive new age man, also helped the two films soft-pedal the fact that the heroes' final, noble atonement for their duality and duplicity was a victory won at many women's expense.

Drawing on other aspects of the Malkovich image, *Mary Reilly* also seems to invoke the sublime ruthlessness of Malkovich's Mitch Leary character in *In the Line of Fire*. As portrayed by Malkovich, mesmerising intensity and a drive toward complete self-destruction define both the demented assassin and the scientist gone mad. Hyde's repeated, sexually charged assaults on Mary serve as the most convincing proof that Jekyll is, in spite of his soft voice and grey hair, truly a man. The film doubles that character's dangerous masculinity by invoking associations with the decade's collection of action-adventure figures whose threatening physical presence served as evidence of their callous masculinity. By combining Malkovich's associations with dangerous masculinity with the decade's widely circulated images of hard masculinity, the film moves yet another step farther from the image of the Victorian dandy. In 1996 Hyde is not only more sadistic than Jekyll, he is also more buff.

CONCLUSION

Audiences for Barrymore's portrayal of Jekyll and Hyde in 1920 encountered the character(s) through the filter of the actor's star-image shaped by his performances as a matinée idol, embellished by reports of his off-stage/off-screen excesses, and then amended by his landmark performances as Richard III. With his star-image mediating interpretations, Barrymore presented audiences with an alluring but disturbing portrayal of an impetuous youth whose impatient gaiety made him vulnerable to men like George Carew. With March's performances as brash young men in romantic comedies providing the basis of his portrayal of a tormented Victorian gentleman, the 1931 film used March's unsullied bio and intellectual, outsider status to make Jekyll's impatient gaiety a comforting counterbalance to the film's sadistic violence against women. Replacing the 'effete' image of the gentleman with the more virile image of the self-made man, the 1941 film with Tracy depended on audiences recalling Tracy's award-winning performances as men of virtue to make the flamboyant sadism of its central character a sign of masculine potency. Maintaining the emphasis on sadism as a sign of masculinity, the 1996 film used Malkovich's performances in films such as *Dangerous Liaisons* and *In the Line of Fire* to give credence to the idea that Jekyll's sexual aberrations actually proved his masculinity.

Drawing on their stars' images, the four adaptations depict masculinity in two dominant ways: characters prove their manhood by battling to subdue their violence or by committing horrific acts of violence. Amendments in the films from 1920 to 1996 depend on how the films have negotiated or weighted these two intertwined features of twentieth-century masculinity. The films with Barrymore and March emphasise Jekyll's ethical struggle, his 'virtuoso asceticism'. By comparison, the films with Tracy and Malkovich underscore the sadism that marks the central character. A distinct bond exists, however, between the Barrymore and Malkovich films. By having the characters end their own lives, the Barrymore and Malkovich characters become more sympathetic, tragic and pitiable. In addition, the 1920 and 1996 films include scenes that feature pure-hearted women embracing Jekyll as he dies, and they exclude scenes in which transgressive women declare their hatred of Hyde. These choices make Jekyll less guilty, his violence more forgivable and more intrinsic to his sexual allure – Jekyll becomes the deformed Richard III.

In the Barrymore and March films, Jekyll needs Hyde to move from youth to manhood. In the Tracy and Malkovich films, Hyde is Jekyll's invigorating escape from the oppression of wives, mothers and children. In all four adaptations, Hyde is the key to the actors' successful performance of masculinity. Hyde provides a foil for Barrymore and March's giddy matinée idol youthfulness, Tracy's inert stoicism, and Malkovich's foppish new age softness. What unites the adaptations and joins them as well to their literacy source is that however the narrative is framed, Hyde guarantees its success, for the '"something wrong" in the story – that is, Hyde – [is precisely what] accounts for its popularity' (Brantlinger and Boyle, 1988: 274). First published in January 1886, the novella 'sold forty thousand copies [became] the subject of pulpit sermons ... and consolidated Stevenson's literary reputation' (Rose, 1996: 42) because it offered readers an antidote to models of masculinity embodied by 'the gentleman, the prophet, the dandy, the priest, and the soldier' (Adams, 1995: 2). More than 100 years later, the story is now threadbare, even if its vision of masculinity is not.

---

1 In his study of the star system, Richard DeCordova explains that by 1910 'picture personalities' had started to coalesce around certain actors working in film and that audiences were identifying an actor with the characters he or she played in a series of pictures. As described by DeCordova, an actor's picture personality 'existed as an effect of the representation of character ... across a number of films' (1990: 86). By 1914, audiences began

encountering certain actors as stars, that is, as individuals whose 'existence outside his or her work became the focus of discourse' (1990: 98). These categories have never been mutually exclusive. As DeCordova points out, audiences encounter certain individuals who appears in films 'as actor (as a professional manipulator of signs), as picture personality (as a personality extrapolated from films), and as star (as someone with a private life distinct from screen image)' (1990: 146–7).

2 Gaylyn Studlar, for example, offers a detailed account of relationships between selected star-images and masculinity in the 1920s. Studlar argues that the intersection between audience expectations and the star-images of actors such as Douglas Fairbanks, John Barrymore, Rudolph Valentino and Lon Chaney reveals that in this period, masculinity depended on 'different guises or "masquerades"', and that it was 'a process, a liminal construction, even a performance' (1996: 4).

3 For an account of the earliest adaptations, see Rose (1996: 42). For the most recent index of film adaptations see Charles King (1997).

4 Mansfield's legacy can be seen in the *New York Times* article (15 February 1920) which discusses the growing interest in the forthcoming film of 'the Stevenson tragedy of dual personality which Mansfield played for so many years'.

5 Act I concluded with Hyde murdering Carew in his home; Act II took audiences through Hyde's pursuit and escape; Act III presented audiences with Hyde's transformation into Jekyll in full display before Dr Lanyon; Act IV presented audiences with Jekyll alone in his laboratory, a design that called for Mansfield to hold the stage alone for 20 minutes with only one interruption.

6 Some might argue that Mary is not Utterson but instead that the reader takes the place of Utterson who reads the 'journals' collected in the novel. To consider such questions, see the 'Afterword' in Valerie Martin's *Mary Reilly* (1990).

7 For a full discussion of the influence which the Jack the Ripper case had on subsequent adaptations of Stevenson's novella, see Geduld (1983: 6–7).

8 In the two portrayals, Barrymore helped to shape a new style of performance. As Joseph Garton points out, 'it is indisputable that the styles of acting since World War I are significantly different than the style of acting before 1900. An absolute master in both modes of acting, John Barrymore is the link between nineteenth and twentieth century styles of acting' (1980: 4–5). For an outline of the two styles, see Garton's discussion on nineteenth-century acting (1980: 7–12).

9 In addition to Jekyll and Hyde, Mansfield had set the pattern for productions that were some of the most important performances in Barrymore's career; these include *Richard III* (1920, USA), *Beau Brummel* (1924, USA) and *Don Juan* (1926, USA). Barrymore's commitment to serious dramatic undertakings is suggested by his taking an apartment in New York's Washington Square that he named the 'Alchemists Corner' (Paul Rudnick, 'Living', *Vogue*, July 1989: 131). The dispersal of his creative energy is also suggested by the contrast between his New York apartment and the estate which he developed in Hollywood.

10 See Morrison's discussion of this period in Barrymore's career (1997: 69–90, 116) for an account of Barrymore's concomitant development of his portrayals for *Richard III* and *Dr Jekyll and Mr Hyde*. For a parallel account, see Garton's (1980) discussion of Barrymore's work in *Richard III* (1980: 29–32) and *Dr Jekyll and Mr Hyde* (1980: 79–83).

11 As touchstones of contemporary responses to the film, see the *New York Times* (2 January 1932) and *Variety* (5 January 1932). As examples of commentary that continues to valorise the film, see Nash and Ross (1985), Virginia Wright Wexman (1988), John McCarty (1993), Brian Rose, who refers to the film as 'the most effective and intriguing of later film adaptations' (1996: 54), and Anne Edwards, who names the 1931 adaptation as the film 'considered by movie buffs to be by far the best of the many film adaptations of Robert Louis Stevenson's classic' (1990: 222).

12 For examples of March's public bio, see the 1933 article 'Who's Who This Week in Pictures' (*New York Times*, 26 November 1933), referring to March as 'one of the less conspicuous members of the Beverly Hills colony', a man who returns each year to his birthplace, Racine, Wisconsin, to visit his father. See also Edwards (1990:

222) who calls attention to the collaboration between March and his wife, actress Florence Eldridge, in design-ing their Beverly Hills home, and the fact that the couple spent time in Los Angeles and New York.

13 Malkovich's Oscar-nominated performance in *In the Line of Fire* anticipates his portrayal of Jekyll and Hyde in very specific terms. There are two instances in *Line of Fire* when Malkovich's image, once in a sketch, another time in a hotel mirror, morphs from one persona to another. Moreover, the narrative makes it overly clear that Malkovich's villain and Eastwood's hero are two sides of one bureaucratic entity. Audience interest in Malkovich as a villain with 'psychological sophistication' can be seen in Howard Hampton's 1993 essay. The following year, *Psychology Today* (July 1994: 26–30) carried an interview with Malkovich about portraying the dark side of human nature. In 1997, *Us* magazine (July: 70–3) interviewed Malkovich about playing villains. Typecast as an interesting sexual marauder, in 1996 Malkovich played the lead in a stage production of *The Libertine* and the part of the dissolute rake in Raul Ruiz's film *Time Regained* (2000, Italy/France).

14 The bravura moment of the piece, the transformation from one persona to another, was taken out of the actor's control and replaced by special effects that left many audiences giggling. As was the case with Tracy's 'naturalistic' portrayal, Malkovich's performance called attention to the incongruity of an American midwest-erner playing a British Victorian gentleman. Critics noted that there was no explanation for the fact that Malkovich was 'the only one in London with the flat prairie vowels of the American Midwest' (Michael Medved, *New York Post*, 23 February 1996: 49) and insisted that 'Malkovich's toneless, self-satisfied whine of a voice [had] never been more distracting' (David Ansen, *Newsweek*, 26 February 1996: 66). With pointed humour ready at hand, reviewers explained that 'all Malkovich does is posture, splutter and stagger furiously through his anti-hero's episodic trajectory' (Chris King, *Sight and Sound*, May 1996: 55), that with Malkovich 'oozing oil and menace [his Mr Hyde gave] the film a particularly smarmy psychosexual undercurrent' (Gary Daupin, *Village Voice*, 5 March 1996: 48), and that Malkovich's 'libido-crazed Hyde would be more appropri-ate to a novel written by Fabio' (Kenneth Turan, *Los Angeles Times*, 23 February 1996: 1).

15 With the release of Spike Jonze's film, Malkovich became a part of American popular culture. An article in the *Village Voice* ('Here's a Trend for Jack Valenti: Men Without Guns', 26 October 1999: 164) joked that *Being John Malkovich* created a new trend by equating the actor's mind with a birth canal; a Taco Bell ad campaign was designed as a take-off on *Being John Malkovich* (MacArthur and Cuneo, *Advertising Age*, 31 July 2000: 3, 62); an article in *People Weekly* (Michelle Tauber *et al.*, 'On the Block: Lodging with John Malkovich', 12 June 2000: 26) reminded readers that in addition to visiting the actor's brain they could stay in his hotel in Wales; and to call attention to a report on HSX, a faux online market that allows people to buy shares in film pro-jects, *Inc.* magazine (August 2000: 30) selected the title 'Buying John Malkovich'.

16 For a more detailed discussion of Malkovich's star-image see Baron (2002).

17 *Mary Reilly* places a female character at the centre of the narrative. Yet in contrast to the 1920, 1931 and 1941 films that present audiences with fiancées who grace domestic spaces and exotic mistresses who can create enticing performances on stage, *Mary Reilly* eliminates women's performative presence from domestic and public arenas. The change brings with it two deeply troubling corollaries. First, with women removed from the centre of domestic space, it becomes more plausible for male characters (first Mary's father and then her master, Dr Jekyll) to take control of domestic space. Second, as suggested by the glimpses we receive of Mrs Farrady's brothel, removing women from public arenas designed for men's pleasure does not eliminate men's sexual violence against women; instead, the film tacitly suggests that it perhaps increases the intensity of that violence. Disconnecting women from specific (traditional) sites seems, however, to be what frees Mary to cross symbolic boundaries. Not confined to public display or domestic 'protection', Mary is able to become the nursemaid who attends to the master of the house, the witness to Hyde's acts of manliness, and the angel who serves as the guarantor of Jekyll's forgiveness. For discussions about considerations such as these, see the analysis by Chris Foss (2000), who argues that *Mary Reilly* justifies male violence and uses female forgiveness to assuage male guilt about violence against women.

Chapter Fourteen

SCRAMBLING HOLLYWOOD: ASIAN STARS/ASIAN AMERICAN STAR CULTURES[1]

Julian Stringer

DO THE RICE THING

Consider this quote:

> My view of sexy is quite different from the mainstream. I find sexy to be revealed in the person, how they carry themselves and their characteristics, not in the looks. I think for many people, Chow Yun-Fat is sexy because he conveys confidence and a strong sense of self-esteem that most people are not used to associating with Asian men.
>
> *(Geraldine Kudaka, quoted in 'Rice is Nice',* Yolk: For the Generasian Next *5(2), 1998: 57)*

Form a picture of Chow Yun-Fat in your head: large dove's eyes, cute dimples, toothy grin. Perhaps the image you have is more than this, however; perhaps it is an image of him totin' guns and mowing down throngs of adversaries, as in *A Better Tomorrow* (1986, HK), *Hard Boiled* (1993, HK) and countless other Hong Kong action titles. Or maybe you are thinking of Chow wearing slick suits and carrying a large wad of cash, as in *God of Gamblers* (1989, HK) and *God of Gamblers' Return* (1995, HK). Perhaps you are even struggling with the question of why you cannot quite recall having seen Chow Yun-Fat have sex in a movie – certainly not with Cherie Cheung in *An Autumn Tale* (1988, HK), Jodie Foster in the Hollywood production *Anna and the King* (1999, USA), or Michelle Yeoh in the US–China collaboration *Crouching Tiger, Hidden Dragon* (2000, US/China), and definitely not with Danny Lee in *The Killer* (1989, HK) or Simon Lam in *Full Contact* (1992, HK). Not with anyone, ever, in fact.

You might find upon reflection that the quote requires further consideration. The fact that Geraldine Kudaka, editor of the first anthology of Asian American erotic literature ever published in the US, responds to the question 'Who do you think is the sexiest Asian

American male?' with the answer that, 'for many people' it is famed Hong Kong movie icon Chow Yun-Fat, may seem surprising, if not baffling. Simply put, given this particular actor's mega-star status in many regions of the world, it is widely known (if, crucially, not universally so) that Chow is a Chinese star, not an Asian American star. Yet it appears in this quote as if the lines are being blurred, as if no distinction is being drawn between the 'Asian American male' and non-US 'Asian men' such as Chow Yun-Fat.

Many observers may be oblivious to this rhetorical slippage, this elision of fundamental cultural distinctions between Asian America and Asia. (Herein lie the roots of a racist worldview that formulates 'Orientals' as always already the same, wherever they are from.) However, given that the interview from which the quote is taken was for *Yolk*, a leading Asian American style magazine, it is fair to assume that the implied reader will be aware of the complexities involved. She or he will probably recognise the need for such categorial elasticity, and so will have little problem accepting Chow Yun-Fat as an Asian American star. (Indeed, the desire to form bonds between diverse Asian and Asian American individuals and societies is characteristic of the broader Asian American project of pan-ethnic community building and political solidarity.) According to this formulation, stars like Chow Yun-Fat are not just Chinese; they are also 'cousins' of their Asian American fans and admirers, and as such, *de facto* Asian Americans.

On another level, though, Kudaka's response raises a point of possible dissent. This may be taken as indicative of the potentially volatile differences that characterise Asian American communities with distinct national and ethnic identities and heritages. When looked at closely, the quote reveals how Kudaka skilfully side-steps the requirements of a personal answer. The question 'Who do *you* think is the sexiest Asian American male?' is answered with a speech act concerning what 'many people' and 'most people' may consider to be sexually attractive in 'Asian men'. I find two aspects of this speech act particularly interesting.

To begin with, in light of the highly particularised nature of *Yolk*'s readership, here is an unusually ambiguous and unexplained appeal to 'the mainstream'. It is not clear, for example, whether Kudaka is talking about the mass US (or non-US?) audience, or about the 'mainstream' Asian American community of *Yolk* readers – which she implicitly, and cryptically, sets herself against. Secondly, I also find a quiet resistance, an intriguing stubbornness and refusal, in her answer. *They* may find Chow Yun-Fat sexy, but *my* view of the sexy Asian American man is different; more than that, *I am not going to explain what my view actually is!* The quote seems to suggest that Asian American sexiness must retain an 'inner', virtually secret, dimension. Push the logic of these observations one step further, and Kudaka's words come to imply a number of different perspectives on the subject of Asian stars and Asian American audiences. In this quote, she could by turns be validating, criticising or rejecting Chow Yun-Fat's relevance for Asian Americans. She could be promoting some delicious – because barely formed – Asian American erotic programme or political manifesto.[2] Equally, Kudaka could be offering confirmation that confidence and self-esteem, as well as 'character' and 'personhood', are indeed of crucial importance to America's favourite 'model minority'. Her quote could be read as carrying all of the above implications.

In this chapter, I want to discuss developments in the role of Asian stars in Hollywood in the 1990s. I am concerned with one key question: to what extent can and should Asian stars such as Chow Yun-Fat be deemed more significant participants in the discourse of Asian American stardom, purveyors of greater confidence and greater self-esteem, than home-grown US talents? As we pursue this subject, is there a way in which we can unscramble some of the above without falling into Orientalist traps?

SCRAMBLING HOLLYWOOD

> **scramble** v. & n. 1. v.i. Make way as best one can over steep or rough ground by clambering, crawling, etc.; move hastily and anxiously; take part in physical or other struggle with competitors for as much as possible of something; (of aircraft or pilots) take off quickly in emergency. 2. v.t. Mix together indiscriminately; deal with hastily or awkwardly; cook (eggs) by breaking into pan with butter, milk, etc., stirring slightly and heating; . . . alter frequencies of transmitted speech of (telephone conversation etc.) so as to make it unintelligible except to recipient using similar process . . .
>
> (Oxford English Dictionary, [1911] 1978: 1017)

For the past decade or so, the Hollywood film industry has been under the sway of an intense, not to say at times hideous, fascination with the cinemas of East Asia, particularly its dynamic action genres and charismatic action stars. Aside from Chow Yun-Fat, performers such as Jackie Chan from Hong Kong, Joan Chen and Jet Li from China, and Michelle Yeoh from Hong Kong/Malaysia have made their mark on US public life by appearing in, and often carrying, major star productions. The proliferation of compelling images of Chinese and other Asian identities in 1990s Hollywood can be tracked through a viewing of these stars in titles such as *Anna and the King*, *The Corruptor* (1999, USA), *First Strike* (1999, HK), *Lethal Weapon 4* (1999, USA), *Romeo Must Die* (2000, USA), *The Replacement Killers* (1998, USA), *Rumble in the Bronx* (1998, HK), *Rush Hour* (1998, USA), *Rush Hour 2* (2000, USA), *The One* (2001, USA) and *Tomorrow Never Dies* (1997, UK/USA).

In addition, a second tier of famous Asian actors have appeared in less obviously showcase roles, providing 'local colour' and supporting performances that contribute nevertheless to what US print journalists are fond of terming the 'Asian Invasion' of

231

popular cinema (see, for example, 'The Asians are Coming! The Asians are Coming!' *Time*, 13 September 1993: 68; 'Asian Invasion', *Time*, 14 August 1995: 42; 'Chinese Takeout', *Newsweek*, 19 February 1996: 55–69). Examples include Hong Kong diva Maggie Cheung's role in *Chinese Box* (1997, France/Japan), as well as the presence of Japanese icons Toshiro Mifune in *Picture Bride* (1993, USA), Takeshi Kitano in *Johnny Mnemonic* (1995, USA), and Ken Takakura and Yusaku Matsuda in *Black Rain* (1989, USA). Moreover, despite the post-1997 bursting of the Hong Kong movie-craze bubble, there is little sign that such rampant Asiaphilia will dissipate. For example, as I write, Korean actor Park Joong-hoon – star of Lee Myung-se's *Nowhere to Hide* (1999, South Korea), among others – has been cast to play a major role alongside Mark Wahlberg in director Jonathan Demme's *The Truth About Charlie* (2003, USA).

At the same time as Hollywood has been looking to draw stars from a pool of select Asian film industries, it has also opened up a greater role for Asian American actors in feature film production. These talented men and women are in the process of introducing new thematics into the contemporary US media landscape. Putting aside the related subject of the ubiquity of Asian American images and personalities on network television (Hamamoto, 1994), a provisional shortlist of these performers would include Jason Scott Lee (especially in the Bruce Lee bio-pic, *Dragon* (1994, USA)), the excellent John Lone in many critically underrated roles (starting with *Year of the Dragon* (1985, USA) and reaching a peak in *M. Butterfly* (1993, USA)), Margaret Cho (*It's My Party* (1996); *Face/Off* (1997, USA); *I'm the One That I Want* (2000, USA)), Lucy Liu in *True Crime* (1999, USA), *Charlie's Angels* (2000, USA), and *Shanghai Noon* (2000, USA) and Mark Dacascos (*The Island of Dr Moreau* (1996, USA); but particularly *Drive* (1995, USA), recently re-released on DVD to cash in on the success of *Rush Hour* (1998, USA) and *The Matrix* (1999, USA)). These names have benefited from Asian Americans' greater institutional presence in recent film-making practices. Over the past few years, the commissioning of movie projects for both a relatively large number of Asian directors (Ronnie Yu, Peter Chan, Tsui Hark, John Woo, Ringo Lam) and Asian American directors (Ang Lee, Wayne Wang, Steve Wang) has built upon the increasing numbers of Asian American technicians and Hollywood crew members entering the industry after graduating from film school. A small number of young actors have also made themselves known through appearing in the few Asian American independent features to have been given theatrical release, including Michael Idemoto and Eric Nakamura's *Sunsets* (1997, USA), Chris Chan Lee's *Yellow* (1997, USA), Quentin Lee and Justin Lin's *Shopping for Fangs* (1997, USA), and Rea Tajiri's *Strawberry Fields* (1996, USA).

Hollywood's investment in Asian faces and stars is not new. Recent revisionist film criticism has played an important role in fleshing out the complex story of how previous Asian and Asian American actors were treated by the movie industry they worked within – a story of assimilation and resistance at once depressing and empowering.[3] What is different about more contemporary activity is two linked developments. On the one hand, corporate film-making has forged clear connections with Asia through the global restructuring taking place along the Pacific Rim, particularly via the influx into Los Angeles of the Hong Kong movie talent listed above.[4] On the other hand, Asian American movie audiences have grown significantly as a market force. For such audiences, any Asian performer – whether Asian American or drawn from a non-US film industry – may be welcomed as a cultural icon to be embraced and, ultimately, scrutinised. Certainly, debate over the social and political efficacy of performers such as Jet Li among Asian American communities often revolves around questions concerning the limits of representation. In electronic discussion forums on websites such as **asianamericanfilm.com**, questions are raised as to whether 'minority' images can ever be deemed 'adequate', in the knowledge that if they are, calls for Hollywood to project a more 'positive' image of Asians may sound less than compelling.

However, when it comes to the wider marketing and critical reporting of such images, the lines which separate Asian from Asian American in the US imaginary remain imprecise. In mass-market publications and advertising, Asian movies are indiscriminately lumped in with Asian American themes and concerns; Asian and Asian American performers are seldom differentiated in terms of cultural background or affiliation; and Asian American-themed films are deemed to be of interest primarily, or sometimes solely, to marginal 'Asian' groups perceived as still loyal to foreign homelands. The argument of this chapter is that it is vital that basic separations be made and understood at all times between Asian and Asian American screen cultures. It is my further argument, however, that while 'mainstream' media seldom promote this understanding and separation, the world of Asian American star culture scrambles such distinctions in a most suggestive fashion.

FLUID BODIES

Robert G. Lee (1999) provides a comprehensive analysis of the processes through which Asian American and Asian images have historically been elided in US popular culture. In this reading, the history of Asians in the US has been a continuous struggle against racial exclusion and subordination as 'Orientals'. Asian American cultural and political workers have fought against this oppressive edict and for their own particular birthright, namely a central position in the forging of America's destiny. They have been obliged to point out that Asian Americans are entitled to all the rights and privileges promised in the Declaration of Independence and the US Constitution.

The slipperiness of 'Oriental' discourse – the pernicious assumption that Asian Americans are really foreigners in disguise; the inability to distinguish between different kinds of ethnic Asian groups – can be made to work on occasion for, rather than against, Asian American cultural formations. If we consider the *Oxford Dictionary* definition of the word 'scramble' quoted above, these possibilities become a little clearer. I want to explore these

233

in relation to some of the new images of Asian stardom advanced by Hollywood in the 1990s.

> Make way as best one can over steep or rough ground by clambering, crawling, etc; move hastily and anxiously; take part in physical or other struggle with competitors for as much as possible of something.

It is hard when reading the above words not to think of Asian actors performing in the role of action stars. The commercial Hollywood titles listed above largely comprise cop, espionage or gangster movies, and male 'hard body' Hong Kong stars in particular (e.g. martial arts experts such as Jackie Chan and Jet Li) have been offered Hollywood contracts whereas equally talented actors with 'softer' or more sensitive images (Leslie Cheung, Lau Ching-Wan, Tony Chiu-Wai Leung) have not. Being an Asian star in the US has its advantages and disadvantages. 'About a year ago, watching David Letterman's *Late Show* on CBS, I was surprised to find that Jackie Chan was the show's second guest,' recalls Kwai-Cheung Lo. Lo continues:

> Chan showed off his athleticism live by somersaulting to his chair and kicking bottles from a table. He teasingly told Letterman that his American fans had asked him to come to kick the host's butt. Letterman responded by exchanging his jacket with Chan's and trying it on to demonstrate that he was bigger than the Asian star. For a while, the show was full of jokes about bodies. I felt embarrassed afterwards. In front of the American audience, Chan played the role of silent film comedian or cartoon character. I worried about his representativeness for Hong Kong. Would the American audience see the Hong Kong subject as a muscular, though slight, man who only knows how to use his body to amaze them and make them laugh?
>
> (Lo, 1996: 105–6)

What is passed over in the above statement is the possibility, indeed likelihood, that Chan's 'American fans' in the cited example include a substantial number of Asian American supporters. From this perspective, Chan's potency as a 'representative' for Hong Kong is of less importance and relevance than his embodiment of values and attitudes familiar to Asian groups in the US. Chan's star-image potentially holds together both of these possibilities.

Consider the opening few minutes of the feature-length *Jackie Chan: My Story*, a Hong Kong television production from 1998. The voiceover narration which introduces this film poses the question: 'Who is Jackie Chan?', to which a range of commentators then provide answers. The question signals the star's multi-dimensional appeals – the way in which he embodies different things for different people, and is used accordingly as a form of cultural currency, or for purposes of self-legitimation. (It also refers to his film, *Who Am I?* (1998, HK), and print autobiography *I Am Jackie Chan*.) For example, *Jackie Chan: My Story* opens with a quote from Buster Keaton ('Only things that one could imagine happening to real people, I guess, remain in a person's memory'), but other more contemporary voices are soon intercut talking directly about the matter at hand. These speech acts emanate from the mouths of such luminaries as Quentin Tarantino ('One of the greatest movie stars in the history of movies'), Eddie Murphy ('Jackie's my hero'), Bruce Willis ('Jackie Chan? He's a great man!'), Sylvester Stallone ('He puts his life on the line. . . . He's a great guy'), numerous Hong Kong and Hollywood movie industry personnel ('He must be one of the heroes'; 'He loves and respects his work'; 'He's a born entertainer'; 'He's the best stuntman that ever lived'; 'I was working with an actor'), and an unidentified Asian American woman ('He's a role model for all of us'), among others. It is certainly significant that Hollywood stars are being foregrounded here as a way of framing Jackie Chan's global significance and so demonstrating the respect and affection he is accorded in the USA. Equally, however, the point is made that Jackie Chan is many things to many different people, depending on who you are and what you want him to be.

One of the things this particular Hong Kong title claims Chan to be, then, is a 'role model' for Asian Americans. Given this orientation, the very fact that Chan is seen on network television 'struggling' with a white competitor for as much available airtime and exposure as possible, suggests a re-narrativising project. This emphasises the question of agency, the active processes through which Asian American audiences construct counter-visions of US society in line with their experiences and outlooks. As further support for this point of view, consider by way of a contrast to or modification of Kwai-Cheung Lo's words the perspective adopted by Asian American media scholar Jun Xing:

> Jackie Chan has become the biggest action star in Hollywood since Bruce Lee. Chan was interviewed by David Letterman and was presented [with] a Lifetime Achievement Award on MTV. Without the usual steamy sex, dirty jokes, and hero-wins-it-all plot-line, Chan brings to the American cinema a creative vision in on-screen martial arts that he terms 'happy-go-lucky'.
>
> (*Xing, 1998: 200*)

There are clear problems with conceptualising the significance of Asian stars in contemporary Hollywood primarily through the significance of their bodies, especially when martial arts is distinguished so clearly from 'steamy sex' (the absence of which so often structures media stereotypes of Asians in the US). After all, the body has provided one of the prime locations for the 'Orientalising' project. The body is what makes signs of racial difference visible; it constitutes a suitably 'primitive' technology, at least when compared with the materiality and statecraft of white American culture. Yet the signs are that when re-narrativised in Asian American reception contexts, this emphasis on bodily struggle and ability takes on more positive connotations. At the very least, the recognition of the familiarity of narratives of struggle and fighting-against-the-odds structures writing on Hollywood action movies published in Asian American fanzines such as *Bamboo Girl*, *Full-on Asian Action*, and *Secret Asian Man*.

Mix together indiscriminately; deal with hastily or awkwardly.

Watching movies such as *Anna and the King*, *Lethal Weapon 4*, *Rumble in the Bronx*, or *Tomorrow Never Dies* one becomes aware of a certain disjuncture between the prior images of the films' world-famous Asian stars, and the peculiar narratives into which those star-images are inserted. Andrew Britton ([1984] 1995: 14) claims that Hollywood history 'provides numerous examples of a radical discrepancy between the nature of a star's popular image and the kinds of thing which, in the films themselves, the star actually does'. This is certainly true of 'ethnic' stars obliged to bear the burden of a minority's hopes and dreams. Judging from the available evidence, Asian Americans are acutely aware that contemporary Hollywood's particular brand of Asiaphilia is in the process of constructing a generic image of 'Asian-ness' that blurs, and hence devalues, the many differences that characterise the diversity of Asian American communities. Such representations are perceived as signalling the continuing social and political work of Orientalising narratives, albeit ones which may be rejected or re-narrativised in the act of reception by Asian American audience members.

In her piece on Chinese American Joan Chen's performance in the television series *Twin Peaks*, Greta Ai-Yu Niu discusses 'fluidity' as a key term in the analysis of Chen's star image in relation to the character of Josie Packard. Discussing the 'mysterious' Asian woman's resistance to definition on this show, her concomitant manipulation of other characters, and the ways in which she inevitably becomes caught within a web of Orientalising assumptions and expectations, Niu notes that

'Passing' and my term 'fluidity' are not synonymous. Josie seems to pass, she seems to be an agent, but she acts out what other people want her to be and to do. Fluidity is not something she does, it is something she is, a quality that other characters assume she possesses. Fluidity describes the ease with which she is absorbed into a discourse of stereotypes.

(Niu, 1998: 120)[5]

Niu is talking specifically here about how this Asian female character uses her fluid body so as to manipulate other people's perception of her for her own suspicious ends. Yet the word has a wider applicability to the workings of Asian ethnicities in contemporary

Hollywood cinema. Take the example of actor Jason Scott Lee. This third-generation Chinese Hawaiian actor – a 'local hero' on the islands ('Local Hero: Jason Scott Lee', *Hawaii International Film Festival 1994*, official brochure: 14–15) – has been cast as 'the Asian' in a variety of different roles, among them *Dragon: The Bruce Lee Story*, *Map of the Human Heart* (1992, USA), *Rapa Nui* (1994, USA), Disney's *The Jungle Book* (1994, USA), and *Arabian Nights* (2000, television movie). Each of these films demanded that Lee play a character of different Asian heritage – Filipino, Chinese, Korean, Japanese, and so on. Historically, this is certainly not an unheard of phenomenon in Hollywood (see 'Latin lovers' such as Rudolph Valentino), but what is different about recent developments in Asian representation is the large variety of possible responses such generic stereotyping, or fluidity in terms of casting, may draw from a large, loyal and increasingly diversified Asian American fan base.

The Asian American response to pan-Asian stars therefore operates on two levels at once. It strives to recognise the potentially volatile differences that characterise communities divided by distinct national and regional heritages. Yet at the same time – and in line with the political demands made by Asian American political and cultural activists over the past decades – it attempts to bring such distinctions together under a collective vision of common experiences and aspirations. In this sense, the fact that Jason Scott Lee, Chow Yun-Fat or Jackie Chan have largely been confined to playing the generic Asian role in Hollywood movies matters less than the fact that Asian images are visible in the first place. Moreover, the fluid nature of those images can be scrambled, mixed together indiscriminately, so as to make them speak to the differing experiences and expectations of Asian American communities linked by continuing subjection to Orientalising tendencies. 'But what about Jet Li's fans?', wrote Martin Wong in *Giant Robot* in 1998, about the Chinese star's impending face-off with Mel Gibson in *Lethal Weapon 4*.

> How will they feel when the national hero of China gets waxed by a bunch of pretty-boy American actors who can't really fight? When they see Li return to the Hong Kong screen in *Hitmen* (1998, USA), won't his perfect record be tainted? It's taken 35 years for Godzilla to try taking his belt back. (*Godzilla* 1985 doesn't count.) It had better not take that long for Jet Li to return and kick some gweilo ass.
>
> ('*King Kong vs. Jet Li*', Giant Robot *11(Summer) 1998: 31*)[6]

> Alter frequencies of transmitted speech of (telephone conversation etc.) so as to make unintelligible except to recipient using similar process.

Mass Asian and Hispanic immigration to the US over the past two decades has challenged the hegemony of English as the lingua franca of the nation-state. This fact has been reflected, among other places, in some of the movies listed above, where Asian languages (sometimes accompanied by English subtitles, sometimes not) have been preserved on occasion so as to signify 'Asian-ness' and/or to enhance narrative interest. For example, while Jet Li's character in *Lethal Weapon 4* is originally presented as a Chinese speaker, the perception that he also understands English becomes an important point of tension between him and his white adversary. Indeed, the use of Chinese as a 'sanctuary', a language that White and African American characters cannot understand, becomes an explicit point of discussion and contestation in the film, a way of introducing themes of racial antagonism and intolerance. Similarly, English dubbing of the various Hong Kong Jackie Chan movies released state-to-state throughout the 1990s has only drawn attention to the question of how 'ethnic' speech is modified for a perceived mass audience.

A frequent point of discussion in Asian American culture magazines, as well as fan-based websites and chat rooms, is the linguistic diversity, not to mention sheer unfamiliarity, of Asian languages. Given the basic assumption that access to the lingua franca is a key pre-requisite for broad-based cultural acceptance and political power, but that links to imagined homelands and Asian cultures remain important, Asian American star culture has generated its own internal debate about the value, or otherwise, of retaining or forging connections to Asian linguistic traditions. In magazines such as *Giant Robot*, this often takes the form of 'teach yourself' guides to Japanese, Chinese, and so on. Certainly, the reten-tion of 'Oriental' linguistic traits in the star-images and roles of Chow Yun-Fat and other actors allows for a critical reading of the cultural semiotics of linguistic diversity in con-temporary Hollywood. Moreover, 'Yellow' criticism, that is to say work orientated around an Asian American perspective, can seek to unscramble this tower of Babel by exposing its embedded power relationships.

EVERYBODY IS A STAR

The reception of Asian stars by Asian American audiences can be traced through writings about cinema published in the abundance of Asian American style magazines and fanzines that have sprung up over the past decade or so. In addition, a flourishing reception context for such images has been created through Asian American film festivals in cities such as Los Angeles, San Francisco and Seattle, as well as on many college campuses, and by the innovative programming strategies of niche distribution companies such as the National Asian American Telecommunications Association (San Francisco) and Asian Media Access (Minneapolis). Yellow Entertainment Network (YEN) has recently been estab-lished so as to feature Asian American television programming, and various other cable and access stations in major cities already service distinct Asian American communities.

In lieu of the full institutional analysis which alone can properly contextualise the recent emergence of this unique cultural formation, I want to focus for a moment on certain Asian American film-making activities. These can generally be found in the independent sector, and constitute one important means by which contemporary Asian star images are translated into the terms of Asian American identity politics. Such film-making practices offer direct evidence of how distinct audiences form and maintain star–audience identifications. They provide a powerful indication of the processes through which the contemporary demands of a specific US citizen base are negotiated through the consumption of ostensibly non-American star images.

A short, highly selective and by no means definitive list of such titles should be enough to indicate something of their proliferation. The following are all films or videos (usually shorts) which engage in one way or another with the question of Asian stars and/or celebrities (as well as a few non-Asian famous faces) and what they mean to Asian American audiences: *Beyond Asiaphilia* (Valerie Soe, 1997, USA), *Cunanan's Conundrum* (Stuart Gaffney, 1997, USA), *A Critique of Game of Death* (Kip Fulbeck, 1994, USA), *My Mother Thought She Was Audrey Hepburn* (Sharon Jue, 1992, USA), *O.J. Simpson My Father* (Rajendra Roy, 1995, USA), *Picturing Oriental Girls: A (Re)Educational Videotape* (Valerie Soe, 1992, USA), *Sex, Love and Kung Fu* (Kip Fulbeck, 2000, USA), *Slaying the Dragon* (Deborah Gee, 1988, USA), *Yuki Shimoda: Asian American Actor* (John Esaki, 1985, USA).

Such works are characterised by two features. First, they engage with what might be termed the discourse of Asian American stardom – that is, they confront the nature of stardom, its attractions, its significations, the functions which stars may fulfil and the roles they may play in the imaginative and material lives of Asian Americans. This focus on the discourse of stardom is also to be found in style magazines, fanzines and programming initiatives of Asian American film festivals. Second, the films share a preoccupation with the power and fluidity of prior images of Asians and Asian Americans. As part of their engagement with the legacy and ideology of the 'Oriental', they re-appropriate media representations to propose counter-narratives, other ways of viewing and comprehending the stories that lie behind the stereotypes. In the case of the earlier titles, such as the well-known documentary *Slaying the Dragon*, this takes the form of a compendium of Hollywood images of Asians, together with a running commentary on the hideousness of their pernicious assumptions. In recent work the emphasis has shifted more towards the audience itself.

For example, in *Beyond Asiaphilia* images of Jet Li's Hong Kong movies provide a visual background to interviews with Asian American men. Positioned in the foreground of the frame, as befits their 'star' status and billing in the short, these men provide alternative perspectives on Asian movies, talking about why they respond so positively to their compelling representations of masculinity. Similarly, director Valerie Soe positions herself as a further centre of narrative interest, explaining at the start of the film that she can not figure out why she, a Chinese American woman, has after two decades of pursuing blue-eyed White boyfriends, suddenly fallen in love with Chow Yun-Fat. In this way, the iconic beauty of Chow in the accompanying clips from *A Better Tomorrow* (1986, HK) are made subservient to the primary narrative of Asian American subjectivity advanced through such re-contextualisation of prior images.

In short, these examples of independent Asian American film-making scramble Hollywood's images of Asians and Asian Americans. They illustrate the uphill struggles experienced by pioneer actors, and the hastily and awkwardly put together stereotypes that litter the landscape of the US corporate media. Yet they also suggest the various ways in which such images can be made intelligible, re-invested with meaning from a 'Yellow' perspective. In this sense, the films may be considered further kinds of Asian American speech acts – rhetorical positionings that centre the Asian American experience at every turn. Picking up on the implications of the Asian American discourses surrounding Hollywood films, they demand an active reading. When watching these kinds of shorts, you have to work to make the connections between images of stars and the implied political perspectives of the film-makers. A sense of the fluidity of Asian media representation is preserved, but this has been turned on its head. Instead of promoting generic 'Asian-ness', fluidity now suggests the range of potential Asian American reading positions opened up in the act of reception.

In his work on Asian American eroticism, Darrell Hamamoto takes a cue from Marvin Gaye's black soul classic 'Let's Get It On' (1973) in 'proposing a full-frontal approach to sexual healing in racist society' (Hamamoto, 2000(a): 4). In a similar spirit, I would like to appropriate a different US soul classic, this time the chartbuster 'Everybody is a Star' (1970) by Sly and the Family Stone, to suggest the forward-looking dynamics of this Asian American cultural sensibility. Such musical references are suggestive both of the African American/Asian American pan-ethnic links demonstrated in titles such as *Drive* and *Rush Hour* (as well, more generally, as the political activities of the Yellow Brotherhood; the fetishisation in the fanzines of actors like Jim Kelly (from *Enter the Dragon*, US/HK, 1973)), and of the structuring importance of the discourse of stardom. The process I am describing can briefly be characterised as one that moves from appropriating and reclaiming prior images of Asian stars, to one where the Asian American individual himself/herself – her or his 'character' and cultural identity – are validated as the centre of attention and selfhood.

One recent film which pulls these issues into sharp relief is the documentary *Sex: The Annabel Chong Story* (1999, USA). A chronicle of the life and work of the star of the porn best-seller *The World's Biggest Gang Bang* (1995, USA), *Sex* seeks to investigate what makes the woman who became famous after having on-screen sex with 251 men in a ten-hour period tick. Chong, who is originally from Singapore and lived in London before moving to the US to study at the University of Southern California (USC), may be termed an Asian American counter-star. The documentary utilises the discourse of stardom to raise the spectre of what this particular Asian woman represents in US media culture. More than that, the fact that Chong works in the porn industry provides an ironic inversion of all the tropes of Hollywood stardom. Whereas Hollywood icons are glamorously sexy, Chong proudly wears a T-shirt bearing the legend 'SLUT'; where stars perform or act for the camera, Chong proclaims to enjoy her sexual routines; while stars live in opulent luxury, and stay trim and healthy, Chong rents a seedy apartment, receives a pittance for acting in her porn tapes, and is in constant danger of contracting the AIDS virus from her industry colleagues.

Sex: The Annabel Chong Story is a significant movie, albeit a deeply ambiguous and therefore disturbing one.[7] Whereas Asian American star culture tends to focus on the lives and images of Asian star 'cousins' *in lieu of the anticipated success of future Asian American stars*, the first film specifically about Asian American stardom to be given a wide theatrical release concerns a porn icon. The significance of this might be said to lie in the fact that if a porn star can be granted such visibility and be given such stellar treatment, any Asian American can therefore aspire to be a 'star'.

We return, then, to where we started from – namely, an Asian American 'erotic feast'. Geraldine Kudaka raised the question of what constitutes 'sexiness' in the Asian American male, although the example she used to illustrate this subject – Chow Yun-Fat – has remained curiously sexless throughout his screen career (particularly, it must be said, in Hollywood). Coming at this subject from a different direction, *Sex: The Annabel Chong Story* reverses these erotic dynamics. Whereas Chow Yun-Fat is perceived by some to have introduced Asian eroticism into the imaginative lives of Asian America, Chong is shown in her movie to have implanted US sex culture back 'home' to Asia, more specifically into Singapore. In what are probably the most moving scenes of the entire film, Chong reveals her secret to her mother and cousin – she works as a porn star in America, she has 'disgraced' the family name. Such scenes illustrate – as do moments of cross-cultural travel and arrival in *Anna and the King, Rumble in the Bronx*, and *Rush Hour* – that global dynamics, in Asia and elsewhere, play a continuous role in the formation of Asian American subjectivities.

CONCLUSION

It would be remiss of me not to mention the fact that I am acutely aware of the gender implications of the material I have been exploring. Simply put, in some of the examples cited, Asian male stars appear to connote stylishness and confidence, whereas Asian female stars appear to connote deviousness and hyper-sexuality. On one level, these divergences are entirely predictable; after all, such distinctions merely reproduce the gender polarities that so often characterise the representation of Asians across US media culture. There is an urgent need to recognise and explore the gender discriminations of contemporary Hollywood's compelling images of Chinese and other Asian identities. However, such analyses shall have to wait for another day. For now, I hope that this chapter contributes to the work of challenging such distinctions by merely questioning their continuing status and validity.

---

1 This chapter is concerned with the culture of some Asian Americans, namely that category of person Darrell Y. Hamamoto (2000a: 1) identifies as 'Yellow people in the United States'. As such, the term 'Asian' should here be differentiated from its more common usage in the UK, i.e. to refer to Brown people in Britain of Indian descent.

   Following the convention used by many Asian Americans in the US, I have chosen not to hyphenate the two terms 'Asian' and 'American'. This is to signify the distinctiveness of the two separate terms as well as their combination into a wholly new third term (that is, Asian American). These dimensions are lost when a hyphen is inserted.

2 On the cultural politics of Asian American media eroticism, see Hamamoto (2000b), and film-maker Greg Pak's spoof 'infomercial' *Asian Pride Porn* (at **www.gregpak.com**).

3 The three most important Asian stars of the classical Hollywood period were Sessue Hayakawa, Nancy Kwan and Anna May Wong. For revisionist accounts of these actors from an Asian American perspective, see Kirihara (1996), Feng (2000) and Liu (2000). For historical overviews of Asian images in US film, yellowface and patterns of Orientalist stereotyping, consult Oehling (1980), Marchetti (1993), Shohat and Stam (1994), Carson (1995), and Bernstein and Studar (1997). On the dynamics of white ethnicity, assimilation and celebrity from the silent era to the present, see Negra (2001).

4 See Stringer (2000) for a discussion of the implications for a nascent Asian American film-making practice of the convergence of the Hong Kong and Hollywood film industries.

5 A comparable analysis, this time in the context of literature written by Japanese American women, is Yamamoto's (1999) utilisation of the trope of the 'mask' and its relevance for the formation of distinct Asian American subjectivities.

6 'The story goes that when *King Kong vs. Godzilla* (1962, Japan) came out, there were two endings. In America, the guy in the monkey costume won. In Japan, it was the rubber suit. . . . Today, another East vs. West battle is taking place on the big screen' (Martin Wong, 'King Kong vs. Jet Li', *Giant Robot* 11 (Summer), 1998: 30).

7 Framed initially by footage of Chong's depiction as a feminist icon-freak on *The Jerry Springer Show*, the movie opens with a montage of different images. We see *cinema verité* shots of her trying to avoid the documentary camera on the street; her porn publicity work and publicity photos; a glamour shot taken on the day she delivered an address at Oxford University; Chong waking up in her Los Angeles apartment; attending class at USC; meeting up with Dick James, president of her fan club, to discuss strategy. In an interesting spin on the ambivalences of how this film might be read, John Anderson reports that when *Sex: The Annabel Chong Story* was screened at the 1999 Sundance Film Festival, the post-screening question and answer session included a request that director Gough Lewis confirm whether or not Chong had a financial stake in his documentary: 'He said she did – thereby altering the perception of the film among the entire audience' (Anderson, 2000: 11–12). Anderson does not clarify what these altered perceptions actually were. However, the very fact that an audience might alter its response so completely testifies to the indeterminate nature of the diverse signs of 'Asian-ness' projected by Chong throughout.

Chapter Fifteen

'PETER PAN'S MY DAD?!?' THE MAN-CHILD PERSONA OF ROBIN WILLIAMS

Ewan Kirkland

Robin Williams is a somewhat contradictory figure within contemporary popular cinema. Rising to prominence in the 1970s for his role in the sitcom *Mork and Mindy*, he became known for his manic, rapid-fire delivery style as a stand-up comedian during the 1980s, before emerging as a regular of the family feature film in the 1990s. Glancing at Williams' filmography, one is struck not only by the extent of his output, but also its range: 1996 saw Williams starring in *The Birdcage* (USA), a remake of gay farce *La Cage aux Folles* (1978, France/Italy), Kenneth Branagh's *William Shakespeare's Hamlet* (UK/USA), *Joseph Conrad's The Secret Agent* (UK), Francis Ford Coppola's *Jack* (USA) and Disney's video follow-up *Aladdin and the King of Thieves* (USA) in which he reprises his 1992 role as genie of the lamp. Williams is interesting for the apparent ease with which he straddles the child-orientated genre of 'family comedy', and the adult-orientated sphere of 'serious drama'. In 1997, the same year as Williams earned a Best Supporting Actor Oscar for his role in Gus Van Sant's *Good Will Hunting* (USA), a film dealing with class prejudice, social deprivation and child abuse, he also took the lead in Disney's *Flubber* (USA) in which he plays the bumbling, flying car-driving inventor of green anthropomorphised slime.

In his study *Stars*, Richard Dyer relates a popular film star's image to the struggle between dominant and competing or subordinate ideologies. Stars can be understood as negotiating these conflicts, either through displacement, the suppression of one discourse in favour of another, or by working a '"magic" reconciliation of the apparently incompatible terms'. Thus Lana Turner's synthesis of sexiness and ordinariness, or Marilyn Monroe's combination of knowing sexuality and sexual innocence, both serve to reconcile the conflicting desire within American culture for women to be at once sexy, pure and ordinary (Dyer, 1998: 26); Dyer observes parallels between Monroe's film persona and discourses surrounding female sexuality during the era of her popularity (1998: 31). This suggests that the attraction of film stars stems from their ability to unify competing discourses, an act of ideological reconciliation cemented by the star's existence outside the film text. I shall argue that Robin Williams, both in terms of the roles he has played and the range of films in which he has starred, characterises many of the tendencies of recent Hollywood cinema. The central conflict which Williams serves to reconcile is between adult and child, synthesised in what might be termed his 'man-child' persona. While serving to stabilise various generic problematics inherent within the contemporary family film, this merging of adult and child has significant ideological dimensions, in terms of Hollywood's representation of men and masculinity, and children and childhood.

ROBIN WILLIAMS AND THE CHILD IN THE AUDIENCE

Notions of children's cinema, and the even more complex concept of the implied child audience member, are recurring themes in discussion of recent American film. Production trends in 1980s Hollywood – the concentration on visual and special effects, nostalgia for Saturday-morning matinée features, the absence of sexual or contentious subject matters, paternal reassurance and what is perceived as the concurrent narrative 'infantilisation' of cinema – are described by Robin Wood as resulting in 'children's films conceived and marketed largely for adults' (Wood, 1986: 163). Many writers have observed that this industrial strategy facilitates a media machine geared towards audience maximisation. John Hartley makes a similar argument concerning the 'paedocratic regime' apparent in 1980s television industrial discourses, in which audiences are constructed as children in order to attract the highest possible viewing figures. According to Hartley, the larger a medium's target or potential audience, the more pronounced paedocratic tendencies become (Hartley, 1987: 127), hence their prominence within blockbuster cinema. In his study of the American box office, John Izod emphasises the financial importance of the holiday seasons, and the film industry's reliance upon a small number of big films, which will attract the otherwise irregular family audience. Since the mid-1970s, Izod argues that, in order to draw in this essential demographic, Hollywood films have combined elements considered appealing to children with more sophisticated adult-orientated pleasures (1988: 182). Exploring what he calls the 'family-adventure' movie, Peter Krämer argues that many of the most successful recent American films combine the children's film, family film and adventure movie, providing both 'childish delight' and 'adult self-awareness and nostalgia' (1998: 304–5).

While Krämer acknowledges the infantilising pleasures of many recent Hollywood films, he takes issue with, among others, Wood's assumption that audiences for such features are predominantly composed of adults (1998: 297). This underscores a certain critical confusion at the level of generic definition, exacerbated by developments which parallel the infantilisation of films for adults: the 'adultification' of film forms traditionally aimed at children, eroding their position as primary audience. Such tendencies are apparent in the sophisticated jokes, cultural and cinematic allusions of *Casper* (1995, USA), *Toy Story* (1995, USA), *A Bug's Life* (1998, USA) and many recent Disney feature cartoons, of which *Aladdin* (1992, USA) is an obvious example. Here Williams' performance is integral. While the frenetic slapstick animation of the genie seems designed to appeal to children,

Williams' dialogue, a rapid succession of frequently adult cinematic references and impressions, including Robert de Niro, Peter Lorre and Jack Nicholson, seems aimed at more mature members of the audience. A large number of Williams' family film roles contain similar sequences.

In discussion of such texts, the exclusive category of 'children's film' gives way to the inclusive label 'family film'. While the family film has much in common with children's cinema, Bazalgette and Staples note important points of departure resulting from their significantly increased budgets and subsequent requirement to appeal not just to children, but also to mums, dads and teenagers. The stars that feature in such vehicles are almost exclusively adult stars. They enjoy the greatest share of screen time, from Dick Van Dyke and Julie Andrews in *Mary Poppins* (1964, USA), to Williams in *Hook* (1991, USA) and *Aladdin*. Consequently child actors as figures of identification for child audiences are diminished, as adult stars take centre stage. When children do feature their roles are comparatively marginal, predominantly functioning as problems for adults to solve or as helpless characters for adults to rescue, the narrative privileging adult over children's perspectives and agency (Bazalgette and Staples, 1995: 95–6).

In many ways, Williams' filmography characterises the generational blurring apparent in contemporary cinema. A closer exploration of Williams' films and roles reveals a double dichotomy. On one level, his films can be broadly divided into those orientated towards children or family audiences, such as *FernGully: the Last Rainforest* (1992, Australia), *Jumanji* (1995, USA) and *Father's Day* (1997, USA); and those seemingly aimed at more adult viewers such as *Awakenings* (1990, USA), *Good Will Hunting* and *Jakob the Liar* (1999, USA). Williams can therefore be seen as embodying the cross-generation address of American mainstream cinema. Within these films, Williams' roles can be further divided into two categories. In the first he plays a child-figure, an otherworldly innocent. In *Toys* (1992, USA), he stars as the child-like owner of a primary-coloured toy factory. In *Jack*, Williams plays a ten-year-old boy trapped within the body of a 40-year-old man. And in *Bicentennial Man* (1999, USA) he stars as a Pinocchio-esque robot learning how to be human. This is in apparent contrast to the films in which Williams plays a father-figure such as *The Birdcage*, *Being Human* (1994, USA/UK) and *What Dreams May Come* (1998, USA). Significantly, there is no necessary correlation between the adult Williams role and the adult-orientated feature, particularly in his early films. In both *The World According to Garp* (1982, USA) and *Seize the Day* (1986, USA) Williams plays a young man overshadowed by an overbearing mother and father respectively. In *Moscow on the Hudson* (1984, USA) Williams plays an innocent abroad as a naïve Russian defecting to the United States. And in *Good Morning, Vietnam* (1987, USA) Williams is an irreverent army disc jockey, whose schoolboy pranks are a constant source of irritation to his superior officers. None of these could be considered family films. Nevertheless, the child-like persona is indisputably evident.

The developments described above are far from unproblematic for audiences, producers and actors alike. The first inherent tension relates to the construction of adult audiences as children. Taking issue with Wood's assumption that the pleasures of being reconstructed as a child are 'mindless' and 'automatic', Krämer observes that the childhood represented in many family films, undoubtedly like the childhood of many adult audience members, is far from idyllic (Krämer, 1998: 297). In addition, western society has long perpetuated a deeply embedded distinction between adult and child, a distinction which informs the social, political and cultural activities afforded to each by both law and convention. A degree of resistance to the implied infantilising processes is therefore likely, as viewers desire to retain their adult status and sophistication even as they consume these big-budget 'children's films'. The two-tier address and adult–child synthesis of Williams' performances can be understood as appeasing such anxieties, complicating the infantilisation model of spectatorship suggested by both Wood and Krämer. The seemingly improvised asides which form part of his comic contribution to *Toys*, *Mrs Doubtfire*, (1993, USA) and *Hook*, one-liners, including references to Freudian psychology, Richard Nixon, acid flashbacks, *Psycho* (1960, USA), *Dirty Harry* (1971, USA) and *The Exorcist* (1973, USA), can be understood as a series of knowing winks, assurances that despite the films' juvenile generic source, they nevertheless contain pleasures available only to adult audience members. At the same time, in his most child-like roles, Williams might also be understood as a surrogate for the adult-as-child viewer.

This child-like persona has further significance in relation to the problematic nature of the children's film itself, exacerbated by its appropriation and modification for adult consumption. The ambiguous relationship between adult author and child reader, Jacqueline Rose argues, is central to the 'impossibility' of children's fiction (Rose, 1984: 1), an impossibility which applies as much to children's cinema as literature. The modification of the children's film, increasing focus on adult stars, narratives and perspectives, inherently emphasises the adult authorship within the text, threatening to undermine the generic location upon which this project relies.

One of the means of appeasing such contradictions, Rose suggests, is the discursive construction of the text's author as childlike (1984: 19–20) or the notion that those who realise the author's vision are somehow 'in league' with the child in the audience (1984: 32). In an article influenced by Rose's work, David Buckingham undertakes a comparative critique of presenters of children's television. Arguing that children's television embodies similar contradictions and tensions to those observed by Rose, Buckingham notes a distinctive change in tone within recent British children's television, an attempt to erase the divide between adult programmers and child viewers through the infantilisation of the adult presenter (1995: 48). Focusing on Timmy Mallett, presenter of children's television programme *Wacaday*, Buckingham criticises the persona of the adult presenter as clown. Mallett assumes a child-like appearance and behaviour, dressed in luminous striped shirts, paisley shorts, 'outrageous' spectacles and peaked cap, lurching around the studio, gesticulating wildly in a play of anarchy and 'zaniness'. An 'adult in drag' (1995: 51), an adult masquerading as a child, Mallet attempts to address child viewers as equals, while his relationship to his audience is based on a contempt for, rather than affinity with, children, celebrating a patronising and trivialising construction of childhood characterised by anarchy and disorder (1995: 57).

Williams' filmography includes numerous comparative examples of the adult masquerading as child. In *Jumanji* Williams plays Alan Parrish, first seen as a boy in the late 1960s, who becomes trapped within a board game. Emerging as an adult three decades later in the film's present day, Parrish is depicted as a child unnaturally located in a grown-up body. In *Jack* this theme becomes more literal, as Williams plays a young boy suffering from premature ageing, who has the appearance of a 40-year-old man. Arguably the most complex manifestation of such tendencies occurs in *Hook*, a collaboration between Williams and man-child director Steven Spielberg, adapting and contemporising a traditional children's classic. In a key scene, Williams as the now-adult Peter Pan regains the power of flight. Dressed in a dinner suit, he launches into the air, whereupon he is magically transformed into the Pan of Barrie's play, dressed in green-leaf trousers and top, his hair moulded in impish spikes: adult dragged as eternal child. Williams' man-child persona can therefore be understood as personifying the merging of adult-children's cinema. In addition, his prominence within recent American film may also be explained through observed changes within 1990s cinema and its representation of masculinity.

ROBIN WILLIAMS AND 1990s MOVIE MASCULINITY

Susan Jeffords (1993) argues that 1991 (also termed by Fred Pfeil (1995: 37) 'The Year of Living Sensitively') was the year of the transformed American male within mainstream cinema. While the 1980s were dominated by tough, weapon-wielding, independent, muscular hard-bodied heroes, the early 1990s saw the sudden emergence of a softer, kinder, gentler masculinity within popular cinema, typified by the male leads in films like *Regarding Henry* (1991, USA), *Terminator 2: Judgement Day* (1991, USA), *City Slickers* (1991, USA), together with Williams-starring *The Fisher King* (1991, USA) and *Hook*. For Jeffords, the factor which turns the excessively macho superheroes of 1980s cinema into the 1990s 'new man' can be summed up in a single word: 'family'. Not only does 'the family' function as the means by which the hero discovers his gentler side, but the family, as opposed to action, feature film was commonly the arena in which this transformation took place.

For Jeffords, *Kindergarten Cop* (1990, USA) constitutes a precursor to the male transformation films under discussion. Starring Arnold Schwarzenegger, icon of 1980s musculinity, as John Kimball, a tough police officer who goes undercover as a teacher in order to track down a murderous drug dealer, the film charts his gradual emotional awakening, re-discovering his protective paternal instincts, breaking down his psychological barriers to intimacy, and concluding that he 'wants nothing more than to be a father, not a warrior/cop after all' (Jeffords, 1993: 199–200). While *Kindergarten Cop* may chart this change, its potential pitfalls are perhaps best exemplified by a later Schwarzenegger family feature, *Junior* (1994, USA). Here, Arnie plays Dr Hess, an emotionally cold university scientist researching a new fertility drug. When funding is cut, Hess is encouraged by his gynaecologist partner Arbergast (Danny DeVito) to test the drug on himself, and becomes pregnant. Homoerotic subtext abounds, from the scene in which Arbergast impregnates Hess with a phallic syringe, to the pregnant male scientist moving into his 'partner's' estranged wife's bedroom, to Schwarzenegger's performance as insecure and clingy mother-to-be with Arbergast as his henpecked husband. These homoerotic elements are largely defused through the presence of a female academic, Dr Diana Reddin (Emma Thompson), as heterosexual love interest for the feminised Hess. Although initiated by Abergast's insemination, it is through her character that Hess's transformation is realised, culminating in the film's epilogue which sees Reddin pregnant by Hess through more traditional means as proof of his essential heterosexuality. Despite this closure, the film's frequent gay overtones, and subsequent frantic attempts to seal these queer cracks, provide an insight into the 'dangers' of the 1990s feminised man. As Jeffords observes in relation to *Switch* (1991, USA), this was an industrial trend concerned with challenging male gender roles, while maintaining traditional masculine (hetero)sexuality (1993: 203).

The homosexual associations of the domesticated male hero, occasionally verging on the 'sissy man' gay stereotype, perhaps typified by a frilly aproned Michael Keaton on the posters advertising *Mr Mom* (1983, USA), are invariably closed off through an emphasis on fatherhood. The family which features as the motivation for male transformation is unambiguously heterosexual and procreative in nature, emphasised by the prominence of children towards whom the male hero becomes increasingly fatherly. These children may be biological, as in *Regarding Henry*, adopted children like Kimble's unruly kindergarten class, or even non-human, such as the calf which Mitch (Billy Crystal) fosters in *City Slickers*. Later, *Jerry Maguire* (1996, USA) told of an unscrupulous sports agent (Tom Cruise) whose transformation is facilitated by a single mother and her son; while a misanthropic hypochondriac (Jack Nicholson) succeeded in wooing another single mother, partly through his treatment of her sickly son in *As Good as it Gets* (1997, USA). Children perform an important function in these narratives, serving to locate the transformed male within traditional familial structures and sexual relationships.

While Williams' career transformation is not comparable to Schwarzenegger's, his emergence as a prominent figure within popular cinema (his 1990–5 feature roles doubling those of 1985–9) coincides with changes in these representations of masculinity. Children's function in asserting the heterosexuality of the male protagonist is strongly evident in Williams' 1993 family film *Mrs Doubtfire*. A strangely literal example of Buckingham's notion of the adult television presenter dragged as child, Williams plays

Daniel Hillard, an estranged husband and father, disguising himself as an old Scottish housekeeper in order to spend more time with his children, and finally achieving success as a children's television presenter. The queer stigma associated with transvestism is largely defused through Hillard's children, who function as the sole motivation behind his decision to adopt this persona. The superficial feminisation of the protagonist derives from his attempts to infiltrate the family home from which he has been excluded, while his increasing domestication stems from the desire to construct a suitably ordered alternative environment for his children to visit within his own apartment. The transformation of Williams' character from Hillard to Doubtfire, and consequent development from slob to culinary and housekeeping aficionado, far from undermining his masculinity, serves to emphasise his commitment to his children and strengthen his role as father.

These developments in the representation of masculinity have been significantly criticised by writers such as Elizabeth Traube (1992), Jude Davies and Carol Smith (1997), in addition to Jeffords, as entailing the highly selective male appropriation of female-coded roles and qualities, a strategy for perpetuating and naturalising male paternal authority. However, strong elements of infantilisation are also apparent. *Regarding Henry* features Henry (Harrison Ford) as an unscrupulous lawyer who suffers brain damage as the result of a convenience store hold-up. Surviving the incident, he has to learn again how to talk, walk and relate to his family. Returning to this infantile state, Henry emerges gentler, kinder, more loving towards and loved by his wife and child.

Just as the child-like aspects of Williams' roles persist in his adult films, so the paternal qualities are evident in his family features, including those in which the man-child persona is most pronounced. In *Jack*, Williams' character becomes both child role model and father figure to his best friend, Louis (Adam Zolotin). In *Jumanji*, due to the time-loop nature of the narrative, Williams and his girlfriend grow up to become protectors of the two present-day children in the film. In *Hook*, Williams must access his inner child, the eternal Peter Pan, in order to save his children from the villainous Captain Hook. Even in films in which Williams' role is more overtly, if not literally, paternal, *Dead Poets Society* (1989, USA), *Awakenings, Good Will Hunting* and *Patch Adams* (1998, USA), his fatherly style is noticeably benevolent. In contrast to Kimble's military brand of kindergarten instruction, Williams' characters' method of teaching or treating typically involves an erosion of the division between adult doctor or teacher and child pupil or child-like patient, which brings his character into conflict with more officious adult-orientated authority figures.

While this is characteristic of the generational blurring of Williams' career and contemporary cinema, it has significant implications for male familial authority. The fusion of adult and child in an infantilised father invariably enhances the male protagonist's authoritative position within the family unit. In *Mrs Doubtfire* this works to undermine Miranda (Sally Field), Hillard's ex-wife, who in contrast to Williams' character is shown to be cold, stern and unsympathetically 'adult'. An early scene features a chaotic children's birthday party within the family home, characteristic of the anarchic construction of childishness criticised by Buckingham. Upon her arrival, Miranda brings the party to an abrupt halt, and the film is subsequently critical of her inability to appreciate her ex-husband's childish irresponsibility. A 1991 transformation film allowing Williams to represent both officious parent and the benign infantilised father, *Hook* features Williams as Peter Banning, a hard-nosed corporate raider, whose workaholism is eroding his relationships with his wife and children. Banning's estrangement from his own childhood is characterised by the fact he cannot remember anything before he was 12 years old, and his antagonistic relationship with his son whom he regularly reprimands for his immature behaviour. Returning to the Banning's childhood home, Williams' character is confronted not only with the abduction of his children, but the revelation that he is the Pan of Barrie's novelisation. Banning can only save his children by regaining the power to fly, which can only be rediscovered by finding his 'happy thought'. This 'happy thought' is the thought of his own children, and his status as father. Having defeated Hook and rescued his children, Banning and family return to the nursery, shown to be both physically and emotionally reunited, thanks to their father's new-found child-affinity.

This fortification of the male familial position on the grounds of child-like as opposed to feminine-coded qualities, can be seen as a much more sustainable strategy for naturalising paternal authority. The construction of an ideal infantile father figure suggests a simultaneous reaction against feminist discourses privileging women's familial authority through their reproductive abilities, and the emergence of the career mother partially located in the adult-orientated workplace. In *Mrs Doubtfire*, Miranda's motherhood is undermined not because she is lacking in femininity, but through her excessive adulthood which alienates her from her children. While involving considerable softening of on-screen masculinity, the infantilised father circumvents the ambiguities of sexuality inherent in the feminised male, provides a perfect figure for the family-orientated hero of the family feature film, as well as standing as a substitute for the absence of children traditionally at the centre of children's cinema.

ROBIN WILLIAMS AND CHILDHOOD IN 1990s CINEMA

While the appropriation of feminine-coded qualities by male protagonists within recent American cinema has been significantly criticised by feminist writers, there exists no established discourse for engaging with a similar appropriation of child-coded characteristics. Patriarchal dominance within 1980s cinema, persisting in the reaffirmation of male parent figures in the 1990s family film, Wood characteristically interprets as a reaction to gay, Black and feminist movements of the 1960s and 1970s. However, the 'restoration of the father' can equally be understood as a reactionary response to the anti-war protests, radical magazines, university activism and associated youth movements of the same period, and the political rhetoric of student protest emphasising the disparity between the generations. While the impact of what might be labelled 'the youth liberation movement' was minimal, it did constitute a short-lived attack not just on white male heterosexual hegemony, but the very adult-based foundation of ruling authority.

Evidence of a reactionary response to such developments, and the anxiety which children continue to evoke, can be seen in the emphasis on family reconciliation within the family feature, traditionally represented in a final shot framing the male protagonist, together with loving family, from which the camera draws back in an elaborate crane shot (Pfeil, 1995: 38). While it may take various forms, the unified or reunited family is more often than not traditionally hierarchical in organisation. Father, his paternal role reaffirmed through his adventures, resumes central position, mother and children assuming second and third places. No matter what degree of agency is displayed by children within the narrative, either as explorers searching for gold (*The Goonies* (1985, USA)), miniaturised adventurers trekking across the garden lawn (*Honey, I Shrunk the Kids* (1989, USA)) or dinosaur and computer systems experts (*Jurassic Park* (1993, USA)), they finally assume subordinate positions within this family structure. Just as the softer, gentler 1990s man forfeits none of his male privilege, the infantilised father figure does not relinquish any of his adult authority, but emerges more capable and justified in his position as head of his family and children.

Williams' man-child role in such films as *Toys*, *Jumanji*, *Hook* and *Jack* can be understood as further symptomatic of adult ambivalence towards contemporary childhood. Within these four films the absence or marginalisation of child stars is accompanied by an adult actor exhibiting child-like characteristics. While Buckingham's labelling of this process as a form of drag strikes a playful, carnivalesque note, it might more antagonistically be described as a form of minstrelisation, an often-patronising attempt to control the terms within which a subordinate group is represented. Rose discusses the adult process of writing for children as one of drawing in the child in order to possess it (Rose, 1984: 2). Williams' child minstrel goes one stage further by constructing the child in the adult's own image and, in the process, defining childhood according to specifically adult ends.

This redefinition of childhood is an important if not crucial aspect of the kind of contemporary cinema under discussion. If the family film relies for its success upon the pleasurable nostalgia and infantilisation associated with children's cinema, 'the child' such escapism depends upon is of a very specific, and particularly fictional, nature. Negative aspects of being a child – confusion, helplessness, the tyranny of parents and peers – must be exorcised or neutralised. Discussing *The Lion King* (1994, USA), *ET: the Extra Terrestrial* (USA, 1982) and the *Star Wars* trilogy (1977, 1980, 1983, USA), Krämer questions Wood's characterisation of the childhood such films represent as idealised, illustrating the hardship and psychological trauma experienced by Simba, Elliott and Luke Skywalker respectively. Similarly, childhood and adult–child relations are often problematised in Williams' family

251

films. However, equally absent are the more threatening representations of young people contained within such adult, anti-family films as *Fun* (1994, USA), *Heavenly Creatures* (1994, New Zealand) and *Kids* (1995, USA). The man-child persona of Robin Williams' family films serves to resolve these childhood and generational tensions, to banish the bad seed child, and to reconstruct childhood in a fantastical, nostalgia-friendly form. As a distinctly symbolic state, located in the past not the present, this process often involves the privileging of the man-child figure, not only over adult characters, but also over actual children within the narrative.

Given the specificity, selectivity and tenuousness of the childhood which this cinema relies upon, the threat posed to its maintenance by actual children is circumvented by the relegation of child stars, and the prominence of the child-minstrel as their substitute who frequently acts to resolve childhood unhappiness. The narrative of *Jumanji* is framed by Parrish's story, emphasising Williams' centrality within the text; while the child, turned man-child, returned to child, now grown naturally into an adult solves the plight of the orphaned children within the original 1990s storyline by saving their parents from a fatal accident. The discontent of the children in *Mrs Doubtfire*, who despite the significant differences in their ages are virtually indistinguishable from one another, stems from the estrangement of their child-like father. Within *Toys*, which with its fantasy milieu, colourful sets and toy factory setting, has all the iconography of the children's film, children are present only in the opening and closing musical sequences, and in a number of brief scenes where young boys are shown playing computer games as part of the villain's evil scheme to harness children's arcade skills for military purposes. The main children within the film are Williams as Leslie Zevo, and Alsatia (Joan Cusack), his equally infantile sister, who eventually succeed in foiling the villain's plans to corrupt both the toy factory and his unwitting child accomplices.

In *Hook* the fusion of adult and child in the desirable father figure, and the man-child's displacement of the threatening child is a central goal within the narrative. In order to save his children, Banning must lead the Lost Boys in an assault on Hook's ship, usurping the position of their child leader, Rufio (Dante Basco). While the other Boys are depicted in a range of old-English outfits (as cub scouts, sailors, Dickensian street urchins), Rufio's appearance is markedly contemporary, dressed in a leather jacket with tight punky trousers and striped mohican. If the Boys constitute an unthreatening pre-industrial, whimsical version of childhood, the defiant Rufio who is most suspicious of Banning's entry into their ranks, is racially, culturally and sexually coded as the urban juvenile delinquent, threatening the nostalgic construction of childhood which *Hook* means to evoke. Throughout the course of the narrative, Rufio not only surrenders to Banning's paternal-infantile leadership, but dies in his arms, wishing that he had a father like Banning. The absence of a man-child father figure is suggested as the source of the bad seed's deviation from true childhood; while Banning's son's pre-pubescent angst, represented as stemming from the disinterest and frequent chiding of his adult father, is resolved through Banning's personal rediscovery of the child within.

In *Jack*, the man-child is placed within a contemporary setting and generally shown to represent a more authentic and desirable form of childhood than the actual children within the film. Described by Jack's father as 'a bunch of spitting swearing ten-year-olds', the gang of kids who eventually become Jack's friends are depicted in a particularly unfavourable light, shown to be cruel, suspicious and initially unaccepting of the giant in their midst. In contrast to his streetwise contemporaries, Jack is markedly innocent. Showing no interest in the pornographic magazines in which the other boys are so fascinated, when asked if he ever gets an 'erector', he replies no, but he's hoping to get one for Christmas. In the film's penultimate scene, in which all the children in Jack's class celebrate his return, Louis reads an essay on what he wants to be when he grows up, saying he wants to be just like Jack, the perfect grown-up because on the inside he's just a kid, not afraid to learn and try new things, seeing everything for the first time, and freed from the adult trappings of working, making money, and showing off to neighbours. Through this, the child celebrated in *Jack* is shown to have little to do with real children. The figure of the man-child facilitates the configuration of a more acceptable form of both adulthood and childhood, a childhood of which contemporary children, represented as precocious and knowledgeable beyond their years, are shown to fall woefully short.

CONCLUSION

Robin Williams characterises many tendencies within contemporary cinema. Given the dynamics of 'children's films for adults', the emergence of the family feature film and the ways in which children and childhood have come to function in recent Hollywood cinema, it is perhaps not surprising that such a star has emerged. Variously understood as an assurance of the adult pleasures of adult-appropriated children's cinema, a surrogate for the adult-as-child audience member, the children's television presenter dragged as child of adult-constructed visual culture for children, the idealised infantilised father figure, and the minstrel-child: Williams' man-child persona facilitates the generational blurring of contemporary cinema, softening on-screen masculinity as a means of enhancing paternal authority, facilitating the metaphorical function of childhood, and assuaging adult anxieties surrounding contemporary children.

In closing, a number of qualifications need to be made to the above. It must be acknowledged that many of the key films discussed in this essay, *Toys*, *Hook* and *Jack* (also *Popeye* (1998, USA), *Being Human*, *What Dreams May Come* and *Patch Adams*) failed in terms of box office returns, critical response and textual coherence. These 'failures' suggest that the star-figure's reconciliation of incompatible terms or characteristics is far from guaranteed. In addition, these texts are far more complex than the necessarily sketchy descriptions contained within this brief chapter can accommodate. Childhood in *Jack* is variously represented as idyllic, oppressive, socially constructed, innate, a state of joy and wonder, a state of frustration, alienation and misery; and it would be a gross oversimplification to suggest these contradictions are wholly resolved in the film's celebration of the eponymous man-child. Similarly, the appropriation of media forms associated with children may serve radically different functions to those outlined above. The *South Park* series, with its arguably subversive satirisation of the children's cartoon, its conventions and associated construction of childhood is just one example; and Williams' solo performance of a slightly bowdlerised version of the song 'Blame Canada' from *South Park: Bigger Longer & Uncut* (1999, USA) at the 2000 Oscar ceremony admittedly complicates this analysis of his star persona. Finally, my own dislike of Robin Williams must be acknowledged. I find it extremely uncomfortable to watch a grown man acting like a child, particularly in a film which I consider to be aimed at children. This undoubtedly reflects my own ambivalence towards children and adults, my past childhood and present adulthood. Despite my negative reading of the infantilised male which, in various forms, characterises Williams' film roles, I understand the childish adult to be particularly popular among child viewers, on whose behalf in my discussion of the child-minstrel, I have implicitly been speaking.

Section 5
Star controversies

Martin Barker

Film studies has long been prone to a certain mild disease: the affliction of high theory. Perhaps arising from a search for a distinctive kind of respectability, from a will to prove that film, like literature, has high cultural virtues, which can only be truly appreciated by properly educated aficionados, there has been a tendency to a certain grandiosity of theoretical claim about the ways films work and make meanings. In their own way, star studies too have also perhaps been prone to a certain over-egging.

What could be wrong with the notion that the primary distinguishing feature of stars is simply that they are exceptionally *beautiful*? Specimens of ideal body types, with camera-friendly eyes and mouths, and well-sculpted physiques. Once one has admitted this possibility that stars work primarily by being sexually desirable, then why not also allow that in at least some cases – and at least in relation to the range of parts they opt for or are assigned to play – stars are actually *very good actors*? This seems to be a point that may be so obvious that it is just being overlooked in the search for 'deeper' meanings.

In short, the important thing might be that stars look good, and look and sound right, in the parts they play. Assuming this were correct, it would not at all be the end of the story, but it would realign the questions we would ask. We could, for example, explore the shifting ideals of physical attractiveness, and the differing notions of bodies and personalities on display. We could examine how different genres of film generate requirements for kinds and styles of acting. We could study Marilyn Monroe as an embodiment of a certain fleshly perfection with modest acting skills, as against a summary of ideological sexual tensions. We could study Al Pacino and Robert de Niro not primarily as iconic Italian Americans, but for the grain of their individual voices, and their body styles in front of the camera.

Take one emergent star, Halle Berry, whose tearful overflow at the 2002 Academy Award ceremony instantly became iconic.[1] Compare two articles about her in the same newspaper, one day apart. In the first, Berry is celebrated for her post-Oscar progress:

> The 33-year-old has spent the morning at Pinewood Studios in London, where she is completing a four-month stint filming the next Bond movie. A grey baseball cap is crammed over her chic curls, but the peak's shadow fails to conceal the glorious swell of her cheekbones. . . . In *Monster's Ball*, Berry plays Leticia Musgrove, a luckless single mother who becomes entangled with her jailed husband's racist executioner. She turns in an exceptional performance as the feckless, angry young woman who finds an unlikely redemption with a man whose own pain and prejudices are transformed by love.
>
> (*Libby Brooks, 'Now I'm Really at the Party', Guardian, G2,
> 3 June 2002: 10–11*)

Brooks' celebration of Berry's beauty, and of her acting skills, delights in what they seem to promise as new possibilities for Black American women. It is not that all questions about representation have gone away, rather, that the very charismatic qualities that she, as a star, embodies seems to offer a transcendent opportunity.

The second article dismissed *Monster's Ball* (2001, USA) as just another Blaxploitation movie, arguing that Berry is being used as just another 'noble savage':

> What was hailed by many white observers as courageous and groundbreaking was denounced more privately by black Americans as embarrassing and stereotypical. . . . Women in film have had to battle sexual objectification since they first stepped in front of the camera. But race makes that objectification historically and culturally insidious and harder to fight. . . . And contrary to all the critical plaudits, she projects little character, instead alternating between sullenness and all-out hysteria, the sort of emotional extremism long ascribed to black characters.
>
> (*Erin Aubry Kaplan, 'Hollywood Hype, Black Stereotype', Guardian, 4 June
> 2002: 14*)

The difference between these is not simply in the judgements (is her acting exceptional, or exceptionally limited?), but in the critical lexicon. While the first aesthetically appreciates Berry, and her performance, the second examines her representational power. The difficulty is that the second, undoubtedly much more recognisable to star studies, hardly leaves a conceptual space within which it might be possible to enjoy. Or, at best, only after a star and his/her performance had passed health-checks could personal pleasure be acknowledged. Star studies is in danger of only permitting critical, external stances.

In this section we publish just one essay, an honestly polemical contribution by Alan Lovell who has long tried to argue for such a shift in emphasis. Lovell takes to task the tradition of star studies which derives from Richard Dyer's books. He challenges in particular a series of distinctions that have largely been taken for granted. For example, the distinction between stars and character actors: for whom is it true, he asks, that character-actors 'disappear into their roles'. And why is this ability being approved of, when comedy, for instance, virtually requires a gap between actor and character? Lovell asks us to change the terms of the debates about stars, and allow back in the very terms that audiences and reviewers typically use: 'There is a much larger debate underlying the debate I have tried to open up about star studies. It is a debate about how art is defined, how it relates to entertainment, the kind of art cinema is, what political role it plays.' We think that this is a timely challenge with which to close this book.

---

1 The poster for Aberystwyth Students' 2002 May Ball simply presented the overcome, thunderstruck Berry. The image summarised: glamour, completion, exhaustion, an overflow of emotion, and 'that special night'.

Chapter Sixteen

'I WENT IN SEARCH OF☐ DEBORAH KERR, JODIE FOSTER AND JULIANNE MOORE BUT GOT WAYLAID . . .'

Alan Lovell

I wanted to write about star performance. I was interested in the effect of an actor's physical appearance. I was going to make two comparisons: first, between Jodie Foster and Julianne Moore as Clarice Starling in *The Silence of the Lambs* (1991, USA) and *Hannibal* (2001, USA); second, between Deborah Kerr and Julianne Moore as Sarah Miles in *The End of the Affair* (1952, USA, and 2000, USA, respectively). I began my preparation, looked at the DVDs, read the novels and the scripts. And then . . .

My decision to write about performance was not entirely innocent; it was meant as a gentle protest about the way star studies has developed. I felt that performance had been marginalised. Stars are worth studying, it seems to me, because they are, first and foremost, performers. The priority for star studies should therefore be to develop a richer account of performance. My wish to do this was strengthened when I read some recent books about stars (Babington, 2001; Macnab, 2000; Vincendeau, 2000). The overall effect of these experiences was unsettling. I found it hard to focus on the specific performances of Deborah Kerr, Jodie Foster and Julianne Moore, as other issues kept intruding. What follows is an attempt to put a stop to those intrusions.

*

The questions 'Why stardom?' and 'Why such and such a star?' have to be answered in terms of ideology.

(Dyer, 1979: 38)

Richard Dyer's two books, *Stars* (1979) and *Heavenly Bodies* (1986), placed the study of stars squarely within the study of ideology.[1] Dyer's account of ideology was shaped by Louis Althusser's ideas, which were highly influential in film, cultural and media studies when he wrote his books. So, via Althusser, stars and ideology were firmly linked. The link is now one of the givens of star studies.

Dyer did not explain why he concluded that stars and stardom have to be discussed ideologically. This is not surprising: his answer had a quality of obviousness to it. From the early days of cinema, there has been a widespread conviction that films have a powerful effect on the social beliefs and behaviour of audiences. The concept of ideology provides one way of exploring this.

Dyer was writing at a time when the ideas that had emerged from the political upheavals of 1968 were fresh and attractive. Ideology was one of the most prominent of those. It was a key to explaining the puzzle of how, despite their obvious injustices, modern capitalist societies maintained themselves. The mass media were identified as making a major contribution in this area. Althusser's account of ideology seemed to provide a sophisticated intellectual foundation for this position. In established Marxist accounts, ideology had become a crude instrument. Althusser made it sharper, a suitable tool for analysing contemporary capitalism.

Even in the late 1970s, the commitment to ideology, particularly Althusser's version of it, should not have been made so unproblematically, and 20 years later, the attractions seem even less powerful. The problems it raises are more obvious and, consequently, its value for star studies is more contestable. I'll discuss two areas where there are problems.

Dyer's discussion starts from the premise that ideology promotes a particular account of human individuality (Dyer, 1986: 8), that individuals have an essence unique to each individual. These unique individuals are in command of their lives. Stars *embody* this account of individuality. Because of their prominence, stars play a crucial role in keeping it dominant (though sometimes they register the anxieties surrounding it). I will summarise my main reservations about this position.

1. The belief that a particular account of human individuality is central to ideology is not an obvious one. To support it, Dyer draws heavily on Althusser's claim that the fundamental operation of ideology is to make individuals misperceive themselves as subjects. This applies to all human beings throughout history. There appears to be no way out of this – ideology is as universal and fundamental as the air we breathe (and misperception is at the root of human existence). Richard Dyer is forced to adapt this bleak view to make it more persuasive and workable. In his account, 'subject' almost disappears and 'individual' becomes the dominant term. 'Individual' then often elides into 'human being'. So he can write 'Stars articulate what it is to be a human being in contemporary society'. This brings his position close to the traditional view of stars as reflecting deep human needs, ambitions and fantasies.

2. I do not believe that capitalism is dependent on one particular view of human individuality. Dyer cites the philosopher David Hume as an opponent of the view that human beings have a unique essence. He summarises Hume's position as 'all we know of ourselves is a series of sensations and experiences with no necessary connection' (Dyer, 1986: 9). For me, such a view is perfectly consistent with modern capitalism. And the view that human beings have a unique essence does not necessarily lead to conservative politics; it has played a part in a wide range of political activities, from the American Revolution to pacifism.

3. On a different level, film stars are improbable candidates for carrying out the ideological task assigned to them. Their notorious capriciousness seems to point in the opposite direction to stable and unique identities, especially if we take gossip and rumour seriously. In popular imagination, film stars are the polar opposite of the solid bourgeois citizen, and indeed the whole area of acting seems unfavourable territory for this kind of ideological work. Actors as a group are traditionally regarded as frivolous people without a stable identity. When one individual represents another, the uniqueness of individuals is always put into question.

Ideology is an account of how meanings arise, how some become dominant, and how claims for legitimacy are made. I do not think that the main interest of stars (or films) is in the meanings they create. I agree with Geoffrey Nowell Smith's claim that 'Films mean. But they do not just mean. ... Too many of the things that films do evade attempts to subsume them under the heading of meaning' (Nowell Smith, 2000: 16) Applied to stars, I would highlight performance as an area that has been evaded. The exchange between actor and audience has no stable currency. Actors offer bodies, voices, technical skill, beauty, attractiveness, imagination, intelligence. Audiences offer attentiveness, admiration, curiosity, fantasy. Meanings may well be made in the exchange between them, but I do not think its character is adequately captured if this is made central.

There is a passage in the conclusion to *Stars* that articulates the way in which ideology limits the discussion of stars. Richard Dyer writes:

> I should mention beauty, pleasure, delight. ... The emphasis in this book has
> been on analysis and demystification. ... However, we should not forget that
> what we are analysing gains its force and intensity from the way it is
> experienced, and that ideology shapes the experiential and affective as much
> as the cognitive. When I see Marilyn Monroe I catch my breath: when I see
> Montgomery Clift I sigh over how beautiful he is: when I see Barbara
> Stanwyck, I know that women are strong. I don't want to privilege these
> responses over analysis but equally I don't want, in the rush to analysis, to
> forget what I am analysing. And that I must add that while I accept utterly

that beauty and pleasure are culturally and historically specific, and in no
way escape ideology, nonetheless they are beauty and pleasure and I want to
hang onto them in some form or another.

(Dyer, 1979: 184)

There is an uneasiness about the relationship between beauty, pleasure and ideology. The
uneasiness is created in part by the way Dyer links analysis and demystification. This is
an easy link to make since ideological analysis most often takes the form of demystification. However, the link does not have to be made; analysis is not always a form of
demystification. It can as well enhance beauty and delight as destroy them.

*

Acting and stardom are of course by no means necessary to each other, with
stardom depending as much on image as on technique.

(Higson, 2001: 71–2)

This disjunction between stars and acting ability is frequently observed. But is it an
accurate observation? The majority of stars have a background in acting. They have
been to drama school and/or have experience of film or theatre acting before they
become stars. What use they make of the training or experience – how good they are as
actors – is a matter of judgement, and making such judgements is not easy. Much of the
evidence is intangible: the 'grain' of a voice, the size of a mouth or the rhythm of a walk.
Additionally the framework for considering the evidence is weak. Basic issues have not
been adequately discussed. Should actors disappear into their parts? What role does
physical beauty and attractiveness play? How different is acting in the cinema to acting in
the theatre?

I do not want to argue that judgements about acting are inevitably individual and
arbitrary, the product of unchecked subjectivity. There are tangible qualities – technical
skills, the ability to read a script intelligently, inventiveness. More substantial discussion
and debate would make it possible to create a stronger framework. However, the nature
of the activity means that evaluating acting is unlikely to become an exact science!

In the assessment of any human activity where the evidence is not hard and criteria uncertain, cultural prejudices are likely to have an effect. I believe this has been the case in
star studies. Stars have focused the hostility to cinema as a form of mass culture, and
particularly because stars are first thought of in terms of Hollywood and America. In such
a context, the claim that they cannot really act is easy to accept.[2]

Stars who play a limited range of characters are usually cited in support of this belief. This range is supposedly close to their own personality – 'They play themselves.' John Wayne is likely to be cited, but I would describe the example of Wayne in different terms. In any profession there are successful people who have strong but limited technical abilities. They are successful because they carefully choose the areas they work in, are self-conscious about their abilities and stay within their limits. John Wayne's career can be described in this way. He had some obvious qualities as an actor; he had an imposing physique made distinctive by the lightness of his movements ('The big guy moves like a fairy' as director Henry Hathaway 'eloquently' described it); his voice added to his physical distinctiveness; a long apprenticeship gave him a very good understanding of the mechanics of film acting. He used the knowledge and talents to provide vivid representations of a certain kind of heroic character.

My own view is that the majority of stars in the cinemas I am familiar with (British, American and French) are, by and large, the best actors. There are undoubtedly a minority who are not; again, this is no different from other professions. In universities, I would guess there are just as many mediocre lecturers who become professors as mediocre actors who become stars.

*

> One of the endearing aspects of Cary Grant's charm is how good-naturedly he falls in with the women's instinct to play.
>
> *(DiBattista, 2001: 19)*

> ... there always comes a moment in which [Deborah] Kerr is ready to surrender to the force of her own desire and she is interrupted by some external event which prevents full expression.
>
> *(Deleyto, 2001: 128)*

> Nevertheless it is significant that a star [Brigitte Bardot] who incarnated vibrant sexuality and energy should be so violently punished in most of her key films.
>
> *(Vincendeau, 2000: 98)*

Varying degrees of confusion between stars and their roles mark these quotations. The confusion could be the result of a forgivable carelessness. However, it is so prevalent that it demands some explanation.

Certainly, the identification of actors as ideological figures does not encourage an interest in performance, where the interaction between actor and character takes place. Nor do attitudes towards the film script. Ever since the intervention of the *Cahiers du Cinéma* in the 1950s, the contribution a script makes to a film has been downgraded. The key critical terms deployed by the *Cahiers'* writers, *mise-en-scène* and auteur, were in part a polemic against the script. The director was the key creative figure in film-making. What the director did, especially his deployment of *mise-en-scène*, constituted the writing of a film. In such a climate the writer became a secondary figure and the script of limited importance. Not surprisingly, the problems posed by fictional characters in drama, especially for actors, have been ignored. If a strong awareness of stars as ideological figures is combined with a weak awareness of fictional characters, the grounds for confusion between star and character are well established.

The application of the auteur theory to stars did not help. Stars have been written about in the same terms as directors. Their films have been analysed to discover an overall pattern, a meta character which can be constructed out of all the different characters a star plays. There are obvious objections to this approach. Stars have even less control over the characters they play than directors have over the films they make. However, if the approach is adopted, stars rather than writers appear to create characters. It then does not seem incongruous to say that it is the star, Brigitte Bardot, who is punished rather than the characters she plays, or that Deborah Kerr surrenders to the force of her own desire.

The distinction commonly made between stars and character-actors further adds to the confusion. On the face of it, the distinction is puzzling. Like character-actors, stars play characters. The basis for the distinction is a judgement that character-actors disappear into their roles in a way stars do not. I doubt that this is true. Does Eve Arden disappear into her roles more than Joan Crawford does? Marcel Dalio more than Jean Gabin? Norman Rossington more than Albert Finney? Ricky Jay more than Burt Reynolds? Or is it simply the fact that because Crawford, Finney and Reynolds play central roles, they are more familiar than are actors who play minor roles? My own experience is that once I identified a non-star actor, they did not disappear into their characters. I became aware of Ricky Jay in films directed by David Mamet, so when he appeared in *Boogie Nights* (1997, USA) and *Magnolia* (1999, USA) I recognised him immediately. And, for me, fine actor though he was, Elisha J. Cook Jr never disappeared into his characters.

I would challenge the judgement on more theoretical grounds. Is the actor's ability to disappear into a character a universal criterion of good acting? It is most appropriate for drama with naturalistic ambitions, but for genres such as comedy, westerns, horror, melodrama, it is less appropriate. Indeed, I would argue that it is a misleading criterion for all dramatic genres. Just like sport and opera, a fundamental pleasure of arts like cinema and theatre is an appreciation of performance, an awareness of a performer's skills and talents and how effectively they are being used. If the performer disappears, then some of the audience's pleasure is lost.

The distinction between stars and character-actors is another way of suggesting stars cannot act. I believe a more helpful distinction is between actors who play leading parts (stars) and actors who play supporting parts (character-actors).

*

> By stars I mean celebrated film performers who develop a persona or myth, composed of an amalgam of their screen image and private identities, which the audience recognises and expects from film to film, and which in part determines the parts they play.
>
> *(Vincendeau, 2000: viii)*

> Stars are usually discussed in terms of their persona, a sort of meta character built up across several films, a star image which can be carried into each new film.
>
> *(Higson, 2001: 72)*

'Persona' and 'image' are the analytical terms most used in the discussion of stars, and they are used in confusing ways. Ginette Vincendeau distinguishes persona from image; Andrew Higson uses persona and image as interchangeable. Some writers, like Yvonne Tasker, agree with Vincendeau in making persona the dominant term. Others, like Paul McDonald, follow Dyer in making image the dominant term. Vincendeau connects persona to ideology, Dyer connects image to ideology.

This confusion does not help. However, it is less important than the assumptions that underlie the use of these terms. Persona/image points to the fact that stars are more than their individual performances. The individual performances combine with each other and with personal biography, publicity and general media exposure to create the persona/image. In analysing a star, all of these should be considered.

The audience's knowledge of a star tends to be taken for granted. Cinemagoers are assumed to know as much as a scholar does. They have the full awareness of stars' careers, their films and their manifestations in the media that research has made available for the scholar. Is there evidence that this is the case? When the cinema was the dominant form of mass entertainment, it might have been. For a period in the middle of the twentieth century large numbers of people went weekly to the cinema. There was a limited number of media, and film stars had few challengers for the public's attention. In such conditions, cinemagoers might know a lot about their favourite stars. The evidence collected by Jackie Stacey (1994) about cinemagoers in the 1940s and 50s supports this. It is much harder to believe the same of cinemagoers over the last 30 years. The main pattern of filmgoing is irregular and infrequent. There is a wide range of media – music, television and sports stars compete with film stars for our attention. In such a situation, cinemagoers, with the exception of a minority of enthusiasts, are likely to have a limited and vague knowledge of stars.[3]

*

> We may generalise (following Dyer) that British, like other, stars exhibit a
> 'structured polysemy', have meaning in regard to dominant and subdominant
> ideologies, reinforce ruling values, sometimes articulate oppositional
> meanings as they play out the culture's conceptions of individuality,
> masculinity and femininity.
>
> *(Babington, 2001: 19)*

The demonstration of how stars 'reinforce ruling values and sometimes articulate oppositional meanings' has characteristically taken the form of the analysis of texts (films, newspapers, television programmes, advertisements). To be politically meaningful and intellectually convincing, another step is necessary. It has to be shown that audiences respond to films in a way consistent with the critic's discoveries. You can only avoid taking this step if you believe that meanings are expressed in so compelling a way that only one kind of response is possible. Since most accounts of meaning have stressed its instability and openness, few critics have taken this position. Most have simply assumed that audiences respond in a way that is consistent with their account.[4]

Richard Dyer's discussion of Marilyn Monroe vividly illustrates this problem. He argues that Monroe's popularity was the consequence of two discourses which developed in the early 1950s. The first was the *Playboy* discourse, which presented sex as a healthy, guilt-free, natural form of human activity. The second was the *Psycho* discourse, which presented female sexuality as passive, formless in character, and dependent on male sexuality. Trying to establish that Monroe was primarily thought of in terms of sex, he quotes a sociologist's account of how a group of miners and their wives from the north of England responded to Monroe:

> In the bookie's office or at the pit they made jokes about the suggestiveness
> of Miss Monroe, about her possible effect on certain persons present, and
> about her nickname, 'The Body'. Indeed any man seemed to gain something
> in stature and recognition if he could contribute some lewd remark to the
> conversation. On the other hand, in private conversation with a stranger the
> same men would suggest that the film was at best rather silly, and at worst

on the verge of disgusting. Finally the men's comments in the presence of women were entirely different. In a group of married couples who all knew each other well, the women said that they thought Miss Monroe silly and her characteristics overdone; the men said they liked the thought of a night in bed with her. The more forward of the women soon showed up their husbands by coming back with some remark [such] as 'You wouldn't be much bloody good to her anyway!' and the man would feel awkward.

(Dyer, 1986: 23)

The vividness and detail of this description makes it valuable evidence. It certainly establishes that Monroe was primarily thought of in terms of sex! However, I cannot see that, as described here, the responses can be explained by the discourses which Dyer identifies. There is little sense that sex is 'guilt-free'; the strong presence of lewdness and humour suggests it is an area of tension, and it appears to have a taboo quality for the men. They assert their masculinity by breaking the taboo with lewd remarks. The women's response hardly suggests that they regard female sexuality as passive, either for themselves or for Monroe. At one level, what is most striking about the description is the different attitudes of the men and women to sex. The men's attitude is uncritical and inflationary, whereas the women's attitude is critical and deflationary. What is also striking is the way in which the men's attitudes change according to the context.

The description of one group's response to Marilyn Monroe, however it is interpreted, does not prove that Richard Dyer's account of her popularity is wrong. Before conclusions could be reached about its validity, much more evidence would be needed. I want to suggest that independent evidence about audience response should have a much stronger presence in the discussion of stars. If it did, the conclusions reached from textual analysis could be tested and they would carry more conviction.

The kind of evidence about audience response that I have cited is not often available. This is not surprising – most critics have been trained in methods of textual analysis of films, while cinema audiences constitute very different objects for analysis. They are made up of large numbers of individuals divided by class, age, gender, ethnicity and disability. Their responses are informal, often not fully articulated and frequently unstable. Given how different the objects of analysis are, the methods appropriate for the analysis of texts cannot easily be transferred to audiences. Methods that might be appropriate have been developed outside of film studies. Significantly the description of responses to Marilyn Monroe comes from a sociological study of mining communities.[5]

If audiences remain unknown quantities, stars also now seem less knowable. In her thoughtful and well-informed discussion of the present state of star studies, Christine

Geraghty suggests the star is now regarded as 'an unstable and contradictory figure' (Geraghty, 2000: 185). This makes the intellectual situation even more precarious. The relationship that has been at the heart of star studies now seems to be constituted by an elusive phenomenon (stars) and an uninvestigated one (audiences). In such a situation, intellectual caution would seem advisable. Certainly large claims about ideological effects should be avoided.

*

> Interviewer: You must have found it very different when you went to Hollywood, big budgets, stars.
>
> Stephen Frears: No, stars are mainly actors, very good actors.
>
> (Nicky Campbell Programme, *BBC Radio 5*, 18 February 2002)

Can I find my way back to Deborah Kerr, Jodie Foster and Julianne Moore, having profited from these detours? Is there some firmer ground that star studies can be based on? I will make some suggestions.

PERFORMANCE

The most important fact about stars is that they are performers. (I prefer the term 'performer' rather than 'actor' because the latter has limiting connotations.) Whether superb or mediocre, whether they have wide-ranging skills or limited skills, they are still performers. To cope with this, a more substantial account of film performance than presently exists is needed. What technical skills are required? How important is physical presence (bodies, faces, voices, movements)? What kind of knowledge and intelligence do performers need? Giving priority to the discussion of performance should help to make the discussion more intellectually secure. Performance is an area where film critics ought to be able to claim distinctive knowledge and expertise.[6]

SCRIPTS

All performers in dramatic fictions are dependent on scripts. To develop a stronger aware-ness of performance, it is therefore necessary to develop a greater awareness of scripts. This task can be focused more sharply for stars because they are performers of a special kind; they play main characters in narratives. To understand star performance, an aware-ness of the nature of those characters and their relationship to other characters is especially important.[7]

AUDIENCES

An emphasis on performance should support the study of audiences. It would concentrate attention on the one thing which cinemagoers undoubtedly have in common – they have seen stars in films. I have suggested that there should be an independent investigation of audience response. I would like to see that investigation directed towards the audience–performer relationship. How aware are audiences of performance? In which ways does interest in stars' performance guide the choice of films and how people attend to them? What criteria do audiences use to judge performance? Are there any typical languages in which we might trace these criteria? Through what aspects of people's behaviour (their talk or facial expressions or bodily movements as they 'relive' those performances, perhaps) are their responses made public?

ELITES

Emanuel Levy (1990) places his study of stars within the study of elite groups. He provides an illuminating description of the kind of elite group Hollywood stars constitute. His account ought to be developed. Is his description accurate? How does the Hollywood group compare with other elite groups both in the film industry and other industries? It would be especially helpful to develop comparisons of national star groups. Recent interest in stars from countries like France and Britain suggests that star studies has been distorted by a concentration on Hollywood stars.

CELEBRITY

Although discussions of film stars as celebrities have tended to confuse matters, it would be foolish to ignore the issue. My own view is that the study of film stars as celebrities would be much improved if the study of celebrity was developed as an area in its own right. Joshua Gamson's pioneering (1994) work provides an excellent model. He shows an awareness of the work of film scholars that should be repaid in kind.[8]

*

An actor is there for only one purpose: to perform in front of people that must be amused on the highest possible level. And by amusement I mean *Some Like It Hot* or *Hamlet* or *Othello*. The audience is there to be amused.

(Lemmon, 1998: 271)

There is a much larger debate underlying the one I have tried to open up about star studies. It is about how art is defined, how it relates to entertainment, the kind of art cinema is, what political role it plays. For me, the concept of ideology is at the heart of this debate. Most of the reservations I have expressed in this article can be traced back to it. I have become increasingly uneasy not only about the way it is used, but also about the value of the concept itself. Too often it plays the role that phlogiston played in

269

eighteenth-century chemistry, the mysterious substance whose existence conveniently accounts for awkward problems.[9]

Is there another framework for the study of stars I can suggest? My attempt to highlight performance and my unqualified support for Jack Lemmon's demand that the audience be amused make me sympathetic to Geoffrey Nowell Smith's call for 'a return to theories of the aesthetic' (Nowell Smith: 2000: 16). What this would entail deserves more elaboration than I can provide in the last paragraph of an article. So, as a final flourish, I will say that what we should be concerned with are: beauty, pleasure and delight; why somebody *should* catch their breath when they see Marilyn Monroe or sigh over Montgomery Clift's beauty; why somebody should want to write about Deborah Kerr, Jodie Foster and Julianne Moore!

---

1   In fact, there is a change between *Stars* and *Heavenly Bodies*. In the second book, ideology is relegated to the background and discourse becomes the key term. Although this has some consequences, they do not affect the overall position. Discourse is discussed in a way that makes it pretty much interchangeable with ideology. The change mainly marks the way in which Michael Foucault's ideas had replaced Althusser's as the centre of intellectual interest between 1979 and 1986.

2   It would be inaccurate to say that academic writing about stars simply expresses hostility. Admiration is also frequently expressed. Like many writers on mass culture, writers about stars struggle to reconcile the two responses.

3   It would be helpful to have some evidence about this. As part of a course I was teaching I did try to find out about students' knowledge of Susan Sarandon. Almost all of the 99 students who took part in the survey had seen at least two or three of her films. The vast majority knew only two things about her: she was married to Tim Robbins and had won an Oscar for *Dead Man Walking* (1996, USA). It was hardly surprising they should know these two facts as the survey was made just after Sarandon won the Oscar for *Dead Man Walking,* which Tim Robbins directed. Of 99 students only two had what could be described as general knowledge of Sarandon. One had this knowledge because she had a close friend who she described as a real fan of Sarandon. The other had the knowledge because her parents had met Sarandon!

4   Jackie Stacey's (1994) discussion of the audience response to stars is an important exception.

5   Happily, there is an increasing interest within film studies in developing appropriate methods. Some of the issues that arise are illuminatingly discussed in an exchange between Janet Staiger and Martin Barker (2000).

6   There is a welcome interest in performance in Christine Geraghty's essay. She confuses the issue a little, I think, by making a distinction between stars as performers and stars as professionals. I think in both cases she is talking about different ways of approaching performance.

7   Sarah Kozloff's (2000) discussion of film dialogue is an excellent example of the kind of work that needs to be done.

8   The extensive bibliography on film acting that Peter Krämer has produced suggests that there is valuable work in all of these areas that could be drawn upon (Lovell and Krämer, 1999).

9   My rejection of ideology obviously needs more explanation than I have given it here. I found *On Voluntary Servitude* by Michael Rosen (1996) especially helpful in trying to think about the area.

CONTRIBUTORS' DETAILS

Thomas Austin is Lecturer in Media Studies at the University of Sussex. He is the author of *Hollywood, Hype and Audiences: Selling and Watching Popular Film in the 1990s* (2002).

Martin Barker is Professor of Film and Television Studies at the University of Wales, Aberystwyth. His works include (with Thomas Austin) *From Antz To Titanic: Reinventing Film Analysis* (2000) and (with Jane Arthurs and Ramaswami Harindranath) *The Crash Controversy: Censorship Campaigns and Film Reception* (2001).

Cynthia Baron is an Assistant Professor at Bowling Green State University in Ohio. She teaches courses in film studies, women's studies and American culture studies. Recent publications include articles in *Quarterly Review of Film and Video*, *Women's Studies Quarterly*, and *The Velvet Light Trap*. She is co-editor of the forthcoming *More Than a Method: Trends and Traditions in Contemporary Film Performance*.

Sharon Marie Carnicke is Professor and Associate Dean of the School of Theatre at the University of Southern California. An expert on acting theory, she has performed and directed professionally in the United States and Moscow. Her recent book *Stanislavsky in Focus* (1998) examines the complex impact of Stanislavsky's system of actor training on the Method and on Russian training. Her work with Lee Strasberg began in the late 1970s, when she served as an assistant director and interpreter for a Russian director at the Actors Studio in New York.

Dr Máire Messenger Davies is a Reader at the School of Journalism, Media and Cultural Studies, Cardiff University. She was an Annenberg Research Fellow at the University of Pennsylvania in 1993, studying media literacy in children. She is the author of *Television is Good for Your Kids* (1989, 2nd edition 2001), and *'Dear BBC': Children, Television-storytelling and the Public Sphere* (2001). With Roberta Pearson, she is writing a book on *Star Trek* and television.

Christine Geraghty is Professor of Film and Television Studies at the University of Glasgow. She has written extensively on film and television and is the author of *Women and Soap Opera* (Polity, 1991) and *British Cinema in the Fifties Gender, Genre and the 'New Look'* (2000).

Matt Hills is a lecturer at the School of Journalism, Media and Cultural Studies at Cardiff University. He is the co-editor of *Intensities: The Journal of Cult Media* (**www.cult-media.com**) and the author of *Fan Cultures* (2002). He is currently writing *The Pleasures of Horror* and carrying out a one-year AHRB-funded study of media audiences.

Ian Huffer currently teaches Media Studies at the University of Sussex. He is also writing a DPhil on the reception of the films of Sylvester Stallone by British film audiences.

Barry King is Associate Professor and Head of the School of Communications Studies at Auckland University of Technology. He has published in *Screen*, *Afterimage*, *Cultural Studies*, *Semiotica* and the *American Journal of Semiotics*, and in edited collections in the USA, the UK and Germany. He has just completed a book-length study of the star system in the American cinema.

Geoff King is lecturer in Film Studies at Brunel University, and author of *New Hollywood Cinema: An Introduction* (2002), *Film Comedy* (2002), *Spectacular Narratives: Hollywood in the Age of the Blockbuster* (2000) and co-editor of *ScreenPlay: Cinema/Videogames/Interfaces* (2002).

Ewan Kirkland is completing his PhD thesis on children's cinema at the Graduate Research Centre in Culture and Communication, University of Sussex.

Peter Krämer teaches Film Studies at the University of East Anglia. He has published widely on American film and media history in *Screen*, *The Velvet Light Trap*, *Theatre History Studies*, the *Historical Journal of Film, Radio and Television*, *History Today*, *Scope* and numerous edited collections. Together with Alan Lovell, he has co-edited *Screen Acting* (1999).

Joanne Lacey is Senior Lecturer in Visual Culture at the University of Brighton. She has published in the areas of popular culture, class and audience, and is currently researching the history of home movies in Britain.

Alan Lovell recently retired from teaching film at Staffordshire University.

Paul McDonald is Reader in Film and Television Studies at University of Surrey, Roehampton. He is the author of *The Star System: Hollywood's Production of Popular Identities* (1999) and contributed the supplementary chapter updating Richard Dyer's *Stars*.

Roberta Pearson is Reader in Media and Cultural Studies at Cardiff University. Her related work on acting and stardom includes *Eloquent Gestures: Performance Style in the Griffith Biograph Films* (1992) and ' "Bright Particular Star": Patrick Stewart, Jean-Luc Picard and Cult Television' forthcoming in *Worlds Apart: Essays on Cult Television* which Pearson co-edited with Sara Gwenllian-Jones. Together with Máire Messenger Davies she is writing *Small Screen, Big Universe: Star Trek and Television*.

Julian Stringer is Lecturer in the Institute of Film Studies at the University of Nottingham, and an editorial board member of *Scope: An Online Journal of Film Studies*. He is editor of *Movie Blockbusters* (forthcoming).

Paul Wells is Professor and Head of the Media Portfolio at the University of Teesside. He has published widely in the field of animation, including *Understanding Animation* (1998) and *Animation: Genre and Authorship* (2001), and is the Curator of 'Animation at the Ark' at the Children's Cultural Centre in Dublin.

BIBLIOGRAPHY

Abercrombie, Nicholas and Brian Longhurst (2000) *Audiences*, London: Sage.

Abramowitz, Rachel (2000) *Is That a Gun in Your Pocket? Women's Experience of Power in Hollywood*, New York: Random House.

Adams, Cindy (1980) *Lee Strasberg: The Imperfect Genius of the Actors Studio*, New York: Doubleday.

Adams, James Eli (1995) *Dandies and Desert Saints: Styles of Victorian Masculinity*, Ithaca: Cornell University Press.

Allen, Robert C. (1999) 'Home Alone Together: Hollywood and the "Family Film"', in Melvyn Stokes and Richard Maltby, eds, *Identifying Hollywood's Audiences: Cultural Identity and the Movies*, London: British Film Institute.

Allen, T. (1988) 'The Semi Precious Age of TV Movies,' *American Film* (Dec): 41–3.

Altman, Rick (1999) *Film/Genre*, London: British Film Institute.

Anderson, John (2000) *Sundancing: Hanging Out and Listening In at America's Most Important Film Festival*, New York: Avon Books.

Armon-Jones, Claire (1991) *Varieties of Affect*, Toronto: University of Toronto Press.

Auslander, Philip (1999) *Liveness*, London: Routledge.

Austin, Thomas (1999) '"Desperate to See It": Straight Men Watching *Basic Instinct*', in Melvyn Stokes and Richard Maltby, eds, *Identifying Hollywood's Audiences: Cultural Identity and the Movies*, London: British Film Institute.

Austin, Thomas (2002) *Hollywood, Hype and Audiences: Selling and Watching Popular Film in the 1990s*, Manchester: Manchester University Press.

Babington, Bruce, ed. (2001) *British Stars and Stardom*, Manchester: Manchester University Press.

Bacon-Smith, Camille with Tyrone Yarborough (1991) '*Batman*: the Ethnography', in Roberta Pearson and William Urrichio, eds, *The Many Lives of the Batman*, London: Routledge/British Film Institute.

Baker, Wayne E. and Robert Faulkner (1991) 'Role as Resource in the Hollywood Film Industry', *American Journal of Sociology* 97(2): 279–309.

Balio, Tino (1976a) *United Artists: The Company Built by the Stars*, Madison: University of Wisconsin Press.

Balio, Tino, ed. (1976b) *The American Film Industry*, Madison: University of Wisconsin Press.

Barish, J. (1981) *The Anti-theatrical Prejudice*, Berkeley: University of California Press.

Barker, Martin and Kate Brooks (1998) *Knowing Audiences: Judge Dredd, its Friends, Fans and Foes*, Luton: University of Luton Press.

Barker, Martin with Thomas Austin (2000) *From Antz to Titanic: Reinventing Film Analysis*, London: Pluto Press.

Baron, Cynthia (2002) 'Buying John Malkovich: Queering and Consuming Millennial Masculinity', *The Velvet Light Trap* 49 (Spring): 18–38.

Base, Ron (1994) *Starring Roles: How Movie Stardom in Hollywood is Won and Lost*, London: Little, Brown.

Baym, Nina (2000) *Tune In, Log On: Soaps, Fandom and Online Community*, London: Sage.

Bazalgette, Cary and Terry Staples (1995) 'Unshrinking the Kids: Children's Cinema and the Family Film', in Cary Bazalgette and David Buckingham, eds, *In Front of the Children: Screen Entertainment and Young Audiences*, London: British Film Institute.

Beebe, Roger Warren (2000) 'After Arnold: Narratives of the Posthuman Cinema', in Vivian Sobchack, ed., *Meta Morphing*, Minneapolis: University of Minnesota Press.

Benson, Lou (1974) *Images, Heroes and Self-Perceptions: The Struggle for Identity from Mask-Wearing to Authenticity*, Englewood Hills: Prentice-Hall.

Berlin, J., ed. (1996) *Toxic Fame: Celebrities Speak on Stardom*, Detroit: Visible Ink.

Bernstein, Matthew and Gaylyn Studlar (1997) *Visions of the East: Orientalism in Film*, New Brunswick: Rutgers University Press.

Bingham, Dennis (1994) *Acting Male: Masculinities in the Films of James Stewart, Jack Nicholson, and Clint Eastwood*, New Brunswick: Rutgers University Press.

Blandford, Steve, Barry Keith Grant and Jim Hillier (2001) *The Film Studies Dictionary*, London: Arnold.

Bolter, J. and R. Grusin (1999) *Remediation: Understanding New Media*, Cambridge, Mass.: MIT Press.

Boorstin, Daniel (1963) *The Image*, Harmondsworth: Penguin.

Bourdieu, Pierre (1984) *Distinction: A Social Critique of the Judgement of Taste*, Cambridge: Harvard University Press.

Bowser, Eileen (1990) *The Transformation of Cinema 1907–15*, Berkeley: University of California Press.

Branston, Gill (1995) '... Viewer, I listened to him ... Voices, Masculinity *In the Line of Fire*', in Pat Kirkham and Janet Thumim, eds, *Me Jane: Masculinity, Movies and Women*, London: Lawrence & Wishart.

Brantlinger, Patrick and Richard Boyle (1988) 'The Education of Edward Hyde: Stevenson's "Gothic Gnome" and the Mass Readership of Late-Victorian England', in William Veeder and Gordon Hirsch, eds, *Dr Jekyll and Mr Hyde: After One Hundred Years*, Chicago: University of Chicago Press.

Britton, Andrew (1984, 2nd edn 1995) *Katharine Hepburn: Star as Feminist*, London: Studio Vista.

Brooker, Will (1997) 'New Hope: the Postmodern Project of *Star Wars*', in Peter Brooker and Will Brooker, eds, *Postmodern After-Images*, London: Arnold.

Brooker, Will (1999) 'Internet Fandom and the Continuing Narratives of *Star Wars*, *Blade Runner* and *Alien*', in Annette Kuhn, ed., *Alien Zone II*, London: Verso.

Brooker, Will (2000) *Batman Unmasked: Analyzing a Cultural Icon*, London: Continuum.

Brookey, Robert Alan and Robert Westerfelhaus (2002) 'Hiding Homoeroticism in Plain View', *Critical Studies in Mass Communication* 19(1): 21–43.

Buckingham, David (1995) 'On the Impossibility of Children's Television: The Case of Timmy Mallett', in Cary Bazalgette and David Buckingham, eds, *In Front of the Children: Screen Entertainment and Young Audiences*, London: British Film Institute.

Buckingham, David (2000) *After the Death of Childhood*, Cambridge: Polity Press.

Bukatman, Scott (1991) 'Paralysis in Motion: Jerry Lewis' Life as a Man', in Andrew Horton, ed., *Comedy/Cinema/Theory*, Oxford and Berkeley: University of California Press.

Bukatman, Scott (1998) 'Zooming Out: The End of Off-screen Space', in Jon Lewis, ed., *The New American Cinema*, Durham: Duke University Press.

Butler, Judith (1990) *Gender Trouble: Feminism and the Subversion of Identity*, New York: Routledge.

Byars, Jackie and Eileen Meehan (1998) 'Once in a Lifetime: Constructing the Working Woman Through Cable Narrowcasting', *Camera Obscura* 18, May–June: 13–23.

Byrne, Eleanor and Martin McQuillan (1999) *Deconstructing Disney*, London: Pluto Press.

Cabarga, L. (1988) *The Fleischer Story*, New York: Da Capo.

Cardullo, Bert, Harry Geduld, Ronald Gottesman and Leigh Woods, eds (1998) *Playing to the Camera: Film Actors Discuss Their Craft*, New Haven: Yale University Press.

Carnicke, Sharon Marie (1998) *Stanislavsky in Focus*, London: Routledge.

Carnicke, Sharon Marie (1999) 'Lee Strasberg's Paradox of the Actor', in Alan Lovell and Peter Krämer, eds, *Screen Acting*, London: Routledge.

Carroll, Noël (1990) *The Philosophy of Horror*, London: Routledge.

Carson, B. and M. Llewellyn-Jones (2000) *Frames and Fictions on Television: The Politics of Identity Within Drama*, Exeter: Intellect.

Carson, Diane (1995) 'Cultural Screens: Teaching Asian and Asian-American Images', in Diane Carson and Lester D Friedman, eds, *Shared Differences: Multicultural Media and Practical Pedagogy*, Urbana: University of Illinois Press.

Chan, Jackie (1999) *I am Jackie Chan: My Life in Action*, London: Pan.

Chang, Chris (1999) 'Head Wide Open', *Film Comment* 35(5): 6–9.

Cholodenko, A., ed. (1991) *The Illusion of Life: Essays on Animation*, Sydney: Power Press.

Chunovic, Louis (1995) *Jodie: A Biography*, Chicago: Contemporary Books.

Clark, Danae (1995) *Negotiating Hollywood: The Cultural Politics of Actors' Labor*, Minneapolis: University of Minnesota Press.

Cohan, Steve and Ina Rae Hark, eds (1992) *Screening the Male: Exploring Masculinities in Hollywood Cinema*, Bloomington: Indiana University Press.

Cohan, Steven (1997) *Masked Men: Masculinity and the Movies in the Fifties*, Bloomington: Indiana University Press.

Cohan, Steven (1998) 'Censorship and Narrative Indeterminacy in *Basic Instinct*: "You Won't Learn Anything From Me I Don't Want You to Know"', in Steve Neale and Murray Smith, eds, *Contemporary Hollywood Cinema*, London: Routledge.

Cohan, Steven (2001) 'Judy Garland fandom and "the gay thing" revisited', in Mathew Tinkom and Amy Villarejo, eds, *Keyframes: Popular Cinema and Cultural Studies*, London: Routledge.

Corrigan, Timothy (1998) 'Auteurs and the New Hollywood', in Jon Lewis, ed., *The New American Cinema*, Durham: Duke University Press.

Creed, Barbara (1987) 'From Here to Modernity: Feminism and Postmodernism', *Screen* 28(2): 47–67.

Creed, Barbara (2000) 'The Cyberstar: Digital Pleasures and the End of the Unconscious', *Screen* 41(1): 79–86.

Dalton, S. (1980) 'Bugs and Daffy go to War', in Daniel Peary and Gerald Peary, eds, *The American Animated Cartoon*, New York: E. P. Dutton.

Darley, Andrew (2000) *Visual Digital Culture: Surface, Play and Spectacle in New Media Genres*, London: Routledge.

Davies, Jude and Carol R. Smith (1997) *Gender, Ethnicity and Sexuality in Contemporary American Film*, Stafford: Keele University Press.

DeCordova, Richard (1990) *Picture Personalities: The Emergence of the Star System in America*, Chicago: University of Illinois Press.

DeCordova, Richard (1991) 'The Emergence of the Star System in America', in Christine Gledhill, ed., *Stardom: Industry of Desire*, London: Routledge.

DeCordova, Richard (1994) 'The Mickey in Macy's Window: Childhood, Consumerism and Disney Animation', in Eric Smoodin, ed., *Disney Discourse*, New York: Routledge.

Deleyto, Celestino (2001) 'The Nun's Story: Femininity and Englishness in the Films of Deborah Kerr', in Bruce Babington, ed., *British Stars and Stardom*, Manchester: Manchester University Press.

DiBattista, Maria (2001) *Fast-Talking Dames*, New Haven: Yale University Press.

Diderot, Denis (1976) *Rameau's Nephew and D'Alembert's Dream*, trans. Leonard Tancock, London: Penguin Classics.

Doane, Mary Ann (1988) *The Desire to Desire: The Woman's Film of the 1940s*, Basingstoke: Macmillan.

Dovey, Jon (2000) *Freakshow: First Person Media and Factual Television*, London: Pluto Press.

Dyer, Richard (1979, 2nd edn 1998) *Stars*, London: British Film Institute.

Dyer, Richard (1982) 'Don't Look Now', *Screen* 23(3–4), Sept–Oct: 61–73.

Dyer, Richard (1986) *Heavenly Bodies*, London: Macmillan.

Dyer, Richard (1991) '*A Star is Born* and the Construction of Authenticity', in Christine Gledhill, ed., *Stardom: Industry of Desire*, London: Routledge.

Edgerton, G. (1985) 'The American Made for TV Movie', in Brian Rose and Robert Alley, eds, *TV Genres: A Handbook and Reference Guide*, New York: Greenwood Press.

Edwards, Anne (1990) 'Fredric March: Normandy Style for *Dr Jekyll and Mr Hyde*'s Best Actor', *Architectural Digest* 47(4): 222–4.

Ehrenstein, David (2000) *Open Secret: Gay Hollywood, 1928–2000*, New York: Perennial.

Eisner, Will (1985) *Comics and Sequential Art*, Florida: Poorhouse Press.

Elley, Derek, ed. (2000) *The Variety Movie Guide*, New York: Perigee.

Ellis, John (1982) *Visible Fictions: Cinema, Television, Video*, London: Routledge & Kegan Paul.

Evans, A. and G.D. Wilson (1999) *Fame, The Psychology of Stardom*, London: New Vision.

Faludi, Susan (1999) *Stiffed: The Betrayal of the Modern Man*, London: Chatto & Windus.

Featherstone, Mike (1991) *Consumer Culture and Postmodernism*, London: Sage.

Feng, Peter X. (2000) 'Recuperating Suzie Wong: A Fan's Nancy Kwan-Dary', in Darrell Y. Hamamoto and Sandra Liu, eds, *Countervisions: Asian American Film Criticism*, Philadelphia: Temple University Press.

Feuer, Jane (1995) *Seeing Through the Eighties: Television and Reaganism*, Durham: Duke University Press.

Figgis, Mike, ed., (1999) *Projections 10: Hollywood Film-makers on Film-making*, London: Faber and Faber.

Fiske, John (1992) 'The Cultural Economy of Fandom', in Lisa Lewis, ed., *The Adoring Audience: Fan Culture and Popular Media*, London: Routledge.

Foss, Chris (2000) 'When "Good" Men Turn Bad: *Mary Reilly* as Disturbing Allegory of Domestic Abuse', *Literature/Film Quarterly* 28(1): 12–15.

Foster, Buddy and Leon Wagener (1998) *Foster Child: A Biography of Jodie Foster*, London: Arrow.

Friedman, L., ed. (1991) *Unspeakable Images, Ethnicity and American Cinema*, Chicago: University of Illinois Press.

Frow, John (1995) *Cultural Studies and Cultural Value*, Oxford: Clarendon Press.

Gaines, Jane (1991) *Contested Culture: The Image, The Voice, and The Law*, Chapel Hill: University of North Carolina Press.

Gamson, Joshua (1994) *Claims to Fame*, Berkeley: University of California Press.

Garfield, David (1980) *A Player's Place: The Story of the Actors Studio*, New York: Macmillan.

Garton, Joseph W. (1980) *The Film Acting of John Barrymore*, New York: Arno Press.

Garton, L., C. Haythorn-Waite and B. Wellman (1999) 'Studying On-line Social Networks', in Steven G. Jones, ed., *Doing Internet Research*, London: Sage.

Geduld, Harry M., ed. (1983) *The Definitive Dr Jekyll and Mr Hyde Companion*, New York: Garland Publishing.

Geraghty, Christine (2000) 'Re-examining Stardom: Questions of Texts, Bodies and Performance', in Christine Gledhill and Linda Williams, eds, *Reinventing Film Studies*, London: Arnold.

Gergen, K. (1991) *The Saturated Self*, New York: Basic Books.

Giddens, Anthony (1991) *Modernity and Self-Identity*, Cambridge: Polity.

Giles, David (1999) *Illusions of Immortality: A Psychology of Fame and Celebrity*, New York: St Martins Press.

Gitlin, Todd (1983) *Inside Prime Time*, New York: Pantheon Books.

Gledhill, Christine, ed. (1991) *Stardom: Industry of Desire*, London: Routledge.

Goffman, Erving (1979) *Gender Advertisements*, Basingstoke: Macmillan.

Goldman, William (1985, 2nd edn 2001) *Adventures in the Screen Trade: A Personal View of Hollywood*, London: Abacus.

Gomery, Douglas (1983) 'Television, Hollywood and the Development of Movies Made for Television', in E. Ann Kaplan, ed., *Regarding Television*, New York: University Publications of America.

Gomery, Douglas (1986) *The Hollywood Studio System*, London: Macmillan.

Grieveson, Lee (1999) 'Stars and Audiences in Early American Cinema', author's mss., published as 'Nascita del Divisimo. Stars e Pubblico del Cinema dei Primordi', in G. Brunetta, ed., *Storia del Cinema Mondiale*, Turin: Einaudi.

Gripsrud, Jostein (1989) 'High Culture Revisited', *Cultural Studies* 3(2): 194–207.

Grodal, Torben (1999) *Moving Pictures*, Oxford: University of Oxford Press.

Gunning, Tom (1990) 'The Cinema of Attractions: Early Film, Its Spectators and the Avant Garde', in Thomas Elsaesser, ed., *Early Cinema: Space, Frame, Narrative,* London: British Film Institute.

Hamamoto, Darrell (1994) *Monitored Peril: Asian Americans and the Politics of TV Representation*, Minneapolis: University of Minnesota Press.

Hamamoto, Darrell (2000a) 'Introduction: On Asian American Film and Criticism', in Darrell Hamamoto and Sandra Liu, eds, *Countervisions: Asian American Film Criticism*, Philadelphia: Temple University Press.

Hamamoto, Darrell (2000b) 'The Joy Fuck Club: Prolegomenon to an Asian American Porno Practice', in Darrell Hamamoto and Sandra Liu, eds, *Countervisions: Asian American Film Criticism*, Philadelphia: Temple University Press.

Hampton, Howard (1993) 'Sympathy for the Devil: In the Cinematic Sniper's Nest', *Film Comment* 29(6): 36–41.

Handel, Leo (1950) *Hollywood Looks at its Audience*, Chicago: University of Illinois Press.

Hansen, Miriam (1991) *Babel and Babylon: Spectatorship in Silent American Film*, Cambridge, Mass.: Harvard University Press.

Hartley, John (1987) 'Invisible Fictions: Television Audiences, Paedocracy, Pleasure', *Textual Practice* 1(2): 121–38.

Higson, Andrew (2001) 'Britain's Finest Contribution to the Screen', Flora Robson and Character Acting, in Bruce Babington, ed., *British Stars and Stardom*, Manchester: Manchester University Press.

Hills, Matt (2002) *Fan Cultures*, London: Routledge.

Hinerman, Stephen (2001) 'Star Culture', in James Lull, ed., *Culture in the Communication Age*, London: Routledge.

Hirsch, Foster (1984) *A Method to Their Madness*, New York: W. W. Norton.

Hobbes, Thomas (1975) *Leviathan*, ed. Crawford MacPherson, London: Penguin.

Holliss, Richard and Brian Sibley (1988) *The Disney Studio Story*, London: Crown.

Hollway, Wendy and Tony Jefferson (2000) *Doing Qualitative Research Differently*, London: Sage.

Hornby, Richard (1992) *The End of Acting: A Radical View*, New York: Applause Theatre Books.

Hoxter, Julian (2000) 'Taking Possession: Cult Learning in *The Exorcist*', in Xavier Mendik and Graeme Harper, eds, *Unruly Pleasures*, Guildford: FAB Press.

Humphrey, Daniel (1997) 'John Malkovich', in Amy L. Unterburger, ed., *International Dictionary of Films and Filmmakers*, New York: St James Press.

Izod, John (1988) *Hollywood and the Box Office, 1895–1986*, Basingstoke: Macmillan.

Jarvie, Ian (1991) 'Stars and Ethnicity: Hollywood and the United States, 1932–5', in Lester D. Friedman, ed., *Unspeakable Images: Ethnicity and the American Cinema*, Urbana: University of Illnois Press.

Jeffords, Susan (1993) 'The Big Switch: Hollywood in the Nineties', in Jim Collins, Hilary Radner and Ava Preacher Collins, eds, *Film Theory Goes to the Movies*, New York: Routledge.

Jeffords, Susan (1994) *Hard Bodies: Hollywood Masculinity in the Reagan Era*, New Brunswick: Rutgers University Press.

Jenkins, Henry (1992) *Textual Poachers: Television Fans and Participatory Culture,* New York: Routledge.

Jensen, Joli (1992) 'Fandom as Pathology: The Consequences of Characterization', in Lisa Lewis, ed., *The Adoring Audience: Fan Culture and Popular Media*, London: Routledge.

Jewett, Robert and John Shelton Lawrence (1977) *The American Monomyth*, New York: Anchor Press.

Jones, Alan (2001) *Lara Croft: Tomb Raider – The Official Film Companion*, London: Carlton Books.

Jones, Steven G., ed. (1999) *Doing Internet Research: Critical Issues and Methods for Examining the Net*, London: Sage.

Kapsis, Robert E. (1992) *Hitchcock: the Building of a Reputation*, Chicago: University of Chicago Press.

Karney, Robyn (1993) *Who's Who in Hollywood*, London: Bloomsbury.

Kaufman, Stanley (1997) 'Timeless Acting', *Salmagundi* 114 (Spring/Summer): 49–57.

Keller, Alexandra (1999) '"Size Does Matter": Notes on *Titanic* and James Cameron as Blockbuster Auteur', in Kevin S. Sandler and Gaylyn Studlar, eds, *Titanic: Anatomy of a Blockbuster*, New Brunswick: Rutgers University Press.

Killick, Jane (1995) *The Making of Judge Dredd*, London: Boxtree Books.

Kindem, Gorham (1982) 'Hollywood's Movie Star System: A Historical Overview', in Gorham Kindem, ed., *The American Movie Industry: The Business of Motion Pictures*, Carbondale: Southern Illinois University Press.

King, Barry (1989) 'The Burden of Max Headroom', *Screen* 30(1–2): 122–38.

King, Barry (1985) 'Articulating Stardom', *Screen* 26(5): 27–50.

King, Barry (1986) 'Stardom as an Occupation', in Paul Kerr, ed., *The Hollywood Film Industry: A Reader*, London: Routledge.

King, Barry (1991) 'Articulating Stardom', in Christine Gledhill, ed., *Stardom: Industry of Desire*, London: Routledge.

King, Barry (1992) 'Stardom and Symbolic Degeneracy: Television and the Transformation of Stars as Public Symbols', *Semiotica* 92(1–2): 8–44.

King, Charles (1997) '*Dr Jekyll and Mr Hyde*: A Filmography', *Journal of Popular Culture* 25 (Spring): 9–20.

King, Geoff (2001) *Spectacular Narratives: Hollywood in the Age of the Blockbuster*, London: I. B. Tauris.

King, Geoff and Tanya Krzywinska (2000) *Science Fiction Cinema*, London: Wallflower Press.

Kirihara, Donald (1996) 'The Accepted Idea Displaced: Stereotype and Sessue Hayakawa', in Daniel Bernardi, ed., *The Birth of Whiteness: Race and the Emergence of US Cinema*, New Brunswick: Rutgers University Press.

Kirkham, Pat and Janet Thumim, eds (1993) *You, Tarzan: Masculinity, Movies and Men*, London: Lawrence & Wishart.

Klapp, Orrin (1962) *Heroes, Villains and Fools*, Newport, RI: Aegis Publishing.

Klaprat, Cathy (1985) 'The Star as Market Strategy: Bette Davis in Another Light', in Tino Balio, ed., *The American Film Industry*, Madison: University of Wisconsin Press.

Klein, Naomi (2000) *No Logo: Taking Aim at the Brand Bullies*, London: Flamingo.

Klein, Norman (1998) 'Hybrid Cinema', in Kevin S. Sandler, ed., *Reading the Rabbit*, New Brunswick: Rutgers University Press.

Kleinhaus, Chuck (2002) 'Pamela Anderson on the Slippery Slope', in Jon Lewis, ed., *The End of Cinema as We Know it: American Film in the Nineties*, London: Pluto Press.

Klinger, Barbara (2001) 'The Contemporary Cinephile: Film Collecting in the Post-Video Era', in Melvyn Stokes and Richard Maltby, eds, *Hollywood Spectatorship: Changing Perceptions of Cinema Audiences*, London: British Film Institute.

Kozloff, Sarah (2000) *Overhearing Film Dialogue*, Berkeley: University of California Press.

Krämer, Peter (1998) 'Would you Take your Child to See this Film? The Cultural and Social Work of the Family-Adventure Movie', in Steve Neale and Murray Smith, eds, *Contemporary Hollywood Cinema*, London: Routledge.

Krämer, Peter (1999a) 'A Powerful Cinema-going Force? Hollywood and Female Audiences since the 1960s', in Melvyn Stokes and Richard Maltby, eds, *Identifying Hollywood's Audiences*, London: British Film Institute.

Krämer, Peter (1999b) 'Women First: *Titanic*, Action-Adventure Films and Hollywood's Female Audience', in Kevin Sandler and Gaylyn Studlar, eds, *Titanic: Anatomy of a Blockbuster*, New Brunswick: Rutgers University Press.

Krämer, Peter (forthcoming a) '"Want to take a ride?": Reflections on the Blockbuster Experience in *Contact*', in Julian Stringer, ed., *Movie Blockbusters*, London: Routledge.

Krämer, Peter (forthcoming b) 'The Rise and Fall of Sandra Bullock: Notes on Starmaking and Female Stardom in Contemporary Hollywood', in Andy Willis, ed., *Hollywood, Film Stars and Beyond*, Manchester: Manchester University Press.

Krasner, David (2000) 'I Hate Strasberg: Method Bashing in the Academy', in David Krasner, ed., *Method Acting Reconsidered: Theory, Practice, Future*, New York: St Martins Press.

Kripke, Saul (1980) *Naming and Necessity*, Oxford: Oxford University Press.

Krutnik, Frank (1995) 'A Spanner in the Works? Genre, Narrative and the Hollywood Comedian', in Kristine Brunovska Karnick and Henry Jenkins, eds, *Classical Hollywood Comedy*, New York: Routledge.

LaValley, Albert J. (1985) 'Traditions of Trickery: The Role of Special Effects in the Science Fiction Film', in George Slusser and Eric S. Rabkin, eds, *Shadows of the Magic Lamp: Fantasy and Science Fiction in Film*, Carbondale: Southern Illinois University Press.

Lacey, Joanne (1999) 'Seeing through Happiness: Hollywood Musicals and the Construction of the American Dream in Liverpool in the 1950s', *Journal of Popular British Cinema* 2: 54–65.

Landon, Brooks (1992) *The Aesthetics of Ambivalence: Rethinking Science Fiction Film in the Age of Electronic (Re)production*, Westport: Greenwood Press.

Lane, Christina (1995) 'The Liminal Iconography of Jodie Foster', *Journal of Popular Film and Television* 22(4): 149–53.

Lee, Robert G. (1999) *Orientals: Asian Americans in Popular Culture*, Philadelphia: Temple University Press.

Lemmon, Jack (1998) 'Conversation with the Actor', in Bert Cardullo, Harry Geduld, Ronald Gottesman and Leigh Woods, *Playing to the Camera*, New Haven: Yale University Press.

Levy, Emanuel (1990) 'Social Attributes of American Movie Stars', *Media, Culture and Society* 12(2): 247–67.

Lewis, Lisa, ed. (1992) *The Adoring Audience: Fan Culture and Popular Media*, London: Routledge.

Liu, Cynthia W. (2000) 'When Dragon Ladies Die, Do They Come Back as Butterflies?: Re-Imagining Anna May Wong', in Darrell Hamamoto and Sandra Liu, eds, *Countervisions: Asian American Film Criticism*, Philadelphia: Temple University Press.

Lo, Kwai-Cheung (1996) 'Muscles and Subjectivity: A Short History of the Masculine Body in Hong Kong Popular Culture', *Camera Obscura* 39 (September): 105–25.

Lovell, Alan and Peter Krämer, eds (1999) *Screen Acting*, London: Routledge.

Lupton, Deborah (1998) *The Emotional Self*, London: Sage.

Lusted, David (1991) 'The Glut of the Personality', in Christine Gledhill, ed., *Stardom: Industry of Desire*, London: Routledge.

Machin, David (2002) *Ethnographic Research for Media Studies*, London: Arnold.

Macnab, Geoffrey (2000) *Searching for Stars*, London: Continuum.

Magder, Ted and Jonathan Burston (2001) 'Whose Hollywood? Changing Forms and Changing Relations Inside the North American Entertainment Economy', in Dan Schiller and Vincent Mosco, eds, *Continental Order? Integrating North America for Cyber-Capitalism*, Lanham, MD: Rowman and Littlefield.

Maltby, Richard (1995) *Hollywood Cinema: An Introduction*, Oxford: Blackwell.

Maltby, Richard (1998) ' "Nobody Knows Everything": Post-classical Historiographies and Consolidated Entertainment', in Steve Neale and Murray Smith, eds, *Contemporary Hollywood Cinema*, London: Routledge.

Mann, C. and F. Stewart (2000) *Internet Communication and Qualitative Research*, London: Sage.

Marchetti, Gina (1993) *Romance and the 'Yellow Peril': Race, Sex and Discursive Strategies in Hollywood Fiction*, Berkeley: University of California Press.

Marill, A. (1980) *Movies Made for Television*, New York: Da Capo Press.

Marshall, P. David (1997) *Celebrity and Power: Fame and Contemporary Culture*, Minneapolis: University of Minnesota Press.

Martin, Valerie (1990) *Mary Reilly*, New York: Doubleday.

McCarty, John (1993) *Movie Psychos and Madmen: Film Psychopaths from Jekyll and Hyde to Hannibal Lecter*, New York: Citadel Press.

McDonald, Paul (1995) 'Star Studies', in Joanne Hollows and Mark Jancovich, eds, *Approaches to Popular Film*, Manchester: Manchester University Press.

McDonald, Paul (1998) 'Reconceptualising Stardom', supplementary chapter in Richard Dyer, *Stars*, London: British Film Institute.

McDonald, Paul (2000) *The Star System: Hollywood's Production of Popular Identities*, London: Wallflower Press.

McLaughlin, Margaret, Steven B. Goldberg, Nicole Ellison and Jason Lucas (1999) 'Measuring Internet Audiences: Patrons of an On-Line Art Museum', in Steve Jones, ed., *Doing Internet Research: Critical Issues and Methods for Examining the Net*, Thousand Oaks: Sage.

Medhurst, Andy (1991) 'Batman, Deviance and Camp', in Roberta Pearson and William Urrichio, eds, *The Many Lives of the Batman*, London: Routledge/British Film Institute.

Meredith, Burgess (1965) 'Preface', in Robert H Hethmon, ed., *Strasberg at the Actors Studio*, New York: Theatre Communications Group.

Miller, Toby (1998) 'Hollywood and the World', in John Hill and Pamela Church Gibson, eds, *The Oxford Guide to Film Studies*, Oxford: Oxford University Press.

Miller, V. (2000) 'Search Engines, Portals and Global Capitalism', in David Gauntlett, ed., *Web Studies: Rewiring Media Studies for the Digital Age*, London: Arnold.

Mitroff, I. and W. Bennis (1989) *The Unreality Industry*, Secaucus, NJ: Birch Lane Press.

Modleski, Tania (1983) 'The Rhythms of Reception: Daytime Television and Women's Work', in E. Ann Kaplan, ed., *Regarding Television: Critical Approaches: An Anthology*, Los Angeles: American Film Institute.

Modleski, Tania, ed. (1986) *Studies in Entertainment: Critical Approaches to Mass Culture*, Bloomington: Indiana University Press.

Mordden, Ethan (1988) *The Hollywood Studios: House Style in the Golden Age of the Movies*, New York: Blackstone.

Morrison, Michael A. (1997) *John Barrymore: Shakespearean Actor*, Cambridge: Cambridge University Press.

Moser, James D., ed. (2000) *International Motion Picture Almanac*, La Jolla: Quigley.

Munn, Michael (1997) *The Sharon Stone Story*, London: Robson Books.

Naremore, James (1988) *Acting in the Cinema*, Berkeley: University of California Press.

Nash, Jay Robert and Stanley Ralph Ross (1985) *The Motion Picture Guide: 1927–1983*, Chicago: Cinebooks.

Ndalianis, Angela (2000) 'Special Effects, Morphing Magic and the 1990s Cinema of Attractions', in Vivian Sobchack, ed., *Meta Morphing*, Minneapolis: University of Minnesota Press.

Ndalianis, Angela and Charlotte Henry, eds (2002) *Stars in Our Eyes – The Star Phenomenon in the Contemporary Era*, Connecticut: Greenwood Press.

Negra, Diane (2001) *Off-White Hollywood: American Culture and Ethnic Female Stardom*, London: Routledge.

Nickson, Chris (1999) *Will Smith*, New York: St Martins Press.

Niu, Greta Ai-Yu (1998) 'Consuming Asian Women: The Fluid Body of Josie Packard in *Twin Peaks*', in Yingjin Zhang, ed., *China in a Polycentric World: Essays in Chinese Comparative Literature*, Stanford: Stanford University Press.

Nowell Smith, Geoffrey (2000) 'How Films Mean, or, from Aesthetics to Semiotics and Half-way Back Again', in Christine Gledhill and Linda Williams, eds, *Reinventing Film Studies*. London: Arnold.

Oehling, Richard A. (1980) 'The Yellow Menace: Asian Images in American Film', in Randall M. Miller, ed., *The Kaleidoscopic Lens: How Hollywood Views Ethnic Groups*, Englewood: Jerome S. Ozer.

O'Toole, Lawrence (1998) *Pornocopia: Porn, Sex, Technology and Desire*, London: Serpent's Tail.

Palmer, R. Barton (1996) 'Fredric March', in Nicolet V. Elert and Aruna Vasudevan, eds, *International Dictionary of Films and Filmmakers*. New York: St James Press.

Peters, Anne K. and Muriel G. Cantar (1982) 'Screen Acting as Work', in J. Ettema and D. Whitney, eds, *Individuals in Mass Communications Organisations*, London: Sage.

Peters, Margot (1994) 'John Barrymore: The Great Profile on Tower Road', *Architectural Digest* 51(4): 130–5.

Peterson, Deborah C. (1996) *Fredric March: Craftsman First, Star Second*, Connecticut: Greenwood Press.

Peterson, Richard A. and Roger M. Kern (1996) 'Changing Highbrow Taste: From Snob to Omnivore', *American Sociological Review* 61(3): 900–7.

Pfeiffer, Glenn, Robert Capettini and Gene Whittenberg (1997) '*Forrest Gump* – Accountant: A Study of Accounting in the Motion Picture Industry', *Journal of Accounting Education* 15(3): 319–44.

Pfeil, Fred (1995) *White Guys: Studies in Postmodern Domination and Difference*, London: Verso.

Pidduck, Julianne (1998) 'Of Windows and Country Walks: Frames of Space and Movement in 1990s' Austen Adaptations', *Screen* 39(4): 381–400.

Pierson, Michele (1999) 'CGI Effects in Hollywood Science-fiction Cinema 1989–95: the Wonder Years', *Screen* 40(2): 177–92.

Plantinga, Carl and Greg M. Smith, eds, (1999) *Passionate Views*, Baltimore: Johns Hopkins University Press.

Powdermaker, Hortense (1950) *Hollywood: The Dream Factory*, Boston: Little, Brown.

Prince, Stephen (1996) 'True Lies: Perceptual Realism, Digital Images and Film Theory', *Film Quarterly* 49(3): 27–37.

Pullen, K. (2000) 'I-Love-Xena.com: Creating Online Fan Communities', in David Gauntlett, ed., *Web Studies: Rewiring Media Studies for the Digital Age*, London: Arnold.

Rein, Irving J., Philip Kotler and Martin R. Stoller (1997) *High Visibility: The Making and Marketing of Professionals into Celebrities*, Lincolnwood, NTC.

Roberts, Thomas J. (1990) *An Aesthetics of Junk Fiction*, Athens: University of Georgia Press.

Rojek, Chris (2001) *Celebrity*, London: Reaktion Books.

Rose, Brian (1996) *Jekyll and Hyde Adapted: Dramatizations of Cultural Anxiety*, Connecticut: Greenwood Press.

Rose, Jacqueline (1984) *The Case of Peter Pan, or the Impossibility of Children's Fiction*, London: Macmillan.

Rosen, David (1993) *The Changing Fictions of Masculinity*, Chicago: University of Illinois Press.

Rosen, Michael (1996) *On Voluntary Servitude*, Cambridge: Polity Press.

Sammon, Paul M. (1997) *The Making of Starship Troopers*, London: Little, Brown.

Sanello, Frank (1997) *Naked Instinct*, Secaucus, NJ: Carol Publishing Group.

Schatz, Thomas (1993) 'The New Hollywood', in Jim Collins, Hilary Radner and Ava Preacher Collins, eds, *Film Theory Goes to the Movies*, New York: American Film Institute.

Schulze, Laurie (1988) 'The Made-for-TV Movie: Industrial Practice, Cultural Form, Popular Reception', in Tino Balio, ed., *Hollywood in the Age of Television*, Boston: Unwin Hyman.

Schulze, Laurie, Anne Barton White and Jane D. Brown (1993) '"A Sacred Monster in Her Prime": Audience Construction of Madonna as Low-Other', in Cathy Schwichtenberg, ed., *The Madonna Connection: Representational Politics, Subcultural Identities and Cultural Theory*, Boulder: Westview Press.

Seger, Linda (1996) *When Women Call the Shots: The Developing Power and Influence of Women in Television and Film*, New York: Henry Holt.

Seidman, Steve (1981) *Comedian Comedy: A Tradition in Hollywood Film*, Ann Arbor: UMI Research Press.

Sennett, Robert (1998) *Hollywood Hoopla: Creating Stars and Selling Movies in the Golden Age of Hollywood*, New York: Billboard Books.

Sergi, Gianluca (1998) 'A Cry in the Dark: The Role of Post-Classical Film Sound', in Steve Neale and Murray Smith, eds, *Contemporary Hollywood Cinema*, London: Routledge.

Shepherd, Donald and Robert Slatzer (1986) *Duke: The Life and Times of John Wayne*, London: Sphere.

Sher, Anthony (1996) *Year of the King*, London: Methuen.

Shohat, Ella and Robert Stam (1994) *Unthinking Eurocentrism: Multiculturalism and the Media*, London: Routledge.

Sigelow, Greg (1993) 'The Distance Between You and Me: Madonna and Celestial Navigation (Or You Can Be My Lucky Star)', in Cathy Schwichtenberg, ed., *The Madonna Connection: Representational Politics, Subcultural Identities and Cultural Theory*, Boulder: Westview Press.

Singer, Michael (1995) Batman Forever: *The Official Moviebook*, London: Mandarin.

Singer, Michael (1997) Batman and Robin: *The Making of the Movie*, London: Titan Books.

Smith, Murray (1995) *Engaging Characters: Fiction, Emotion and the Cinema*, Oxford: Oxford University Press.

Spada, James (1993) *More Than a Woman: An Intimate Biography of Bette Davis*, London: Warner Books.

Speidel, Suzanne (2000) 'Times of Death in Joseph Conrad's *The Secret Agent* and Alfred Hitchcock's *Sabotage*', in Robert Giddings and Erica Sheen, eds, *The Classic Novel from Page to Screen*, Manchester: Manchester University Press.

Stacey, Jackie (1994) *Star Gazing: Hollywood Cinema and Female Spectatorship*, London: Routledge.

Staiger, Janet (1991) 'Seeing Stars', in Christine Gledhill, ed., *Stardom: Industry of Desire*, London: Routledge.

Staiger, Janet (1993) 'Taboos and Totems: Cultural Meanings of *The Silence of the Lambs*', in Jim Collins, Hilary Radner and Ava Preacher Collins, eds, *Film Theory Goes to the Movies*, New York: Routledge.

Staiger, Janet and Martin Barker (2000) 'Traces of Interpretation', *Framework* (Summer), **www.frameworkonline.com**.

Stallone, Sylvester (1991) *Sylvester Stallone: A Life on Film*, London: Hale.

Stone, D. (1984) 'TV Movies and How They Get That Way', *Journal of Popular Film and Television*: 146–8.

Street, Sarah (2000) '*A Place of One's Own*? Margaret Lockwood and British Film Stardom in the 1940s', in Ulrike Sieglohr, ed., *Heroines without Heroes: Reconstructing Female and National Identities in European Cinema 1945–51*, London: Cassell.

Stringer, Julian (2000) 'Cultural Identity and Diaspora in Contemporary Hong Kong Cinema', in Darrell Hamamoto and Sandra Liu, eds, *Countervisions: Asian American Film Criticism*, Philadelphia: Temple University Press.

Studlar, Gaylyn (1990) 'The Perils of Pleasure? Fan Magazine Discourse as Women's Commodified Culture in the 1920s', *Wide Angle* 13(1): 7–33.

Studlar, Gaylyn (1996) *This Mad Masquerade: Stardom and Masculinity in the Jazz Age*, New York: Columbia University Press.

Swern, Phil with Mike Childs (1995) *Guinness Book of Box Office Hits*, London: Guinness.

Tasker, Yvonne (1993a) *Spectacular Bodies: Gender, Genre and the Action Cinema*, London: Comedia.

Tasker, Yvonne (1993b) 'Dumb Movies for Dumb People: Masculinity, the Body and the Voice in Contemporary Cinema', in Steve Cohan and Ina Rae Hark, eds, *Screening the Male: Exploring Masculinities in Contemporary Hollywood*, London: Routledge.

Tetzlaff, David (1993) 'Meta-textual Girl', in Cathy Schwichtenberg, ed., *The Madonna Connection: Representational Politics, Subcultural Identities and Cultural Theory*, Boulder: Westview Press.

Thompson, John O. (1978) 'Screen Acting and the Commutation Test', *Screen* 19(2): 55–69.

Thompson, John O. (1985) 'Beyond Commutation: A Reconsideration of Screen Acting', *Screen* 26(5): 64–90.

Thorburn, David (1987) 'Television Melodrama', in Horace Newcomb, ed., *Television: The Critical View*, Oxford: Oxford University Press.

Traube, Elizabeth G. (1992) *Dreaming Identities: Class, Gender and Generation in 1980s Hollywood Movies*, Boulder: Westview Press.

Tudor, Andrew (1974) *Image and Influence: Studies in the Sociology of Film*, London: George Allen and Unwin.

Uricchio, William and Roberta E. Pearson (1991) ' "I'm Not Fooled by that Cheap Disguise" ', in Roberta Pearson and William Uricchio, eds, *The Many Lives of the Batman*, London: Routledge/British Film Institute.

Vincendeau, Ginette (2000) *Stars and Stardom in French Cinema*, London: Continuum.

Vineberg, Steve (1991) *Method Actors: Three Generations of an American Acting Style*, New York: Schirmer Books.

Walker, Alexander (1970) *Stardom: The Hollywood Phenomenon*, London: Michael Joseph.

Walkerdine, Valerie (1986) 'Video Replay: Families, Films and Fantasy', in Victor Burgin, James Donald and Cora Kaplan, eds, *Formations of Fantasy*, London: Methuen.

Wark, McKenzie (1999) *Celebrities, Culture and Cyberspace*, Annandale: Pluto Press.

Wells, Paul (1998) *Understanding Animation*, London: Routledge.

Wells, Paul (2001) ' "Roughnecks": Reality, Recombinancy and Radical Aesthetics', *Point* 11, Spring/Summer: 48–56

Wernick, Andrew (1999) *Promotional Culture*, London: Sage.

Wexman, Virginia Wright (1988) 'Horrors of the Body: Hollywood's Discourse on Beauty and Rouben Mamoulian's *Dr Jekyll and Mr Hyde*', in William Veeder and Gordon Hirsch, eds, *Dr Jekyll and Mr Hyde: After One Hundred Years*, Chicago: University of Chicago Press.

Whatling, Claire (1997) *Screen Dreams: Fantasising Lesbians in Film*, Manchester: Manchester University Press.

Williams, Simon (2001) *Emotion and Social Theory*, London: Sage.

Winokaur, Jon (1992) *True Confessions*, New York: Plume.

Wood, Robin (1986) *Hollywood from Vietnam to Reagan*, New York: Columbia University Press.

Wyatt, Justin (1994) *High Concept: Movies and Marketing in Hollywood*, Austin: University of Texas Press.

Wyatt, Justin (1998) 'The Formation of the "Major Independent": Miramax, New Line and the New Hollywood', in Steve Neale and Murray Smith, eds, *Contemporary Hollywood Cinema*, London: Routledge.

Xing, Jun (1998) *Asian America Through the Lens: History, Representation, and Identity*, Walnut Creek: Alta Mira.

Yamamoto, Traise (1999) *Masking Selves, Making Subjects: Japanese American Women, Identity, and the Body*, Berkeley: University of California Press.

Zizek, Slavoj (2000) *The Fragile Absolute*, London: Verso.

INDEX

2D/3D animation 95
60 Minutes (TV programme) 180
100% Nude Celebrity Pics 35–6
1941 (1979, USA) 10
ABC 192
Abercrombie, Nicholas 60
Abramowitz, Rachel 208, 212–13
Absolute Fake Celebs 37
Academy Awards 23, 204, 211,
  219, 220, 223, 255–6
Accused, The (1988, USA) 203,
  205–6
Ace Ventura: Pet Detective (1994,
  USA) 136
acting gurus 121, 122
action genre 15, 138, 139, 141,
  159–63
  see also specific films
Actors Fund 126
Actors Studio 121, 122, 125, 126,
  129, 133
Adams, Cindy 124, 126, 129
Adams, James Eli 226
adaptations, classic 106–10,
  112–14, 115, 116
Adler, Jacob 119, 120
Adler, Luther 120
Adler, Stella 120, 122–3
Adult Sites Against Child
  Pornography (ASACP) 36
adult/child opposition 75–6, 78–9,
  81–2, 85, 86, 88–9, 200
  see also man-child persona
adultification 244–5, 246, 253
advance impressions 67–8
advertising 21, 192
Advertising Age 12
Affairs of Anatol, The (1912, USA)
  218
affect 26, 74–82, 84–9
  see also emotional work
  audiences' dislike of stars 26,
    76, 77–82, 84–9
  audiences' love of stars 74–5,
    76, 82, 89, 151
  and cognitive opposition 75–6
  controlled 132

fan's investment of 80–1
affective discourses 74, 79, 80–1,
  86, 88, 89
  see also discourses of affect
affective memory 120, 121,
  131–2
African Americans 240, 256
age
  and Hollywood women 201–2,
    213
  and star-power *173*, 174, 175,
    179, 181
agency 27, 235
A.I. (2001, USA) 10
Aladdin (1992, USA) 20–1, 95,
  244–5
Aladdin and the King of Thieves
  (1996, USA) 243
Alexander, David 129, 131, 133
Ali (2001, USA) 70, 71
Alien 204, 206, 211
alienation 157–8
Allen, Robert 135–6
Allen, Tim 94, 95, 101
Allen, Tom 126
'allergic haters', of Jar Jar Binks
  26, 76, 77–82, 84–9
Althusser, Louis 13, 259–60
Altman, Rick 68
Ambassador Theater, Broadway
  170, 178
Amblin Entertainment 63, 68, 70
AMC Entertainment 34
America Online (AOL) 34
American Beauty (1996, USA) 19,
  20
American Laboratory Theatre
  119–20
American Music Awards 2000
  67
American Pie (1999, USA) 2
analysis, and demystification
  261–2
...And Justice for All (1978, USA)
  123, 126, 127–8, 133
Anderson, Gillian 38
Anderson, Pamela 25

Andrews, Julie 245
Angels With Dirty Faces (1938, USA)
  12
animated stars 21–2, 26–7, 91–9,
  101, 102
  iconic form 83, 94, 99, 101
  and the paradigms of stardom
    92, 93–4, 95–6
  symbolic identity 97
animation 20–2, 90–102
  see also computer-generated
    imagery
  2D/3D 95
  and live action 83, 84
  and special effects 94–7
  traditional 96–7
  and virtual stars 83, 84, 85,
    86–7, 88, 89
Anna and the King (1999, USA)
  211–12, 229, 231, 236, 241
Ansen, David 204, 206
Ant and the Aardvark, The (1969,
  USA) 94–5
Antoine, André 119
Antz (1998, USA) 94, 95
'appearing to be' 57
Arabian Nights (2000, television
  movie) 237
Arbuckle, Roscoe 'Fatty' 30
Arden, Eve 264
Arden, Hal Mark 133
Armon-Jones, Claire 79
As Good as it Gets (1997, USA)
  248
'Asian Invasion' 231–2
Asian languages 237–8
Asian Media Access 238
Asian/Asian American stars
  199–200, 229–42
Asiaphilia 236
aspirational status of stars 161
Assassins (1995, USA) 156
assimilation 232
attention
  doubled 84
  objects of 131, 132
Attitude 156

audiences 5, 151–3, 266–9
  see also fans; star-audience
    relationship
  affect 26, 74–82, 84–9, 151
  Asian American 235, 236, 239
  child 244–7
  construction of adult as child
    246
  cultural mobility/permeability of
    153, 169, 171, 172, 176, 177,
    178–82
  disappointment in stars 152
  effect of star-power on the tastes
    of 178–82, *179*
  female, and made-for-television
    movies 151, 187, 188–90,
    191, 192, 193, 194–7
  knowledge of the stars 265–6
  male, and action heroes 155,
    156–66
  mass 169
Auslander, Philip 178
Austen, Jane 106, 112
Austin Powers films 8
Austin, Thomas 25–8, 47, 75–6,
  82–3, 103–4, 135–49, 155,
  163, 199–200
auteurs 27, 86
  directors as 134, 264
  stars as 50, 55
authenticity 46, 49, 51, 58, 87–9
  authenticating 93
  of computer-generated imagery
    91, 92, 96, 98–9, 102
  construction through character-
    star matching 140
  construction through star dislike
    79
  of virtual stars 82
autobiographies 158, 159, 235
autographic phase of stardom
  52
Autumn Tale, An (1988, HK) 229
Awakenings (1990, USA) 245, 249

Babington, Bruce 12, 259, 266
Baby Dance, The (1998, USA) 212
Babylon 5 (TV series) 193
Bacon, James 129
Bad Boys (1995, USA) 70
Baker, Wayne E. 49
Baldwin, William 54, 58
Balio, Tino 4, 5
Bamboo Girl (fanzine) 236
Bancroft, Anne 125
Banderas, Antonio 11
bankability 1
Bardot, Brigitte 263, 264
Barish, J. 46

Barker, Martin 1–24, 74, 75–6,
  77–8, 84, 94, 95, 151–3, 155,
  255–7
Baron, Cynthia 199, 215–28
Barrie, J.M. 250
Barrymore, Drew 35
Barrymore, John 199, 216, 217,
  218–19, 220, 221, 222, 225,
  226
Barthel, John 121, 127, 129, 130,
  131, 133
Barton White, Anne 77
Basco, Dante 252
Base, Ron 17
Baseline.Hollywood.com 34
Basic Instinct (1992, USA) 53–4, 55,
  56–7, 58, 59
Basinger, Kim 10
Batman: The Animated Series (1992)
  136
Batman (1989, USA) 65, 135,
  137–8, 141
Batman Beyond (1999) 136
Batman films 65, 104, 135–49
  casting for 137–41, 146
  constructions of masculinity in
    138, 139, 140, 141, 142,
    144, 145
  homosexual undertones 145–6
  physical appearance in 138,
    139–40, 141–3, 144–5
  place of the villain in 142–5
  use of costume in 135–6, 138,
    139–40, 142–3
  use of voice in 142, 144, 145
Batman Forever (1995, USA) 104,
  135, 138, 140, 141–6
Batman Returns (1992, USA) 135
Batman and Robin (1997, USA) 135,
  138, 140–1, 142, 143
Batsuit 135–6, 138, 139–40,
  142–3
Battlefield Earth (2000, USA) 10
Baxter, Meredith 193
Bayley, John 116
Baym, Nina 193
Bazalgette, Cary 245
Beatty, Warren 1
Beauty and the Beast (1989, USA)
  95
Beebe, Roger Warren 88
Beetlejuice (1988, USA) 137
Begley, Ed, Jr 145
Being Human (1994, USA/UK)
  245, 253
Being John Malkovich (1999, USA)
  221
'being like' 60
'being in public' 47, 51–2, 53

'being taken as being' 47
Bellini-Witkonski, Barbara 190
Bennis, W. 49
Benson, Sheila 203–4, 205–6
Bergman, Ingrid 221
Berlin, J. 52, 56, 57
Bernard, Jami 204, 206
Bernstein, Leonard 124
Berry, Halle 255–7
Bertinnelli, Veronica 193
Best, Ahmed 81
Better Tomorrow, A (1986, HK) 229,
  240
Betty Boop 96, 97
Beyond Asiaphilia (1997, USA) 239
Bicentennial Man (1999, USA) 245
Big Willie Style (album) 63, 64
Bill and Ted's Excellent Adventure
  (1989, USA) 18
Billboard online 67
biography 23, 119–23, 191
  see also autobiographies
  authorised 53, 58
  public 53, 59
  spatialisation of 51
  unauthorised 58
Birdcage, The (1996, USA) 243,
  245
bisexuality 53–4, 58, 209
Black Rain (1989, USA) 232
Blair Witch Project, The (1999, USA)
  2
Blandford, Steve 7
Blaxploitation 256
Blockbuster Video 162
blockbusters 19
Blood Vows: Story of a Mafia Wife
  (1987, USA) 190–1
Boardwalk (1979, USA) 123, 126,
  133
body
  see also physical appearance
  ideal types 255
  narrative purpose of 111–12
  use in the action genre 160–1
  use in the Batman films 141–3,
    144–5
  use by Asian stars 234, 235–6
  use in heritage films 107, 108,
    109, 110–12, 113–14
  use in the Jekyll and Hyde films
    218
body-building 161
Bodyguard, The (1992, USA) 208
Bogart, Humphrey 52
Boleslavsky, Richard 120
Bolter, Jay David 42
Bonham Carter, Helena 108
Boogie Nights (1997, USA) 264

Boorstin, Daniel 50
Bourdieu, Pierre 153, 168, 176
Bowser, Eileen 29
box office, imperative of 50, 65
Boxleitner, Bruce 191, 194
Boyle, Richard 226
Boys Town (1938, USA) 220
Bradshaw, Peter 116
Bram Stoker's Dracula (1992, USA)
    18, 221
Branagh, Kenneth 243
Brando, Marlon 125
brands
    film brands 136
    star brands 12, 19, 68–73
    TV channel 189, 192
Branston, Gill 142
Brantlinger, Patrick 226
Braund, Simon 164
Brest, Martin 130, 132
Bringing Out the Dead (1999, USA)
    2
Britain
    failure to produce a star system
        12
    made-for-television movies 188,
        190, 191
    stars 103, 105–12, 113, 116
Britton, Andrew 236
Bronson, Charles 17
Brooker, Will 74, 79
Brookey, Robert Alan 10
Brooks, Kate 74, 84, 155
Brooks, Libby 256
Brown, Georgia 210, 224
Brown, Jane D. 77
Buckingham, David 75, 246–7,
    248, 250, 251
Buffy the Vampire Slayer (TV series)
    179
Bugs Bunny 94, 96, 97
Bug's Life, A (1998, USA) 244
Bukatman, Scott 9, 144
Bullock, Sandra 38, 202, 203
Burke, Jonathan 9
Burns, George 123, 132
Burston, Paul 146
Burstyn, Ellen 125
Burton, Tim 10, 137, 139
Butler, Judith 45
'buzz' 66, 67, 70
Buzz Lightyear (*Toy Story*
    character) 26, 27, 91, 92,
    93–4, 95–6, 98, 99, 100–2
Byars, Jackie 189
Byrne, Eleanor 95

C4I 188, 190
Cabarga, L. 97

cable television 50, 188
Cage, Nicholas 2, 52, 72
Cagney, James 12, 52
Cahiers du Cinéma 264
Cameraman's Revenge, The (1911,
    Russia) 94
Cameron, James 10
Campbell, Joseph 211
Campbell, Neve 35
Canby, Vincent 132, 133
Canterville Ghost, The (1995) 170
Cantor, Muriel G. 103
capitalism 6, 13, 260, 261
capriciousness, of actors 261
Captains Courageous (1937, USA)
    220
Cardullo, Bert 12
Carey, Jim 160
Carlton Television 188
Carney, Art 123, 132
Carnicke, Sharon Marie 104,
    118–34, 120, 121, 128
CarolCo 8
Carrey, Jim 65, 104, 142, 144–5
Carroll, Noël 75
Carson, B. 188
Carson, Johnny 143
Carter, Linda 193
Casino (1995, USA) 53, 55
Casper (1995, USA) 244
Cassandra Crossing, The (1977, USA)
    123
casting, for the Batman films
    137–41, 146
Cat People (1942/1982, USA) 71
categorisation
    of the movie industry 162
    of stardom 155–6, 162–3, 165,
        166
CBS 234
celebrity 13–14, 269
    commodification of 13
    defining contemporary 93
    industry's responsibility for the
        creation of 93
    'ordinary' 13–14
celebrity journalism 51
celebrity nudes 25–6, 34–7, 42–3
    fake 37–8
CelebsXposed 35–6
Centropolis 70
Champlin, Charles 124, 127,
    129
Chan, Jackie 160, 231, 234–5, 237,
    238
Chan, Peter 232
Chang, Chris 222, 223
Chanko, Kenneth M. 208, 209
Channel 5 21

character-star interface 257, 263,
    264–5
    gulf between 55–7, 59, 136, 146
    in heritage adaptations 106, 107
    matching star-actors and
        characters 136–41
    merging of 20, 46–7, 194–6
    similarities between 45, 46–7,
        57–8, 59
    and virtual stars 82–3, 84
characterisation, grammar of 47
characters, existential portability
    of 47
Charlie's Angels (TV Series) 193
Chen, Joan 231, 236
Cher 201, 202
Cheung, Cherie 229
Cheung, Leslie 234
Cheung, Maggie 232
child audiences 244–7
child-minstrels 251, 253, 254
child/adult opposition 75–6, 78–9,
    81–2, 85, 86, 88–9, 200
    see also man-child persona
childhood
    in 1990s cinema 250–4
    adult ambivalence towards 251,
        253, 254
    idealisation of 251–2, 253, 254
children
    marginalisation of 200
    roles in children's films 245, 251
children's fiction, impossibility of
    246
children's television presenters
    246–7
Chinese Box (1997, France/Japan)
    232
Chinese stars 230, 231, 238,
    241–2
Ching-Wan, Lau 234
Cho, Margaret 232
Chong, Annabel 240–1
Christmas Carol, A (1999) 168, 170
Christmas Miracle in Caulfield (1977,
    USA) 193
Chunovic, Louis 211
'cinema of attractions' 102
CinemaSource 34
Cinergi 8, 14
City Slickers (1991, USA) 247, 248
Clark, Danae 103
class status
    and acting 103, 105, 106, 108,
        110–11, 112, 113, 114, 115
    and cultural consumption
        168–9
Cliffhanger (1993, USA) 156, 165
Clift, Montgomery 261, 270

Clooney, George 35, 47, 104, 135, 139, 140–1, 142, 143
Close, Glenn 201
Close, Meryl 56
Clurman, Harold 120
Cobra (1986, USA) 157–8, 159
Coburn, James 22
Code Red (album) 67
cognitive film theory 75–6, 79, 80
Cohan, Steven 54, 193, 220
Columbia Pictures 2, 5, 11, 63, 64, 68, 70, 71, 73, 124
Columbia Records 63, 69, 72
commercialism 27
    of crossover stars 26, 62–3
    of Jodie Foster 209
    of Lee Strasberg 125–6
    of licensed merchandising 135–6, 142
    of *Star Wars* 79, 81, 82, 88, 89
commodification
    of celebrities 13
    of stars 29, 33, 41, 43
common sense audience theory 75–6
computer games 96
computer-generated imagery (CGI) 25, 26, 27–8, 84–6, 88, 90, 95, 102
concerted cynosure 46
constancy 47, 60
consumer activism, of fans 41, 42, 43
consumption
    cultural 168–9, 178–81
    stardom as phenomenon of 6
Contact (1997, USA) 211, 212
context 98, 100
contracted semioticians 21
control 86
Cook, Elisha J., Jr 264
Copland (1997, USA) 156, 160, 161, 162, 164–5
Coppola, Francis Ford 119, 127, 128, 130, 133, 243
Corliss, Richard 2–3, 19, 142, 210, 211, 223
Corruptor, The (1999, USA) 231
Cosmopolitan (magazine) 222
Costner, Kevin 2, 10
costs 8–9
costume
    and iconic meaning 138
    and matching stars/characters 136, 138, 139–40
    political economy of 135–6
    use in Batman films 135–6, 138, 139–40, 142–3

use in heritage films 106, 107, 109, 110–11, 113, 114
Cousteau, Jacques 124
Cox, Alex 10
Crawford, Cheryl 120, 121
Crawford, Joan 264
Creed, Barbara 82, 84, 87–8, 138
Critique of Game of Death, A (1994, USA) 239
Croft, Lara (computer game/film character) 96
crossover stars
    Hollywood glamour/British class 103, 105–6, 112, 115, 116
    music/film 26, 62–73
    theatre/film/television 152–3, 169–70
Crouching Tiger, Hidden Dragon (2000, US/China) 229
Cruise, Tom 2–3, 13, 38, 191, 248
Crystal, Billy 248
cultural consumption 168–9, 178–81
cultural identity 199
    Asian/Asian American 229–42
    multi-dimensionality of 234–5
cultural magnets 169, 171, 176, 177, 178, 181–2
cultural mobility/permeability 153, 169, 171, 172, 176, 177, 178–82
cultural resistance 41
cultural studies 76–7
Cunanan's Conundrum (1997, USA) 239
Curry, Tim 22
Cusack, Joan 252
Cutthroat Island (1995, USA) 8
cyber stars *see* virtual stars
Cybernet Ventures Inc. 36

D-Tox (2002, USA) 156
Dacascos, Mark 232
Daily Mail (newspaper) 22
Dalio, Marcel 264
'dames' 105, 106, 108, 109, 114, 116
Damon, Matt 35
Danae Clark 4, 6
Dangerous Liaisons (1988, USA) 221, 224, 225, 226
Dangerous Lives of Altar Boys, The (2002, USA) 213
Dargis, Manohla 146
Darley, Andrew 9, 26, 85, 86
Darnton, Nina 205
Davies, Bette 4, 6, 18–19
Davies, Jude 249

Daylight (1996, USA) 156
de Niro, Robert 123, 125, 245, 255
De Patie-Freleng 94–5
de Souza, Steven 15
Dead Poets Society (1989, USA) 249
Death of a Salesman (play) 180
DeCordova, Richard 3, 29, 30, 33, 36, 43
definitive performances 46
Deleyto, Celestino 263
Demme, Jonathan 203, 206, 232
Demolition Man (1993, USA) 156, 162, 165
demystification, and analysis 261–2
Denby, David 204, 206, 209, 210–11
Dench, Judi 105, 108, 116
Derek, Bo 201
DeVito, Danny 73, 248
Devlin, Dean 70
Diabolique (1996, USA) 55
Diaz, Cameron **31**, 32–3, 35, 38–9, 202
DiBattista, Maria 263
DiCaprio, Leonardo 35, 111
Dick Tracy (1990, USA) 1
Diderot, Denis 45
Dieckmann, Katherine 201, 207, 212
Dietrich, Marlene 6, 11
difference, marks of 190
differentiation, programme 5
digital television 188
Dillon, Matt 32
directors
    Asian 232
    as *auteurs* 134, 264
    and Method acting 130, 134
    as stars 9–10
    stars as 10–11, 207–8, 213
Dirty Harry (1971, USA) 246
discourse determinism 80
discourses
    see also star discourses
    extratextual 87–8, 92, 94, 99, 165
    moralistic 38
    personality-type 29
    Playboy 266, 267
    Psycho 266
    unification of competing 14, 17, 243
discourses of affect 74, 79–81, 82, 88, 89
    see also affective discourses
dislike, audiences' of stars 26, 76, 77–82, 84–9

Disney Corporation 1, 8, 13, 20, 22, 72, 94, 95, 97, 205, 237, 243, 244
  see also Touchstone imprint
dispersible text 146
Diva (1982, France) 71
Doane, Mary Anne 56
docusoaps 14
Donald Duck 96, 97
doubled attention 84
Douglas, Kirk 217
Douglas, Michael 53, 54
Dovey, Jon 13–14
Dr Jekyll and Mr Hyde (1931, USA) 219–20, 225–6
Dracula (1931, USA) 219
Dragon: The Bruce Lee Story 237
DreamWorks 70, 94
dress see costume
Driven (2001, USA) 156
Dumb and Dumber (1994, USA) 144
Durgnat, Raymond 7
DVDs 10, 23
Dyer, Richard 5, 6–7, 12, 14–15, 17, 30, 74–5, 92, 93, 94, 96, 98–9, 106, 155, 243, 257, 259–62, 265, 266–7

E! Networks 34
E! Online 33–4
Eastern Review 123
Eastwood, Clint 10–11, 17, 70, 223–4
Edgerton, G. 187, 192
education, and star-power 177, 177, 181
Egg Pictures 208, 212, 213
Egyptian Theater, Hollywood 119
Eisner, Michael 1
Eisner, Will 93–4
elaborative ignorance 47
elasticity, of the self 45–61
Elfman, Danny 63
elites 269
Ellis, John 27, 32, 47, 155, 188
Ellison, Harlan 137–8
Ellison, Nicole 193–4
Emma (1996, USA) 103, 112–14, 115
Emmerich, Roland 70
emotional work
  see also affect
  of animated stars 91, 96, 98, 99–102
Empire (film magazine) 1, 10, 140, 141, 146, 164
Empire Strikes Back, The (1980, USA) 79, 81
empowerment, female 56–7

End of the Affair, The (1952/2000, USA) 259
Enemy of the State (1998, USA) 68, 70
entertainment news 33–4, 42
Entertainment Weekly 58, 66, 68, 70, 206
equilibrium, star's maintenance of 156
ER (TV series) 140, 141, 170
Esaki, John 239
Eszterhas, Joe 54
ET: the Extra Terrestrial (1982, USA) 251
ethnicity
  see also racial issues
  and star-power 176–7, 176, 181
ethnographic methods 151
Evans, A. 45
Evans, Robert 58
Even Cowgirls Get The Blues (1993, USA) 18
Excite 34
existential portability 47
Exorcist, The (1973, USA) 80, 81, 246
extratextual discourse 87–8, 92, 94, 99, 165

failure 14–17
fall of stars 2–3
Faludi, Susan 165
fame, absolute 50
family feature films 104, 145, 243
  generational blurring in 244, 245, 246, 247, 250, 251, 253
  licensed merchandising of 135–6, 142
family structures 251
Family Ties (TV Series) 193
Famous Players 34
fans
  see also audiences; star-audience relationship
  affection of 74–5, 76, 82, 89, 151
  of Batman 137
  dislike of stars 26, 76, 77–82, 84–9
  'good' 79, 82, 86, 89
  as hysterical crowd 40
  identities 78, 80, 81, 82
  on the internet 26, 38–42, 43, 51, 74, 76, 77–82, 84–9
  as isolated and lonely 40
  negative image of 40, 41
  positive image of 40–1
  shared fate concept 60

and star personae 59–60
  of Star Wars 74, 76, 77–82, 84–9
  textual productivity of 40–1
fanzines 38
FAO Schwarz 97
fascism 15–17
father, restoration of 247–51, 252–3
Father's Day (1997, USA) 245
Faulkner, Robert 49
'fear for'/'fear of' 91
Featherstone, Mike 101
Feeling Minnesota (1996, USA) 33
Felix the Cat 96
feminine identities, fragile/transient nature of 151–2
feminism 189, 250
FernGully: the Last Rainforest (1992, Australia) 245
Feuer, Jane 187, 189, 195
Field, Sally 201, 249–50
Figgis, Mike 199
Fight Club (1999, USA) 18
film brands 136
Film Four 18
film franchises 8, 13, 146
film promotion, on the internet 32–3, 42
film release, performance pressures 50, 65
film reviews 65, 164–5
film-music synergies 26, 62–9, 72–3
Fincher, David 213
Finney, Albert 264
'first look' deals 69–70
First Strike (1999, HK) 231
First Studio, The 120
First World War 219
Fisher King, The (1991, USA) 247
Fiske, John 41
F.I.S.T. (1978, USA) 156
Five Corners (1988, USA) 205
Flamm, Matthew 206
Fleischer Bros 94
Flextech television 188
Flora Plum (2004, USA) 213
Flubber (1997, USA) 243
fluidity 236–7, 240
folk theory, of audience reception 75–6
Fonda, Henry 6
Fonda, Jane 6, 125, 201
For Love of the Game (1999, USA) 2
Forbes magazine 12
Ford, Harrison 2, 18, 249
Forrest Gump (1997, USA) 101

Fortune Hunter, The (1909, USA) 218
Foster, Buddy 209
Foster, Jodie 199, 201, 202, 203–13, 229, 259, 268, 270
  autobiographical nature of her films 210
  commercialism of 209
  Contact (1997, USA) 211, 212
  Egg Pictures 208, 212, 213
  films as reflections on her career 210–11
  heroism of 201, 206–7, 211, 213
  and the Hinckley case 203, 205, 206, 212
  as icon 213
  Little Man Tate (1991, USA) 207–8, 210–11, 212
  Maverick (1994, USA) 208, 209
  motherhood 212, 213
  Nell (1994, USA) 208, 209–10, 211
  Panic Room (2002, USA) 213
  power of 202, 207
  rise of 203–7
  salary 212
  sexual orientation 208–9
  Sommersby (1993, USA) 208, 209
  as star, director and producer 207–8, 213
  The Silence of the Lambs (1991, USA) 199, 201, 202, 203–4, 206–7, 209, 211
Fox Searchlight Pictures 170
franchises
  film 8, 13, 146
  star 62, 68
Frank, Scott 210
Frankenstein (1931, USA) 219
Frears, Stephen 221, 268
Freer, Ian 164
Fresh Prince of Bel Air, The (TV series) 70
From Dusk Til Dawn (1996, USA) 140
Frow, John 169
Full on Asian Action (fanzine) 236
Full Contact (1992, HK) 229
Fun (1994, USA) 252

Gabin, Jean 264
Gable, Clark 4–5
Gaffney, Stuart 239
Gaines, Jane 47
Gamson, Joshua 45, 51, 76, 269
gangster genre 104, 116, 190
  see also specific films
Garfein, Jack 125
Garfield, David 119, 120

Garland, Judy 6, 193
Garton, L. 193
Gay Times 156
Gaye, Marvin 240
gaze 115, 151
Geduld, Harry M. 215, 216, 217
Gee, Deborah 239
gender issues
  see also masculinity
  Asian/Asian American stars 241–2
  gender roles under threat 219–20
  gendered nature of acting styles 116
  and star-power 174–5, *174*, 181
  women in Hollywood 199, 201–2, 204, 207, 210–12, 213
generation
  and female stars 199, 201–2, 213
  generational blurring 244–7, 249–53
  and *Star Wars* fans 74, 78, 79
genre
  and acting style 103–4, 106–14, 115, 116
  action 15, 138, 139, 141, 159–63
  gangster 104, 116, 190
  heritage 103–4, 106–14, 115, 116
  and video 162
Geraghty, Christine 11, 76–7, 84, 103–4, 105–17, 155–6, 157, 159, 162, 166, 267–8
Gere, Richard 52, 209
Gergen, K. 50
Gertie the Dinosaur (1914, USA) 90
Get Carter (2000, USA) 156
Giant Robot magazine 237, 238
Gibson, Mel 209, 237
Giddens, Anthony 45
Gilbert, Melissa 153, 187–8, 190–1, 193
  appearance 196–7
  biography 191
  internet presence 193–7
  merging with the Laura Ingalls character 194–6
  star status 197–8
Giles, David 5
Gitlin, Todd 192
glamour 109, 112, 113–14, *114*, 115
Gledhill, Christine 7, 91–2, 93, 96, 105, 188, 197–8
Gloria (1999, USA) 55

God of Gamblers (1989, HK) 229
God of Gamblers' Return (1995, HK) 229
Godfather, Part II, The (1974, USA) 104, 119, 123, 124, 125, 126–7, 128–30, 131–2, 133
Goffman, Erving 52
Going In Style (1979, USA) 123, 129, 132
Goldberg, Whoopi 22, 201, 202, 208
Golden Globes 211
Goldman, William 23
Gomery, Douglas 5, 187, 191
Good Morning, Vietnam (1987, USA) 20, 245
Good Will Hunting (1997, USA) 243, 245, 249
Goodfellas (1990, USA) 116
Goonies, The (1985, USA) 251
Gordon, Ruth 123
Gosford Park (2001, UK/USA) 116
gossip 50, 51
Gotham Knights (1997) 136
Gow, Gordon 124, 129
Graham, Heather 35
Granada Television 188
Grant, Cary 263
Grant, Hugh 106
Grasshopper and the Ant, The (1953, USA) 94
Green Grow the Lilacs (1931) 120
Grieveson, Lee 38
Griffith, Melanie 11
Gripsrud, Jostein 168–9, 174, 181
Gritten, David 222, 223
Grodal, Torben 75
Group Theatre 120–1, 122, 133
Grove, Lloyd 53
Grusin, Richard 42
Guardian Editor 57, 58
Guardian (newspaper) 2, 10, 11, 21, 116, 256
Guardian Weekend 53
Gulbeck, Kip 239
Gunning, Tom 102

Hackman, Gene 17
Hager, Steve 119, 123, 130
Hallmark 168, 170
Hamamoto, Darrell 232, 240
Hampton, Christopher 221
Handel, Leo 17
Hanks, Tom 13, 20, 94, 95, 101
Hannibal (2001, USA) 259
Hansen, Miriam 136–7
Hard Boiled (1993, HK) 229
hard/soft opposition 222
Hardy, Thomas 110

Hark, Tsui 232
Harlow, Jean 53
Harris, Thomas 203
Harryhausen, Ray 95
Hartley, John 244
Hartley, Mariette 193
has-beens 193
Hathaway, Henry 263
Hawn, Goldie 201
Hays Code 97
Heat (1995, USA) 116
Heath, Chris 163
Heavenly Creatures (1994, New
    Zealand) 252
Heinlein, Robert 16
Hello! magazine 158, 159
Hepburn, Audrey 38
heritage genre, and acting styles
    103–4, 106–14, 115, 116
heroism, feminine 201, 206–7,
    211, 213
heteroglossia 80
Heyerman 120
high culture 168–9, 177
Highway to Heaven (TV series) 195
Higson, Andrew 262, 265
Hills, Matt 26, 74–89, 193
Hinckley, John, Jr. 203, 205, 206,
    212
Hinerman, Stephen 76
Hirsch, Foster 121, 125, 126, 127
historical development of stardom
    3–5
Hitman (1998, USA) 237
Hobbes, Thomas 46
Hoberman, J. 204, 210, 211
Hoefler, Jonathan 202
Hoffman, Dustin 130
Holliss, Richard 97
Hollway, Wendy 80
Hollywood Media Corporation 34
Hollywood Online 55
Hollywood Pictures 8
Hollywood Reporter, The 63, 65, 67,
    70–1, 73, 123, 127, 129
Hollywood.com 33–4
home base, and star-power 178,
    178
Home for the Holidays (1995, USA)
    208
Home Improvement (TV sit-com) 101
homosexuality 145–6, 156, 157,
    208–9, 248
Honey, I Shrunk the Kids (1989,
    USA) 251
Hong Kong stars 231, 234–5, 238,
    239
Hook (1991, USA) 245, 246, 247,
    249, 250, 251, 252, 253

Hopkins, Anthony 203–4, 207
Hopkins, Arthur 218
Horn, John 206
Hornby, Richard 133
Horrocks, Jane 22
Hotel New Hampshire (1984, USA)
    205
Houston, Whitney 208
Hoxter, Julian 80, 81
Hoyts 34
'hub and spoke' model 42
Huffer, Ian 152, 155–66
Hume, David 261
humiliation, of stars 38
Hunter, Jimmy 98

I Am Jackie Chan (Chan's
    autobiography) 235
I Dreamed of Africa (2000, USA) 10
Ice Age (2002, USA) 21
Ice Cube 62
iconography 136, 138, 143
icons 195, 255
    animated 83, 94, 99, 101
    Asian 233, 239–40
    female 213
Idemoto, Michael 232
identification, fans' with stars 151,
    157–8, 159, 161
identity
    of the Batman film characters
        144
    cultural 199, 229–42
    equation of masculine with
        violence against women
        216, 219
    fan's construction of through
        star dislike 78, 80, 81, 82
    national 103, 105–16, 116, 199
    popular 191, 197
    stars' 45, 46, 49, 50, 51, 53, 60
        and celebrity nudes 36
        commodification of 33, 41, 43
        construction following the
            naming of performers 29
        and the internet 26, 33, 41,
            43
    symbolic 97
identity-formation approach 5
ideology 6, 7, 12, 14–15, 87,
    243–4, 259–62, 264, 268,
    269
    and audience attachment to
        stars 75
    and individuality 260–1
    and persona 265
    and star image 265
ignorance, elaborative 47
image *see* star image

imagination 120, 129
Impact 156
In the Line of Fire (1993, USA) 221,
    223–4, 225, 226
inauthentication by perfection 50
income
    see also salaries
    and star-power *175*, 176, 181
Independence Day (1996, USA) 9,
    64, 70, 85
independent production
    companies 8, 238–41
individuality, and ideology 260–1
infantilisation 244, 246–7, 249–50,
    251, 252, 253, 254
inner life, of the character, creation
    130
Inside Film (magazine) 20
Insider, The (1999, USA) 180, 181
instantiation 101
Insurrection (1998, USA) 180
intellectual property issues 35–6
intellectualisation 165
intelligence, constructing
    masculinity through 222–3,
    224
intelligent/stupid truths opposition
    81, 82
internet 22, 25–6, 29–44, *31*
    Asian stars on 233
    celebrity nudes 34–8, 42–3
    entertainment news 33–4, 42
    fans on 26, 38–42, 43, 51, 74,
        76, 77–82, 84–9
    film promotion 32–3, 42
    hate sites 51
    Melissa Gilbert on 193–7
    rise of 25
    and star discourse 26, 30–2, 36,
        42–4, 89
    and star personas 50–1
Internet Movie Database 22
Interscope Records 72
Intersection (1994, USA) 55
intertextuality 194, 196
Interview with the Vampire (1994,
    USA) 221
Iris (2002, USA) 116
irony 107, 108–9, 112–13, 114
It Happened One Night (1934, USA)
    207
Izod, John 344

Jack (1996, USA) 243, 245, 247,
    249, 251, 253–4
Jackie Chan: My Story (TV
    production) 234–5
Jagged Edge (1985, USA) 203
Jakob the Liar (1999, USA) 245

Japanese stars 232
Jar Jar Binks (virtual character) 26, 27, 74, 76, 77–89
Jarvie, Ian 48
Jason and the Argonauts (1963, USA) 95
Jauss, Hans Robert 76
Jaws (1975, USA) 65
Jay, Ricky 264
Jefferson, Tony 80
Jeffords, Susan 15, 247, 249
Jekyll and Hyde narratives 199, 215–28
    Barrymore in 199, 216, 217, 218–19, 220, 221, 222, 225, 226
    love interests in 217–18
    Malkovich in 199, 216, 217, 220, 221–5, 226
    March in 199, 216, 217, 219–20, 221, 222, 225–6
    and picture personalities 216, 219–20, 225
    portrayal of masculinity in 215–16, 218–19, 220–1, 224–6
    theatre productions 217, 218
    Tracy in 199, 216, 217, 220–1, 222, 224, 226
    transition between Jekyll-Hyde personae 220–1
    use of body in 218
Jenkins, Henry 41
Jensen, Joli 40
Jerry Maguire (1996, USA) 248
Jersey Films 73
Jest, The (1921, USA) 218
Jewett, Robert 146
Jewison, Norman 128
Jive Records 67
Johnny Mnemonic (1995, USA) 18, 232
Johnson Over Jordan (2001) 170
Jolie, Angelina 9
Jones, Alan 9
Jones, Chuck 94
Jones, Robert Edmund 218
Jones, Steve 193
Jones, Tommy Lee 63, 142
Joong-hoon, Park 232
Joseph Conrad's the Secret Agent (1996, UK) 243
Jude (1996, USA) 109–10
Judge Dredd (1995, USA) 8, 13, 14, 15–17, 156
Jue, Sharon 239
Jumanji (1995, USA) 245, 247, 249, 251, 252
Jungle Book, The (1994, USA) 237

Junior (1994, USA) 248
Jurassic Park (1993, USA) 2, 26, 85, 95, 251
Justman, Robert 167

K-Pax (2001, USA) 70
Kael, Pauline 127, 129
Kakutani, Michiko 123
Kalem 216
Kane, Bob 141
Kaplan, Erin Aubry 256
Kaplan, James 206
Katzenberg, Michael 1, 2, 20
Kazan, Elia 121, 122–3
Keaton, Buster 235
Keaton, Michael 104, 135, 137–40, 141, 248
Kelly, Jim 240
Kern, Roger 169
Kerr, Deborah 259, 263, 264, 268, 270
Kessler, David 119
Kidman, Nicole 140, 145–6
Kids (1995, USA) 252
Killer, The (1989, HK) 229
Killick, Jane 15, 16
Kilmer, Val 38, 104, 135, 139, 140, 141–3, 144, 145, 146
Kindem, Gorham 5
Kindergarten Cop (1990, USA) 247–8
King, Barry 4–5, 26, 45–61, 68, 98, 155, 164, 166
King, Geoff 9, 26, 62–73, 87
King Kong (1933, USA) 95
King of Texas (2002) 170
Kirkham, Pat 15
Kirkland, Ewan 200, 243–54
Kitano, Takeshi 232
Klapp, Orrin 48
Klaprat, Cathy 18–19
Klein, Naomi 12–13, 48
Klein, Norman 85
Kleinhans, Chuck 25
Klinger, Barbara 10
Knick Knack (1989, USA) 90
Knight, Arthur 128
Knots Landing (TV Series) 193
knowledge, fan 80–1
Kondazian, Karen 118, 119, 121
Kotler, Philip 93
Krämer, Peter 12, 103, 199, 201–14, 244, 246, 251
Krasner, David 118
Kripke, Saul 46
Kroll, Jack 210
Krzywinska, Tanya 87
Kubrick, Stanley 10
Kudaka, Geraldine 229–31, 241

La Cage aux Folles (1978, France/Italy) 243
labour
    real v formal subsumption modes 4
    stardom as a mode of 4–5, 11, 28
Lacey, Joanne 153, 155, 187–98
'ladies' 105, 106, 108, 109, 112, 116
Lam, Ringo 232
Lam, Simon 229
Lancaster, Burt 4–5
Landon, Brooks 9
Landon, Michael 195
language
    Asian languages 237–8
    use in heritage films 107–9, 112–13, 115
Lansky, Meyer 129
Lara Croft: Tomb Raider (2000, USA) 9
Lasseter, John 27, 90
Lassiter, James 69, 71
Last Action Hero, The (1993, USA) 1–2
Last Dance (1996, USA) 55
Last Supper, The (1995, USA) 33
Last Tenant, The (1978, USA) 123, 130
Late Show (TV programme) 234
Laughter (1930, USA) 219
LaValley, Albert J. 9
Lawrence Gordon Productions 70
Lawrence, John Shelton 146
Lee, Ang 106, 107, 232
Lee, Bruce 235
Lee, Chris Chan 232
Lee, Danny 229
Lee, Jason Scott 232, 237
Lee, Quentin 232
Lee, Robert G. 233
Lee, Tommy 25
Legend of Bagger Vance, The (2000, USA) 70
Lemmon, Jack 269, 270
lesbians 208–9
Lethal Weapon 4 (1999, USA) 231, 236, 237, 238
Letterman, David 234, 235
Leung, Chiu-Wai 234
Levin, Bob 25
Levy, Emanuel 269
Lewis, Jerry 144, 216–17
Lewis, Robert 120, 121, 122–3
Li, Jet 231, 232, 234, 237, 238, 239
licensed merchandising 135–6, 142

licensed withdraw 52
Lifetime 188, 191
Lin, Justin 232
Lion King, The (1994, USA) 22, 75, 251
Lion of Oz (2000, USA) 22
Little House on the Prairie (TV series) 153, 187, 194–6
Little Man Tate (1991, USA) 207–8, 210–11, 212
Liu, Lucy 232
live-action, and animation 83, 84
Livewire 97, 98
LivingTV 188–9, 190–3
   re-branding of 189, 192
LL Cool J 62
Llewellyn-Jones, M. 188
Lo Bianco, Tony 130
Lo, Kwai-Cheung 234, 235
Lock Up (1989, USA) 156, 158, 162
Lockwood, Margaret 105
Lone, John 232
Longhurst, Brian 60
Lopez, Jennifer 35
Loren, Sophia 123
Lorre, Peter 245
Los Angeles Herald Examiner 128–9
Los Angeles Times (newspaper) 64, 203, 205–6, 209, 211
love, audiences' of stars 74–5, 76, 82, 89, 151
Love II Love 70
love interests 217–18
Lovell, Alan 12, 103, 257, 259–70
low culture 168–70, 177
low-Other 77–82, 88
Lowe, Rob 191
Lucas, George 10, 27, 78–9, 82, 85, 86, 87, 88
Lucas, Jason 193–4
Lupton, Deborah 79, 80
Lusted, David 188
Luxo Jnr (1986, USA) 90
Lyons, Donald 130

McCay, Winsor 90
MacDonald, Bill 57
McDonald, Paul 4, 6, 7, 11, 25–6, 29–44, 65, 89, 155, 166, 168, 191, 192, 197, 265
Machin, David 151
McLaughlin, Margaret 193–4
Macnab, Geoffrey 12, 259
McQuillan, Martin 95
McTierney, John 1
Made in America (1992, USA) 70
made-for-television movies 187–93, 196

origins of 191–2
physical appearance of female stars 196–7
'quickies' 189, 192
Madonna 11, 45, 49, 77
Magnolia (1999, USA) 264
Making of books 22–3
Malkovich, John 199, 216, 217, 220, 221–5, 226
   appearance 222
   intelligence 222–3, 224
   star-image 223, 225
Mallett, Timmy 246–7
Malpaso 70
Mamet, David 264
Mamoulian, Rouben 219
man-child persona 200, 244, 245, 246, 247, 249–50, 251, 252–3, 254
Manhunter (1986, USA) 203
Mann, C. 193
Mann, Michael 203
Mansfield, Marsha 219
Mansfield, Richard 217, 218
Map of the Human Heart (1992, USA) 237
March, Fredric 199, 216, 217, 219–20, 221, 222, 225–6
marginalisation
   of children 200, 251
   of Hollywood women 207, 210–12
   of star performance 259, 261, 262–5
Marill, A. 187
Mark, The 70
Marshall, P. David 13, 76
Martin, Dean 144
Martin, Valerie 217
Marxism 260
Mary Poppins (1964, USA) 245
Mary Reilly (1996, USA) 217–18, 221, 224–5
Mary Shelley's Frankenstein (1994, USA) 221
masculine/feminine opposition 222
masculinity
   of the 1990s new man 200, 222, 226, 247–50, 253
   of action heroes 15, 138, 139, 140, 141, 142, 144, 145
   construction in the Batman films 138, 139, 140, 141, 142, 144, 145
   construction in the Jekyll and Hyde films 200, 215–16, 218–19, 220–1, 224–6
   construction through intelligence 222–3, 224

construction through violence 218, 219, 220–1, 222, 223, 224, 226
   dangerous 225
   exaggerated 138
   feminised 248–50, 253
   hard 223–4, 225
   heightened models of 161
   heroic 139
   ideals of 200, 218, 219
   post-War/Cold War constructions of 221
   shifting constructions of 200, 215–16, 218–19, 220–6
   under threat 220
Mask, The (1994, USA) 33, 136
mass audiences 169
Masterpiece Theater (TV anthology programme) 179, 180, 181
Mathews, Jack 210
Mathews, Tom Dewe 2
Matrix, The (1999, USA) 18
Matsuda, Yusaku 232
Maverick (1994, USA) 208, 209
Me, Myself and Irene (2000, USA) 144
meaning 92, 98–9, 100, 261, 266
   in Asian film-making 240
   gained by audiences from stars 151–66
   iconic 138
   and made-for-television movie stars 191, 192, 194–5, 197, 198
Medved, Michael 209
Meehan, Eileen 189
Meisner, Sanford 122–3
men
   male audiences 155, 156–66
   male gaze 151
Men in Black (1997, USA) 26, 62, 63–4, 65, 66, 67–8, 70, 73
   earnings 63, 65
   music of 63–4, 65
   television rights 66
   on video 66
Men in Black II (2002, USA) 70
Men in Black ride 73
Meredith, Burgess 125, 129
Mesmerized (1986, USA) 205
Messenger Davies, Máire 152–3, 167–86
metaphorical servitude 48, 59
Method acting 59, 104, 108, 116, 118–19, 120, 121–2, 127
   affective memory 131–2
   objects of attention 131, 132
   realism of 128–9, 133

Strasberg's use of 128–32, 133–4
metonymic servitude 47–9, 59
MGM 5, 25, 70
Mickey Mouse 96, 97
Microsoft Network (MSN) 34
Midler, Bette 201, 202
Mifune, Toshiro 232
Mighty, The (1998, USA) 55
Mill, Bert 212
Miller, Arthur 168, 170, 171, 172, *173*, 174–8, *174–8*, 179–81, *179*
Miller, Toby 13
Miller, Vincent 42
Mills, Donna 190, 193
Minsky, Terry 137, 140, 141
minstrelisation 251, 253, 254
Mirabella, Alan 205
Miramax 8
Mirren, Helen 116
mise-en-scène 264
  nostalgic 195
  use in Batman films 135
  use in heritage films 107, 110
  use in made-for-television movies 192
Mission Impossible 2–3
Mitroff, I. 49
Moby Dick (1997) 168, 170
mocking, of stars 38
modality, shifts in 95
Modleski, Tania 189
Molson 12
Monroe, Marilyn 6, 14–15, 53, 54, 125, 171, 255, 261, 270
  sex appeal 266–7
  and the unification of competing discourses 14, 17, 243
Monster's Ball (2001, USA) 256
Monsters Inc. 22
Montgomery, Elizabeth 193
Moon for the Misbegotten (play) 180, 181
Moore, Demi 35, 202
Moore, Julianne 259, 268, 270
Moore, Mary Tyler 52
moralistic discourses 38
Mordden, Ethan 5
Mork and Mindy (TV sitcom) 243
morphing 88
Morrison, Michael 218
Moscow Art Theatre (MAT) 119, 120, 122
Moscow on the Hudson (1984, USA) 245
Moser, James D. 201
Motion Picture Association of America 8

Motion Picture Classic (fanzine) 38
Motion Picture Story Magazine (fanzine) 38
Movie Chart Show (TV programme) 21
Movieline 52
MovieTicket.com 34
Mr Bug Goes to Town (1941, USA) 94
Mr Mom (1983, USA) 137, 248
Mrs Doubtfire (1993, USA) 246, 248–50, 252
MSNBC 34
MTV 64
Much Ado About Nothing (1993, USA) 18
Muerhen, Dennis 95
multiple media systems 30
Mulvey, Laura 11
Munn, Michael 53, 54, 55, 56, 57
Murphy, Eddie 235
musculinity 15
music industry 12–13
music-film synergies 26, 62–9, 72–3
My Best Friend's Wedding (1997, USA) 33
My Mother Thought She Was Audrey Hepburn (1992, USA) 239
My Own Private Idaho (1991, USA) 18
Myers, Mike 8
Myung-se, Lee 232

Nakamura, Eric 232
naming performers 29, 42
Naremore, James 11–12, 59, 106, 107, 116, 159
narrative images 32
narratives 95, 99, 145
  and actresses use of the body 111–12
  disruption through use of film title music 65
  feminine 189
  in made-for-television movies 189, 192
Nash, Jay Robert 220
Nathan, Ian 140, 141, 164
National Amusements 34
National Asian American Telecommunications Association 238
National Association of Theater Owners (NATO) 33
National Center for Missing and Exploited Children 206
national identity

  and acting style 103, 105–16, 116
  of Asian/Asian American stars 199
National Theatre 125
naturalistic acting styles 107
NBC television 217
NBCi 34
Ndalianis, Angela 88
Nell (1994, USA) 208, 209–10, 211
Nemesis (2002, USA) 167
Neumeier, Edward 16
New Kids on the Block 13
'new man' concept 200, 222, 226, 247–50, 253
New Republic 133
New York Daily News 205, 206, 208, 209, 212
New York magazine 209, 211
New York Post 204, 205, 206, 209
New York Times 205, 210, 212, 220
New York Times Magazine 52
news, entertainment 33–4, 42
Newsday 204
newspapers 22
Newsweek 86, 204, 206, 210, 232
Nicholson, Jack 137, 245, 248
Nickelodeon's Kid's Choice Awards, 2000 67
Nickson, Chris 67, 70
Night Shift (1982, USA) 137
Nighthawks (1981, USA) 156
Nightmare on Elm Street (1984, USA) 8
Niu, Greta Ai-Niu 236
'noble savage' 256
nostalgia 101, 151, 194–5, 244, 251, 252
Nowell Smith, Geoffrey 261, 270
Nowhere to Hide (1999, South Korea) 232
Nutty Professor, The (1963) 216–17

objects of attention 131, 132
O'Brien, Willis 95
O.J. Simpson My Father (1995, USA) 239
O'Malley, Suzanne 122
One Fine Day (1996, USA) 140
One Flew Over the Cuckoo's Nest (1975, USA) 207
One, The (2001, USA) 231
O'Neill, Eugene 180
online clubs 39–42, 43
Orientalising project 230, 231, 233, 235, 236, 237, 238
Orion Pictures 206–7
Osborne, Robert 133
Oscar (1991, USA) 156, 159, 161

Othello (1997) 170
Other, low 77–82, 88
O'Toole, Laurence 35, 37
Over the Top (1986, USA) 156, 158
Overbrook Entertainment 69, 70–2, 73
Overbrook Records 69
ownership of stars
  fan 80–1, 89
  studio 18–19

Pacino, Al 104, 122, 123, 125, 126–7, 128, 131, 255
paedocratic tendencies 244
Palmer, R. Barton 219
Paltrow, Gwyneth 35, 103, 105–6, 112–16
Panic Room (2002, USA) 213
paradigms of stardom 91–4, 98–9
  animated stars 92, 93–4, 95–6
Paramount 4, 5, 70, 167, 212, 213, 218, 219
Parr, Chris 190
Parsons, Estelle 131
Parton, Dolly 201
Pascal, Amy 71
Patch Adams (1998, USA) 249, 253
paternal authority, naturalisation 247–51, 252–3
patriarchy 6, 219
Patterson, John 11
Pearson, Roberta 138, 141, 152–3, 167–86
Pearson television 188, 190
Peirce, C.S. 138
Pennington, Ron 124
People Magazine 125, 167
perfectionism 50
performance *see* star performance
Perkins, Anthony 46
personae 26, 48–60, 265
  actor/character matching 136, 137, 141
  and animated characters 20, 94, 99, 101
  archetypal millennium 19–20
  of contracted semioticians 21
  elastic 26, 60
  guaranteed inherent properties of 60
  gulf between person and 55–7, 59
  John Malkovich's 223
  Kevin Spacey's 19–20
  Lee Strasberg's 126–8
  man-child persona of Robin Williams 200, 244, 245, 246, 247, 249–50, 251, 252–3, 254

Marilyn Monroe's 6, 14, 17, 243
  meta-textual 49–52
  as process 46–7
  Sharon Stone's 26, 53–9
  similarities between person and 45, 46–7, 57–8, 59
  and star brands 68
  Sylvester Stallone's 16, 17
  of television stars 188
  transition between Jekyll-Hyde personae 220–1
  tying to the private life of the star 51
  used to defray perceived tension 14, 17, 243
  Will Smith's 67
personal development/maturation, audience/star's 101, 162, 163–5
personality discourse 29
Peter Ibbetson (1917, USA) 218
Peters, Anne K. 103
Peterson, Richard 169
Pfeiffer, Michelle 11, 202
Pfeil, Fred 247, 250
Phantom Menace, The (1999, USA) 26, 74, 79, 81, 82, 85–6, 87, 88
photo opportunities 51
Photoplay (fanzine) 38
physical appearance 27, 51, 255, 259, 261–2, 263, 270
  see also body; sex appeal
  in the Batman role 138, 139–40, 141–3, 144–5
  of female stars in made-for-television movies 196–7
  ideal 255
  of male action stars 138, 139
  masculine 139, 140, 141
  non-standard (Malkovich) 222, 225
Picasso, Pablo 21
Picture Bride (1993, USA) 232
picture personalities 26, 29, 34, 41, 42
  and the Jekyll and Hyde films 216, 219–20, 225
  John Malkovich's 223, 225
  Michael Keaton's 137
Picture Play (fanzine) 38
Picturegoer (film magazine) 105, 106
Picturing Oriental Girls: A (Re)Educational Videotape (1992, USA) 239
Pidduck, Julianne 107, 110
Pierson, Michele 9, 26

Pinocchio (1940, USA) 94
Pitt, Brad 18, **31**, 32, 35, 38–40, 48, 195
PIXAR 90
Places in the Heart (1984, USA) 223, 224
Plantiga, Carl 75
Play Misty for Me (1971, USA) 71
'Play for Today' 170
'*Playboy* discourse' 266, 267
Playboy magazine 56, 57
Playgirl magazine 167
pleasure 261–2, 270
'points' 1
political economy 7, 11
  of costume 135–6
  of television 188
PolyGram 208, 212
Popeye (1998, USA) 253
Popeye character 96
popular culture 168–70, 177
popular identities 191, 197
pornography 25, 34–8, 42–3, 240–1
portability, existential 47
post-human stars 26, 27
  see also virtual stars
post-photographic film 102
posters 33
Postgate, Oliver 90
Postman, The (1997, USA) 10
Powdermaker, Hortense 5
power of stars 1–3, 202, 207
Premiere (film magazine) 57, 58, 139, 141, 201, 202, 207, 213
power list 202, 207
presence 51
press kits 33
Pretty Woman (1990, USA) 201, 202
Priestley, J.B. 170, 181
Prince, Stephen 9, 26, 83, 85
privacy, for actors 122
private life of the star 19–20, 30
  absence in virtual stars 27, 82
  audience connections to 157, 158–9
  and celebrity nudes 36–7
  public fascination with 4
  tying of personas to 51
production, stardom as phenomenon of 6
programme differentiation 5
promotion, film, on the internet 32–3, 42
Psycho (1960, USA) 46, 246
Psycho (1998, USA) 46
'*Psycho* discourse' 266

psychoanalytic theory 151–2
public biography 53, 59
Pullen, Kirsten 38, 41

qualitative audience research
    152–3
quantitative audience research
    152–3, 167–86
questionnaires, audience research
    156, 162, 170–1, 178–9,
    183–6, 194, 196
Quick and The Dead, The (1995,
    USA) 55
Quigley's top ten 201–2, 207

racial issues 138
    see also ethnicity
Rainer, Peter 209, 211
Rambo: First Blood Part 2 (1985,
    USA) 17, 153, 156, 158, 162
Rambo III (1988, USA) 156, 158,
    162, 163
Random Hearts (1999, USA) 2
rap music 67
Rapa Nui (1994, USA) 237
re-categorisation, of stardom 165
Reagan, Ronald 203, 204, 205
realism 128–9, 133
    and virtual stars 83–4, 85
RealNetworks 34
Red Herring (magazine) 8–9
Redgrave, Lynn 22
Reeves, Keanu 18, 38
Regarding Henry (1991, USA) 18,
    247, 248, 249
Rein, Irving J. 93
Reiniger, Lotte 94
relaxation, in Method acting
    130–1
Replacement Killers, The (1998,
    USA) 231
Replacements, The (2000, USA) 18
reputation building 202
Reservoir Dogs (1991, USA) 116
resistance, cultural 232
reviews 65, 164–5
Reynolds, Burt 264
Rhinestone (1984, USA) 156
Rich, Frank 132
Richard III (1920) 218, 225
Ride Down Mt Morgan, The 168,
    170–2, 181
Riefenstahl, Leni 213
Rigg, Lynn 120
Roberts, Julia 195, 201, 202, 203,
    208, 212, 225
Roberts, Thomas J. 77
Robeson, Paul 6
Robocop (1987, USA) 8, 136

Rocky (1976, USA) 8, 16, 17, 156,
    158, 162, 163, 165
Rocky II (1979, USA) 156, 165
Rocky III (1982, USA) 156
Rocky IV (1985, USA) 156
Rocky V (1990, USA) 156
Roddenberry, Gene 167, 175
Rojek, Chris 13
role models 235
Romeo Must Die (2000, USA) 231
Romney, Jonathan 223
Rose, Brian 215, 226
Rose, Jacqueline 246, 251
Rosen, David 223
Ross, Stanley Ralph 220
Rossington, Norman 264
Roy, Rajendra 239
Royal Family of Broadway, The (1930,
    USA) 219
Royal Family, The 219
Royal Shakespeare Company 170
Rumble in the Bronx (1998, HK)
    231, 236, 241
Rush Hour (1998, USA) 231, 240,
    241
Rush Hour 2 (2000, USA) 231
Ryan, Meg 202, 212
Ryder, Winona 37

Sabrina (1995, USA) 18
sadism 218, 226
St Luke's advertising agency 21
salaries 63, 212
    see also income
Sammon, Paul M. 16
San Sebastian Film Festival 221
Sanello, Frank 58
satellite television 50
Saturn Films 72
Saving Private Ryan (1999, USA)
    101
Scarlet Letter, The (1995, USA) 8
Schatz, Thomas 9
Scheuer, Philip K. 123, 124, 128
Schiffman, Jeff 118, 119, 121
Schulze, Laurie 77, 187, 189, 190,
    191, 192
Schumacher, Joel 140–2, 146
Schwarzenegger, Arnold 1–2, 8,
    54, 138, 143, 160, 161, 247–8
science fiction 211
Scott, Ridley 10
Scottss.com Fake Nudes Gallery
    37
Screen Actor's Guild 28
Screen International 25, 190, 208
scripts
    down-grading of 264
    importance of 268

rendition of 105
Seagram group 69
Secret Asian Man (fanzine) 236
Seize the Day (1986, USA) 245
self
    elasticity of 45–61
    'playing yourself' 263
    sense of 161
self-actualisation 58, 60
Selig 216
Sennett, Robert 33
Sense and Sensibility (1995, USA)
    103, 105, 106–10, 111, 112,
    115
sequels 136
Sergi, Gianluca 2
Sex: The Annabel Chong Story (1999,
    USA) 240–1
sex, and Asian stars 229, 235,
    240–1
sex appeal 223, 255
    and Asian stars 229–31
    Marilyn Monroe's use of 266–7
    Sharon Stone's use of 53–4, 55,
    56–7, 58
Sex, Love and Kung Fu (2000, USA)
    239
sexual deviancy/aggression 218,
    220, 223, 226
SFX 84–5, 86, 87
Shadyac, Tom 73
Shaeffer, Carl 125
Shakespeare in Love (1998, UK) 115
Sheldon, Edward 218
Shepherd, Donald 17
She's the One (1996, USA) 33
Shnayerson, Michael 208, 209
Shone, Tom 165
Shootist, The (1976, USA) 17
Shopping for Fangs (1997, USA) 232
Sibley, Brian 97
Sigelow, Greg 45
Sight and Sound 146
signifiers 94
Silence of the Lambs, The (1991,
    USA) 199, 201, 202, 203–4,
    206–7, 209, 211, 259
Silver, Joel 16
Simon, John 131, 133
Singer, Bryan 170
Singer, Michael 141, 143
Six Degrees of Separation (1993,
    USA) 70
Skokie (1981, USA) 123
Slatzer, Robert 17
Slaying the Dragon (1988, USA)
    239
Sliding Doors (1997, UK/USA) 103,
    114–16

Sliver (1993, USA) 54–5, 57, 58
Sly and the Family Stone 240
Smith, Carol 249
Smith, Greg M. 75
Smith, Liz 127, 133
Smith, Maggie 105, 108, 116
Smith, Murray 75
Smith, Sean M. 213
Smith, Will 26, 62–73
Snyder, John K. 217
Sobchack, Vivian 88
social identity 156, 161, 166
Soe, Valerie 239
Sommersby (1993, USA) 208, 209
Sonnenfeld, Barry 67–8
Sony Corporation 2, 63, 64, 68, 70, 73
Sony Dynamic Digital Sound (SDDS) 2
Sony Pictures Entertainment 33
South Park: Bigger, Longer & Uncut (1999, USA) 254
South Park (TV series) 254
Spacek, Sissy 201
Spacey, Kevin 19–20, 70
spatialisation 51
special effects 51, 84–6, 87, 88, 94–7
and animation 94–7
pulling power of 172
as stars 8–9
Speed (1994, USA) 18
Spelling, Aaron 192
Spelling, Ian 208
Spelling, Tori 193
Spice Girls 12
Spielberg, Steven 2, 9–10, 63, 247
Stacey, Jackie 76, 151–2, 155, 266
Staiger, Janet 3
Stallone, Sylvester 8, 13, 14, 16–17, 50, 138, 152, 155, 156–66, 235
Stammers, Kate 21
Stanislavsky, Konstantin 119, 120, 122
Stanwick, Barbara 261
Staples, Terry 245
star brands 12, 19, 68–73
star discourses
Asian/Asian American 239
and the Internet 26, 30–2, 36, 42–4, 89
and the private lives of stars 30
in television movies 193
star image 6, 265
Asian 234, 236, 239, 240
John Barrymore's 216, 225
John Malkovich's 223, 225
Sylvester Stallone's 16

and the unification of competing discourses 243
Will Smith's 62, 63
star performance 11–12, 103–4, 105–17, 118–34, 255
acting as feminine career 199
acting as manly career 199, 216
in the Batman films 135–49
and class status 103, 105, 106, 108, 110–11, 112, 113, 114, 115
'dames' 105, 106, 108, 109, 114, 116
definitive 46
in the heritage genre 103–4, 106–14, 115, 116
'ladies' 105, 106, 108, 109, 112, 116
marginalisation of 259, 261, 262–5
Method acting 104, 108, 116, 118–19, 120, 121–2, 127
as most important aspect of the star 268
'Star Power' survey 63, 65
star systems 4, 5, 25–8, 74–89
and an elastic self 45–61
animated stars 20–2, 90–102
crossover stars 26, 62–73
McDonald's model 191, 192, 197
online 29–44
of television movies 193
virtual stars 26–8, 74, 82–8
Star Trek product 168, 169, 170, 171, 174, 175, 179, 180, 182
Star Trek: The Next Generation (TV series 1987-94) 167, 170
Star Trek (TV series 1966-9) 167
star vehicles 17–20
Star Wars 9, 251
fandom 74, 76, 77–82, 84–9
Star Wars (1977, USA) 79, 81, 251
Star Wars: The Special Edition 88
star-as-celebrity 11, 157, 159
star-as-performer 11
star-as-professional 11, 159
star-audience relationships 269
and made-for-television movies 190, 191, 194–7
and the virtual star 74–5, 76, 77–82
star-character interface *see* character-star interface
star-led production companies 69–73
star-power factor 172–82
and audience age *173*, 174, 175, 179, 181

and audience tastes 178–82, *179*
and education 177, *177*, 181
and ethnicity 176–7, *176*, 181
and gender differences 174–5, *174*, 181
and home base 178, *178*
and income *175*, 176, 181
Starewich, Wladyslaw 94
Stargate (1994, USA) 136
Starship Troopers (1996, USA) 16, 85
Statistical Package for the Social Sciences (SPSS) 172
Staunton, Imelda 106
Stealing Home (1988, USA) 205
Steiner, Griselda 118
stereotyping, of women 55
Sterritt, David 209, 210, 211
Stevenson, Robert Louis 215, 216, 217, 218, 220, 226
Stewart, F. 193
Stewart, Patrick 152–3, 167–8, 169–70, 171–8, *173–8*, 179–82, *179*
Stiller, Ben 32
Stoller, Martin R. 93
Stone, Sharon 26, 35, 53–9
Stop Or My Mom Will Shoot! (1992, USA) 156, 159, 161
Strange Case of Dr. Jekyll and Mr. Hyde (Stevenson) 215–16, 217, 218, 220, 226
Strange Case of a Hyde and a Seekyl, The 215
Strasberg, Anna 129
Strasberg, Lee 104, 118–34
biography 119–23
commercialism of 125–6
film debut as actor 119, 123, 124, 126–7, 128–30, 131–2, 133
hypocrisy of 126
paternal image 127
performances as reflections of his teaching 128–32
persona as teacher/star maker and image as actor 126–8
star-struck nature of 125
stardom of his last years 123–6
Strawberry Fields (1996, USA) 232
Streep, Meryl 56, 201, 202
Street, Sarah 105
Streisand, Barbra 35, 125, 201, 202
Stringer, Julian 199–200, 229–242
Stuart, Jan 204
Student of Arts and Drama 120
studios
see also specific studios

and the creation of celebrity 93
and independent production
    companies 8
and star ownership 18–19
and star-led production
    companies 69–73
and Strasberg 121
Studlar, Gaylyn 4, 218
sub-contractors, stars as 4, 5
sub-genres 160
subtext 99
Sullivan, Thomas Russell 217
Sundance Festival 8
Sunday Mirror (newspaper) 17
Sunday Times, The (newspaper)
    164–5
Sunsets (1997, USA) 232
Superman (TV series) 193
Sutherland, John 77–8
Svengali (1983, USA) 205
Svetkey, Benjamin 66, 68
Switch (1991, USA) 248
symbolic identity 97
synergy, film-music 26, 62–9

Taitz, Sonia 205
Tajiri, Rea 232
Takakura, Ken 232
Tarantino, Quentin 235
Tasker, Yvonne 15, 138, 265
Taxi Driver (1975, USA) 203, 205
technological instrumentalism 102
technological progress 27–8, 102
Teenage Mutant Ninja Turtles (1990,
    USA) 8
teenagers 162–3, 165
television
    see also made-for-television
        movies
    Asian 238
    mass nature of 169
    as means of promoting cultural
        mobility/permeability
        169–70
    political economy of 188
television personalities 188
television presenters, children's
    246–7
television series, derived from film
    brands 136
television stars 188, 191, 192–3,
    196–8
Tempest, The (1995) 170
Terminator 8, 211
Terminator 2: Judgement Day (1991,
    USA) 26, 247
Tetzlaff, David 49
texts 99
    dispersible 146

pulling power of 172
textual authenticity 87–9
textuality 98–9
theatre 167, 168, 169–72, *173–8*,
    174–8, 180–2
    Jekyll and Hyde productions
        217, 218
Theatre Guild 120
Thelma and Louise (1991, USA) 18
There's Something About Mary (1998,
    USA) 32–3
Thompson, Emma 103, 105,
    106–8, 109, 112, 113, 115,
    248
Thompson, John O. 115, 138
Thorburn, David 192
Thornton-Sherwood, Madeleine
    125
Thumim, Janet 15
Thunderbirds 90
Thurman, Uma 35
Time magazine 3, 124, 125, 130,
    132, 142, 207, 210, 232
Time Out (magazine) 146
Time Warner empire 68–9
Tin Toy (1988, USA) 90
Titanic (1997, USA) 8, 26, 103,
    109, 110–12, 212
Tomorrow Never Dies (1997,
    UK/USA) 231, 236
Tootsie (1982, USA) 130
Top Hat (1935, USA) 145
Total Recall (1990, USA) 8, 54, 56
Touchstone imprint 68, 70
Townes, DJ 'Jazzy' Jeff 67
Toy Story (1995, USA) 13, 20, 26,
    90, 93, 96, 98, 99, 100–2, 244
Toy Story 2 (2000, USA) 90, 93, 96,
    98, 99, 100–2
toys 97–8, 100
Toys (1992, USA) 245, 246, 251,
    252, 253
Toys 'R' Us 97
toys-come-to-life stories 90, 96, 99
Tracy, Spencer 199, 216, 217,
    220–1, 222, 224, 226
trailers 85–6
Tramell, Catherine (*Basic Instinct*
    character) 53–4, 55, 56–7, 58,
    59
Traube, Elizabeth 249
Travolta, John 10
TriStar Pictures 221
True Male Celebs 35, 36
truth 98, 99
Truth About Charlie, The (2003,
    USA) 232
Tudor, Andrew 5
Turner, Kathleen 201

Turner, Lana 220, 243
TV Guide (American magazine)
    167, 169
Twentieth Century Fox 33, 70, 72,
    121
Twin Peaks (TV series) 236

United Artists (UA) 4, 70
Universal City complex, Los
    Angeles 69
Universal Music Group 72
Universal Studios 69, 70, 71–3,
    219
Universal Studios theme park,
    Florida 73
unknowableness of stars 267–8
Uricchio, William 138, 141
US National Endowment for the
    Arts 125
USA Today 65
Uspenskaya, Maria 120
Usual Suspects, The (1995, USA) 19,
    20

Valenti, Jack 8
Valentino, Rudolph 237
Van Dyke, Dick 245
Van Sant, Gus 243
vanity deals 10–11, 72
Vanity Fair (magazine) 53, 208, 209
Variety (magazine) 72, 119, 133,
    218
Vaughn, Vince 46
Verhoeven, Paul 57, 58
victimhood, female 204, 205,
    206–7, 209–10
video 66, 162
video recorders 50
View from the Bridge, A (play) 180
Village Voice 123, 124, 125, 126,
    128, 201, 204, 210
villains, place in the Batman
    movies 142–5
Vincendeau, Ginette 12, 259, 263,
    265
Vineberg, Steve 129, 132, 133
virtual stars 26–8, 74, 82–8
    lack of referentiality/indexicality
        83
    realism of 83–4, 85
Vivendi 69
voice 255
    use in *Batman Forever* 142, 144,
        145
    use in heritage films 107–9, 110,
        111, 112–13, 115
voiceovers 20–2
volume of information 22–3
voyeurism 37

Wacaday (TV programme) 246–7
Wager, Michael 121, 126
Wagner, Lindsey 193
Wahlberg, Mark 35, 232
Waking the Dead (2000, USA) 213
Walker, Alexander 5, 7
Walkerdine, Valerie 161
Wall Street Journal 11
Wallace, Amy 213
Wang, Steve 232
Wang, Wayne 232
Wark, McKenzie 76
Warner Brothers 11, 19, 68, 69,
    70, 72, 94, 97, 135, 136, 138
Washington, Denzel 72
Wayne, John 6, 17, 263
Weaver, Sigourney 72, 204, 206
Weinraub, Bernard 210, 212
Wells, Paul 22, 26, 90–102
Wernick, Andrew 48
West Wing, The (TV series) 170
West Yorkshire Playhouse 181–2
Westerfelhaus, Robert 10
What Dreams May Come (1998,
    USA) 245, 253
Where the Day Takes You (1992,
    USA) 70
Who Am I? (1998, HK) 235
Who's Afraid of Virginia Woolf?
    (2001) 170
Wild Wild West (1999, USA) 26,
    62, 63, 64, 65–6, 67–9, 70, 72,
    73
    as box office failure 65–6
    earnings 65
    music products of 64, 65, 66,
        68–9
    television rights 66
    on video 66
Willennium (album) 64, 69
William Shakespeare's Hamlet (1996,
    UK/USA) 243

Williams, Linda 105
Williams, Robin 20–1, 243–54
    man-child persona 200, 244,
        245, 246, 247, 249–50, 251,
        252–3, 254
Williams, Simon 80
Willis, Bruce 48, 235
Wilson, Earl 124
Wilson, G.D. 45
Winfrey, Oprah 13
Winokaur, Jon 52
Winslet, Kate 103, 105–6, 108–12,
    113, 116
Witherspoon, Reese 35
witnesses, female 215–16
Wolf, Michael J. 12
women
    empowerment through sexuality
        56–7
    in the gangster genre 190
    and made-for-television movies
        151, 187, 188–90, 191, 192,
        193, 194–7
    professional opportunities in
        Hollywood 199, 201–2,
        204, 207, 210–12
        age factors 201–2, 213
        marginalisation 207, 210–12
        reputation building 202
        salaries 212
        and science fiction 211
    as stars in made-for-television
        movies 192–3
    symbolic annihilation through
        stereotyping 55
    victimisation of 204, 205, 206–7,
        209–10
    violence against 216, 219,
        220–1, 223, 224, 225,
        226
    as witnesses 215–16
Wong, Martin 237

Woo, John 232
Wood, Robin 244, 246, 250, 251
Woods, Rowan 99
Woody (*Toy Story* character) 13,
    20, 26, 27, 91, 92, 93–4, 95–6,
    98, 99–102
World According to Garp, The (1982,
    USA) 245
World Wide Web (WWW) 32,
    42, 89
World's Biggest Gang Bang, The
    (1995, USA) 240
Wray, Fay 95
Wyatt, Justin 8, 65, 137

X-Men, The (2000, USA) 153, 168,
    170–1, 172, 178, 180, 181
Xena: Warrior Princess (TV series)
    38
Xing, Jun 235

Yahoo.com 34, 39, 41–2
Yellow (1997, USA) 232
Yellow Entertainment Network
    238
Yeoh, Michelle 229, 231
Yiddish Progressive Dramatic
    Club 119
Yolk magazine 230
Young, Jeff 123
youth liberation movement 251
Yu, Ronnie 232
Yuki Shimoda: Asian American Actor
    (1985, USA) 239
Yun-Fat, Chow 229, 230, 231, 237,
    238, 239–40, 241

Zanuck, Darryl 121
Zimmerman, Paul 131
Zizek, Slavoj 86, 87
Zolotin, Adam 249